contents

chapter 3
Youth in Trouble 81

chapter 4
Reading Theory and Research with Problem Adolescents
and Chronically Disruptive Youth 137

chapter 5
Institutionalization: History, Influence, and the Problem
of Recidivism 181

preface

This book is written for educators by educators. In this book we shall attempt to articulate what the literature contains concerning youths in trouble in the community, their homes, institutions, schools, and in transition from one place to another.

The home, community (including peer groups of all descriptions), and school appear to be the three most influential factors in any adolescent's life. What happens precisely to influence some youth to anti-social aggressive-disruptive behavior is not clear. Most of the past generalities formed from the sociological studies of groups do not appear to explain the behavior for a given member of that group. Similarly, psychological study of one youth can seldom be generalized to include an accurate description of another. True enough, there are many common group characteristics, and most certainly there are personality factors which affect or are affected by norm-violating and chronic disruptive behavior. But, the practicing educator has frequently had little relevant information related to instructional materials or delivery systems.

We have attempted to focus on the salient issues related to facts, attitudes, beliefs, and misbeliefs which directly affect the population. Unlike other book material, we have attempted to interpret these data emphasizing special educational needs of adolescents in trouble. Long overdue is the massive mobilization of efforts in our country to vastly reduce the number of adolescents engaged in norm-violating and chronic disruptive types of behavior. For the educator preparing professionally to work with norm-violating adolescents, this book will furnish necessary informational competencies and a personal reference point. For the practitioner in the public schools; community agencies, and correctional facilities, the information should serve to reinforce, support, or cast doubt upon current beliefs and best practice procedures. For those in law enforcement, community consideration, and educationally related disciplines, these materials should provide a one-stop consolidation for the vast body of information that defines the current state-of-the-art in the study of norm-violating secondary school youths. For the other interested readers, concerned laymen, and parents, we dedicate this reading.

DAS
AJM

norm-violating secondary school youth: demographic findings

DAVID A. SABATINO

This chapter provides teachers, pupil personnel workers, and administrators of public and private institutions with usable plans of action, current theorization, and research findings on chronic norm-violating disruptive youth. It addresses the age-old demographic issues of describing difficult to classify—but easy to observe—behaviors, by relating the characteristics, definitions, and concomitant handicaps, to demographic findings reported over the last quarter century. The following chapters discuss these characteristics in light of assessment, and plans for management of chronic norm-violating disruptive youth in communities and specialized settings. These selected readings are written for educators; and unlike most other resources available, they approach the topic from an instructional frame of reference. They represent the practices and theorization of sociologists, behaviorists, psychiatrists, anthropologists, nutritionists, and other associated professionals.

We do not wish to imply that the materials, ideas, suppositions, postulates, or practices reviewed or expressed within these pages represent the sum and substance of all there is to know about the educational and behavioral management of chronic norm-violating disruptive youth. Rather, it should set forth contributory information that may assist educators in assessing their current practices, feeling supported in their beliefs or gaining new insights. We invite you to read, agree, disagree, and

1

update this work with that of your own. Our purpose is to provide for the mutual struggle to identify the best practices in the state-of-the-art for the educational amelioration of what we fear is a much wasted part of humanity at a critical crossroad—secondary school age chronic norm-violating disruptive youth.

NORM VIOLATION AND CHRONIC DISRUPTION

Chronic norm-violating disruption, adjudication, behavioral disorders, social–emotional disorders, and *neglect* are terms that have both legal and human implications. The laws of most states cite neglect, delinquency, and incorrigibility as the three major contributors necessary for initial investigative and/or judicial action against youth, parents, or guardians. Neglect, incorrigibility and delinquency are used as terminology in most states' legal codes regarding court and social agency involvement with children and youth. Neglect is the term most frequently found in affidavits charging parents with failure to discharge their duty responsibly.

The *physical* component of neglect is not hard to substantiate in court: a youth is malnourished, sick, ill-clothed, battered, or generally in a miserable physical state. But the *emotional* component of neglect, to which legal codes in many states refer, is difficult to establish, even though we know that it is prevalent in families at all socioeonomic levels. Emotional neglect typically reflects on the quality of the parent–youth relationship, but a host of factors such as religion, ethnic background, race, values, beliefs, and the immediate conditions of the larger society, as well as the respective home, are also involved. Black urban, rural Appalachian, and native American cultures and subcultures are distinctly different, and their differences are magnified in child-rearing practices. A reservation Indian family may walk twenty miles to a package liquor store where youths will be front-row observers as mother and father drink to intoxication. For this particular culture, however, this does not constitute neglect, leading possibly to delinquency as it might for others. Rather, it is an established cultural expectation of regular occurrence; one consequence is that it is likely to reproduce itself in the next generation.

One may find dogmatic statements in the literature on such matters as chronic disruptive behavior (incorrigibility and delinquency). Reckless (1967) for example, has stated that youths from the same home, living in an urban renewal area in a major city, who share similar physical and possibly emotional experiences, have an equal chance of becoming criminals or law enforcement officials. The fact is, however, that we do not presently possess comprehensive knowledge of the causes of norm-violating behaviors nor why particular youths in given families respond negatively or positively to child-rearing practices and attitudes they experience in homes or secondary social institutions. Certainly, there is no single theory which offers *the* answer. A patchwork of theories does exist. These theories include:

1. *Genetic Transmission Theories.*   Early naturistic criminologists believed in inherited criminality or degeneracy, contending that behavior is biologically determined. This idea held for two decades and implied that physical structure dictated social functioning.

2. *Bad Parents.* Most criminologists have attributed norm-violating behavior to lack of parental guidance and discipline. They point out that increases in broken homes parallel the rise in delinquency.

3. *The Bad Boy Theory.*   The antithesis of the bad parent theory is the bad boy theory which states that disruptive behavior begins in the youth's ear—"You are a bad boy." But youths tend to role play within the expectations of their parents or friends. If told they are bad, punished frequently, and provided positive reinforcement for certain acts, they may incorporate such a view of self and attempt to actualize the role placed upon them.

4. *The Defective Parent-Youth Relationship.*   This is the generation gap concept which states that the parents just do not understand the clothes, music, dances, or even the vocabulary of the *now* generation. The insistence from both of these groups that a real difference exists in nature only amplifies the tendencies of one or the other group to actually be different. Communication, its absence or difficulty, is the "whipping boy" in this theory.

5. *The School's Fault Theory.*   This theory emphasizes the school's dominant role in the life of students as society moves from a primary social system centering on the home to a community-based urban setting. The school is considered as having failed to communicate appropriate values to students. Grades, not honesty, are said to have been emphasized as an example of the loss in real human values.

6. *The Economic Pressure Theory.*   Since most neglected and disruptive youths are black, from the inner city, or both, their chronic disruptive behavior is seen as being directly related to poverty, housing, and associated family conditions.

7. *The Delinquent Gang Theory.*   This theory emphasizes association with bad boys since "evil communications corrupt good manners." The argument is that social values of the gang serve to un-

balance and replace the value structures of the larger society which the subgroup feels are not applicable to the cultural settings where the gang operates.

8. *The Mental Illness Theory.* This theory holds that all who are neglected or neglect others must suffer from psychopathology. There is a widely held belief that norm-violating youth are emotionally maladjusted and need psychotherapy.

9. *The Asocial Theory.* This theory maintains the position that some youths simply do not learn the appropriate values and mores congruent with society; they live for and value what is appropriate or expedient for the moment.

10. *Other Theories.* There are other theories stressing inadequate recreation facilities, physical weakness, underdeveloped expressive vocabularies resulting in physical aggression (Billy Budd Syndrome), hostility toward an alien culture, rejection by parents or the home for a multitude of reasons, and the message of crime and violence conveyed through mass media.

SOCIAL MALADJUSTMENT

Central to an understanding of most norm-violating behaviors is recognition of a youth's specific problem or disability. Awareness that the youth has a definite handicap, chronic illness, or some acute problem that needs attention will help us to both understand and obtain services for him or her. It is very difficult in studying social maladjustment to determine whether genuine differences exist among the socially maladjusted youth who exhibit adjustment problems to the relative social situation in which they find themselves. The hostility, aggressiveness, or withdrawn behavior a youth may exhibit might rightly or even necessarily be considered part of the youth's normal adjustment processes depending on the stresses of that environment. Normal adjustments to life can require youths to react in a manner magnified out of proportion according to the standards of the so-called normal adult world, or its regulatory institutions. Much norm violation occurs in the eyes of the beholder. If every youth were adjudicated who committed a punishable offense, most youth would establish court records.

Any situation which is threat-producing to a youth poses a danger to his or her physical or emotional well-being. Emotional neglect, multiple mothering, and parental rejection are stressful threatening. An adolescent may fear his parents' pending divorce. These fears may attack the youth's other emotional supporting structures, such as feelings of security at home, personal identity, and feelings of belonging to a protective family. A youth's emotional reactions in themselves are adjustment processes. Adjustment implies that a youth is interacting in a satisfactory or unsatisfactory manner with a particular environment or environmental situation in which he finds himself. Within a given period of time, all of us adjust or readjust to constant environmental changes. For the majority of youths, maladjustment is a temporary process which will pass with the time that it takes to remove the threat and residual anxiety.

The rules which govern behavior in our society sometimes provide situations in which a person may exhibit anger, fear, affective warmth, or hostility, and still be seen as showing normal adaptive mechanisms. A soldier may display extreme emotionality under wartime conditions and still be considered as demonstrating normal behavior. However, the same reaction by the same person in a peacetime office where the stress might be equal to battlefield stress would be considered evidence of maladaptive behavior under society's rules.

SOCIAL–EMOTIONAL MALADJUSTMENT

Two distinct concepts are usually implied by the terms emotional and social maladjustment. One may distinguish social from emotional maladjustment by examining the interaction of the individual under stress. Basically, an emotionally maladjusted youth lives with total disregard for most social-environmental situational interactions. Such a youth's response to a given social situation is impaired by faulty adjustment mechanisms which result in extremes of overt withdrawal from people and things. Emotional maladjustment is neither temporal nor related to the immediate situation or environment.

Social adjustment or maladjustment, on the other hand, tends to be depended upon, or interrelated with, the context of the immediate environment. It is generally regarded as emerging over difficulties in interpreting societal rules, or the inability or unwillingness to adapt to particular environmental situations. Socially maladjusted youths exhibit behaviors such as aggressiveness, withdrawal, and other behaviors which may be reinforced by their securing attention. Common examples of social maladjustment are seen in disruptive acts committed by juveniles. Pate (1963) describes social maladjustment as follows:

> *Socially maladjusted* children are chronic juvenile offenders who regularly disregard broader social values and rules as a matter of course, substituting in their stead the values and rules of their peer group. They make

up delinquent gangs who are constantly in trouble with the law. Their accepted code of conduct is truancy, fighting, and defiance against constituted authority. Socially maladjusted children are handicapped by their provincial patterns of social values. . . . (p. 240)

The psychosocial adaptation of a given individual to one's environment represents a total adjustment process; that is, each person is molded by how well one thinks he or she feels, what is happening in one's immediate family and vocational life, as well as one's ability to use psychological adjustment mechanisms. Equally important, overt behavior does not always provide a true picture of one's personal state; pseudo-adjustment phenomena are real. An individual may present a state of good adjustment when, in fact, he or she is troubled. It seems necessary to develop systematic ways of looking at human adjustment and/or how each aspect interacts to promote or inhibit that process. One may look at psychosocial adjustment as being influenced by biological, sociocultural, and psychological concerns. (See Figure 1.1.)

The adaptation of man to this world is dependent upon a variety of identifiable features or variables. The biological factor includes how one's body performs, the absence or presence of physical pain, and the benefits of normal sensory functioning. Biological fact is basic to man's view of self and of the world. Nevertheless, it is the total interaction of all factors—the biological, sociocultural, and psychological—which form the complex whole involved in adaptation. Not all youths want to be football players, but some do because of a desire for the social recognition football players receive. Physically a boy may not have the size or endurance to play football, so he must then either adapt or enter a non-adjusted phase of living. More pressing, he may be asked to "rip-off" the record store, and if he doesn't, he will not achieve acceptability with his peers.

Similarly, a high school senior girl who wants to be a nurse may have been reared in a setting which gave her limited opportunities to develop academically. She may have entered school with an underdeveloped speech and language faculty, consequently evidencing poor reading and disliking school. Her academic progress in the elementary grades may have suffered to the extent as to deprive her of the opportunity to learn the skills necessary to undertake algebra, physics, and chemistry when she entered junior high or high school. Consequently, as a senior, her applications for nurse's training are rejected. Again, this is due to biological, sociocultural, and psychological variables acting together. As a result the girl, 18 years of age, must now readjust her dream and expectations for life or suffer continuing frustrations. Whether she can modify her expectations and accept the lower status of nurse's aide,

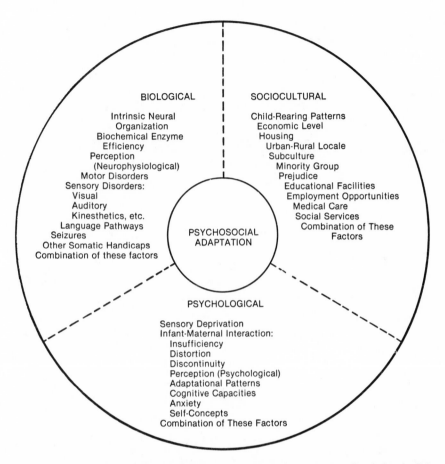

From: J. B. Richmond, "Introduction," *Mental Retardation: A Handbook for the Primary Physician,* p. xiv, 1964. Reproduced with the permission of the *Journal of the American Medical Association.*

Figure 1.1   Psychosocial Adaptation

working in the hospital kitchen or laundry, while successfully working toward other goals will depend upon the strength and balance of her psychosocial adaptive mechanisms.

TYPES OF SOCIAL MALADJUSTMENT

Three major types of social maladjustment are generally defined—in relation to social values—as *asocial, dysocial,* or *antisocial.*

Asocial implies being without knowledge of social rules or morals. An example may be given in the case of a five-year-old boy who was brought to a hospital outpatient clinic for a preschool examination. He has little language except grunts and gestures. His overt behavior is filled with gross, aggressive acts of hitting, biting, and kicking. His social adjustment is comparable to the "negativism" characteristic of a two-year-old, yet shows normal intelligence on commonly used nonverbal intelligence tests. The case history showed that he had been in seven different homes, has had multiple mothering, and never knew his father. It is not surprising that he fails to act appropriately in a social sense; he has not internalized societal rules, not even those normally in the repertoire of a five-year-old.

A *dysocial* type of maladjustment represents an intrapersonal conflict with events or positions reflecting important social values. The youth has learned that rules are not to be broken; for example, he should never steal from others. Upon entering school he may find that youths from other homes steal, and they have regard for one conduct rule only—it is wrong to be caught. The youth in question is now confronted with dysocial values; that is, two opposing views which seemingly apply to the same social situation.

The third type, the *antisocial* condition, characterizes the public's view of most norm-violating youths who are brought to the attention of the court. The antisocial youth has indeed learned values consistent with those taught by society. As a result of gang or personal pressure, the youth violates those values and thus comes into confrontation with society's norms and the law.

Two other diagnostic categories associated with social disability are *character disorders* and *transient situational personality disorders.*

Character disorders are manifested as habitual types of behaviors which draw unfavorable attention to the person. They are not the result of either mental retardation or psychopathology; the person is not mentally disturbed. Character disorders may simply be described as an individual's possession of some behavioral characteristic that disturbs others. An example is the youth described as having a *mean streak;* she bullies smaller youths. The youth is not psychotic or does not have a mental disorder in the sense that her behavior is driven by neurotic anxieties. The youth likes to boss, direct, and influence weak and smaller youths, perhaps because she cannot express this need for dominance with youths of similar age.

The following example distinguishes the character disorder from the psychopathological personality disorder. One youth expresses aggressive, hostile behavior in a socially disapproved manner by bullying smaller youths. Another youth tends to withdraw, unable to express frustrations and hostility openly, and displays such behavior as lighting fires in homes. The former displays a character disorder while the latter exhibits a more serious personality disorder. There is a large gray area between the youth who recognizes that she should not bully smaller youths, and the withdrawn youth whose anxiety causes him to express feelings and impulses that he cannot explain and seemingly has no power to control.

Between the character disorder and acute personality disorder is the area of *transient situational personality disorder.* It falls under the heading of social maladjustment and not emotional maladjustment because of its transient nature. The most important characteristic of the transient situational personality disorder is that while the youth frequently displays the more severe manifestation associated with neurotic anxieties, the resulting overt behaviors that the youth displays can be explained in rational terms and understood when sufficient information is presented.

THE WITHDRAWAL-AGGRESSION CONTINUUM

A first step in the management of a youth's reaction to a stressful situation (when possible) is to isolate the triggering mechanism. Once this is understood by both the teacher or interested adult and the youth, a relationship may be established which will reduce the stresses and negative emotion involved. This relationship will promote a sense of security which will assist the youth in dealing with other stresses. If this does not happen, the youth's disturbed behavior will continue and the situation may eventually produce the kinds of maladjusted responses frequently associated with passive-aggressive and passive-withdrawn personality disorders.

The youth with a passive-aggressive personality disorder suffers from repeated anxiety attacks which, for the most part, are well controlled; but, he can only defend himself against anxiety by seeking a more passive state which contrasts with the aggressive behavior displayed when anxieties become too strong. To offset a further buildup of anxiety, the youth finds an outlet for his frustrations. Perhaps, he breaks a window in the presence of the school principal or hits a student twice his size in the restroom after recess. He seems tense, though still able to talk about his problems; then suddenly he becomes violently aggressive, apparently fully expecting and wanting punishment for the aggression.

Such behaviors are caused in part by the youth's inability to understand and isolate the anxiety-inducing problems, which are real and have a situational base. At the same time, the foreboding fears of other anxieties are building up which may not have any basis in reality. This combination results in the transient changing of behavior from a passive state to an overt-withdrawn or overt-aggressive state.

Students with such problems draw attention to themselves in classrooms and corridors a great deal of the time. It is difficult to generalize about the etiology of their condition, but some of the more common reasons are rejection by parents, inability to meet parental expectancy, fears promoted by unsuccessful social interaction, academic or other performance failure, and fears instilled by peers or parents. The taxing dilemma is the simultaneous need for acceptance and punishment. His or her need is for consistent rules which he understands, administered with positive feeling, to consistently guide and structure his life's decisions reducing his need to manipulate the social or personal situation in search of "rules." Any search which will bring about a desired change in an adolescent will generally promote manipulation of the adults involved. Youth constantly test the boundaries which define the relative rules of the social order in any given situation (home, school or street) and attach feelings of acceptance or rejection to those rules and the rule makers. These feelings of acceptance or rejection are primarily aimed at the rule makers' sincerity and reasons rather than the rules themselves. It is little wonder that most adolescents manipulate the boundaries set by rule makers, when in fact, the reasons for the rules which determine social order are rarely explained. Most youth hear only the consequence for transgressing, which is but a challenge in the adolescent's struggle for independence.

JUVENILE DELINQUENCY

One of the major categories of norm violation is juvenile delinquency. It is so closely linked to sociocultural problems that delinquency appears most frequently in areas where there is poverty, adult crime, or a constellation of community conditions that are grouped under the names of anomie or social disorganization. Susceptibility to influences of the physical environment, intellectual level, and family background interact and affect a person's leaning toward norm-violating or norm-accepting behavioral values. Research on the delinquent, his social group, and his community indicates that sociological and psychological factors, personality, and social pressures are all determinants of norm-violating behavior.

Quay (1965), focusing on the "legal sense" of the term, defines delinquency as follows:

The delinquent is a person whose misbehavior is a relatively serious legal offense, which is inappropriate to this level of development; is not committed as a result of extremely low intellect, intracranial organic pathology, or severe mental or metabolic dysfunction; and is alien to the culture in which he has been reared. Whether or not the individual is apprehended or legally adjudicated is not crucial. (p. 12)

Delinquency, of course, is a form of misbehavior, but not all misbehavior is delinquency, even when it is inappropriate for the age of the individual. Both the quality of the behavior and the degree of social deviance are factors in judging an antisocial act appropriately.

Gibson and West (1970) studied 87 boys who were classified as unofficial early delinquents on the basis of delinquent acts or reports made by teachers and community members. Also included in the study were 294 additional boys, up to age 14, free of any delinquent act or referral. A third group of delinquents consisted of 411 boys in the age range of eight to nine when first seen. In the older half of the sample were boys 15 years of age or more. Their offenses were almost exclusively petty stealing. The boys were classified according to family type, and seven characteristics of social handicaps were defined. These seven component items were: supported by family, low occupational status of father, poor housing, poorly kept accommodations, inadequate income, six or more children in the family, and physical neglect.

Essentially, the implications that low to average intelligence is a feature of early delinquents rather than delinquents in general complement evidence that has been gathered by a number of researchers. On the measures of verbal and nonverbal ability at the earlier age, on the scale of social handicapped, the boys who subsequently became chronically disruptive were found to be substantially lower in IQ, and to have come predominantly from the most impoverished and socially deprived families. These findings seem compatible with everything that we know, and the uniqueness of the findings in this case is the predictability for intervention with young pre-delinquent offenders. The word "young" is critical in this case and implies youth who may well be brought to the attention of legal officials by age eight at the latest. That means, as odd as it sounds, that preventative activities need to be initiated in kindergarten of the public schools.

Of course, when we described the youth as having low intelligence, we are not suggesting mental retardation. We are suggesting a relationship between two common social variables. Verbal ability and language comprehension, two products of society, are also related to social status of the family. It is well recognized that reading scores in verbal intelligence tests and socioeconomic factors correlate highly with most identifiable samples of youth. The added component for delinquency in this case is one more symptomatic outgrowth of poverty: an inability to utilize education to lift oneself, and the attitude of families towards school as an imposing authority within the life structures once it has been established that a family is on the bottom of the social pile. Thus, a comedy of tragic errors results which is cyclic and self-reinforcing. The major social question is where and how to break it.

What are the causes of delinquency? Certainly, the inconsistencies and incontinuities between theoretical positions as to the nature of delinquency have impeded the understanding of what its causes are. Delinquency is a mosaic—it has no single cause, just as it has no single concomitant. The sequel of a delinquent act is also a multidimensional aspect.

Hirschi (1969) has advanced a control theory which postulates that adolescent behavior is an extension of the individual's bond to society's weaknesses as that individual determines them. This empirically tested approach is based on the theory that the bonds annoy humans: attachment; caring about others—their opinions, their expectations; the time and energy committed to self; the time and energy committed to school, work, family, hobbies, recreation, etc.; provide a belief in the values of the societal order which tend to produce the behavior observed in secondary school age adolescents. Hirschi views these components as generally related and as having some independent effects on the possibility that youth will initiate chronically disruptive behavior.

Delinquency is represented in the nature, interpretation, reinforcement, frustration, or hostility that is experienced as a bond between himself and society. The bulk of Hirschi's analysis focuses on his group of approximately 1,300 white males in California. His major dependent variable is the recency index which is composed of several questions regarding the involvement in delinquent behaviors. His questions include: "Have you ever taken little things that did not belong to you?" "Have you ever taken things of large value that did not belong to you?" "Have you ever taken a car for a ride without the owner's permission?" "Have you ever banged up something that did not belong to you on purpose?" "Not counting fights that you have had with a brother or sister, have you beaten up on anyone or hurt anyone on purpose?" These questions are used to establish the recency index (bond), as a simple sum across all acts.

Part of Hirschi's control theory postulates that attachment to school is similarly related to delinquency. Those who do poorly in school reduce their bond and hence have school-related difficulties which, in part, are delinquent acts—for example, truancy. The attachment to peers, depending on the peer's value structure, can be of a similar nature. Commitments to conventional kinds of activities are suggested: an athlete, committed to sports' principles, is less likely to be a delinquent than a youngster who admires big cars and certainly cannot own one but could steal one.

Control theory is brief and to the point, postulating that delinquency does not result from a failure to interact with the social order, but instead occurs because the youth adopts beliefs that disruptive behavior is a viable alternative to the social order. Specifically, it is Hirschi's position that attachment to parents generates a wider concern for the approval of persons in positions of authority, and ultimately a belief that societal norms bind one's conduct. Thus, attachment to conventional beliefs and the moral validity of their roles are not independent. The question of delinquency seems always to be one of cult—peer expectancy, peer pressure, or the gang. The general assumption is that most delinquency is a group or gang phenomenon. The literature on chronic disruptive behavior seems to suggest that many delinquents depend upon the values of the gang. The history of delinquent gang structures started with Shaw and McKay (1942) whose original data show that the predominance of disruptive acts involves more than one youngster. For all practical purposes, gang members are often defined as "frequent offenders who had committed more of their offenses in the presence of a companion" (p. 15).

Thrasher (1963) and Sutherland (1955), who worked on group structure in urban settings, further brought about the emphasis on groups of youth who seem to have as their purpose the displaying of chronically disruptive behavior. Cloward and Ohlin's (1960) book, *Delinquency and Opportunity: A Theory of Delinquent Gangs,* established an almost sociological tradition of focusing on gang delinquency. Tannenbaum (1966) issued a theory showing that the cornerstone of all chronically disruptive acts is group phenomena.

DeFleur (1967) stressed the importance of not confusing peer groups with gangs. She determined "among the sixty-three hard-core delinquents, forty-nine planned to be members of some type of group with regular associations" (p. 136). Two such groups were made up of only two persons, and for the present analysis these were eliminated. The remaining 47 respondents were found to have some general degree of gang membership but little allegiance. It was her work that for the first time seemed to stress the fact that most of the theories on gang structures were generalities.

Empey (1967) cites that the incidence of group delinquency is 60–90%. He cites six separate studies to confirm these figures and adds that most studies confirm the results. In another study, Empey and Rabow (1961) state: "The greater part of delinquent behavior is not that of individuals engaging in highly secretive deviations, but is a group phenomenon—a shared deviation, which is a product of differential group experience in a particular subculture" (p. 685).

The problem, then, is one of agreeing on a definition of group or gang. Klein (1969) takes issue with most group delinquency theories criticizing sloppy terminology. He would have us adopt a neutral term rather than gang or group, such as *companionate behavior.* Haney and Gold (1973) in *Psychology Today,* clearly state their opinion in a review of recent research that delinquency is companionship in crime-shared experiences, but not necessarily a gang experience. These authors studied 433 teenagers committing 2,490 delinquent acts. The majority of these acts, 70%, were in the presence of others. The lone offense tended to be the impulsive one, such as striking a parent, running away, etc.

Usually the delinquent acts are shared experiences. About 41% were with one other person, 23% with two others, 15% with three others, 9% with four others, and only 12% with five or more. The offender and companion were generally the same sex (70%) and the delinquent rarely committed an offense with the same partner twice. In fact, in that study only 11 teenagers committed more than half of his or her offenses with a most frequent companion. Those 11 youths committed 134 offenses. It is also interesting to note that of the 11 who committed frequent crimes in companionship frequently with the same people, 4 were girls. It may be that female gang membership is higher than male. There was also some evidence that children of parentage in higher socioeconomic classes tend to be more gang oriented than the more commonly thought of youngsters from the lower socioeconomic classes. If that can be verified, it will greatly reverse earlier theorization.

It would appear that two different issues have coincided to the point that an assumption has been made about their relationship. The myth that delinquency is gang-oriented behavior is derived from the fact that as one proceeds down the socioeconomic ladder, incidence of delinquency seems to increase. There is a clustering of youth who are prone to have difficulty with the school, difficulty with constructive community acts, and are plagued with trouble. In the eyes of many, this group comprises a gang. It may be that they hang out in the same places, that they are seen together, and upon occasion they even commit delinquent acts together. However, the frequency of those commitments is rare.

Secondly, there are a multitude of theories that delinquency is a result of peer pressure and gang relationships, and that the values of the gang are the ones that the delinquent holds most dear. Most of those theories have not been proven and in almost any attempt to define the values or mores of a gang, it is learned that delinquency is generally an impulsive act, not a planned one. Running away, truancy, stealing a car, and destructive behavior are generally not planned or premeditated. The act occurs on the spur of the moment. In fact, one of the largest distinctions between blue-collar and white-collar crime, between crime of youth and crime of adults, is the amount of impulsivity versus the amount of preconception that precedes it.

The controversy over whether delinquents have been fairly described as constituting a gang subculture is certainly not answered. Rathus and Siegal (1973) attempted to study the attitudes of delinquent gang members toward the rest of society. They hypothesized that if a subculture existed, then there would be variance between the attitudes that subculture held toward conventional groups, and that a clear pattern of self-esteem among the constituents of the delinquent subpopulation would be discernible. In their research, delinquents were defined as youth on probation. Nondelinquents were defined as students with no record of adjudication.

Sixty-three male delinquents, ranging from 12 to 16 years of age, were randomly selected from 300 offenders in upper New York State. A semantic differential technique was used to evaluate adjective pairs that have opposite meaning on a seven-point scale. The concepts rated were: self, policemen, law, education, work, managing money, and crime. The delinquents did not differentiate themselves in attitudes from nondelinquents on the education, work, and saving money variables. They did distinguish themselves in the negative relationship between delinquents' attitudes.

While any given sociological, psychological, and educational factor may be related to delinquency, that relationship should not be interpreted as one of cause and effect. What is important to recognize is that a socioeconomic condition may be associated to delinquency by the fact that a large group of delinquents are from lower socioeconomic homes. However, that does not imply predictability for a given delinquent. Nor does any one sociological, educational, or psychological factor seem to relate to any one type of offense, reason for adjudication, length of sentence, recidivism, or number of offenses. In summary, there are a number of determinates which do appear to contribute to delinquency, but that factor which triggers any one person's norm-violating act can rarely be determined.

Important considerations in delinquency

Sex.   In most western countries, the ratio of male to female delinquents is about six to one; in some countries, it is ten to one. Parsons (1967) holds that this ratio is the most illustrative indication of societies' different standards for the sexes. A society might look favorably on a male who takes a "joy ride" in a stolen car. His adventure may be regarded as an assertion of masculinity. The same behavior by a woman would be frowned upon since obedience and gentle behavior are expected from women. Something similar may be true of a boy's feelings toward his mother at puberty. The stronger the mother's control, the stronger the act of breaking it. In families of low socioeconomic status, when the father image is weak or even absent, relatively many crimes are committed by adolescents. However, the crimes committed by girls in this situation are generally quite different from those of boys.

Age.   The age at which an individual performs his first deviant act is very important. Glueck and Glueck (1956) found that, on the whole, if the acts of delinquency begin very early in life, they are abandoned at relatively early stages of adulthood. Conversely, if such acts begin later, they may be abandoned provided the natural processes of maturation are not interfered with by a treatment agency, school, parent, or community. In most western countries, mean age in delinquency is decreasing. In industrial countries, rate of crime by adults is going down; crime by juveniles is going up. The incidence of delinquency is generally highest during early adolescence; a mean age of 14 years is found in many countries. By age 21, the amount of criminal activity decreases quite substantially; however, severity of the crimes usually increases with age.

Social Class.   The social class to which a person belongs, as well as the culture, influences what he learns to accept as correct norms to observe. Cohen (1965) writes: "What we see when we look at the delinquent subcultures . . . is that it is nonutilitarian, malicious, and negative" (p. 25). It is defined by its *negative polarity* to the norms of *respectable society*. In delinquent subcultures, behavioral norms and values are at variance with those of the culture at large. The delinquent's conduct is normal by the values of his subculture, but wrong according to the larger culture.

THE FAMILY AS THE PRIMARY SOCIAL SUBCULTURE

The home is the primary subcultural environment in which the parents establish tone and conditions and, to a large extent, shape their children's behavior. Yet a youth's interaction with parents and immediate environment always remains at an individual level. Though their environment might be conducive to producing delinquent youths, one can only discuss a particular delinquent youth in the light of the particular events that have interacted to produce the behavior which society sees as inappropriate. In speaking about a particular individual and his delinquency, precise observations must be made in reference to the causative factors, time events, and place of his delinquency behavior.

Delinquency studies in high-risk neighborhoods in various cities have sometimes found that even brothers in the same family may differ considerably in regard to their respect for social values. It may happen that a policeman, a minister, and a criminal come from the same family. The obvious fact is that no two people are alike genetically nor respond to their environment in similar ways. Even if it were possible to create an ideal environment at home and school, it would not be so for more than one person. The mother who works to treat all her children alike, denying one a birthday party because his brother does not want one, has not treated her children as individuals. She may have denied one the very consideration that would have promoted his social growth. On the other hand, to force both brothers to have birthday parties would be just as inequitable, especially if one brother were as socially retiring as the other was socially outgoing.

Family breakdowns are occurring in our society with increasing regularity as evidenced by rising divorce rates, changes in role relationships among family members, and the social disorganization that accompanies advancing urbanization. Delinquency is also increasing steadily, which may suggest a relationship of the above factors to both family stability and the social adjustment of children. Except for orientals and blacks, delinquency occurs about twice as frequently among the children of immigrants as among those of native-born parents (Conger & Miller, 1966). Parental prestige, the foreign language factor, and the change from a simple rural to a complex urban environment are all contributing factors. First-generation parents may themselves have difficulty adapting to the new environment. Parental inability to guide their children, due to their own limited experience in a new cultural setting, may contribute to role model deficiencies. One middle-class culture frequently restricts boys from lower classes in the achievement of material possession. In considering this matter, Cloward and Ohlin (1960) noted that delinquents repeatedly wanted big cars, flashy clothes, and swell dames.

> These symbols of success, framed primarily in economic terms rather than in terms of middle-class life styles suggest . . . that the participants in delinquency subcultures are seeking higher status within their own cultural milieu. If legitimate paths to higher status become restricted, then the delinquent subculture provides alternative avenues. . . . (p. 96)

Other studies have shown delinquents to be either highly motivated to obtain material possessions and comforts (Cartwright, Howard, & Short, 1966) or frustrated by a lack of economic and social status. They cite the emphasis upon gang membership among lower-class youths as one way of meeting the needs for feelings of personal worth and peer acceptance to overcome what they feel are deficiencies in material possessions and social position.

INCIDENCE OF SOCIAL MALADJUSTMENT

The purpose of examining delinquency in some detail was to acquaint the reader with the factors that are associated with it. However, there are many socially troubled youths who do not violate society's values but whose problems interfere with their own adjustment.

In 1954, MacFarlane, Allen, and Honzik reported data collected longitudinally since 1929 on 252 children who were part of the Berkeley survey. The survey drew its sample from one of every three children born between January 1, 1928, and June 30, 1929. Eighty-six youths were available for study in their 14th year, enabling the investigators to sample 46 possible problem areas. The results showed that problems of speech, elimination of fears, thumbsucking, overactivity, destructiveness, and temper declined with age. Nailbiting was the only problem to increase with age, subsiding by age 14. Problems such as insufficient appetite and lying rose to a peak and then subsided. Several problem areas showed a twin peaking effect, one occurring at the time of school entrance and the other at adolescence. These were evidently situational problems likely to appear when a child is under stress. Included in this group were restless sleep, disturbing dreams, physical timidity, irritability, attention demanding, overdependence, somberness, and jealousy.

The only problem which had no evident relationship to age was that of oversensitivity, which persisted in girls throughout the years of the study but dropped dramatically in boys after age 12. Oversensitivity in an observable behavior, frequently displayed as a reaction to a fear, such as a meeting expectancy (measuring up to what others think). The early adolescent girl may fear a social situation such as a party, because she has facial acne; or she may have too timid a voice to receive a part in the junior play.

Another major finding in this study was the differing patterns in sibling birth order. First-born boys were more withdrawn and tended to internalize their problem much more than those occupying another position in the birth order. Younger children were seen to be more aggressive and competitive than their older siblings. First-born girls appeared to have more problems and difficulty in coping with stress situations. Of all the findings presented by MacFarlane et al., the most important one was that most problem behaviors did not persist throughout the age range. Children seem to enter periods when several problems are manifest, around 5 to 7 years of age, subsiding by 11 to 12. Although this data was collected in the late 1920's, it is not outdated and Table 1.1 should be studied carefully. The authors concluded with a rather concise statement:

May we pay our respect to the adaptive capacity of the human organism, born in a very unfinished and singular dependent state into a highly complex and not too sensible world. Unless handicapped by inadequate structure and health, and impossible and capricious learning situations, he treads his way to some measure of stable and characteristic patterning. . . . (p. 154)

Table 1.1. THE PREVALENCE OF SOME BEHAVIOR CHARACTERISTICS IN A WEIGHTED REPRESENTATIVE SAMPLE OF 482 CHILDREN AGED 6 TO 12 AS REPORTED BY THEIR MOTHERS

	Percent
1. Fears and worries, seven or more present	43
2. Bedwetting within the past year	
all frequencies	17
once a month or more	8
3. Nightmares	28
4. Food intake	
less than "normal"	20
more than "normal"	16
5. Temper loss	
once a month or more	80
twice a week or more	48
once a day or more	11
6. Overactivity	49
7. Restlessness	30
8. Stuttering	4
9. Unusual movements, twitching, or jerking (tics)	12
10. Biting nails	
all intensities	27
nails bitten down (more severe)	17
11. Grinding teeth	14
12. Sucking thumb or fingers	
all frequencies	10
"almost all the time"	2
13. Biting, sucking, or chewing clothing or other objects	16
14. Picking nose	26
15. Picking sores	16
16. Chewing or sucking lips or tongue or biting inside of mouth	11

Another study of maladjustment (Lapouse & Monk, 1959) used the survey technique to study a sample of 482 children between 6 and 12 years of age by interviewing mothers in their homes in Buffalo, New York. They found more intense and higher incidences of worries and fears in lower socioeconomic children and black children. An examination of the characteristics covered by the survey suggests that most of the concerns manifested by children could be considered normal.

Adolescents live under many stress situations, a stress situation being defined as one that denies comfort and tends to promote threat. A trip to the family physician may be a pleasant visit for an adult, but for the youth it may produce fears and worries that result in many inappropriate and attention-getting behaviors. The overt behaviors listed in Table 1.1 may not have clear direct relationships with the real fears or worries that may produce them. They may be only symptomatic representations of the youth's real problems, or no problem at all. Youth A may bite his fingernails to alleviate anxiety produced from the fear of failing to achieve his parents' expectancies. Youth B may bite his fingernails to remove irritating dirt. Fingernail biting is a symptom; the point is, a symptom of what?

The relativity of problem behaviors, or at least troublesome behaviors or misbehaviors, is reflected in Zeitlein's (1957) report that as high as 41% of the entire student age school population was cited once or more for misbehaving during the school year. Of the misbehaviors reported, 82% involved problems of disturbance, disobedience, and disrespect. Boys were more frequent offenders than girls. It was also reported in this study that children from higher socioeconomic homes, with higher IQ's, did better academically in school, and children with greater popularity were better adjusted than children who lacked these attributes.

Incidents of problems in delinquent youth were reported in a study by Eisner (1969). He analyzed data from San Francisco, dividing the youth according to several variables. Making separate tabulations for boys and girls found in other studies, boys showed delinquent behaviors averaging six times higher than girls. The ratio varied in different city census tracts, the lowest ratio being 3½ to 1. In one San Francisco census tract, the boys' rate was nine times that of the girls. Dividing the individual groups of boys and girls by race and age and comparing four age divisions among the five groups, the author viewed the problems of delinquency for each sex and race at each age.

The data in Table 1.2 indicate that the delinquency rates varied considerably with race. The lowest delinquency rates for both boys and girls were among Chinese. This fact was true at all ages except for the very youngest boys (8 to 10 years old). In order of increasing delinquency

Table 1.2. DELINQUENCY RATES (1960) PER 1,000 BY SEX, RACE, AND AGE

INTERACTIONS	MALES (Age in Years)				FEMALES (Age in Years)			
	8–10	11–13	14–16	17	8–10	11–13	14–16	17
All Interactions:								
White	10	47	167	210	1	6	28	27
White-Spanish	18	62	251	444	2	9	36	33
Negro	35	146	381	575	5	39	86	60
Chinese	8	26	54	72	0	1	10	3
Other	3	82	189	310	0	20	54	46
Juvenile Court Cases:								
White	8	33	84	86	0	6	22	10
White-Spanish	13	36	99	173	2	9	31	13
Negro	29	118	252	295	5	37	78	36
Chinese	5	20	40	46	0	1	10	3
Other	2	67	124	184	0	18	49	22

From: Eisner, *The Delinquency Label*, 1969, p. 35. Reproduced with permission. Random House, Inc.

TABLE 1.3.   JUVENILE COURT DELINQUENCY RATES (1960) BY SEX, RACE, AND INCOME

Race	MALES				FEMALES			
	0–$2,500	$2,500–$5,000	$5,000–$10,000	Over $10,000	0–$2,500	$2,500–$5,000	$5,000–$10,000	Over $10,000
White	20	70	20	3	8	19	3	0
White-Spanish	18	62	11	2	9	13	3	0
Negro	81	104	121	3	30	22	9	0
Chinese	3	11	14	2	0	2	2	0
Other	6	63	21	0	12	18	4	0

From: Eisner, *The Delinquency Label*, 1969, p. 37. Reproduced with permission. Random House, Inc.

rates, the racial breakdown showed a progression from Chinese to white, "other," white-Spanish, and black. The highest rates for both sexes at all ages were for blacks. The black group displayed rates many times higher than those of the average Chinese youth. Seventeen-year-old blacks, in fact, had an average delinquency rate of 575 per 1,000; over half were either warned by the police or sent to juvenile court in the course of a year. The rate of juvenile court citations for the black group as a whole was 295 of 1,000.

Table 1.3 represents the delinquency rates by race, sex, and family income. Unexpectedly, the highest rates did not appear in the lowest income groups except for black girls. The majority of delinquents appears in the family annual income levels between $2,500 and $5,000. The highest rates of delinquency were black and Chinese boys whose parents were in the $5,000 to $10,000 annual income bracket. The findings that maximum rates of delinquency were in middle-income groups were true for this study and do not agree with many studies which frequently report most delinquents to come from the lower-income groups.

Table 1.4 takes into account the number of parents in the home. The preliminary results showed that the number of parents in the home was a factor that affected delinquency labeling. However, the study of this factor did not produce consistent data. The presence of two parents in the home was associated with low delinquency rates. The highest rates were found when there was only one parent; the speculated reasons being the lack of a role model and in-home control. However, the pattern seems clear. Juveniles who have no parents (no parents suggests guardians, custodians, or other conservers in wife-husband assembly) in their homes have delinquency rates slightly above those who have both parents. Adolescents with delinquency rates were also more likely to come from broken families.

Eisner (1969) contended that both the definition and statistics of delinquency need overhauling. The common statistic that 4% of the 10- to 17-year-old group are apprehended by policemen in a year is misleading.

> The delinquency rates of high-risk groups are sufficient, I believe, to force a complete reevaluation of the usual concept that delinquents are deviants, that is, that they differ in their attributes from the "normal" boys of the community. If three out of four 17-year-old Negro boys in two large districts of San Francisco are recorded as delinquent in the course of a year, I submit that the deviant in this group is the one boy in four who does not become delinquent. But if delinquency is not due to deviant members of the group, one is driven to the conclusion that the entire group, at least by police standards, must live a life that is opposed by the rest of the community. We should speak of deviant groups, not deviant individuals. The delinquent in this group is the normal member of his society. Psychotherapy

Table 1.4. JUVENILE COURT DELINQUENCY RATES (1960) BY
SEX, RACE, AND NUMBER OF PARENTS IN THE HOME

| | MALES | | | FEMALES | | |
| | Number of Parents | | | Number of Parents | | |
Race	2	1	0	2	1	0
White	20	65	23	3	18	10
White-Spanish	19	64	28	5	15	6
Negro	44	100	47	11	31	14
Chinese	9	15	22	1	3	0
Other	27	34	35	10	9	14

From: Eisner, *The Delinquency Label*, 1969, p. 38. Reproduced with permission. Random House, Inc.

> will not cure his delinquency; and a cure of delinquency will not help him to get along in his society—indeed, it may very well alienate him from his friends and associates.   (p. 43)

The citizenry of the great middle-class culture have many status needs, but they frequently fail to recognize the status needs of youth who reside in different subcultures. There is no general society for them; the society we know is the particular subculture in which we live. Why, then, do we repeatedly ask others to join our society when we fail to understand theirs?

Middle-class values are the standards by which most behaviors are judged. That suggests that an obvious discrepancy exists between two value structures that are commonly called social classes—the middle class acting in the capacity of judge; the lower social classes are the judged. It is probably true that " . . . more lower status youngsters commit delinquent acts more frequently than do higher status youngsters" (Gold, 1966, p. 27). The fact still remains that one class of society sets the relative social condition by which others are determined adequate or inadequate. The types of delinquent acts between lower, middle, and upper classes are not different. There is evidence (Voss, 1966) that directly disputes the claims of Cloward, Ohlin, Cohen, and Merton, namely, that boys in the higher social strata are just as involved in delinquency affairs as are boys in the lower strata. Frease (1973) writes:

> While our data do not deal with kinds of delinquent behavior but rather delinquent behavior *per se*, it is engaging to note that a variation on all these themes involves the kinds of delinquent behavior observed *vis-a-vis* class position. Some show on the one hand that the higher status boys become

more involved in property destruction and the more "serious" kinds of offenses, while low status youth are "more inclined to smoke regularly, skip school, fight, and use narcotics." On the other hand, Cohen theorizes that lower-class delinquency is characterized, in part, by its destructive and malicious nature." (p. 444)

However, it is true that being born white and middle class gives a youth advantages in securing a person's position in society. As a result, blue-collar youngsters tend to rise in the system, displacing white-collar youth. The consequence of this mobility is to blur visible class boundaries. The language, dress, and manner of all classes of youth in the 1930s made it virtually impossible for the officials to distinguish blue-collar delinquents from middle-class youth.

Empey and Erickson (1966, p. 549) add that: "It was our impression that virtually all of these officially serious respondents had low status roots . . . it was not until we gathered objective data on their background that we discovered that we were wrong. The regular 'uniform' was being worn by middle as well as low status boys."

In effect, even if the police were interested in differential law enforcement by class, it may be virtually impossible to do so. The intragroup similarity of delinquents would prevent this. At any rate, social class, using our data, does not appear to be a satisfactory criteria for predicting delinquency. What, then, might be a better predictor? Frease (1973) writes:

It is a basic truism in an industrial culture that material success and amount of formal education are positively correlated so that for the most part, later occupational and material achievement require earlier educational triumphs of at least modest proportions.   (p 448)

Frease advances several reasons for the problems associated with lower- and middle-class difficulties having a common antecedent with school. The first reason is that of poor school achievement by middle-class youth, no matter what the reason. Certainly, many youth, expecially males, fail in school, and it is more than pure speculation that the pressure of home and school alike are greater for middle-class youth. Frequently, a middle-class youth failing the system takes refuge in lower-class attitude, dress, and rebellious attitude, with the primary rebellion against the school and other authority. Frease (1973) states:

If a person perceives himself as relatively worthless, a poor student, and an object of derision, it is quite likely he will behave accordingly. With this category of individual, we would expect poor school and work performance. Since these two areas of school and work are so inexorably bound together in an industrial culture, performance in one is often positively correlated with performance in the other.   (p. 450)

LABELING, EXPECTANCY, AND SOCIAL PERFORMANCE

Labeling has become a major factor in special education in the last four or five years. It is now recognized that labeling youth has a major two-dimensional consequence. On the one hand, youth who are labeled take on the characteristics implied by the label. The second aspect of labeling is the teacher's self-reinforcing attitude that he or she need not teach because the student cannot make use of the teaching. Dunn (1968) states the relationship between the labeling process and the self-fulfilling prophecy: "We must expect that labeling a student 'handicapped' reduces the teacher's expectancy for him to succeed" (p. 9). According to the model presented, this lowered expectancy can be communicated to the student, who in turn is less likely to succeed. Even without direct communication of the lowered expectancy to the student, a deleterious effect of labeling can be expected through altered perceptions of the student's behavior due to a "halo" effect. The phenomenon may affect the student in subtle or obvious ways to induce behavior change.

Palardy (1969) investigated the relationship between teacher expectations and pupil performance by sending a questionnaire to obtain 42 first grade teachers' indications of how successful they thought first grade boys were in reading compared to first grade girls. The teachers were divided into two sections, a high and low expectancy group. Palardy noted that boys assigned to low expectancy teachers achieved significantly poorer scores than boys assigned to high expectancy teachers. Differences were not noted for boys and girls with high expectancy teachers, or for girls under either expectancy condition.

Seaver (1973) postulated that the performance of students would be directly related to the performance of their older siblings. If the older siblings had been good students, the students they studied would fare positively. If the older siblings were poor students, a negative expectancy would exist. The author reports that the teachers' experiences with older siblings generated a teacher-bias which transferred to the younger siblings affecting academic performance.

The process of labeling a student as "special" has come under considerable attack in recent years (Jones, 1972; Gallagher, 1972; Blatt, 1972; Meyen, 1971). Gallagher (1972) states: "The problem with labeling a student educably mentally retarded, for example, and placing him in a special program is a current suspicion, backed by respectable research, that such a placement does *not* lead to effective treatment" (p. 529). Gallagher and others have noted that the labeling process generally implies a deficiency, congruent with the medical model, but gives little educational guidance as to appropriate treatment.

The labeling process has been seen as a preliminary step in the exclusion of students from normal activities (Gallagher, 1972) despite the idealistic philosophy of normalcy often espoused by special educators (Reynolds & Balow, 1971). Dunn (1968) points out that this exclusion from normalcy works to the detriment of the student excluded. Blatt (1972) criticized the labeling process in saying that " . . . there is widespread usage of systems for labeling youths that dehumanize and stigmatize both these youth and their families" (p. 543). He further points out that labeling emphasizes deviancy, and makes a unidimensional problem a multidimensional one. Other criticisms include: problems of misidentification involved in the labeling process and the frequent assignment of minority group youths to disability status (Mercer, 1971). Maurer (1972) likens the labeling process to the establishment of anti-hero or scapegoat groups and encourages a complete reappraisal of the evaluation system through which some youths are categorized as special.

Foster (1974) notes that:

> One of the more recent disability categories to receive widespread attention is that of learning disabled. A relatively new area, widespread agreement has yet to be reached concerning the criteria to be used in labeling the learning disabled youth or the prevalence of this problem within the educational setting. (p. 4)

Ford (1971) defends labeling the learning disabled on the grounds that it is a break with the traditional medical model and an attempt to give education its own terminology. He further points out that the definition stresses normal intelligence. Maurer (1972), however, suggests that the learning disabled category has reduced the percentage of youths seen as normal to an unacceptable level.

The most influential but controversial research dealing with teacher expectancy effects was published by Rosenthal and Jacobson in 1968. Despite harsh criticism (Thorndike, 1968) of the methodological and design errors, *Pygmalion in the Classroom* focused the attention of all those working with children on the problem of expectancy. Rosenthal and Jacobson's research was conducted under the guise of validating a nonlanguage group intelligence test called the Harvard Test of Inflected Acquisition. This test was presumed to identify students who would demonstrate increased academic performance during the coming school year. In reality, it was the Test of General Ability.

A randomly selected 20% of the students were designated as potential spurters by the researchers. The teachers were informed this group was capable of doing better. Of this group, 47% gained 20 or more total IQ points in comparison to 19% of the students in the control group.

In discussing the relationship between deficiency labels and performance on academic tasks, Jones (1972) concludes: "There has been no work which supports the belief that deficit labels actually affect the learning and performance of those so labeled'' (p. 557). This followed two attempts to demonstrate the deleterious effects of labeling on academic performance.

In approaching the labeling controversy from a different perspective, Jones (1970) attempted to measure the expectancies generated in a group of student teachers by labeling a student as "culturally deprived." In terms of the model outlined, Jones was measuring the transference of expectancy to an intermediate agent by the stimulus of a deficiency label. The School Morale Inventory (Wrightman, Nelson, & Tanto, 1968) was completed under two conditions by 163 undergraduate college students (75% of whom were prospective teachers). In the experimental condition 119 subjects were given the following instructions:

> Please fill out the enclosed inventory according to the instructions on the booklet. However, instead of answering the questions as you normally would, answer as you think the person described below would respond: A 12-year-old culturally deprived boy in the 6th grade in an inner-city school. Remember, you are to answer as you feel this person would.   (p. 559)

Identical instructions were given to 44 students in the control group except that the boy was not described as culturally deprived or as having an inner-city background. Significant differences were noted between the experimental and control groups for all seven morale areas measured by the inventory, with the deprived condition yielding consistently lower morale scores.

Ross (1974) investigated the extent to which physical attractiveness could influence teacher judgements concerning four factors: (1) possible special class placement; (2) future problems in peer interactions; (3) need for psychological assessment; and (4) future academic problems. Psychological reports were provided to each of 76 second, third, and fourth grade teachers. Written portions of these reports were identical except for pronouns referring to the sex of the youth. Reports were designed to balance evidence that was supportive and non-supportive for decision making. A photograph depicting either an attractive male, an unattractive male, an attractive female, or an unattractive female was attached to each psychological report. Attractiveness of the child constituted the chief independent variable under investigation. Results indicate that teachers exposed to the psychological reports containing the unattractive photographs gave significantly more negative ratings to each of the four factors than did teachers exposed to the more attractive photographs.

Beeze (1970) conducted an expectancy study designed to measure both the experimenter bias effect resulting from high and low teacher expectancies, and to note the types of teacher behaviors responsible for the expectancy transference. In his design, Beeze randomly assigned 60 headstart students and 60 tutors (education students) to either a high or low expectancy condition. Expectancies were manipulated by biased psychological reports presented to the tutors. Tutors were to teach a series of words to their student during a 10-minute teaching session. A jigsaw puzzle task was then presented to the student while an observer recorded the number of cues presented to the student. Finally, the student was retested by the observer on the number of words retained. The tutor indicated the level at which he or she thought a student could succeed on an intelligence test. He or she completed a rating sheet on the student indicating how it was believed the student would compare to students in the regular classroom on intellectual ability, achievement, and social competency.

The tutor summarized the data by noting that teachers, responding to the biased expectancies, presented fewer words to the low expectancy group, who in turn learned fewer words. The created expectancies were not altered, even when students with low ability performed as well on the puzzle task as did students with high ability. No difference in number of cues given on the puzzle task was noted between the two groups. Teachers of the high expectancy group felt the puzzle task was appropriate for their students while the tutors of the low expectancy group felt the task was too difficult. Most teachers of both groups thought the psychological reports helpful.

Schain (1972) explored the possibility that low expectancies affect both pupil learning and teacher behavior for low ability youths. He identified 30 low ability kindergarten children (Primary Mental Abilities Test IQ's between 71 and 89) and randomly assigned each child to one of 30 tutors under three different expectancy conditions: (1) high expectancy condition; (2) low expectancy condition; or (3) unlabeled expectancy condition. A biased psychological report was mailed to the tutors before teaching sessions began. Schain reported no differences in the number of words learned between the three expectancy conditions. No differences were found in pupil response to tutor requests or recorded teacher behaviors (number of words presented, number of definitions given, verbal reinforcers, words reviewed, total time of task and teaching techniques employed).

Carter (1969) reported the results of a study similar in methodology to the work of Beeze and Schain. Carter's pupil population consisted of 60 kindergarten subjects previously determined to be functioning at the level of educable mentally retarded children. Correspondingly, 60 tutors were chosen from 200 college undergraduates enrolled in elementary methods courses. They were chosen on the basis of Rotter's I-E Control Scale (Rotter, 1966) to yield a group of 30 internally controlled and 30 externally controlled tutors. The two groups were each randomly assigned to a high or low expectancy condition, expectancies being manipulated through biased psychological reports. The results failed to demonstrate any difference between externally controlled groups and expectancy conditions. For the internally controlled tutors, however, significantly more words were presented under high expectancy conditions than under low expectancy conditions. Carter interprets this finding as evidence that

> internally controlled teachers may more readily receive, process and act upon available information because they feel outcomes are a direct result of human interventions rather than fate or chance. (p. 79)

The combined high expectancy groups did not learn more words than did the combined low expectancy groups although this difference did approach statistical significance. Carter suggests psychological reports fail to establish a strong expectancy.

SOCIAL MALADJUSTMENT AND OTHER HANDICAPS

Earlier in this chapter delinquency was related to all types of social, family, and economic conditions; however, we did not relate delinquency to other handicaps, since few studies have been conducted to interrelated the variable of social disability and other handicaps. Youths with social maladjustments are generally thought to have normal mental and physical attributes, but some have other handicaps. A youth handicapped with a social maladjustment is not usually considered multihandicapped because the social disorder is secondary to a primary mental or physical handicap. A primary handicap is used to describe an adolescent with a disability unrelated to any other handicap. Social maladjustment is generally considered an overlay to a primary mental or physical handicap and is, therefore, a secondary handicap. It is important that the teacher, with the assistance from other professionals, make a distinction between secondary and primary social maladjustments, evidenced by the handicapped persons.

The so-called defective delinquent is a youth with mental retardation and delinquency. In 1951, Westwell reported that a committee of members from the American Association on Mental Deficiency (AAMD) met to study the problems of the defective delinquent. They concluded:

A mentally defective delinquent is any person affected with intellectual impairment from birth, or from an early age, to such an extent that he is incapable of managing himself and his affairs; who is charged with, arraigned for, or convicted of a criminal offense; and who for his own welfare and the welfare of others in the community, requires supervision, control, or care; and who is not insane or of unsound mind to such an extent as to require his commitment to an institution for the insane. (p. 285)

There seems to be no real relationship between the degree of intelligence and delinquency. Kvaraceus (1964) has interpreted defective delinquency in terms of Dollard's theory that frustration leads to aggression. This is borne out in the retarded delinquent because he or she has less tolerance for frustration. However, it is not true, that there are more delinquents in the retarded range of intelligence. The mentally retarded are seemingly more easily apprehended by the police, whether or not they had a major or minor role in the delinquency act performed. The most significant attribute relating IQ and delinquency is the variable of social-cultural influences. These range for the delinquent from poor home conditions and parental training to mistreatment with a poor nonunderstanding community environment. Blackhurst (1968) reviewed information on various aspects of mental retardation and delinquency and reported on twelve alternative hypotheses to account for the relationship between delinquency and retardation other than low IQ. They were:

1. There is a "relatively higher incidence of mental retardation among the socially, economically, and culturally deprived segment of our population, which also produces the proportion of prison inmates." (Allen, 1966, p. 4)

2. When negative correlations between intelligence and delinquency are found, they can be attributed "to the association with delinquency of that constellation of cultural factors which adversely affect the test score."
(Woodward, 1955, p. 282)

3. There are more commitments and fewer paroles for mentally retarded individuals accused of crimes; thus, one might expect the incarcerated population to be lower in intelligence. (Glueck, 1935, p. 555)

4. Many times, retarded individuals are used as pawns by more intelligent ring leaders and are apprehended more easily.
(Wallace, 1929, p. 95)

5. Delinquent individuals from good homes, and who have high IQ scores, are often returned to their homes, if it appears

that the parents are able and willing to provide adequate control. (Mann & Mann 1939, p. 355)

6. The retarded often make more mistakes while committing crimes and are not clever in eluding pursuit.
(Wallace, 1929, p. 94)

7. Very often, delinquency is accompanied by emotional instability, which can result in lower scores on intelligence tests. (Burt, 1923, p.172)

8. Retarded females who engage in illicit sexual activities are more frequently apprehended than normal females who engage in similar acts. (Wallace, 1929, p. 95)

9. Criminals often score lower on tests of intellectual ability because of errors of a specific sort; they disobey instructions and are more impulsive in the testing situation. This is characteristic of extroverts, and there are more extroverts in the delinquent than in the normal population.
(Payne, 1961, p. 92)

10. Often, the retarded do not have sufficient funds to provide for adequate defense counsel and are subsequently convicted.
(Wallace, 1929, p. 93)

11. Delinquents may have low educational attainment, thus handicapping them on verbal IQ tests. For example, one group of delinquents had mean verbal IQ scores of 82, but had mean performance IQ scores of 98 on the WISC.
(Payne, 1961, p. 85)

12. Many times a diagnosis of mental retardation in the criminal population has been arrived at by using a mental age score of 11 or 12 years as a criterion. Wallin (1924) indicated that with this as a criterion, 47% (44,556,000) of whites and 89% (9,309,400) of Negroes would have been classified as mentally retarded in 1922 (based on World War I army records). It is apparent that the use of norms established for children, as in the example above, is an unacceptable practice when testing adults and would lead to inflated estimates of lowered intelligence in the criminal population.
(Zeleny, 1933, p. 376)

Mulligan (1969) wrote concerning the origin and characteristics of dyslexia (reading disability) and concomitant delinquency problems. He confirmed earlier studies about illiteracy and its association with anti-social behaviors. He found the 60% of most known delinquents were youths with two or more years of academic reading retardation. He also described the need for closer diagnostic study of delinquent nonreaders to determine if both conditions could have common antecedents. A criminologist (Keldgod, 1969) attempted to establish brain damage as a common antecedent of delinquency and other problems in a study of apprehended youths. Taylor (1969) reviewed the literature and reported on 100 epileptic youths. He concluded that aggressiveness in these patients was less likely to be a result of present interference in brain structures and more likely to be a result of early brain damage to mental control structures. His findings suggest that to prevent learned behavior problems, parental management and special training considerations are needed early.

Believing that the handicapped must be recognized as people, Gruhn and Krause (1968) examined the psychological and social adjustment of 35 female and 38 male vocational high school students with significant handicaps of all types by means of sociometric procedure and standardized questionnaires completed by students and teachers. In comparing these handicapped individuals to a nonhandicapped group, both showed similar adjustments on the sociometric scale, self-concept, and teacher evaluation. The handicapped had a far greater need for friends, were rigid in view of self, and had a significantly reduced level of aspiration.

Mitchell (1970) investigated differences in *Barrier* scores between groups assessed as either high or low in their adjustment to the stress induced by severe physical disability. The Barrier score, an index of adjustment to reality, was constructed of positive social and vocational goals. The subjects were 48 paraplegics and 48 quadraplegics. The high- and low-scoring paraplegics were significantly different on various social, adaptive, and personality measures. There was no significant difference between quadraplegic groups who scored high and low. The study indicated that the amount of physical involvement does not critically interfere with adjustment until that point where the lack of physical function interferes with personal and vocational success and, therefore, independence.

Ossowski (1969) found that the motivation of blind youth to respond to stress—consisting of heightened emotional tension, action to satisfy primary drives, or basic needs—was determined by the types of stress, perception of stress, self-appraisal capabilities, resistance to stress, and whether one's disability might be exposed by counteracting stress. Their choice of actions was motivated by:

1. Fear of being juxtaposed with the public.
2. Fear of being made aware of their handicaps.
3. Striving to show that blindness is not the worst handicap.

Nihiro, Foster, and Spencer (1968) established the need to understand the basic parameters of coping behaviors, which in the retarded vary considerably in nature and content, according to the level of retardation in the physically handicapped. Even if this is so, it may be very hard for normal social reactions to occur because the disability itself seemingly attracts so much attention. This in turn detracts from an interpersonal relationship between the handicapped and the physically normal person. Davis (1961) found that the interaction between the physically impaired and normal person was characterized by an overcompensation of the normal person for the handicapped. This limited the relationship; the behaviors were rigid, and the sentence structures in consideration were short.

It is useful to understand how the normal person reacts to physical impairment in others. Aesthetic aversion can be seen in the reactions of normal youths to physical deviance (impairment) in other youths (Barker, 1964). For example, over 600 10- to 12-year-olds consistently ranked youth's pictures according to their liking of them in the following order (from most to least liked): a normal youth, a youth with crutches and a leg brace, a youth in a wheel chair, a youth with a left forearm amputation, a youth with a slight facial disfigurement, and an obese youth (Richardson & Royce, 1968). The same order was found using a social distance technique with drawings in a high school sample. Youths who had an aesthetic impairment were the least liked by girls; and the forearm amputee, who had a functional impairment, was the least liked by boys in both age groups (Matthews and Westie, 1966). Racial variables made no difference in the rank ordering (Richardson & Royce, 1968).

Unfortunately, youth's negative attitudes seem to increase with age (Billings, 1963) and are not overcome by social contact with the deviant (Richardson, 1969). Shears and Jensema (1969) suggested, on the basis of 94 young adults' social distance evaluations and rankings of 10 anomalies with respect to desirability in a friend and as a self-affliction, that six dimensions combine and interact to form attitudes toward deviants: visibility, communication, social stigma, reversibility, degree of incapacity, and difficulty in daily living. Perhaps youth are more critical of physically visible and social stigma in their consistently high rejection of the obviously handicapped youths. This possibility is suggested by 186 high school students' responses of 12 exceptionalities, using a paired comparison questionnaire (Jones, Gottfried, & Owens, 1966). In this study, the more visible disabilities led to greater rejection regardless of the social context described; but the ordering of less visible anomalies interacted with social context.

The nature of social interaction and social status relates closely to an individual's emotional adjustment, whether judged by self-concept (Wylie, 1967) or by personality traits (Coopersmith, 1967). In study after study, the social acceptability of youths from preschool to college age, has been found to relate significantly and positively to personality or emotional adjustment and negatively to anxiety. The criteria for adjustment included teachers' ratings (Kwall, Smith, & Lachner, 1967), degree of initiation of verbal interaction with peers, independence from adults, responses to projective techniques such as the Rorschach (Northway & Wigdor, 1947), creative thinking (Yamamoto, Lembright, & Corrigan, 1966), and responses to anxiety scales (Ueda, 1964). Usually, however, researchers have examined responses to self-concept and/or social-personal adjustment on questionnaires. The nature of the relationship is unclear, but a slight positive relationship occurs quite consistently in experimental studies, regardless of the size, sex, socioeconomic status, or heterogeneity of the sample. Therefore, one would expect socially unaccepted youths, such as physical deviates, to show poorer emotional adjustment than more accepted youths.

> In view of their generally negative public reception and of the "looking-glass" nature of self-concepts, it is no wonder that those who are deviant are inclined to be frustrated, unhappy, and often hostile . . . No matter how visible their stigmata, individuals well attempt to "cover" them; the extra "performance" required (Goffman, 1959) drains the deviants' energy and their failure to minimize their defects tends to discourage them.   (p. 113)

In conjunction with the above opinion of Yamamoto, et al., (1966) is the finding that self-descriptions of 107 9- to 11-year-old handicapped youths, when compared to those of nonhandicapped youths, showed more expression of personal inadequacy and uncertainty and more general self-depreciation.

(Richardson, Hastorf, & Dornbusch, 1964)

CONCLUSION

Hopefully, this chapter provided a sense of proportion on the critical issues relating to chronic norm-violating disruptive youth. The legal issue cannot be avoided; historically, youth were not viewed as being in trouble until they were adjudicated, and pre-delinquency was not seen as a communtiy or public school problem. Changes in adjudication practices, the rapid expansion of community-based treatment, and modification of attitude by public school persons have contributed to viewing norm-violating behaviors as a school related issue, particularly since youth are within the public schools domain before they enter an institution and after they return. In addition, recidivism reflects that isolated, non-articulated public school and institutional programs only breed failure.

Although, still a legally meaningful term, the focus is the prevention and the reference on identifiable target behavior. In essence, it is no longer the youth that can summarily be called bad—only certain identifiable behaviors. Even the use of the label *bad* may well initial a chain of self-fulfilling prophecy. More importantly, there can be no understanding of a bad adolescent that lends itself to correction. On the other hand, target behaviors can be identified and focal work toward modification can be applied. Maybe what is still in effect is a basic belief that behavior, crippled by environment, poor models, limited socially approved reinforcement, repeated school failure, and outweight scorn of the middle citizenry, can be altered.

On some library shelf is a master's thesis that tells the story of a young looking, mid-20-year-old student majoring in education who forged a set of papers, stating he had just been released from the state boarding school for boys. He visited 20 odd high schools to be rejected 19 times and admitted once on probation. Maybe it is still our attitude that a bad apple spoils the barrel, and that good apples are corrupted by bad apples. Youth are not apples, and behaviors though communicated, can be shaped to yield productive lives. The option: mix bad apples with bad apples and have one behavioral standard remains counterproductive to solid citizenry.

REFERENCES

Allen, R. C. "Toward an Exceptional Offenders Court." *Mental Retardation* 4 (1966): 3–7.

Barker, D. G. "Concepts of Disabilities." *Personnel and Guidance Journal* 43 (1964): 371–374.

Beeze, W. "Influence of Biased Psychological Reports on Teacher Behavior." Unpublished doctoral dissertation, Indiana University, 1970.

Billings, H. K. "An Exploratory Study of the Attitudes of Noncrippled Children Toward Crippled Children in Three Selected Elementary Schools." *Journal of Experimental Education* 31 (1963): 381–387.

Blackhurst, A. E. "Mental Retardation and Delinquency." *Journal of Special Education* 2 (1968): 379–391.

Blatt, B. "Public Policy and the Education of Children with Special Needs." *Exceptional Children* 38 (1972): 537–543.

Burt, C. "Delinquency and Mental Defect." *British Journal of Medical Psychology* 3 (1923): 168–178.

Carter, R. "Locus of Control and Teacher Expectancy as Related to Achievement of Young School Children." Unpublished doctoral dissertation, Indiana University, 1969.

Cartwright, D. S.; Howard, H. K,; and Short, J. F., Sr. "The Motivation of Delinquency." Unpublished manuscript, 1966.

Cloward, R. A., and Ohlin, L. E. *Delinquency and Opportunity: A Theory of Delinquent Gangs.* Glencoe, Illinois: Free Press, 1960.

Cohen, A. *Delinquent Boys.* Glencoe, Illinois: Free Press, 1965.

Conger, J. J., and Miller, W. C. *Personality, Social Class, and Delinquency.* New York: John Wiley & Sons, 1966.

Coopersmith, S. *The Antecedents of Self-Esteem.* San Francisco: W. H. Freeman & Co., 1967.

Davis, F. "Deviance Disavowal: The Management of Strained Interaction by the Visibly Handicapped." *Social Problems* 9 (1961): 120–132.

DeFleur, L. B. "Delinquent Gangs in Cross-Cultural Perspective: The Case of Dordoba." *Journal of Research in Crime and Delinquency* 4 (January 1967): 132–141.

Dunn, L. "Special Education for the Mildly Retarded—Is Much of it Justifiable?" *Exceptional Children* 35 (1968): 5–22.

Eisner, V. *The Delinquency Label: The Epistemology of Juvenile Delinquency.* New York: Random House, 1969.

Empey, L. T. "Delinquency Theory and Recent Research." *Journal of Research in Crime and Delinquency* 4 (January 1967): 28–42.

Empey, L. T., and Erickson, M. L. "Hidden Delinquency and Social Status." *Journal of Social Forces* 44 (1966): 546–554.

Empey, L. T., and Rabow, J. "The Provo Experiment in Delinquency Rehabilitation." *American Sociological Review* 26 (October 1961): 679–695.

Ford, J. "New directions in special education." *Journal of School Psychology* 9 (1971): 147–153.

Foster, G. "Expectancy and Halo Effects as a Result of Artificially Induced Teacher Bias." Unpublished Ed.D dissertation, The Pennsylvania State University, 1974.

Frease, D. E. "The Schools, Self-Conceptual Juvenile Delinquency." *British Journal of Criminology* 12 (1972): 133–146.

Frease, D. E. "Delinquent Social Class in the School." *Sociological and Social Research* 4 (1973): 443–459.

Gallagher, J. "The Special Education Contract for Mildly Handicapped Children." *Exceptional Children* 38 (1972): 579–583.

Gibson, H. B., and West, D. J. "Social and Intellectual Handicaps of Precursors of Early Delinquency." *British Journal of Criminology* 10 (1970): 21-32.

Glueck, E. T. "Mental Retardation and Juvenile Delinquency." *Mental Hygiene* 19 (1935): 549-572.

Glueck, E., and Glueck, S. *Physique and Delinquency.* New York: Harper & Brothers, 1956.

Gold, M. "Undetermined Delinquent Behavior." *Journal of Research in Crime and Delinquency* 3 (January 1966): 27-46.

Gruhn, H., and Krause, S. "On the Social Behavior of Physical Handicapped Children and Teenagers." *Probleme and Ergebnisseder Psychologie* 23 (1968): 73-86.

Haney, B., and Gold, M. "The Juvenile Delinquent Nobody Knows." *Psychology Today* 7 (1973): 49-55.

Haywood, H. "Labeling: Efficacy, Evil and Caveats." Paper presented at Joseph P. Kennedy, Jr. Foundation International Symposium on Human Rights. Washington, October, 1971.

Hirschi, T. *Causes of Delinquency.* Berkeley, California: University of California Press, 1969.

Jones, R. "Labels and Stigma in Special Education." *Exceptional Children* 38 (1972): 553-564.

Jones, R. "Labeling Black College Students Culturally Disadvantaged: A Search for Behavioral Correlates." Paper presented at the meeting of the California Educational Research Association. April, 1970.

Jones, R.; Gottfried, N. W.; and Owens, A. "The Social Distance of the Exceptional: A Study at the High School Level." *Exceptional Children* 32 (1966): 551-556.

Keldgold, R. E. "Brain Damage and Delinquency: A Question and a Challenge." *Academic Therapy* 4 (1969): 93-99.

Klein, M. W. "On the Group Context of Delinquency." *Social Science Research* 54 (1) (1969): 63-71.

Kvaraceus, W. C. "Mental Retardation and Norm Violation." *Journal of Education* 147 (1964): 17-24.

Kwall, D.; Smith, J. T., Jr.; and Tanner, F. "Functional Relationships between Sociometric Status and Teacher Ratings, Aspiration Level, Academic and Parent-Child Variables." Proceedings of the 75th Annual Convention of the American Psychological Association, 1967, pp. 285-286.

Lapouse, R., and Monk, M. A. "Fears and Worries in a Representative Sample of Children." *American Journal of Orthopsychiatry* (1959): 803-818.

MacFarlane, J. W.; Allen, L.; and Honzik, M. P. *A Developmental Study of the Behavior Problems of Normal Children Between Twenty-One Months and Fourteen Years.* Berkeley, California: University of California Press, 1954.

Mann, C., and Mann, H. "Age and Intelligence of a Group of Juvenile Delinquents." *Journal of Abnormal Psychology* 34 (1939): 351-360.

Matthews, V., and Westie, C. "A Preferred Method for Obtaining Rankings: Reactions to Physically Handicaps." *American Sociological Review* 31 (1966): 851–854.

Maurer, A. "Whatever Happened to Witches?" *Journal of School Psychology* 19 (1972): 107–110.

Mercer, J. "The Labeling Process." Paper presented at the Joseph P. Kennedy, Jr. Foundation International Symposium on Human Rights. Washington, October, 1971.

Meyen, E., *The Missouri Conference on the Categorical/Non-Categorical Issue in Special Education.* Columbia: University of Missouri, 1971.

Mitchell, K. R. "The Body Image Barrier Variable and Level of Adjustment to Stress Induced by Severe Physical Disability." *Journal of Clinical Psychology* 26 (1970): 49–52.

Mulligan, W. "Study of Dyslexia and Delinquency." *Academic Therapy* 4 (1969): 177–187.

Neurmberger, R. "Review of Pygmalion in the Classroom." *Personnel and Guidance Journal,* 37 (1969).

Nihiro, K.; Foster, R.; and Spencer, L. "Measurement of Adaptive Behaviors: A Descriptive System of Mental Retardates." *American Journal of Orthopsychiatry* 31 (1968): 381–387.

Northway, M. L. and Wigdor, B. T. "Rorschach Patterns Related to Sociometric Status of School Children." *Sociometry* 10 (1947): 186–199.

Ossowski, R. "Behavior of Blind Youth Under Stress." *Przeglad Psychologiczny* 18 (1969): 85–102.

Palardy, J. "What Teachers Believe, What Children Achieve." *Elementary School Journal* 69 (1969): 370–374.

Parsons, R. W. "Psychological and Behavioral Change in Delinquents Following Psychotherapy." *Journal of Clinical Psychology* 22 (3) (1966): 337–350.

Parsons, R. W. Relationship Between Psychotherapy with Institutionalized Boys and Subsequent Community Adjustment." *Journal of Consulting Psychology* 31 (2) (1967): 137–141.

Pate, J. E. *Exceptional Children in the Schools.* Edited by L. M. Dunn. New York: Holt, Rinehart, and Winston, 1963.

Payne, R. W. "Cognitive Abnormalities." *Handbook of Abnormal Psychology,* edited by H. J. Eysenck. New York: Basic Books, 1961

Quay, H. C *Juvenile Delinquency.* Princeton, New Jersey: D. Van Nostrand, Co., 1965.

Rathus, S. A. and Siegal, L. J. "Delinquent Attitudes and Self-Esteem." *Adolescence* 8 (30) (1973): 265–276.

Reckless, W. C. *The Crime Problem.* New York: Appleton-Century-Crofts, 1967.

Reynolds, M., and Balow, B. "Categories and Variables in Special Education." *Exceptional Children* 3 (1972): 357–366.

Richardson, S. A. "The Effect of Physical Disability on the Socialization of a Child." *Handbook of Socialization Theory and Research,* edited by D. A. Goslin, pp. 1047–1064. Chicago: Rand McNally, 1969.

Richardson, S. A.; Hastorf, A. H.; and Dornbusch, S. M. "Effects of Physical Disability on a Child's Description of Himself." *Child Development* 39 (1964): 467–480.

Richardson, S. A. and Royce, J. "Race and Physical Handicap in Children's Preference for Other Children." *Child Development* 39 (1968): 467–480.

Richmond, J. B. "Introduction." *Mental Retardation: A Handbook for the Primary Physician.* A report of the American Medical Association Conference on Mental Retardation. Chicago, Illinois: April 9–11, 1964.

Rosenthal, R. and Jacobson, L. "Teachers' Expectancies: Determinants of Pupils IQ Gains." *Psychological Reports* 19 (1966): 115–118.

Rosenthal, R. "The Effect of the Experimenter on the Results of Psychological Research." *Progress in Experimental Personality Research. Vol. 1,* edited by B. A. Maher, New York: Academic, 1964.

Rosenthal, R. and Jacobson, L. *Pygmalion in the Classroom,* New York: Holt, Rinehart, and Winston, 1968.

Rosenthal, R. and Fode, K. "Psychology of the Scientist: Three Experiments in Experimenter Bias." *Psychological Reports* 12 (1963): 491–511.

Ross, M. B. "Attractiveness as a Biasing Factor in Teacher Judgments Regarding Special Class Placement and Related Factors." Unpublished doctoral dissertation, The Pennsylvania State University, 1974.

Rotter, J. "Generalized Expectancies for Internal Versus External Control of Reinforcement." *Psychological Monographs* 80 (1966).

Schain, T. "Learning of Low Ability Children and Tutor Behavior as a Function of the Self-Fulfilling Prophecy." Unpublished doctoral dissertation, University of Illinois, 1972.

Seaver, W. B. "Effects of Naturally Induced Teacher Expectancies." *Journal of Personality and Social Psychology* 28 (1973): 333–342.

Shaw, C. and McKay, H. D. "Social Factors in Juvenile Delinquency." Report on the Causes of Crime. Washington, D.C., US GPO, 1931, no. 3, vol. II. C. Shaw and H. McKay, *Juvenile Delinquency and Urban Areas.* Chicago Press, 1942. Rev. ed. introduction by James F. Short, Jr., 1969.

Shears, L. and Jensema, C. J. "Social Acceptability of Anomalous Persons." *Exceptional Children* 36 (1969): 91–96.

Sutherland, E. H. *Principles of Criminology.* 5th ed., rev. Donald R. Cressey. New York: J. B. Lippincott Co., 1955.

Tannenbaum, F. "Point of View." *Juvenile Delinquency: A Book of Readings.* Edited by Rose Giallombardo. New York: John Wiley and Sons, 1966, 69–79.

Taylor, D. C. "Aggression and Epilepsy." *Journal of Psychosomatic Research* 13 (1969): 229–236.

Thorndike, R. Review of Rosenthal, R. and Jacobson, L. "Pygmalion in the Class-room." *American Educational Research Journal* 5 (1968): 708-711.

Thrasher, F. M. *The Gang: A Study of 1,313 Gangs in Chicago.* Abridged, introduction by James F. Short, Jr. Chicago: University of Chicago Press, 1963.

Ueda, T. "A Study of the Stability of Sociometric Status Among Elementary School Children: On the Stability of Choice Received." *Journal of Nara Gakugei University* 12 (1964): 135-154.

Voss, H. L. "Sociometric Status and Reported Delinquent Behavior." *Social Problems* 13 (1966): 314-324.

Wallace, G. L. "Are the Feebleminded Criminals?" *Mental Hygiene* 13 (1929): 93-98.

Westwell, A. E. "The Defective Delinquent: *American Journal of Mental Deficiency* 56 (1951): 283-289.

Woodward, M. "The Role of Low Intelligence in Delinquency." *British Journal of Delinquency* 5 (1955): 281-303.

Wrightman, L.; Nelson, R.; and Tranto, M. "The Construction and Validation of a Scale to Measure Children's School Morale." Unpublished paper, George Peabody College for Teachers, 1968.

Wylie, R. C. *The Self-Concept.* Lincoln, Nebraska: University of Nebraska Press, 1967.

Yamamoto, K.; Lembright, M. L.; and Corrigan, A. M. "Intelligence, Creative Thinking, and Sociometric Choice Among Fifth Grade Children." *Journal of Experimental Education* 34 (1966): 83-89.

Zeitlein, H. "Phoenix Reports on High School Misbehavior." *Personnel and Guidance Journal* 35 (1957): 384-387.

Zeleny, L. D. "Feeblemindedness and Criminal Conduct." *American Journal of Sociology* 38 (1933): 564-576.

2

prevention, punishment, education and rehabilitation

DAVID A. SABATINO

The major descriptors of the intervention strategies used in educational programs with norm-violating youths are *prevention, punishment, education,* and *rehabilitation.* These overlapping program descriptors may represent the biblical four horsemen comprising the chronically disruptive apocalypse, thereby permitting intervention strategies. In fact, describing these four generic treatment categories as apocalyptic may be more than a symbolic relationship. The apocalypse is defined as the ultimate destruction of evil and restoration of good. The reduction and eventual elimination of socially and emotionally disruptive behaviors in juvenile populations are the ultimate goals of correctional educators. To accomplish that goal, the four intervention categories must be mounted and maintained simultaneously, without one inhibiting another, or promoting one at the expense of another. The inability to construct and coordinate a comprehensive network of programs may be the primary reason secondary school and institutional programs for norm-violating youth have not succeeded in many instances.

DIFFERENTIATING PROGRAM TYPOLOGIES

Norm violators may be viewed at three different treatment levels. The community level provides the basis for preventative programs. Next, cooperative community and residential treatment provides rehabilitation efforts. For some, punishment before rehabilitation, and for others, punishment and not rehabilitation is a means of protecting society in institutional programs. Education affects all levels.

A first-order undertaking is to describe the program within the context of the person needing service. Traditionally, the reverse has happened. Secondary youth have received available intervention on the basis that the program should work for all those placed into it, no matter what their diagnosis, behavioral responses, or categorical label.

The Strategy and Planning Conference on child health and mental health, preceded by two White House conferences on youth, resolved an identified need for a systematic study of the problems of norm-violating youth. The participants at that conference suggested that a six-step process was necessary to derive a procedure for dealing with the problems of youth. This process-oriented systematic view should be used in obtaining a definition of the role and function of the various agencies involved in working with youth in trouble. It should also be used to define program content. The six steps in the breakdown of the systematic process are:

1. First-order problems with the youths themselves are associated with disadvantage or disability: abandonment, drug abuse, delinquency, etc. Or, they are problems derived from normal-stream development, for example, children who suffer from the inadequacies of public education or other social classifying systems.

2. Second-order problems are, in effect, redefinitions or interpretations of first-order problems. For example: the problems of broken or inadequate families, or the dehumanizing physical and social environment of public housing projects.

3. Problems of the institutions are directly involved with youth, for example, youth guidance clinics, elementary schools, and day-care centers.

4. Systems problems in the interaction, horizontal or vertical, of organizations and agencies within the system.

5. Problems of innovation and change begin with obtaining meaningful research data on youth, using research results to develop innovative programs and diffusing innovations.

6. Problems of policy formation encompass the difficulties of establishing clear, sustained national policy relating to the well being of youth, and the problems of making that policy effective at the state and community level.

There is continual support for evidence which demonstrates that norm-violating youth respond very differently to given treatment approaches. That is, treatment specific for one group of youths may, in fact, be detrimental for another group of youths.

Lunden has prepared an excellent review of the major theories which have propelled treatment since the early 1900's.

> In the past fifty years or more, successive theories have been "created" which were supposed to have "solved crime." At one time the solution centred on environmental manipulations (bad housing causes crime; therefore, clear the slums and build better houses). Then came the psychological protagonists (mental deficiency is the cause; therefore, develop clinics to deal with antisocial people). Hard upon the heels of these rode the physical education champions who advocated more and better sports and recreation. Then came the special contingent of psychiatrists who did battle with the problem of deep personality conflicts, ego suppression, and "fractured chunks of unorganized conscience." These demanded more and better psychiatric clinics to uncover the personality disorders of offenders. Latest to arrive on the field of battle is the "total child approach: groups who have found the cause and the cure of crime in improved child-rearing formulae." Now, just coming over the horizon, appears still another brigade of researchers in shining armor (with unlimited funds) to enter the lists, flying the banner of psychosomatic involvements, searching out the delinquency-prone individuals in society. In addition, there are a number of axillary groups under various flags of "group dynamics," group therapy, and "child-parent revitalization approaches." Each and all of the "warriors against crime" represent noble and laudable ambitions and efforts to prevent crime, but the fact remains that we already know more about the causes of delinquency than we do about the means of controlling it. Furthermore, it does appear that crime is more of a "hydra" than a fire-breathing dragon which may be killed by one well-directed thrust of the Siegfriedian sword. (Lunden, 1968, p. 27)

The outstanding difficulty in developing a continuum of connected treatment typologies has been the absence of a conceptual framework for planning interventions. A successful conceptual framework is essential for both administrative understanding and programmatic decision making. One of the reasons for the absence of a conceptual framework is that all chronically disruptive youth are viewed as a group having similar characteristics. There has not been a major effort to establish an appropriate range of treatment settings in the community. Youth are still assigned to an institutional program or, in particular, a school program on the basis of IQ, age, interests, and what they are doing in the home, community, school, or job, far more often than on the basis of their social skills or attitude toward society at large. Rehabilitation is generally applied to everyone, based solely on the belief that it should be good for them. The greatest difficulty with rehabilitation is that it cannot be given to the consumer, it must be accepted.

It will remain impossible to enumerate many specific treatment interventions until sufficient data on chronically disruptive or norm-violating youth is available to diagnostically differentiate them. It is even difficult to find behavioral classification systems which have demonstrated validity, especially from an educational reference. It is our belief that before a prevention, rehabilitation, or punishment program can be undertaken, some effort to describe the essential characteristics of a given youth is necessary. Many of these means have been reported in Chapters 7 and 8. The factors listed below are a few of the meaningful variables useful in determining a given youth's program needs.

1. Philosophy and treatment aims for specific programs.
2. Setting for treatment, including size and nature of living groups.
3. Budgeting and administrative control.
4. Relationship of community agencies to residential programs.
5. Type of intake selection data.
6. Determining sentence, release, or pre-release conditions.
7. Age groupings.
8. Selection and qualities of treatment personnel.
9. Inservice training and development of staff awareness, understanding, insight, and the ability to take part in a wide range of relationships.
10. Balancing residential treatment and living with community treatment and living.
11. Role and nature of punishment.
12. Facilities consideration.
13. Recreational consideration.
14. Medical participation.
15. Specific preventative measures designed to inhibit delinquent subculture and attitudes.
16. Family involvement and preparation for return to the community with continuation of preventative programs.

Punishment

Eisner wrote the following description of the prevention-punishment-rehabilitation continuum:

Measures for combatting delinquency can be divided into punishment of individual delinquents, rehabilitation of delinquents or pre-delinquents, and changes in the environment that produces delinquency. . . Both punishment and rehabilitation have a place in delinquency control, and it is not suggested that we abandon them; nevertheless, I believe that we have overused punishment in the past and should now restrict its use and that we must undertake rehabilitation with a new viewpoint before we can do it successfully.   (Eisner, 1969, p. 3)

Eisner's reasoning is derived from both good judgment and factually proven work with socially disruptive youth. Probably because of the political instability reflected in law enforcement, corrections, and even education, there is a tendency to "try this and then try that" approach. Seldom have we sought to achieve a balanced continuum of programs and services representing prevention, punishment, and rehabilitation, or more importantly, a means of reliably differentiating youth into one or more of the programs that are outgrowths of three programmatic areas of concern. Far too frequently, an administrator finds fault with a current correctional practice, only to have some other person find fault and change programs again. There are only so many alternatives under the umbrella of prevention, punishment, and rehabilitation that can be utilized. Why, then, do we continue to discard or abandon this one or that one? Punishment is certainly an example of a programmatic format to correct norm-violating behavior that is highly criticized. There are those who believe that punishment is the absolute antithesis of everything that is positive and good, and that it must be replaced by modern day behavioral modification. Those who believe that punishment has no place in treatment alternatives are naive and have failed to recognize it as one of the primary principles underlying behavioral modification. For those who think only positive reward valances modify behavior, their understanding of behavioral modification is not complete. Eisner and Tsuyemura have taken a very sound position when they suggest that:

We can no more abandon punishment of delinquents than we can abandon the medical treatment of a patient who has contracted cholera. But punishment is an effective measure of social control only when it is applied to a small proportion of the population. If too many people are punished, the result can be rebellion. If only a few people who have committed the worst offense are punished, others will be deterred from similar offenses. In an ideal situation, delinquency labeling should become what K. T. Erickson (1964, pp. 13-14) has called a "boundary maintaining mechanism." In his view, the interactions of members of a society with law-enforcement officers serve as a visible reminder to other members of the society of the limits of permissible conduct in that society. These interactions serve to mark the outside limits of the area within which the norm has jurisdiction, and in this way assert how much diversity and variability can be contained within the system before it begins to lose its distinct structure, its cultural integrity.   (Eisner & Tsuyemura, 1965, p. 689)

The difficulty with punishment is that some have seen it as a routine form of treatment for undifferentiated populations. When youthful residents in correctional institutions successfully respond to rehabilitation but are mixed indiscriminately with others who do not, the values of rehabilitative efforts appear reduced, and the effect on treatment staff and public attitude toward rehabilitative treatment is tragic.

Hardy and Cull (1973) see most institutions as a natural extension of criminal training. They describe a first offender as a youth who has stolen an automobile and is now incarcerated. Initiation to prison life may consist of being forced into homosexual behavior by the stronger inmates. Third- and fourth-time offenders can teach a great deal about how to be more successful in stealing automobiles and committing other socially injurious acts. The possiblity of meeting others who have connections to make crime pay and to get jobs in crime once prison training is completed is a very real happening as it is difficult to get legitimate work with an institutional record. Institutions have their own values and they may be totally in opposition to rehabilitation for some inmates.

> The taking from the weak by the strong is accepted. Those who can defraud others and get away with it are the most highly respected members of this community. The person who can "con" the psychologist or the counselor or the other inmates is also highly respected.   (Hardy & Cull, 1973, p. 12)

The use of prisons as societal vaccines has actually increased the amount of criminal behavior which the public must bear. There must be massive rehabilitation programs to provide for those who can be returned to society with new social attitudes and skills for living. For others, full length sentences and protection of society must be provided. That is not to say that we are in support of punishment. We are not in support of any one sole programmatic effort; rather, we support a coordinated and balanced program of prevention, rehabilitation, and punishment depending upon a realistic determination of the resident's current attitude, abilities, and other traits. The determination will be based on ascertaining meaningful information not yet available through current personological measurement and observation. It is certainly an error that the opportunity to develop predictive measures and even test their validity with pre-release and community-based populations has failed to occur on any scale at all. Many other errors of human judgment have also occurred in the name of prison reform and rehabilitation.

The modern social scientist has continued to view punishment as the antithesis of treatment. He points to the history of penology and notes that it has failed to deter criminal behavior. Punishment as an entity in preventing crime is an outworn concept. The behavioral scientist has made an aggressive attack on society's maintenance of punishment. It should be understood that when the social sciences began this attack, there was really no alternative other than punishment as a treatment typology. The neo-Freudians advocated that punishment only tended to increase criminal behavior because it supplied the criminal with the unconscious drive to commit forbidden acts. Reik (1959) has written that punishment is

> Under certain psychological extremely common conditions in our culture, the most dangerous unconscious stimulus for crime because it serves the gratification of the unconscious feelings of guilt, which presses toward a forbidden act. (p. 65)

Certainly the promise of the psychological explanations to chronic disruptive norm-violating behavior and its prevention have proven to be more disastrous than punishment. Cruel, harsh capital punishment is obviously extracting a full measure of payment from a nonconfroming act against society. Long uninterrupted sentencing may also be on shaky ground as it fails to differentiate the reformable individual from the unreformable. Until such time that accurate prediction can be established between those rehabilitable and those who will only return to crime, the crudeness of punishment as a defensive action against criminal acts must be maintained. Society provides punishment for other reasons than to treat or extract its "pound of flesh." It provides punishment to clarify in the minds of the societal members what is good and what is bad for the welfare of the social order. Punishment is a basic consideration in establishing a code and a moral structure for society. It is true that the enforcement of moral structure can be detrimental to the society it was designed to protect. Moral structure, as it is applied to the governance of society, can be corrupted. Laws and their enforcement are accomplished by men; the human elements of fear, prejudice, and hatred can overpower the balance of societal maintenance necessary for a stable order. Lunden provides a sobering summary on the current reality which underlies human behavior.

> No matter how intricate a theory may become, the fact remains that, if there is no social or moral force behind efforts to keep criminals from doing wrong, how can the social order be preserved? If or when theoreticians advance some means of maintaining social solidarity other than by punishment, then it may be discarded as an outmoded principle of control or prevention. Though it may seem brutal, as long as man remains a nonrational being, it appears that society will have to protect itself. Here, then, is

another barrier to crime prevention—the failure to understand that the basic
issue in crime prevention is a moral issue and that the bonds which hold
society together are moral bonds.   (Lunden, 1968, p. 24)

View punishment as you will—an insult to the human race, a necessary evil, an absurd act counterposed to love, kindness, humanness, the
spoiler of behavioral modification—it still remains necessary at this time.
It, like rehabilitative interventions has been offered as a single cure for
society. That is not true and never will be. But to remove the right of society
to retaliate against those who abuse the weaker of society's members, or
take advantage of society, a balance of controlling power would dominate
the land. We must achieve a balanced program of events, identifying
through differentiation where and with whom punishment, prevention, or
rehabilitation is necessary. There is also a strong presence in adolescents, as
they begin to choose lifestyles, for the necessity to know the consequence of
an act. Adults, society, and our secondary schools administer social values
inconsistently, at best. Public school personnel are afraid to punish students
for disruptive acts on the social order of the school or abusive acts on
another person housed in its confines.

Prevention

Workers in the mental health fields have constructed three levels of
prevention: primary, secondary, and tertiary. *Primary prevention* has as its
aims the early identification and eradication of a problem before it draws
attention to itself as a disability or debilitating condition. It is not
uncommon to hear kindergarten or early elementary teachers describe a
student as one who is likely to be brought to the attention of the school and
juvenile court officials at some time in his life. The reason usually revolves
around two factors: (1) the family attitude and previous history of the
siblings; and (2) the child's attitude toward peers and authority figures. The
major difficulty with early identification is that delinquency in a legal sense
is either black or white—the child has been adjudicated or he has not. The
shadow cast by a continuum tendency toward delinquency has been a very
sensitive issue. Consider how difficult it might be for an elementary school
counselor to address the parents of a kindergarten student as to his or her
potentiality for becoming a delinquent.

Secondary prevention is the much more common approach. It, too,
requires identification, but of an acute problem at a time of crisis. The
major aims of a secondary preventative effort are to provide a program
geared to eliminate the cause of the problem before the symptoms become
any more severe. Special reading programs for particular groups of
students, tutorial-therapy programs which provide for increased academic
achievement, and a change of attitude toward self and school are examples.

One example which has achieved a good deal of praise as a highly successful venture is so-called crisis intervention. The aim of crisis intervention is to have a teacher with specialized preparation in human interaction skills confront the student at the time of crisis, during the time of an aggressive act, passive withdrawal state, or emotional blow-up in the classroom or on the playground.

Tertiary prevention can be used synonomously with the term rehabilitation. It is preventative only in that if intervention alleviates a chronic problem, the individual may be restored to a state of useful functioning in society.

Bower (1964) lists five major deterrents to implementing primary and secondary preventative programs.* They are as follows:

1. The complexity of the problem has the capability of stumping the various disciplines which work on it. In scope of size alone it is easier, and frequently a necessity, to confront crisis and forget about gathering storms. Issues such as school failure, school attendance, poverty, racial difficulties, can be understood as full-blown problems but not as issues in the making.

2. Therefore, most professional workers view themselves as active interveners once a problem has been identified, not passive planners directed at preventing a problem.

3. The attitudes of society and the schools have much to do with the inability to find the funds to prepare preventative programs. Societies attitude generally reflects the attempt to maintain law and order, and a clean definition of societal right and wrong, but only after the fact—only after it is clear that a criminal act has been committed.

   There are those who would say that if wrong is chosen, then how could the values defining the choice have been prevented? There is also the right of those who would feel the finger of prevention as discriminatory, racist, and an invasion of privacy. Most parents are not willing to accept emotionally a delinquent child's behavior, even when evidence is readily available. The defense mechanism of parental denial is frequently in operation.

4. The values of good and evil are frequently seen by society as resulting in their own reward. If a youth falls error to evil, then he must pay the price. If there is a right to commit a crime, then there is a responsibility to suffer the consequences.

---

*Copyright, the American Orthopsychiatric Association, Inc. Reproduced with permission.

5. Finally, professionals do not agree as to what constitutes prevention. If the norm-violating youth is a problem of human values, how can chronic disruptive acts be prevented except by providing one set of societal values, and is not that an obstruction of the democratic process—the right for each man to choose?

PRIMARY PREVENTION: A RESPONSIBILITY OF THE SCHOOLS

There is a passage in an introductory text in educational administration that raises the question as to the legal and moral responsibility of the schools. The issue was—should a school provide books? If books are provided on the basis of a free public school education designed to enhance the maximum potential of all students, then shouldn't schools provide nourishing lunches? If nourishment has a direct relationship on learning, then shouldn't schools provide shoes? The point of the discussion is well taken. Where is the end? With the advent of the right-to-education decision, the public schools in many states have the responsibility for finding and educating subtrainable (severe and profoundly retarded) youths. Traditionally, the public schools have never been sure of their legal or moral resonsibility to teach values or interfere in predicting a problem and advising parents of a potential difficulty.

Oppenheimer and Mandel (1959) have reported that youngsters do manifest symptoms of social-emotional maladjustment prior to kindergarten entrance. They concluded that students likely to experience later emotional problems could be identified at the first grade level. Lambert and Bower (1961) have reported that 90% of elementary school age students identified as being potentially norm-violating youth by teachers were also found to be so labeled by clinicians. Public school teachers do have the ability to reliably detect norm-violating proneness. It must be remembered that only one-third to one-half of all youth committing chronic disruptive acts do come to the attention of the court. Early norm-violater youths who do not become recidivistic or show chronic disruptive behaviors do not become adult criminals, although those with chronic disruptive or recidivistic patterns do. In short, the relativeness of a criminal act makes the prediction of norm violation quite a different matter than predicting mental retardation or dental cavities. It is even true that some students outgrow social disruption before it becomes chronic. It is also true that some adolescents enter short-term norm-violating periods. Chronic disruptive norm-violating youth are a relative social concern; they are about as easy to identify early as they are to rehabilitate. Our success at both has been minimal.

Early identification and early prevention

Since false positives and false negatives can be identified in any population of youth in a search to distinguish those who may demonstrate chronic disruptive behavior, a wiser course of action may be initiating programs designed to instruct all youth in social values, not just known adjudicated youth. A sound action is to avoid labeling a youth while directing program instruction at teaching values, developing self-concept, and preparing one for life's experiences. Labeling has the risk of encouraging the youth to become what he is called. Self-fulfilling prophecy has long been held as one possible contributor in generating chronic disruptive behavior. By convincing a youth he is bad he will have reason to live up to that expectation. Norm-violating behaviors could have their beginning in the teacher's or parent's comments and attitudes that are reinforced in the youth's mind.

The term *prevention* is somewhat confusing and means different things to different people. To some, any youth who develops reasonable social responsibility has been prevented from becoming norm violating, simply because the opportunity to display disruptive behavior was there. To others, prevention must be predicted upon a measure or by observation, or other indices which predict occurrences before norm violation occurs. To a third group, prevention is synonymous with early intervention occurring at the onset of an initial norm-violating behavior. It is preventative in the sense that the youth will not enter into an institution, or be removed from his home. To many, any community based program prevents adolescents from becoming deviants from that community by remaining in it, and avoid the youth the recidivistic classification which has become the high water mark of institutionalization.

An instructional approach

One instructional approach has been described by Ojemann (1967) which emphasizes a causal orientation to the youth's world. By incorporating behavior-science concepts into a curriculum which focuses on the causes or motivations of human behavior—as opposed to the observable behavioral aspects—Ojemann hoped that the student would be better prepared to solve problems confronting him at this time and in the future. The basic rationale is that a person who becomes more fully aware and appreciative of the dynamics of human behavior in general, and of his own in particular, is better able to cope with personal and social crises. As a dynamic approach, it involves an awareness of the probabilistic nature of human behavior, an attitude of flexibility and tolerance, and an ability to view a given situation from another's perspective.

Ojemann contends that a sensible arrangement is to establish a foundation in the causal approach to behavior, starting in kindergarten. Then, as the student continues through the grades, he can add to this foundation and apply such a base to the study of marriage and family relationships, employer-employee interactions, and so forth. This approach not only enables the youth to surmount current crises, but also establishes a foundation for the solution of crises in later development. Ojemann stresses the need for the teacher to live a causal approach in the classroom. As a modeling procedure, daily associations with a teacher who handles situations in an understanding way can go far in developing a causal approach to life.

One teacher strategy used during the primary grades consists of narratives in which observable and causal approaches are contrasted. In kindergarten and first grade, the teacher reads the narratives. In later grades, the student reads them by himself. Each narrative depicts a situation in which a character in the story must respond initially, and then once again after he has thought through the situation a second time. Realistic stories are used. To promote a more generalized approach, stories are described involving children older and younger than himself as well as those from different environments. Discussion focusing on the meaning and causes of the behavior in question follows each narrative.

At the elementary and secondary levels, the social sciences and English literature offer numerous opportunities to study the forces influencing the behavior of people. Even in areas such as math and science, the teacher can serve as a model for this type of approach. Evaluations of this method to date have been promising. The results of more than a dozen research studies indicate that an

> appreciation of the dynamics of behavior is accompanied by significant changes in such dimensions as manifest anxiety, tendency to immediate arbitrary punitiveness, anti-democratic tendencies, conception of the teacher, and tolerance of ambiguity. (Ojemann, 1967, p. 199)

Lafferty, Dennerll, and Rettich (1964) have contrasted the so-called surface and causal classroom teacher pupil interaction schemes. (See Table 2.1.)

The classroom, home base for prevention

The following descriptions under the next two subheadings relate two effective public school chronic disruptive programs. It would appear appropriate before initiating program descriptions to discuss the alternate reason for success or failure of preventative efforts in the public

Table 2.1. THE SURFACE VERSUS THE CAUSAL APPROACH OF THE TEACHER TO CHILD BEHAVIOR (SURFACE VERSUS CAUSAL APPROACHES TO CHILDREN'S BEHAVIOR)*

Surface	*Causal*
1. The teacher responds to the "what" of the situation in an emotional way.	1. The teacher responds to the "why" of the situation objectively.
2. The teacher does not appear to think of the causes of behavior when he: a. responds to the action rather than to the reason for the action. b. labels behavior as "good," "bad," etc. c. makes generalizations to apply to every situation, e.g., "all boys are like that." d. responds with a stock solution or rule of thumb procedure, e.g., lateness is punished by staying in after school.	2. The teacher appears to be thinking of the causes of behavior when he: a. runs over in his mind possible reasons for the action. b. seeks the meaning of the behavior and avoids snap judgments or hasty interpretations. c. searches for specific and concrete clues derived from details of the behavior. d. varies the method; uses a tentative approach, i.e., will try other ways of dealing with a situation if one does not work. In seeking a solution, he takes into account motivating forces and particular method used.
3. The teacher does not take account of the multiplicity and complexity of causes.	3. The teacher thinks of alternative explanations for the behavior. The proposition that behavior has many causes may be elaborated as follows: a. the same cause may result in a variety of behaviors. b. a variety of causes may result in similar behavior.
4. The teacher fails to take into account the later effects of the techniques employed and assumes the effects.	4. The teacher checks for the effects of the method he employs and considers its effects before using it.
5. The "surface" approach is characterized by a rigidity of techniques, essentially static.	5. The "causal" approach is characterized by a flexibility, a tentativeness, a trying-out technique, which accommodates new information as it is accumulated, essentially dynamic.

schools—attitude. The attitude of the principal and teachers in a given building—that they can be bothered. The belief, indeed, that they make a difference.

There is a prevailing attitude among teachers and principals that:

1. The public schools are not the appropriate arena for behavioral change.

2. The public schools are not accountable for prior learning and the stimulus situation present there.

3. There are many other people hired by the schools who know how to treat delinquency.

It appears that all teaching is the analysis of behavior, the judgment as to what learner characteristics are or are not responsive in a given atmosphere, and concern for the immediate antecedent and consequential conditions which promote or inhibit academic or social learning. There are probably many reasons why teachers are uncomfortable with instructing values, or creating an atmosphere in which human responsiveness can be learned. There is a feeling of comfort and security in presenting highly structured subject matter by following textbooks, workbooks, and teacher guides rigorously. Reger, Schroeder and Uschold (1968) have aptly pointed out that many teachers do not feel they have the responsibility (lacking the security) to alter the decisions on what is to be taught, and how it is to be taught in their classrooms. Yet, realism dictates that if a classroom teacher does not offer intervention strategies, no one else will. It is certainly easier for teachers to go beyond the all-important teaching objective if they have help from support personnel in the school (e.g., school psychologists, counselors, curriculum supervisors, and administrative support). However, if support personnel only report IQ scores, meaningful personality descriptors, traditional special education labels, and other non-instructional gibberish, the time delays in referring youth outweigh the meagerness of the information sent back by social workers, school psychologists, and community agencies. This may explain why school psychologists spend more than 85% of their time in the elementary schools, in comparison to the high schools. It is very unusual for inservice training and follow-up support activities for secondary school personnel to include instructional or behavioral management techniques directed toward the chronic disruptive youth.

An elementary school preventative effort

A preventative services coordination program in elementary schools is described by Powell. A statewide survey of more than 600 agency representatives was conducted by the unit in an effort to pinpoint youth problems and develop a statewide plan to cope with delinquency. The survey revealed an overwhelming need for preventative programs, and especially those for students in the early grades of public school. Addressing the problem, Powell determined eight factors which must be considered in an elementary school preventative effort.

1. A teacher's "worry clinic" was organized, bringing a psychologist from a local agency to meet monthly with teachers to discuss related issues.

2. A tutoring program was developed, utilizing volunteers from a church in the community and members of a Future Teachers of America club.

3. A big brother-, big sister-type program was begun, involving volunteers from a local university.

4. Four counseling groups were initiated—three for students and one for parents.

5. A community club was formed which provided manpower for constructing a schoolroom and bought playground equipment.

6. A local civic club provided books.

7. Nursing students took an active role.

8. Consultation by university personnel was provided to help teachers with acute reading problems.

(Powell, 1973, pp. 383–384)

In this project, the coordinator communicated with parents about their children's problems, assisting them in identifying and utilizing appropriate resources, following-up to assess the effectiveness of the service, and providing feedback to the source of referral. The coordinator attempted to involve parents and agency representatives in school programs, and school representatives and parents in other community activities.

Service coordinators (social workers) were placed in four elementary schools as referral resources to school personnel, the basic target group being kindergarten through third grade. The coordinators were not counselors; rather, they were to consult with teachers, accept referrals, make contact with parents, and facilitate referral to community resources. Also critical to the role was that coordinators helped existing agencies and groups develop new services to deal with problems for which no resource existed. Thus, the method employed was community organization, in contrast to casework or group work.

(Powell, 1973, p. 385)

A total of 1,043 students made up the target group in the four schools. Specifically, this included all pupils in grades K–3 in two schools, K–4 in one school, and 1–3 in the other. Any of these pupils were eligible for referral to the service coordinator for any reason the teacher deemed appropriate. There were few clinically significant referrals, and fewer dramatic success stories. Most of the students referred needed glasses, dental work, a coat, or help in obtaining counseling services. What many pupils needed most was an advocate for them so that they and their families could tap existing resources.

Of the 1,043 children, 203 (19%) were referred the first year, and 342 (33%) the second year for a wide variety of reasons. These figures tend to support the survey data expressing a need for help in the early grade school years. The schools selected were generally in lower socio-economic neighborhoods; but in these schools a sizable percentage of preprimary and primary grade pupils presented school staff with observable problems requiring some action. Most of the pupils who came to the attention of the service coordinator were referred by teachers for physical reasons. This fact demonstrates the need for schools to have ready access to resources dealing with medical problems, if not within the school system, certainly in the community.

The positive results of the program were not achieved without some difficulties. The primary problems were those normally expected when functioning in any school setting. Some school staff attempted to place the coordinator in a counseling role. Resistance and suspicion of the program were evident in two schools initially. In the final analysis, it was the schools' staffs and service committees that enabled the coordinators to overcome the difficulties. With the willingness of all agency representatives to openly discuss areas of misunderstanding, problems were resolved in an atmosphere of objectivity and concern for pupils. It is impossible to discuss prevention and not be concerned with preschool or elementary age children. Since the focus of this book is secondary students, let us present programs directed at curbing chronic disruptive behaviors before they start.

A secondary school preventative effort

A different type of experimental program was established in secondary schools under California legislation in the Sacramento City Schools in the form of an Opportunity School. The overall goal of the Opportunity School is to accept chronically disruptive students and return them to their home schools as early as possible. Efforts are made to upgrade the student's achievement, attitudes toward school, and awareness of the world of work.

Students may enroll in classes only with the written concurrence of the parent, the psychologist, and the home school principal. In the event parent and principal agreement is not reached, cases may be referred to the district hearing officer. Pupils are assigned for one semester at a time. The following objectives stated by Parker and Masuda must be satisfied before youth can be returned to regular schools:

1. Attendance
   Complete one semester with no more than one truancy or five class tardies.

2. Behavior
   Earn a *B* grade in conduct for one semester based on the following:
   a. Arrive at class on time.
   b. Know and obey school rules.
   c. Obey teachers. Be respectful and courteous.
   d. Respect the rights of others.
   e. Take reasonable care of school property.
   f. Exert reasonable effort to do assignments.
   g. Use no foul language or loud talk.
   h. Do not possess tobacco or narcotic drugs.
   i. Do not fight, threaten, or promote trouble.
   j. Abide by the bus rules.

3. Achievement
   a. Achieve within one grade of school, grade placement, or improve one grade level in reading, arithmetic, and spelling during the period in which enrolled, as measured by standardized tests.
   b. Complete 75 daily units of work satisfactorily in communications and arithmetic.
   c. Complete one course at the home school with a grade of "C/C" or better.

4. Work-World Familiarization
   a. Complete required field trips with satisfactory reports from the teacher.
   b. Submit a verbal or written report to the communications teacher on two work areas after discussing them with parents.   (Parker & Masuda, 1971, p. 41)

Course offerings are flexible, with considerable freedom for teachers to find the best teaching method. The minimum amount of instruction is 180 minutes daily. Heavy emphasis is placed on individual programs tailored to achievement and interest levels. Short-term units of work are preferable. Workbooks, regular books, and special materials were torn apart and reassembled by achievement level and interest. When a student completes a unit, he receives appropriate credit and begins the next unit, in a self-pacing manner.

Two regular class periods in communication serve as the basic teaching unit. It involves verbal and written communication between people. It may also involve public speaking, reading to others or to one's self, basic grammar, spelling, social studies, newspapers, or geography. Math, crafts, homemaking, electronics, and physical education make up the rest of the required schedule. Students are given choices in the elective whenever possible. Crafts seem to be the course with universal appeal to both boys and girls.

Activities that are avoided are general assemblies, field trips, and mandatory homework. Homework is assigned only if the family desires it. All trips are confined to job-related experiences and juvenile prisons.

A paraprofessional teacher assistant is assigned to each class. They are employed on the basis of their proven interest in working with deviant young persons. The ratio of 15 students to one teacher and one aide is always maintained. Both teachers and aides are expected to demonstrate a good sense of humor. They are required to function calmly under pressure and show no reaction to foul language or other forms of misconduct. In the Sacramento city schools, 37% the youth were recommended for full-time return to the regular school program. An additional 30% were recommended for continuance in the Opportunity School program with part-time enrollment at their home schools. The remaining 33% had either showed limited progress or had been in the program only a short time.

Parker and Masuda (1971) write that

> There is no magic involved in this procedure for rehabilitation. There is no unique or unusual experimentation, only constant application of the basic learning and psychological principles that all teachers studied in their general education and psychology courses. There is also an honest effort by the entire staff to maintain at all times *a cool head, a warm heart, and a firm hand.* (p. 45)

The Opportunity School program was well received by both parents and school officials. In the words of the authors, it provided the chronically disruptive juveniles that attended the following benefits:

> Problem students can be helped. Some continue to fail, however, partly due to the school's inability to control the individual's environment completely for an extended period of time. The cost of training or educating such

students is somewhat higher than educating average students in a regular program. Schools and their communities all too frequently are reluctant to face this fact; but, as a consequence, they eventually are forced to accept the financial burden of persons incapable of regular employment after leaving school who swell the welfare rolls as unproductive citizens.

Ethnic, social, and economic factors must be taken into account in the planning and budgeting of a program specially designed for problem students.   (Parker & Masuda, 1971, p. 38)

Vocational preparation as prevention

In still another secondary preventative effort, Shore and Massimo (1969) have described a program which focuses on the theoretical underpinnings found in the concept of alienation. Alienation is a learned attitude or feeling, based on opinion of one's views of self in relationship to society, as being meaningless, bored, or lost. There is the emptiness associated with the loss of any clearly identified social referent. The preventive effort was termed *comprehensive vocationally-oriented psychotherapy*. It was aimed at a target group of youths who had displayed a chronic pattern of antisocial behavior and severe school problems, which were evidenced in suspensions from school or dropping out of school.

The comprehensive vocationally-oriented psychotherapy was based on two principles of crisis intervention. First, the youth was contacted within 24 hours after he had left school. This contact was usually a telephone call suggesting that the therapist meet the boy at his convenience. Second, every effort was made to keep the contact from being associated with a school setting or other social institution. The therapist would suggest that he might be of help in finding the youth a job. The job focus was most appealing to the boys, and it was that focus that gained cooperation.

Jobs in this program had a different orientation from most other programs. Unlike the usual vocational guidance services where the names of employers are taken from a preselected list, the boy was prepared to meet the boss. The therapist might role play a job interview to help the youth deal with the anxieties he might encounter in the interview. The therapist might take the boy on a field trip to explore what openings were available and what skills were needed to obtain a job the boy wanted. Usually, the therapist accompanied the youth to the first job interview. The therapist was available after the interview and if the youth wasn't hired, a discussion of the reasons why were explained very carefully. It was a point the boy and the therapist were able to discuss and, subsequently, work on frustrations resulting from not gaining certain things immediately.

The need for remedial education and help with personal problems also became more and more evident. Within the concrete situation of the job, individualized educational programs were set up. The therapist played many roles. At one time the therapist acted as a teacher, or assisted the youth in getting help from certain remedial resources in the community. As a teacher, he might, for example, help a boy learn the driver's manual. Another time, the therapist played the role of vocational counselor—finding jobs, filling out forms, and dealing with other issues related to employment. The therapist might play the role of therapist and work out personal problems. At all times, even at night, the therapist was available to discuss issues. There was no preset appointment time nor was there a set length or place for the interview. Throughout this preventative effort, the issue was nonverbal, concrete activities that had therapeutic relevance.

Shore and Massimo evaluate their program as a success. Their major findings in this controlled study were that the 10 subjects in the experimental groups improved significantly in all achievement and personality areas measured. Other changes were:

> Clinical insights played a major role in helping the boy not only to obtain work but also to profit from employment and to develop his personality as well as his skills. The importance of the individual and his psychodynamics was always at the forefront of the program. We feel that what we learned from our experience has implications for schools, some of which at the present time are reevaluating their counseling programs for delinquent and predelinquent youths based on a better understanding of the complexity of the problem. As the boys became more socialized and less actively aggressive, they were able to learn in *all* areas.   (Shore & Massimo, 1969, p. 30)

The authors found an increase in verbalization associated with a reduction in antisocial behavior. They found that delinquent boys became less preoccupied with people, especially over hostility and aggressive aspects. The youths used words more descriptively to elaborate positive feelings toward others.

Special summer programs

Georgiady and Romano (1970) report on a summer program called TOPS (Teen-Age Opportunity Programs in Summer). It was instituted to examine existing promising programs for youth in the summer months, and to recommend guidelines for new ones. The three major questions investigated were: (1) What are the unmet needs of youth in the summer? (2) How extensive are the summer youth programs developed by educational agencies and other community agencies now in operation in six states? (3) What suggestions can provide leadership in developing needed summer youth programs?

A survey instrument determined the number of youth summer programs within each of the participating states. The data are summarized by states and by categories. In Michigan, Ohio, New Jersey, and Pennsylvania, a significant number of schools did not provide summer programs. Illinois undertook only a limited number, and Florida conducted a total program.

Local tax funds were used in all states for summer programs. State funds were used predominantly in Florida. Limited funds were available to schools from private or foundation sources. All states except Florida supported their summer programs through tuition fees or a combination of tuition fees and local tax funds. The majority of summer programs in the participating states were held either for the morning period only or all day. A small percent extended from 6:00 P.M. to 10:00 P.M. The vast majority of school-sponsored summer programs were conducted on a voluntary basis.

The basic focus of the summer programs in Michigan and Pennsylvania was on recreational rather than academic purposes. Ohio, Illinois, and New Jersey focused on academic programs. Florida stressed educational enrichment. The majority of the programs were considered to be moderately to highly successful. Forty percent of the Michigan schools reported that positive changes in attitudes and behaviors occurred.

The major findings are well worth a very careful reading, especially in light of our survey of institutional educational programs reported in Chapter 5. One tremendously significant finding drawn from the study was that the majority of the programs (creative and innovative) were administered by agencies free from several restrictions which inhibit nontraditional program development. The major inhibitors, according to the study, were the Carnegie Unit, grades or marks, a close association and pre-occupation with academic courses per se and other similar concerns. Further, it was found that in a number of instances, both students and instructors raised the question of why this freedom from traditional concerns and a refreshing, exciting creativity and innovativeness could not be extended to programs conducted in schools during the school year. Needless to say, this is a much desired development and one which deserves warm encouragement in the future.

Georgiady and Romano conclude that the most pressing problems were the lack of qualified teachers and staff. Their list of creative recommendations for summer programs are excellent.

1. *Cultural Exchanges*—The purpose is to promote the cultural and social development of youth. The exchange includes the desirability of permitting the populace of the host community as well as the guest to learn about each other.

2. *Youth Business Ventures*—This gives youth the chance to work towards tangible goals—money—by becoming involved in community business pursuits which provide practical first-hand experience.

3. *Exploratory Job Experiences*—This provides youth the opportunity to explore interests in one or more given vocations in an effort to ascertain whether those vocations really hold an interest for them.

4. *Summer Theater*—The creative and therapeutic value of the expressive arts provide several benefits including opportunites for self-expression and total enjoyment.

5. *Youth Hostel-Travel*—Youth would be served by the development of better means for them to travel inexpensively and informally.

6. *Beautification and Site Development Programs*—Youth who organize into teams to convert areas into recreational sites are provided with a challenge of substance. This increases the respect for youth by the community.

7. *Voice of Youth Programs*—The programs, usually in the form of a forum, are oriented towards bringing youth into direct constructive contact with problems and issues of their times.

8. *Cultural Enrichment Programs*—This program promotes the "one world" idea where people enjoy "being different together." Vicarious experiences can be provided through documentary films, tapes, and pictures to promote the "one world" concept.

9. *Personal Service Centers*—These centers provide youth with individual and group therapy through "understanding clinic" where they could be involved in solving their own problems.

10. *Hobby Center*—The center is manned and operated by youth who plan a program appropriate to their needs, and it provides them with valuable planning experience and responsibility.

11. *Youth Canteens or Clubs*—These provide a legitimate place for youth to gather and socialize, thus eliminating the street-corner meetings.

12. *Youth Volunteer Service Programs*—A community service office for youth would serve as a clearinghouse for requests for assistance and for youth offering their services.

13. *Summer Youth Olympics*—Athletic competition among youth would promote understanding, cooperation, and sportsmanship.

14. *Fine Arts Festival*—With a fine arts festival, the youth would be offered an opportunity to explore interests in arts and crafts and music. (Georgiady & Romano, 1970, p. 20–21)

Community-based prevention

Poorkaj and Bockelman (1973) have developed a community prevention program drawing on volunteers. It is based on the norm-containment theory of Reckless, Dinitz, and Scarpitti (1962). That theory describes and differentiates the internal control of man over his own actions, and external control of man by the social system. According to the theory, the normal occurrence of well-developed internal controls by adolescents has been lost in a breakdown of family and societal value structures. Therefore, many adolescents don't have the internal controls, and yet they have the instinctive desire to break dependency bonds with controlling social forces. The study was set up under experimental conditions. A total population of 54 students, ages 9 through 12, were assigned to the program (27 to the experimental group and 27 to the control group).

In analyzing current literature describing the predictive instruments that have been developed for use in the prevention of delinquency, it is evident that as yet no scale can adequately predict delinquency proneness. At best, such scales are confined to identifying only those students who score in the extreme ranges of the scales used. For example, there are methodological weaknesses in not only the Glueck Social Prediction Scale, but also in the Kvaraceus Deinquency Proneness Scale and Minnesota Multiphasic Personality Inventory. The criticisms of the predictive devices have been as abundant as the explanations of their use. The following three scales were developed for the present study:

1. *Social Responsibility Scale* (SRS). This scale was designed by Berkowitz and Lutterman to assess a person's traditional social responsibility and orientation toward helping others.

2. *Volunteer's Reporting Form.* This scale was designed to assess the degree of participation with the delinquency-prone child.

3. *Questionnaire on Community Organizations.* Twelve questions with three subcategories were developed to ascertain the child's belonging to or wanting to join a community organization.

Selections of volunteers were made by the county probation department. Criteria for the selection of a volunteer included the general ability to relate to adults and children in a meaningful way, the potential capacity for reflecting an amiable disposition, and, in general, mentally healthy attitudes. Applicants were also screened through an extensive Department of Motor Vehicles' record check.

Several sessions were held for training and answering the many questions of the volunteers. A female volunteer could work with either a male or a female child, but the male volunteer would be matched with a male. In some cases it was decided to assign a couple who volunteered to meet the needs of a child for a family image. The findings did not indicate that interaction with a volunteer substantially reduced misbehavior. The students having a volunteer (experimental group) were less likely to drop out of school than control group subjects.

> Research results from having investigated the effectiveness of a program are among the most difficult to interpret. Aside from methodological difficulties inherent in almost all research, such as measurements, there is the fundamental problem of how to judge success or failure. Commonsensically, most everyone would add criteria such as success in social work, family, and general citizenship. (Poorkaj & Bockelman, 1973, p. 31)

In 1972, Walter and O'Donnell reported on using nonprofessional volunteers as behavior change agents in a community-based program. The principles and techniques of behavior modification were used in training nonprofessionals as change agents and in the treatment of youth in the project. The program evaluation includes an analysis of the various treatment techniques employed. The results indicate that school attendance increased with application of social and material rewards, while other problem behavior was reduced. The findings suggest that peer approval is a crucial ingredient in the changing behavior.

Other preventative efforts

Barclay (1969) reports on the use of art programs and activities to reduce delinquency proneness in delinquent populations. Art was seen as a natural media through which expression could be shown and understanding achieved, overcoming the harsh influence of poverty and cultural or language disadvantagement. Goals for the program aimed at enriching the lives of the pre-delinquent youth, thus reducing their need for violence; and overcoming educational disadvantages by providing a value-rich course of instruction that did not remind the youth of their inability to achieve in daily school scholarly activities.

Cassel and Blum (1969) describe a computer-assisted counseling program. The purpose is to promote congruence between the social skill development of pre-delinquents by providing conforming response choices to societal queries delivered by the computer. The program contains computer-delivered lessons on home and family, inner development, community relations, rules and law, school and education, psychosexual and romance, economic sufficiency, and self-actualization and leadership.

The work on Project Conscience continues at the University of Wisconsin at Milwaukee. The most recent development in Project

Conscience is the development of the Systems Analysis Approach to Counseling (SAAC), depicting to the many delinquent and delinquent-prone individuals with low competency in reading, video-audio loops of alternative choices to certain posed social problems, together with likely hazards for each alternative.

The new thrust at prevention, at least since the mid-1950s, has been the public schools. In fact, the schools are now heavily involved in treatment. Kvaraceus defines the role of the school counselor as an active one in mobilizing the forces of the school to confront delinquency proneness. He outlines three major provisos for the counselor.

> The school counselor can direct his energies against delinquency at three levels: (1) He can aim to improve the school program by making the school a better school. (2) He can attempt to identify the youngsters who are exposed or vulnerable to delinquent behavior, following through with preventative and remedial action, and (3) he can assist those students who have already been adjudicated as delinquents and are on probation, or those who have returned to the community after institutionalization and are still on parole.   (Kvaraceus, 1971, p. 22)

Finkle, Sullivan and Taylor (1968) have described an effort where adjudicated youth attended a citizenship training program established by the Boston Juvenile Court, and were then paid to interview other delinquents. The apparent amount of insight gained by the interviews, plus the status and prestige from the new role, provided them with a new lease on life. The program was ascertained as highly successful, as it brought a sobering, if not therapeutic, process into the lives of these chronically disruptive youths. Kvaraceus has attempted to see the professional disciplines alter their roles. It has been his belief that only youth can solve the delinquency problem.

> Youth-serving agencies in which adults are subjects of the verb *serve* and youth are direct or indirect objects of the verb will be limited in their attempts to prevent and control norm-violating behavior.
> (Kvaraceus, 1971, p. 54)

It is his contention that youth must become the subject of the verb *serve*. He feels that the youthful energies must be organized toward delinquency prevention and control. He has prepared the following assumptions, guiding principles, and participant requirements as a means of guiding a planned organization of youth assisting youth.

Assumptions
1. Every youth needs to feel that there is a significant place for him in his immediate social world as an adolescent person.

2. Every adolescent needs to be able to exercise his intelligence, initiative, and growing maturity in solving problems of real concern to him and to the adult world.

3. Every youth needs to be given the opportunity to learn that his own life situation is not the only one there is.

4. Youth need to be incorporated in order to communicate and deal with the corporate structures maintained by adults, that is, police, school, courts, etc., in urbanized, bureaucratic anonymous society.

5. The emergence of an adolescent subculture characterized by self-directing community participation is not likely to occur without specific adult leadership which:

   a. gives supportive guidance; that is, is responsive to adolescent problems, needs, and interests, both in terms of individuals and the group.

   b. is positive and symbolic; that is, in its behavior encourages identification of relevant values.

   c. practices appropriate manipulations; that is, is sensitive and effective in both intervention and withdrawal tactics designed to maximize self-direction and community participation.

Guiding Principles

Youth involvement in community action programs that aim to prevent and control delinquency will be guided by the following:

1. Self-direction and initiative of youth will be maximized.

2. Participation in vital and significant community activities and operations will be encouraged.

3. Adult role will be supporting and nondirective. The adult theme will be: "You can be free and significant; go ahead and try; you can count on us to help."

4. The first and major emphasis will be on the development of local units; later development will call for regional and state organization.

Participants

All youth up to voting age are eligible. This may call for two major (but overlapping) groups or segments, including the younger membership, 13–14 to 17–18 to 21–22.

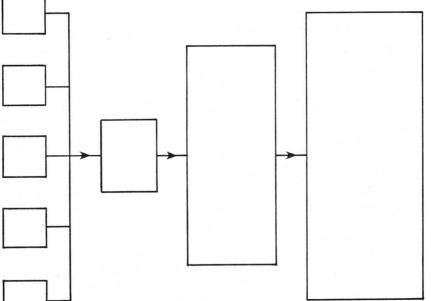

Local
Neighborhood   Central   Regional
Youth Councils City-Town   Metropolitan   State

Youth Participation	Existing Institutional Organization and Power Structure	Program of Activities
Youth Role: planners, data gatherers, deciders, advisors, implementors, participants, evaluators.	Adult Role: enablers, supporters, listeners, beneficiaries, and co-workers.	Research, planning consulting, evaluating, implementing, participating.
Localization of action rather than centralization.	Working with & advising: School Boards Police Department Recreation Centers Courts	Recreation Health & Welfare School Church Unions
Participation of youth as leverage to institutional change and improvement.	City Councils Legislative Bodies Mass Media PTA, Church Community Action Programs Unions	Political Police Courts Participation as: volunteers para-professionals work-study
Election? Selection? Appointment? of participants.	Division of Employment & Security Private Industry (Tel & Tel, etc.)	Youth Council as part of political structure. (Kvaraceus, 1971, p. 56)

Figure 2.1. Organization and Program: Youth Council

Effort will need to be made to insure two way communication without youth's losing linkage and identification with their own primary reference group, that is, avoiding the fink slur.

Participants can be elected, appointed by the mayor or other authority (selectman, governor), or designated as representatives by youth organizations. Various approaches need to be tried out in various situations to insure the most representative and active leadership among neighborhood youth.   (Kvaraceus, 1971, p. 55)

Benning (1968) reports on a five-year longitudinal study of 1,550 children, 384 of whom were intensively studied after being identified by their teachers as demonstrating socially approved or socially disapproved behavior. The disruptive group was lower in academic achievement and social adjustment than the approved group. They displayed socially disapproved classroom behavior and were in frequent contact with law enforcement agencies. It was concluded that teacher disapproval, poor self-concept, and failure to gain scholastic approval significantly reinforce the attitude of the child to continue school underachievement and drop out, or to continue norm-violating behavior and overt criminality. The teacher must identify children exhibiting aggressive behavior and attempt to delineate its exact causes through curricular innovation. Curricular innovation can contribute markedly to a decreased school dropout rate. The difficulty is that methods of motivating and instructing the socially disruptive student are needed.

In first and second year reports on a project in the Cordozo area of Washington, D.C., Fishman and Jones (1965, 1966) sense that the problem is not preventing disruptive behavior in youth but preventing poverty and ghetto influences on behavior.

A school district with a high concentration of low-income Negro youth was used as a target for the project. The research design included a base expectancy study to collect data for delinquency prediction, identify and study an adolescent cohort group of 14- to 17-year-olds. Studies of the cohort families and data on a sample of preschool population in the same district were also included. The preschool children's language responses to different stimuli under varying conditions were studied. It was hypothesized that there would be significant differences between institutionalized and noninstitutionalized youth on such factors as low socioeconomic status, education, family characteristics, intact or broken homes, social class aspirations, peer group behavior, and neighborhood deviancy. Without intervention, the high-risk group would have demonstrated delinquent behavior. The neighborhood centers in the target area appeared to have been effective in reducing juvenile delinquency. It is felt that the experience of this program shows that if interventions are to be more effective, they must concentrate on the specific problems in the ghetto as well as the youth.

In an early study, McGahan (1962) evaluated a preschool clinic's ability to detect the potential norm-violating behaviors of preschool children. All children who were to enter the first grade in the fall visited a spring clinic roundup with one or both parents. An effort was made to detect health problems and to assess the child's social maturation. All families concerned were contacted by telephone, and an appointment was made at the rate of 15 to 20 children per half hour. Visual screening, audiometric evaluations, dental evaluations, and social-emotional-readiness evaluations and assessments were performed by qualified personnel. At least 12 diagnostic functions were required for efficient prediction. Once the child entered the first grade, he either advanced regularly, passed through special transitory classes, or was detained a year to permit maturation.

Dailey (1966) studied the effect of various anti-delinquency school programs using a sample of 1,634 youths, 17 years of age. Of the sample youths, 80% were referred to juvenile court in 1964–1965, and 20% were without court records. The school and community records were used to predict delinquency, almost regardless of such factors as school size, age of building, per pupil expenditure, overcrowding, or class size. Performance in school was directly related to juvenile crime. Schools play a most important role in delinquency prevention in reducing the number of students who failed to read adequately in the primary grades.

Moore (1962) reports on a court and school joint program in Oakland County, Michigan. Using court records before the program began, a 50% reduction in delinquency resulted as a community-wide effort known as child and family protective services was offered. Children and their families were helped before problems or offenses were serious enough to warrant court action. Programs were established jointly by the local school district and the juvenile court. The juvenile court functioned as a community aid by having staff members of the court assigned to advise, assist, and provide casework. The major concern of the effort was the adequate emotional and social adjustment of the child in his family, school, and neighborhood.

A report (Illinois Commission on Children, 1977) of students in two midwestern high schools found that delinquency rates were lower among athletes than non-athletes. The following five general theoretical positions each suggest that participation in interscholastic athletics will have a deterring influence on delinquency. These positions are as follows:

1. *Delinquency as a Result of Differential Association.* Delinquency is posited as a result of exposure to deviant influences. Within a school, the chances of exposure to delinquent subgroups is inversely related to exposure to conforming influences. The strict standards of behavior set by the athletic coach and team are often internalized. The athletes themselves often exert pressure on their teammates to conform with these stand-

ards. Another factor which further reinforces the conforming influences of the team is the athletes' constant public scrutiny, especially in smaller communities.

2. *Delinquency as a Result of Rebellion.* Rebellion is often directed at the school where students are measured against universalistic criteria which they cannot reach. They rebel against failure, lack of perceived payoff, and resentment of punitive sanctions. The athlete, most notably the successful one, finds school a source of success experience and a positive self and public evaluation of himself . . . rebellion is not necessary.

3. *Delinquency as a Result of Boredom.* Athletes are less likely to become bored since their sports activities take up so much of their after-school and weekend time. They are, therefore, less susceptible to delinquent influences than their comparable non-athlete peers.

4. *Delinquency as a Result of Need to Assert Masculinity.* Inter-scholastic athletics, as an institutionalized display of force, skill, strength, and competitiveness, serves as a visible nondelinquent way of demonstrating prowess and competence.

5. *Delinquency as a Result of Labeling.* Social groups create deviance by making the rules whose infraction constitutes deviance and then by applying those rules to particular people, thereby labeling them as outsiders. From this point of view, deviance is not a quality of the act the person commits but rather a consequence of sanctions to an "offender." The deviant is one to whom that label has successfully been applied; deviant behavior is behavior that people so label. For example, a white middle-class youngster may well not be referred to the juvenile authorities for a minor theft. For him, the act is defined as a mere adolescent prank. On the other hand, a lower-class Negro youth is much more likely to be apprehended and referred to the court for the same act.

Similarly, athletes, especially those who are successful and live in small communities, are more likely to be "protected" from apprehension and referral to the court by the public image they enjoy as being clean-cut, all-American boys, even when they commit delinquent acts. They may well be just as delinquent, in fact, but turn up less often in delinquency statistics.

Summary of prevention activities

Berleman and Steinburg (1969) reviewed five major delinquency prevention experiments. A delinquency prevention experiment was defined as having two major characteristics. These were: (1) a social service to chronically disruptive youth who were not yet officially adjudged delinquent; and (2) a research design that permitted a study of the study's effectiveness. The five experiments studied were:

1. Cambridge-Somerville Youth Study
2. New York City Youth Board Validation of Glueck Prediction Scale
3. Maximum Benefits Project
4. Midcity Project
5. Youth Consultation Service

The Cambridge-Somerville Project. A $500,000 grant and a group of well-selected specialists established the Cambridge and Somerville Youth Project. The program became operative in 1939 with the selection of 650 boys, 325 in an experimental group who were given a wide range of treatments, and 325 who remained in the control group. In 1956 a final assessment of the program was made after 17 years of operation. Although the boys in the experimental group were assisted for an average of 5 years, they committed approximately as many crimes as those with no supervision.

New York City Youth Board. The New York City Youth Board, a validation study of the Glueck Social Prediction Scale, offered direct services to 29 experimental subjects for fifty months.

Maximum Benefits Project. The Maximum Benefits Project reported extended services to 111 subjects and their parents over 11 months. The average number of interviews per subject was less than one every two months, and one interview per parent every month.

Midcity Project. The Midcity Project extended services to 205 subjects who were distributed among seven gangs. Service agents contacted these groups on an average of 3.5 times a week over a period of 10 to 34 months.

Youth Consultation Service. The Youth Consultation Service serviced 129 subjects over a 3-year period. Sixteen percent had fewer than 5 contacts, while 44% had more than 20.

Berleman and Steinburg summarize the results of the study in Table 2.2. The overall negative findings of delinquency prevention experiments are disheartening. It is true that the experiments have been plagued by (1) the failure of service agents to expose the experimental subjects to sufficient amounts of attention; and (2) the failure of researchers to report more than a gross evaluation. In spite of the great potential of preventive approaches, as yet there is no usable method of prevention. Those in authority are more interested in stopping crime rather than in studying why it occurs.

Could it be that something as basic to society as breaking its rules is a normal occurrence in nature? Durkheim (1938) suggested that "crime is normal because a society exempt from it is utterly impossible" (p. 38). Crime, Durkheim held, was not only normal, it was necessary. Without crime there would be no evolution in law. Crime is a social problem created

Table 2.2. COMPLETED DELINQUENCY PREVENTION EXPERIMENTS, 1937–1965

| Title | Place | Years | Subjects | | Overall Evaluation of Service |
			Experi-mental	Control	
Cambridge-Somerville Youth Study	Cambridge-Somerville, Mass.	1937–1945	325	325	Ineffective
New York City Youth Board Validation of Glueck Prediction Scale	New York City, N.Y.	1952–1957	29	29	Ineffective
Maximum Benefits Project	Washington, D.C.	1954–1957	111	68	Ineffective
Midcity Project	Boston, Mass.	1954–1957	205	112	Ineffective
Youth Consultation Service	New York City, N.Y.	1955–1960	189	192	Ineffective

Reprinted with permission of the National Council on Crime and Delinquency from *Crime and Delinquency*, October 1969-471-478 by an infraction of a relative practice that will invariably be altered by time and place. Crime must not be viewed as an evil but as a process of faulty education, the inappropriate teaching of society's rules and its values.

Fifty years ago, Burt (1925) recommended six basic pillars of prevention and rehabilitation.

1. All young persons who show tendencies should be dealt with at the earliest possible stage. Parents should be taught that the preschool period is a period vitally decisive . . . Teachers should be urged to watch, and when necessary, to report all who show antisocial inclinations . . . When the school period is over, after-care workers should be persuaded to extend their supervision to the social conduct, as well as the industrial efficiency, of children who have just left; and, above all, special efforts should be made to meet the transitional phase of adolescence.

2. The problem of delinquency in the young must be envisaged as but one inseparable portion of the larger enterprise for child welfare. Crime in children is not a unique, well-marked, or self-contained phenomenon to be handled solely by the policeman and the children's court. It touches the very side of social work. The teacher, the care committee worker, the magistrate, the probation officer, all who come into official contact with the child, should be working hand in hand, not only with each other, but with all the clubs, societies, and agencies, voluntary as well as public, that seek to better the day-to-day life of the child.

3. The delinquent himself must be approached individually as a unique human being with a peculiar constitution, peculiar difficulties, and peculiar problems of his own . . . The court, therefore, and whatever authority has to grapple with such cases, must at all times regard not the offense but the offender. The aim must not be punishment but treatment; and the target not isolated actions, but their causes . . . Such authorities must have access to all available information and possess means to make for every case intensive investigations of their own . . . A special investigator must report upon home circumstances; a medical officer must inspect the child for physical defects; a psychologist must be at hand to apply mental tests, to assess temperamental qualities, and to analyze unconscious motives. A psychological clinic embodying all these different workers studying the same cases scientifically, side by side, is the most pressing need of all.

4. The remedies, in the same way, will be adapted, not to the nature of the offense, but to the nature of the factors provoking it. Probation should be employed with a larger freedom, and at the same time with finer discrimination; it should include, for each separate case, not merely passive surveillance, but active and constructive efforts . . . After-care, in particular, calls for further extension, to lavish a hundred pounds upon the intensive training of a youth in an institution and then suddenly to fling him loose into the old environment, sparing neither time nor trouble for further aid and following up, is not economy but waste.

5. Fuller knowledge is urgently wanted: it is wanted both in regard to causation of crime and in respect of the relative efficacy of different remedial measures. Only from the organization of research can this fuller knowledge come, and organized research means an established criminological department. The fruits of such research should be made immediately accessible to the practical officer, and courses of instruction should be arranged where all who have to deal with the young offender may learn the latest and best accredited results of modern criminology psychology.

6. Finally, society must aim at prevention as well as at cure. Housing, medical treatment, continued education, the psychological study of children in schools, improved industrial conditions, increased facilities for recreation, the cautious adoption of practicable eugenic measures, and above all, sustained investigation into all the problems of childhood—these are but a few of the countless needs to be supplied, if delinquency in the young is to be not merely cured as it arises, but diverted, forestalled, and so far as possible wiped out. (Burt, 1925, pp. 584–587)

REHABILITATION

The third horseman of the chronically disruptive apocalypse is education. Since the entire process and content of education are reviewed in this book, we will omit a discussion of education in this chapter. The fourth horseman is rehabilitation. Before any discussion can proceed on rehabilitation, it is necessary to briefly review the overlap among prevention, punishment, and rehabilitation. Prevention, in the chronic disruptive literature, is generally regarded as the act of prohibiting the occurrence of an unwanted behavioral act. In our review of prevention, we have observed that most prevention is directed at a high-risk group of youth, generally after they have developed, even to maturity, feelings of and attitudes toward society. Very few preventive efforts have occurred early in most children's lives, or have been directed at educating social skills or values. Most preventive methodologies have been devised to remediate symptoms usually following their occurrence. That means, in actuality, most so-called preventive programs are really rehabilitative efforts. Also, the results of most preventive intervention programs have been less than successful. We should probably not be discouraged by these findings as it is this author's opinion that we have yet to understand what it is we are attempting to prevent. Until we truly understand the differentiation in the values, attitudes, or behaviors between various groups of youth, it will be difficult to determine what behaviors are to be curbed, reconstituted, or structured differently. Then, and only then, will we know what it is that needs to be prevented. Prevention, as a concept, sounds like it should occur first, in the natural order of events, when in fact, it is the most difficult to implement and will generally occur last in most treatment paradigms.

Punishment is a very misunderstood concept and has a long history of use. As a concept in corrections, it has been used both as (1) a means of extracting a retribution for the criminally injured; and (2) a supposed deterrent to crime. Neither of these reasons has resulted in the effective use of punishment. The use of punishment to destroy the will of man, to impose the rule of society on the rebellious, to dehumanize, to thwart or repress the spirit of a man is not only amoral in a social sense but also draws a line of criminal demarcation between men. Punishment has two very worthwhile purposes: first, to protect society from injury by those who defy corrective intervention; and second, to clarify that social living is not an inalienable right but an earned privilege. Punishment serves to clearly delineate those behaviors which are unacceptable to man in his relationship to other men, and man in relationship with his environment. Punishment is not the antithesis of rehabilitation that some have made it out to be. It is an alternative form of management of socially nonconforming behavior that is necessary in conjunction with, and at times instead of, rehabilitation.

Rehabilitation, according to Webster's Dictionary, is to restore to a former state of usefulness. Therefore, it may even be an inappropriate term. Habilitation, or the qualifying of a person's ability to perform at some level of function, may be more appropriate. To avoid a meaningless academic play on words, operationally, rehabilitation or habilitation means the restoration or preparation of a nonconforming person to a meaningful life within the framework of social acceptance. Any treatment effort or intervention directed at reducing unfavorable attention received by the person for a disruptive act against self or society could be classified as habilitory or rehabilitory. The next chapter shall consider two important aspects of rehabilitation with that segment of the chronic disruptive population which are adjudicated: the institution as a treatment agent and the problem of recidivism.

REFERENCES

Barclay, D. L. "Dissemination and Implementation of Research on Art Education for the Disadvantaged Child." *Art Education* 22 (5) (1969): 23-24.

Benning, J. J. et al. "Delinquency-Prone Youth—Longitudinal and Preventative Research." Eau Claire County Youth Study, Phase III, 1968.

Berleman, W. C., and Steinburg, T. W. "The Value and Validity of Delinquency Prevention Experiments." *Crime and Delinquency* 15 (1969): 471-478.

Bower, E. M. *The Education of Emotionally Handicapped Children.* Sacramento: California State Department of Education, 1961.

Bower, E. M. "The Modification, Mediation, and Utilization of Stress During the School Years." *American Journal of Orthopsychiatry* 34 (1964): 667-674.

Burt, C. "Delinquency and Mental Defect." *British Journal of Medical Psychology* 3 (1925): 168–178.

Cassel, R. N., and Blum, L. P. "Computer Assist Counseling (COASCON) for the Prevention of Delinquent Behavior Among Teenagers and Youth." *Sociology and Social Research* 54 (1) (1969): 72–79.

Dailey, J. T. "Evaluation of the Contribution of Special Programs in the Washington D. C. Schools to the Prediction and Prevention of Delinquency." 1966.

Durkheim, E. *The Rules of Sociological Method.* Edited by G. E. Gatlin. Chicago: Chicago University Press, 1938.

Eisner, V. *The Delinquency Label: The Epistemology of Juvenile Delinquency.* New York: Random House, 1969.

Eisner, V., and Tsuyemura, H. "Interaction of Juveniles with the Law." *Public Health Republic* 80 (1965): 689–691.

Finkle, D., Sullivan, M., and Taylor, E. "Delinquents Talk About Delinquents." *Law and Disorder* Vol. X, State Government and Public Responsibility, Lincoln Filene Center, Tufts University, Boston, 1968.

Fishman, J. R., and Jones, R. J. "The Impact of the UPO Demonstration Program on a Selected Group of Cordozo Area Youth—A Study of Juvenile Delinquency Prevention." Second year report, 1965–1966.

Georgiady, N. P., and Romano, L. G. "Alternatives to the Long, Hot Summer." *NASSP Bulletin* 54 (344) (March, 1970): 14–28.

Hardy, R. E., and Cull, J. G. *Climbing Ghetto Walls.* Springfield, Illinois: C. C. Thomas, 1973.

Illinois Commission on Children. *News and Views* 14 (May 1977): 1–4.

Kvaraceus, W. C. *Prevention and Control of Delinquency: The School Counselor's Role.* Boston: Houghton-Mifflin, 1971.

Lafferty, J. C. Dennerll, D., and Rettich, P. "A Creative School Mental Health Program." *National Elementary Principal* 43 (5) (April, 1964): 31.

Lambert, N. M. and Bower, E. M. *Bower's Two-Step Process for Identifying Emotionally Handicapped Pupils.* Princeton, New Jersey: Educational Testing Service, 1961.

Lunden, W. "The Theory of Crime Prevention." *Prevention of Delinquency.* Edited by John Stratton and Robert Terry. London: MacMillan Company, 1968.

Massimo, J. L., and Shore, M. F. "The Effectiveness of a Comprehensive Vocationally Oriented Psychotherapeutic Program for Adolescent Delinquent Boys." *American Journal of Orthopsychiatry* 33 (1963): 634–642.

McGahan, F. E. "Early Detection and Programming for Children Who Experience Significant School Adjustment Problems." Galena Park Public Schools, Galena Park, Texas, 1962.

Moore, A. E. et al. How to Cut Delinquency in Half—The Story of Prevention in Oakland County, Michigan. *ERIC Clearing House* No. 05641 September, 1962.

Ojemann, R. "Incorporating Psychological Concepts in the School Curriculum." *Journal of School Psychology* 5 (1967): 195–204.

Oppenheimer, E., and Mandel, M. "Behavior Disturbances of School Children in Relation to the Preschool Period." *American Journal of Public Health* 49 (1959): 1537–1542.

Parker, H. K., and Masuda, R. "Opportunity Schools." *NASSP Bulletin* 55 (354) (April, 1971): 37–45.

Poorkaj, H., and Bockelman, C. "The Impact of Community Volunteers on Delinquency Prevention." *Sociology and Social Research* 57 (1973): 335–341.

Powell, H. "Community Services Coordination in Elementary Schools." *Child Welfare* 52 (1973): 383–391.

Reckless, W. C., Dinitz, S., and Scarpitti, F. "Delinquency Vulnerability: A Cross Group and Longitudinal Analysis." *American Sociological Review* 27 (August, 1962): 515–517.

Reger, R., Schroeder, W., and Uschold, K. *Special Education, Children with Learning Problems.* New York: Oxford University Press, 1968.

Reik, T. *The Compulsion to Confess.* New York: Farran, Strauss, and Cudahy, 1959.

Schultz, E. W.; Hirshoren, A.; Manton, A. B.; and Henderson, R. A. "Special Education for the Emotionally Disturbed." *Exceptional Children* 38 (1977): 313.

Shore, M. F., and Massimo, J. L. "The Alienated Adolescent: A Challenge to the Mental Health Professional." *Adolescence* 4 (13) (1969): 19–34.

Walter, S. C., and O'Donnell, C. R. The Buddy System Model: Community-Based Delinquency Prevention Utilizing Indigenous Non-Professionals as Behavior Change Agents. *ERIC Clearing House* No. 1528 September, 1972.

3

youth in trouble

DAVID A. SABATINO, SHARON G. ROTHMAN, AND MICHAEL H. EPSTEIN

The title of this chapter could read descriptively: Youth and the Problems of Vandalism, Truancy, Dropouts, Overt Classroom and Corridor Aggression, and Traditional Handicapping Conditions. The point is that distinctions are made about people based on the behavior they display. Although it is a struggle to define the underlying causes of these school related difficulties, there are certain characteristics and behaviors which distinguish the individuals involved and bring attention to them and their situation. Most secondary school youth, if not all, face some type of adjustment problem sometime in their school careers. School administrators have sensed this problem and have addressed the issue in part by employing psychologists, counseling psychiatrists, and counselors, and offering clinically related extramural interagency programs and intramural special education programs.

The student with an occasional adjustment problem has a first line of defense to assist him: his counselor. The student with a serious social emotional problem also has the assistance of specialized programs and professional personnel. What about the student in the middle? A chronic problem such as repeated truancy heading toward dropping out, or participation in repeated aggressiveness may place that youth in the gray area: too extreme for the counselor to defend repeatedly to the teachers in their advocacy

81

roles, but not brain-damaged, retarded, or behaviorally disordered enough for a special education program.

DISTINGUISHING A DIFFERENCE

If all adolescents experience difficulty and the period is, as the Europeans call it, a time of storm and stress, why do some adjust and others fail to adjust? Certainly there is no universal answer to such a complex question. Any variable that can sway human adjustment may influence behavior in one direction or another.

There is a persistent assumption in America that secondary school years are a carefree frivolous period. Yet during that period a child must make the transition into adolescence. Adolescence is defined as an interim time, commencing biologically with having the capability to reproduce, and terminating psychologically in maturity. Maturity is difficult to define, but adulthood implies a steady source of income, a job, societal obligations (e.g., military service), and the shared stability of marriage. The vacuum between childhood and adulthood permits teenagers to assume adult responsibility by achieving independent function and decision-making through trial and error, the wisdom of others, and rational thinking. The battle of the balance between independence and dependence with peers and adults shapes that period, and has been cited as one reason for aggression. Youths frequently feel that adults enforce standards and impose limits on behavior to an excessive degree. They feel that they have no rights, no freedom of choice, no privacy, no ear to listen. Adults involve themselves to the point where adolescents feel they must rebel against adult power and control. A "catch-22" situation is in effect. The teenage youth feels an obligation to respect adults and still feels "put down", hence "the inevitable result is conflict, and the teenage response is reluctant conformity, passive resistance, or overt rebellion" (Brammer, 1968, p. 16).

Teenage hostility may be displayed in converse manners. Adolescents may demonstrate hostility through open, aggressive confrontation in the home or school setting. On the other hand, adolescents may vent their hostility through passive resistant behaviors—sullenness, negativism, and resistance to adult suggestion and instruction. The result of the cycle of conflict is a teen culture with its own language, customs, and dress; attending its own movies, and supporting its own multimillion dollar music industries. The social and commercial teen subculture has been documented in works such as Coleman's *The Adolescent Society*. Most adolescents realize they must eventually accept the adult value system, although they may regard it as quite distant.

Incidence

Lest the reader believe the problems of vandalism, truancy, dropouts, and aggression are inconsequential, a closer look at the incidence of such actions is warranted. A discussion of prevalence figures requires a certain degree of critical reservation. There are some incidence reports in which the figures are over-estimated. This is due to (1) definition and identification problems; or (2) use of noneducational frames of reference. In the particular school-problems under study, there may be considerable overlap. Acts of vandalism and assault may be committed by truants and dropouts. The under-achieving truant and dropout often have a history of special education service (i.e., learning disability). Similarly, chronic disruptive youths are often familiar to special personnel dealing with the emotionally disturbed. On the other hand, some prevalence data is under-representative. Few school systems serve all their exceptional youth, yet most often prevalence figures are estimated from the numbers enrolled in special education services. The incidence figures given in this section are intended to convey a range of occurrence rather than an exact rate.

As shown in the 1975 *Digest of Education Statistics* (United States Office of Education, 1975) the percentage of high school graduates in the past 34 years has increased (see Table 3.1). Yet in 1973-74, of those persons 17 years of age only 75% graduated. Of all students who remained in our school systems, 10.7% required special services, and 5.9% were learning disabled, mentally retarded, or emotionally disturbed. This is more than half of all handicapped pupils as, summarized in Table 3.2. A survey on vandalism, theft, and arson was reported in the June, 1973 issue of *School Product News*. Costs of vandalism doubled from 1969 to 1974—from $100 million to $200 million. In 1970-1973 alone, an increase of 14% was recorded in school building burglaries. Schools with enrollments of 5,000 to 10,000 students showed an average vandalism cost of $12,415; schools with 10,000 to 25,000 students reported a cost of $243,952. If these costs were distributed among the nearly 17,000 school districts, acts of vandalism, theft, and arson would approach $500 million.

As cited in *NASSP Bulletin* (Grealy, 1974), a survey compared incidence of overt aggression from 1970-1974. School assault and battery cases were up 58%. School sex offenses had risen 62%. In terms of truancy, Washington (1973) reports that in urban high schools, the average rate of absence is 10%, and in the inner-core areas of large cities the average rate of absence is even higher. If anything, the statistics on truancy and aggression are conservative. In the first situation, unauthorized absenteeism (truancy) causes the school concern in meeting the requirements of the law. In the latter case, many students and teachers are afraid to report crimes committed against them.

Table 3.1.   NUMBER OF HIGH SCHOOL GRADUATES COMPARED
WITH POPULATION 17 YEARS OF AGE: UNITED
STATES, 1969-70 to 1973-74

| School Year | Population 17 Years Old[1] | High School Graduates[2] | | | Number Graduated per 100 Persons 17 Years of Age |
		Total	Boys	Girls	
1	*2*	*3*	*4*	*5*	*6*
1869–70. .	815,000	16,000	7,064	8,936	2.0
1879–80. .	946,026	23,634	10,605	13,029	2.5
1889–90. .	1,259,177	43,731	18,549	25,182	3.5
1899–1900	1,489,146	94,883	38,075	56,808	6.2
1909–10. .	1,786,240	156,429	63,676	92,753	8.8
1919–20. .	1,855,173	311,266	123,684	187,582	16.8
1929–30. .	2,295,822	666,904	300,376	366,528	29.0
1929–40. .	2,403,074	1,221,475	578,718	642,757	50.8
1941–42. .	2,425,574	1,242,375	576,717	665,658	51.3
1943–44. .	2,410,389	1,019,233	423,971	595,262	42.3
1945–46. .	2,254,738	1,080,033	466,926	613,107	47.9
1947–48. .	2,202,927	1,189,909	562,863	627,046	54.0
1949–50	2,034,450	1,199,700	570,000	629,000	59.0
1951–52	2,040,800	1,196,800	569,200	627,300	58.6
1953–54	2,128,600	1,276,100	612,500	663,600	60.0
1955–56	2,270,000	1,414,800	679,500	735,300	62.3
1957–58	2,324,000	1,505,900	725,500	780,400	64.8
1959–60	2,862,005	1,864,000	898,000	966,000	65.1
1961–62	2,768,000	1,925,000	941,000	984,000	69.5
1963–64	3,001,000	2,290,000	1,121,000	1,169,000	76.3
1965–66	3,515,000	2,632,000	1,308,000	1,324,000	74.9
1967–68	3,521,000	2,702,000	1,341,000	1,361,000	76.7
1969–70	3,825,343	2,896,000	1,433,000	1,463,000	75.7
1971–72	3,957,000	3,006,000	1,490,000	1,516,000	76.0
1973–74	4,096,000	3,069,000	1,512,000	1,557,000	74.9

[1] Data from Bureau of the Census.

[2] Includes graduates of public and nonpublic schools.

SOURCES: U.S. Department of Health, Education, and Welfare, National Center
for Education Statistics, *Statistics of State School Systems; Statistics of Public Elementary and Secondary Day Schools, Fall 1974; Statistics of Nonpublic Elementary and Secondary Schools;* and unpublished data.

(Digest of Educ. Statistics, 1975) p. 59

SCHOOL VANDALISM

Perhaps the most conspicuous of the problems discussed in this chapter is vandalism. Across the United States, school vandalism has become a persistent reality for local educational districts. The United States Office of Education in 1969 estimated that school vandalism accounted for over $100 million in property damage. Acts of defacement, theft, arson, and property damage have continued to spiral at an alarming rate. Concommittant with increases in property damage, authorities have documented a parallel increase in the incidence of violent crimes within schools. During the 3-year period between 1970–1973, assaults on teachers increased 77.4%, assaults on students were up 85.3%, robberies increased 36.7%, rapes and attempted rapes increased 40.1%, and homicides and confiscation of weapons jumped 18% and 54.4% respectively. These figures, reported by the U.S. Senate Judiciary Subcommittee on Juvenile Delinquency, are summarized in Figure 3.1.

While these figures are striking in dimension, they are probably unrepresentative of the real destruction taking place in both the elementary and secondary schools. Each year over the past decade, school administrators have quadrupled their maintenance budget to reflect the increase in vandalism, which is compounded by inflation. Most of the small damage to window glass, restrooms, etc., is not even reported. Certain types of property damage are frequently ignored simply because they are not brought to the attention of the law enforcement agencies. In addition, a great deal of this activity is not reported because of a lack of personal complaint, lack of property actually taken that can be used as evidence, or lack of persistence on the part of school officials to follow-up on every minor act. Therefore, as Cohen (1973) reports, many individual acts of vandalism remain anonymous offenses. Although the total cost of vandalism is consequential, each individual act may be too trivial to deal with and is therefore tolerated.

School vandalism has been an isolated concern for school officials for well over 50 years, but recent studies (Weiss, 1974) documenting the cost of vandalism at over $200 million annually in the United States, have broadened the concern of parents and communities to the general public. The Law Enforcement Assistance Administration, United States Department of Justice, has described the problem as having reached epidemic proportions. This crisis level clearly indicates that comprehensive action must be forthcoming. Not only is it vital to curb vandalism because of the financial strain placed on school districts; vandalism also instills fear and/or indifference in students, teachers, and the community, which hinders the effectiveness of our educational programs. Hence it might be inferred that vandalism, when left unchecked, continues as a symptomatic expression whose underlying cause is not understood.

Table 3.2. PUPILS WITH HANDICAPS, PUPILS RECEIVING SPECIAL INSTRUCTION OR ASSISTANCE, AND PROFESSIONAL STAFF FOR THE HANDICAPPED IN LOCAL PUBLIC ELEMENTARY AND SECONDARY SCHOOLS: UNITED STATES, SPRING 1970

	Handicapped Pupils		Handicapped Pupils Served[1]		Professional Staff for the Handicapped			
Type of Handicap	Number	Percent of Total Enrollment	Number	Percent of Handicapped Pupils	Total	Teachers of Separate (Special) Classes	Regular Teachers Who Provided Special Instruction in Regular Classes	Specialized Professional Personnel who Provided Individualized Instruction
1	*2*	*3*	*4*	*5*	*6*	*7*	*8*	*9*
Total[2]	4,752,000	10.7	2,968,000	62.5	464,200	136,000	247,900	80,100
Speech impaired..	1,793,000	4.0	1,224,000	68.3	96,700	35,100	31,400	30,200
Learning disabled........	1,160,000	2.6	648,000	55.9	123,000	27,900	81,400	13,700
Mentally retarded	936,000	2.1	728,000	77.8	102,500	54,300	41,900	6,200
Emotionally disturbed.......	556,000	1.2	253,000	45.5	74,100	11,300	48,800	14,000

Hard of hearing..	131,000	.3	41,000	31.7	21,200	2,000	12,500	6,700
Deaf............	23,000	.1	21,000	90.5	6,200	2,300	3,000	800
Crippled	82,000	.2	30,000	36.6	13,400	1,800	8,200	3,400
Partially sighted..	64,000	.1	17,000	26.7	20,200	800	16,100	3,300
Blind............	6,000	(³)	6,000	94.0	6,900	500	4,600	1,800

¹ Includes pupils receiving instruction or assistance from one or more of the following: Separate (special) classes, special instruction from regular teachers in regular classes, and individualized instruction from specialized professional personnel.

² The totals may be somewhat less than the figures shown because some pupils and teachers may have been reported in more than one category.

³ Less than 0.05 percent.

NOTE—Data are based upon a sample survey and are subject to sampling variability. Percents were computed from unrounded data. Because of rounding, details may not add to totals.

SOURCES: U.S. Department of Health, Education, and Welfare, National Center for Education Statistics, *Number of Pupils with Handicaps in Local Public Schools, Spring 1970*; and *Professional Staff for the Handicapped in Local Public Schools, Spring 1970*.

(Digest of Education Statistics, 1975), p. 38

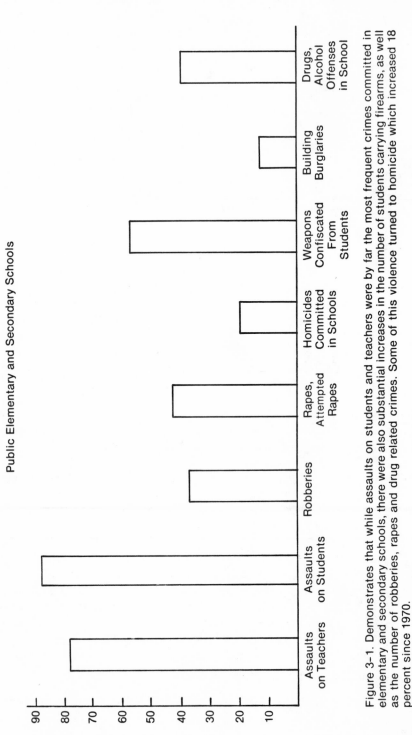

Figure 3-1. Demonstrates that while assaults on students and teachers were by far the most frequent crimes committed in elementary and secondary schools, there were also substantial increases in the number of students carrying firearms, as well as the number of robberies, rapes and drug related crimes. Some of this violence turned to homicide which increased 18 percent since 1970.

Figure 3.1. Increase in school violence and vandalism 1970–1973

Systematic research and analysis of school vandalism did not begin in earnest until 1961 with Martin's study of the nature and prevention of juvenile vandalism. Since then, researchers have been able to relate some aspects of vandalism to such factors as school size, school architecture, community location, or community economic status. The initial studies reporting significant relationships between vandalism and other variables have at times been contradictory. Some investigators, for example, reported that inner-city of ghetto schools have more vandalism than less urban schools (Conant, 1961). Hoerlein (1968), on the other hand, found that there is less vandalism in the center of the city than in the suburbs. The frequency of school vandalism has even differed within the same city. In Houston Independent School District, heavily vandalized and low or non-vandalized schools were spread throughout the city. Even schools geographically close to one another differed, some reporting a high frequency of vandalism and others little, if any. Vandalism touches the larger urban school districts and the smaller rural school districts as well. It destroys schools in economically depressed areas as well as economically affluent areas. Vandalized schools are located in both changing and stable communities. Areas of blue collar workers, white collar workers and business leaders are equally affected. Even exclusive private schools must deal with the effects of vandalism just as our nation's public schools do. From the research evidence to date one conclusive statement can be made: this vast educational problem shows no discrimination (Grieder, 1970).

When our society was smaller, less sophisticated, the constituents of communities held common values and objectives. Smaller scale homogeneous societies may find informal, internal group controls sufficient to maintain effective relations within the community. But these primary control groups would hardly be adequate to manage the complex, highly technological society we have developed. Our population centers are large and diversified. Urbanized communities must deal with a multiplicity of interests and mores which do not present common boundaries for all members. In today's society it has become necessary to supplement informal group controls with more formal institutionalized controls. If we are to establish and maintain a productive society, we must develop a public consciousness, understanding, and control of such social problems as vandalism. It may be symptomatic of the limited amount of data available that it is easier to address the result rather than answer why vandalism has sporadically reached epidemic proportions in our nation's schools. What do we know of the causes of secondary school vandalism?

Characteristics of vandals

Individual acts of vandalism are precipitated by a variety of motives. A review of these motives provides some insight into the social and behavioral characteristics of vandals. Acts of vandalism are generally motivated by financial or property gain, a social cause, nonmalicious play, or the desire to fulfill unmet emotional needs.

Adolescents who commit acts of vandalism for monetary gain or for property that can be acquired may come from a disadvantaged background, may have a drug dependence, or may be a mischievious suburban youth. A socio-economically disadvantaged background is a characteristic of many vandals. Also, minority groups, in relation to their size within the general population, comprise a greater proportion of identified vandals. According to Frost and Hawkes (1970), most vandals are from a lower socioeconomic group and are subject to daily influences on their reputation and interests which are harmful and damaging. Drug dependence is also a factor for property-oriented vandals. Money directly or indirectly obtained through school vandalism may be used to support an expensive drug habit. The money, of course, is acquired by selling stolen property taken from the schools.

For a different reason, teenagers from middle- or upper-middle-class backgrounds are involved in this aspect of vandalism at increasing rates. With greater frequency we see middle-class suburban youth involved in stealing property they could easily obtain legally. Yet the acquisition, processing and black-marketing of these goods are manifestations of the unrest of suburban youth. To these adolescents the money is not as important as the independence and peer association vandalism brings.

A second group of vandals are motivated to commit acts of violence to deliver a message or further a social cause. The secondary school vandal is first of all an adolescent. Whether the person be intellectual or not; high-, middle-, or low-class; urban, suburban, or rural; adolescence will find him striving for self-understanding and self-satisfaction in a world which often challenges such accomplishments. Often adolescents feel their personal values are not reflected in society's mores, resulting in alienation and anger. Vandals may direct their anger toward the schools as the only institution representative of the hostile society with which they have personal contact. In this respect, school vandalism is an indication of rebellion against family, school, or pervading civil, social or political issues.

A third motivating factor for acts of vandalism arises out of nonmalicious play. Any damage derived is done in the context of a game. The individual who commits the vandalous act may be vying for peer acceptance, or he may merely be bored and attempting to create some level of excitement. The end product of this nonmalicious play unfortunately is considerable property damage.

A fourth motivational factor of vandalism is to fulfill unmet emotional needs. Vandals who exhibit manifestations of personal emotional problems have a low trust level. The interpersonal commitments and communication skills of these youths are very low, and they share little satisfactory emotional involvement with others. More specifically, these vandals evidence minimal ability to demonstrate sympathy toward others, to stand alone when necessary, to have close friends, or to be aggressively constructive. This inability to relate to others is supported by Goldman's study (1960) of the Syracuse Public School system where he cited the following factors to a high rate of vandalism: frequent staff turnover, authoritarian administration, and highly formal interpersonal relations.

Vandals who are motivated by unmet emotional needs are characterized as low academic achievers with poor self-concepts. A significantly recurring relationship between self-concept and academic achievement has been verified to some extent (Brookover, Erickson, and Joiner, 1967). Shaw, Edson, and Bell's (1960) study of achievers' and underachievers' self-perceptions indicated that male achievers feel relatively more positive about themselves than their underachieving counterparts. In a closer look at the underachiever, Taylor (1964) listed the following as personality traits: he is self-derogatory, has a depressed attitude about himself, has feelings of inadequacy, and tends to have strong inferiority feelings. A general unhappiness with his personal situation may lead the individual vandal to seek peer acceptance and high self-esteem through acts of vandalism. Cohen (1973) states that vandalism may even be a group offense, whereby "it is situational in character and arises spontaneously out of group interaction" (p. 254).

A sex difference has also been noted. The fact that a negative view toward one's self and one's abilities leads to unsuccessful performances in school holds true more strongly for boys than girls (Bledsoe, 1967; Fink, 1962; Shaw, Edson & Bell, 1960). This is consistent with studies in most Western countries where the ratio of male to female delinquents is about six to one.

In summary, vandals are characterized by immediate motives involving money, property, drugs; historical motives such as cultural, social, or economic backgrounds; or emotional motives including anger, fear, frustration and desire for group acceptance. Whatever the motive, vandals present a real threat to themselves, the schools, and the larger society.

HIGH SCHOOL AND JUNIOR HIGH DROPOUTS

Some 26 million young people will pass through the schools and into the labor market during 1960–1970. It is estimated that 7½ million of these young people will be school dropouts and that 2½ million of them will have had less than 8 years of formal education.   (Metz, 1970)

The idea of dropping out to turn to something other than school is fallacious in that students who leave the secondary school generally do not find success in life. Indeed, secondary schools reflect to a marked degree the harshness of the real world. With academic subject-oriented teachers and measured performance output, schools maintain a climate of conformity. Creativity, consistence in social values, and the expectations of others are relative (as relative, in fact, as any person's value judgment of another person can possibly be). The issue developed to its fullest is simply a dichotomy in which the youth must make the decision to remain in school or leave. Youths who do not succeed in school for a multiplicity of reasons, one of which is the secondary schools' failure to develop curriculum alternatives, must either tolerate obediently the continued failure regardless of the personal cost to self-comfort, or drop out of school.

Dauw (1970) insists the high school dropout rates will not decline until the schools change the curriculum. In 1968, Schreiber estimated the prevalence of dropouts in this country at nearly 700,000 dropouts. He notes that we

> cannot afford to have almost one million youth drop out of school each year to become unwanted and unemployed . . . We must reconstruct our educational system to provide relevant, successful experiences for all children so that they will become and remain an integral part of our society. (p. 6)

Former United States Commissioner of Education Howe (Schreiber, 1968) decreed, "attempts to coax and persuade potential dropouts to stay in school, when the school continues to fail them, accomplish absolutely nothing" (p. 1).

It has been said that "each generation of school administrators discovers dropouts anew" and schools at the turn of the century were no exception. High schools of that period had their dropouts by the thousands, the elementary schools by the tens of thousands. For example, Kingsbury's report from a 1906 state survey in Massachusetts showed 25,000 youths between the ages of fourteen and sixteen were not attending school. Five-sixths of these had not graduated from elementary school. From 1890 to 1912, the percentage of students who, once entered, graduated from high school, remained fairly constant. High school graduates were only 10.7% of the total high school enrollment in 1890. In 1900, that figure was up only slightly to 11.9%. The increasing trend continued to 12.1% in 1910, and 12.5% in 1912. When surveyed, youths at the turn of the century gave a number of reasons for dropping out of school. The factors included poor health, lack of interest, and the need of their services at home. Understandably enough, the adolescents did not mention failure in school as a reason. Other reasons have been cited for dropout statistics of the early 1900s and middle of the century.

Interestingly, some of the reasons cited by the youth of yesterday are relevant today. Among these are attitudes of schools toward culturally different children and youth, the biasing effect caused by standardized tests, and prejudice. Immigrants and their children at the turn of the century were referred to as inferior by social and educational leaders. In 1881, Senator Morrill of Vermont referred to the "weak, vile and hungry outcasts" from Europe who had come to the United States "not only to stay themselves, but to transmit hereditary taints to the third and fourth generation." The Immigration Restriction League decried that Europeans of southern and eastern descent were sending their "illiterates, paupers, criminals, and madmen" into the country, thereby endangering the nation. Ross (1905) described immigrants as "cheap stucco manikins" or "beaten members of beaten breeds," who were either "elbowed aside or left behind" (p. 321) in the path of the mightier European races. Ross claimed that these people could never replace the granite men who fell at Gettysburg and Cold Harbor. This attitude prevailed even among educational leaders. Cubberley (1919), a leading educator of that day, described immigrants as "largely illiterate, docile, lacking in initiative and almost wholly without the Anglo-Saxon conception of righteousness, liberty, law, order, public decency, and government" (p. 338). There may have been some school experiences that led educators to such opinionated statements.

Cohen (1970) found that in New York City in 1909, the Italian child was almost twice as likely to be below grade level according to age than was the native American white. The situation was similar in the 1950s and 1960s. Coleman (1966) in his prestigious report found that blacks in inner-city schools fell further behind the nationwide median in school achievement as they progressed through school. Carmichael and Hamilton (1967) noted that in central Harlem in 1960, while 21.6% of third graders were reading above grade level, 30% were reading below grade level. This situation had seriously deteriorated by the time these youths reached the sixth grade. At that point, 11.7% of the students were reading above and 80% were reading below grade level. The situation was similar in Philadelphia where Nichols observed that 75% of black youths who would graduate that year were functional illiterates (Carmichael and Hamilton 1967).

Intelligence tests further reinforced the view that many ethnic immigrants and blacks were not capable of performing academically at the secondary school level. Educators thought they had scientific data by means of these intelligence tests to support statements of racial inferiority. The data having been "scientifically" collected were used to make judgments regarding the intelligence of students. For example, Murdock (1920) reported the following differences in intelligence scores between Italian immigrant youths and native-born white American youths in New York City: the median intelligence scores for 9- and 10-year-old Italian youths were 73.5 points and 84.3 points, respectively, whereas the native white American registered 108.5 at both ages.

Today, racial differences are still cited by those who report that blacks tend to score lower than whites on intelligence tests. Jensen (1969) noted that on the average, black students score about fifteen points lower than white students on standardized intelligence tests. Charters (1967), in his Social Class and Intelligence Tests, argued that the results described above should be expected. Intelligence tests, he noted, consistently have been biased in favor of middle class students, to the detriment of lower class pupils. Using such "scientific" data as described above, Jensen advocated a theory of "genetic intellectual inferiority among blacks" based solely on their intelligence test data. Similar arguments were advanced relative to the immigrants half a century ago. The questionable use of such standardized tests has contributed significantly to the problems lower-class minorities have faced in schools.

Historically racial prejudice has been another contributing factor to the high rate of dropouts in the black population. Prejudice against blacks was rampant not only in the South where it was part of the legal code, but also in the North. In the South miscegenation laws and segregation of public facilities regulated the blacks to inferior positions. Job discrimination and housing restrictions evoked the same effect in the North. Educationally, blacks were segregated in schools in the South. Even after the famous Brown vs. Board of Education of Topeka Decision (1954) (347 vs. 483, 74 sect. 686, 98 L. Ed. 873), which voted that separate is not equal, many states fought school integration right into the 1970s. Massive resistance, interposition, and violence reminded black youths that mainstream southern society, in and out of school, regarded them as inferior.

Characteristics of the dropout

Many of the historical factors leading to a youth dropping out of school are relevant today. The attitudes of school administrators, lack of readiness for academic achievement, blatant prejudice, and cultural influences all affect the incidence of dropouts. Unfortunately, the conglomeration of factors preclude the identification of common characteristics. However, the incidence of dropouts within specific groups of the youth population, specifically disadvantaged and high ability adolescents, affords the opportunity to delineate a number of characteristics. In this section, the characteristics of disadvantaged and high ability youth and their reasons for leaving school are reviewed.

The District of Columbia's Youth Center which serves the Washington, D.C. public schools was developed to assist youth who came in contact with the courts. Since its inception in 1960, Burke and Simons (1965) noted that about 90% of the youths serviced were dropouts; of these, 95% had long court histories. Burke and Simons surveyed these youths in order to ascertain the factors which led to their leaving school. Interestingly, many of their statements were reminiscent of those historical reasons cited by immigrants and blacks at the early part of the 1900s. The primary reasons stated by most of the delinquent dropouts were: (1) home backgrounds, with little belief in or history of school success; (2) conscious or unconscious prejudice against minority groups, which was evident in the classroom; and (3) a failure of the curricula to match the youths' interests, abilities, or basic academic needs. A search of school records identified a number of characteristics shared by these youths. An academic profile delineates the following factors: (1) inadequate school adjustment; (2) repeated truancy; (3) repeated grade failure; (4) underachievement in reading; and (5) near normal intelligence.

The first factor, lack of appropriate school adjustment, represented perhaps the most prominent factor leading to dropping out. Generally these youths evidenced a disrespect for authority, an inability to relate to peers, fighting, and failure to comply with school rules. Ninety-two percent of those surveyed had histories of chronic disruptive behavior in school.

The second behavior pattern was repeated truancy, where 90% of the respondents were chronic truants prior to leaving school. The most frequently cited reasons for truancy were lack of interest (47%); economic reasons (32%); and dislike of a teacher (10%). While truant, these youths were generally involved in nonproductive activities including aimlessly walking streets (44%); going to the movies (20%); or watching television or entertaining friends (19%). Only 9% of the truants were actively searching for employment. Burke and Simons commented that:

> One wonders if this is a retreat from school—whether in some way adjustments could be made in terms of curriculum, marking system, and grouping to increase the challenge of the schools. There is little need to point up the dangers involved in youngsters taking to the streets and the movies unsupervised and disillusioned. (1965, p. 33)

The remaining characteristics of the profile, problems of academic retardation and school failure, are closely associated with truancy. The habitually truant were repeated failures. Of the respondents, 73% had been retained in school two or more times. A multiplicity of variables accounted for the school failure; of these the primary factors were a lack of academic readiness, cultural distrust in the schools, and truancy. Academically 76% of these dropouts were reading below their grade level. The academic retardation was related more to experiential and cultural factors than to intellectual deficits. As Burkes and Simons argues:

> It could be safely assumed that these limitations in the area of reading really represent early failures and retardations in school. The fact of educational limitations sometimes is not so serious as the frustrations encompassed in at least 11 years of schooling . . .
>
> In terms of intellectual adequacy, what kind of people are these who become dropouts and delinquents and who eventually become incarcerated? Fifty-

nine percent of the sampling falls within the 90 to 110 IQ category. This represents a group with adequate potential for completing high school. When intelligence range is combined with actual achievement, a clear picture of under-achievement emerges. (Burke & Simons, 1965, pp. 33–34)

At the other end of the continuum, the high-ability or gifted dropout has also been a topic of investigation by researchers. In a now classic study, French (1969) compared a group of high-ability dropouts and a group of school attenders. Attitudinal tests and individual interviews were conducted for both groups. High-ability drop-outs and school attenders were given the Minnesota Vocational Interest Inventory (MVII), the High School Personality Questionnaire (HSPQ), the Student Information Blank (SIB), and an attitude scale developed for the project called Attitude Inventory for Youth (AIY). Tests and interviews were administered by 63 school counselors and psychologists located in the schools at which the dropouts had previously been enrolled.

A comparison of personality traits indicated that male dropouts were significantly more assertive, independent, self-assured, rebellious, competitive, cheerful, expressive, frank, happy-go-lucky, and talkative than those students who remained in school. The personal attributes of the high-ability male dropout does not suggest lack of interest toward education, but rather that the school's emphasis on conformity tends to create a stumbling block. Indeed, the high-ability male dropout demonstrated little neuroticism, phobias, or anxiety; and from all predictors, is an emotionally stable person. High-ability female dropouts were similar in most respects to the males.

Personal interviews were conducted to ascertain the reasons for leaving school with high-ability male and female youth. French (1969) observed that youth with measured IQ's exceeding 110 gave these reasons for dropping out:

(1) they did not like school (20 percent); (2) they were asked to leave (18 percent); (3) they wanted to get a job (17 percent); or (4) they wanted to get married (11 percent). Twenty percent of the unmarried female dropouts left school because they did not like it; others left because they wanted jobs (16 percent); because they had failing grades (12 percent); or because they were needed at home (12 percent). A large majority (82 percent) of the female dropouts left school in order to be married. (p. 70–71)

In summary, the high-ability dropout, unlike the disadvantaged dropout, has the academic and intellectual skills to survive in an educational milieu. Furthermore, the personality, traits of these youth, again unlike the disadvantaged dropout, provide a composite profile of a basically emotionally stable person and one who has an inability to adjust to the conformity of school. Interestingly, while academic, intellectual, and personality differences exist between these two groups, they eventually lead to the same startling conclusion—the decision to drop out of school.

A final study serves to recap most of the major characteristics attributed to the dropout. Douglass (1969) defined dropouts on the following nine characteristics:

1. An academic record of low school achievement.

2. A family background of low economic and cultural status, with parents who did little if anything to give the students a good attitude toward school.

3. Poor reading ability despite continued promotion, grade after grade, year after year. The majority of students had not learned to read well enough to complete junior high school level and some intermediate level materials.

4. Markedly lower ability to learn verbal materials.

5. Lack of membership in interest clubs or other types of extracurricular activities. The dropout doesn't belong. He is not a part of the school.

6. A record of absenteeism which may be resultant of factors 2, 3, 4, 8, and 9.

7. A record of anti-social behavior.

8. Associates from among underachieving students and children from culturally disadvantaged homes with inferior morals and morale, including some juvenile delinquents.

9. An unfavorable attitude toward school and teachers.

Obviously, to develop a composite profile of the dropout is a demanding task. Those youths who drop out of school do so for a variety of complex reasons. Familial, cultural, and educational backgrounds vary from individual to individual and prohibit the definition of general group characteristics. Nonetheless, authorities have delineated characteristics shared by a majority of these youths.

There are profiles, studies, trends, and characteristics on the youth who drops out of school. But the research addresses the extremes of our concern: the disadvantaged and the gifted. Perhaps our attention is so involved with the polarities, that adolescents in the middle are unrecognized as distinct dropouts. If there are such youths with distinguishable characteristics and problems, research has been negligent in managing their concerns. The information yields little usable data, simply because knowledge of the group does not provide knowledge for a given individual. The only solution to the problem of school dropouts is a targeted one-on-one examination of those issues related to that youth's reasons for leaving school. Far too frequently the real reasons lie buried in a maze of symptoms.

TRUANCY

Although repeated relationships have been demonstrated between truancy, poor school adjustment, and chronic disruptive behavior in school, in examining the literature on truancy it becomes apparent that little attention and subsequent information has been given to this school problem. References to the topic of truancy are conspicuously absent from general works on school violence, criminology, delinquency, and vandalism. Truancy, it appears, has become a "soft sign" of pervading educational-social ills—an issue often incorporated into our more dramatic, compelling school crises. But can truancy be adequately treated by hard-core delinquency programs? Is the truant's personality the same as our adolescent dropout or offender? Or is the truant more accurately one of our borderline youths entitled to distinct understanding and treatment?

Atypical of earliest material on truancy, most of which is general or circumventive in nature, is Hiatt's (1915) work, *The Truant Problem and the Parent School.* Hiatt studied the characteristics of truants in Philadelphia and recorded detailed information on such demographic factors as age, sex, nationality, and grade distribution. While a study of the causes proved complex, the following were identified as factors contributing to truancy: (1) fault of home environment (29%); (2) dislike of school (26%); (3) bad companions (20%); (4) fault of boy (11%); (5) desire to find a job (10%); and (6) illness (4%).

In 1917 the analysis of truancy in our larger school districts was continued. Abbot's (1917) work, *Truancy and Non-attendance in the Chicago Public Schools,* provided comprehensive and rational consideration of the relationship between the truant and such factors as classroom behavior, home environment, mental and physical abilities of the child, and potentialities for eventual delinquency. Additional studies include the effects of such programs as the parental-school relationship, visiting teachers, school sense, and so-called transfer system on school truancy.

The transfer system problem involves the irregularity of attendance as well as complete truancy from school because of students who take transfers from one school and then delay or fail to enroll in a new school. Statistics regarding the amount of time lost through lack of supervision of transferred students were distinctly related to these early statistics of absence. At that time, school officials had additional social considerations such as the actual need and justification of compulsory attendance laws and changing immigrant populations. Although these concerns have been investigated, the answers have been evasive.

Modern society has created new concerns and the reasons for truancy are even more serious. Modern truancy is symptomatic of a large number of school and societal ills. As early as 1933, Hick reported that only

50% of school absences were due to illness. Early estimates of truancy in large city high schools showed absences of 10% of the total student body. For inner-city schools in lower socioeconomic communities these figures were even higher. In 1963, data contrasting truancy at elementary school and high school levels in Chicago showed the percentage of absence from school tended to increase with the age of the youth. Therefore a concentration on the truancy problems in secondary schools may seem more appropriate.

The truant of the past may be viewed as a mischievous easy-going youth, more interested in a harmless ball game, swim, or leisure play than his school work; a Huck Finn character from the pen of Mark Twain. But today's truant, according to many school and police officials is often involved in crime. A 1972 effort to attenuate truancy in Los Angeles, California, is illustrative of this criminal aspect. Over a four-day period juveniles were apprehended for truancy violations in the city's highest crime-rate area. In this four-day period police statistics revealed that daytime burglaries dropped 30%, and daytime auto thefts decreased 75%.

The schools are greatly concerned with truancy for several reasons. First, schools must meet attendance law requirements, which in turn determine the amount of state aid they receive. This financial aspect directly affects the educational resources of the school districts, with a subsequent adverse affect on the quality of educational programs. Secondly and more important, truancy disrupts the continuity of experiences and instruction students receive. Interpreting integral aspects of the continuous development offered by secondary schools, it is little wonder that chronic truants are underachievers who tend to fall further behind in their academic and social growth.

The truancy problem is a major problem reaching many nonpublic school agencies. It is generally agreed that truancy is symptomatic of the child's problems at home, at school, and in the community. The school continues to spearhead a systematic examination at the source and/or nature of the student's problems by focusing on his needs, problems, and interests. Courts, child welfare agencies, and private and public clinics have all become involved. As a truant, one's name is frequently seen on the agenda of many of these agencies.

Characteristics of truants

According to Washington (1973), all truants must be viewed as potential dropouts from school. Generally they are upset with the world today and often unhappy with their immediate home environment as well. Truants are not a homogenous group of youths, which limits any definitive statement of common characteristics. However, certain researchers have identified some common characteristics shared by a majority of truants. The reader is asked to exercise extreme caution in generalizing from the groups described to a larger population of truants.

Washington (1973) studied 56 truant high school students from a Midwestern city. The socioeconomic background of this group was characterized by unemployment, poverty, and deprivation. Findings indicated that failure to adjust to academic requirements troubled most of these students. It follows that these truants were aware of their academic weaknesses and felt the need to exclude themselves from the classroom and school. Inadequate reading, writing, and speaking skills produced a fear of failure, which was further compounded by a low frustration level. The combination of an inability to meet with success, fear of failure, and low tolerance level culminated in repeated acts of truancy.

The second greatest problem area for truants is that of personal-psychological relations. The truant was constantly confronted with personal-psychological problems manifested by such behavior as daydreaming, loss of temper, or taking things too seriously. It might be inferred that truants have a desire to learn, but due to frustration, have moved to avoidance behavior.

The next area of great truant concern involves money. Washington (1973) found the two most frequently cited problems statements on the

Table 3.3. THE SIXTEEN MOST FREQUENTLY CHECKED PROBLEM STATEMENTS BY PUPILS CLASSIFIED AS TRUANTS (N = 56)

Statement No.	Statement Content	Frequency
116	Wanting to earn some of my own money	25
119	Needing to find part-time job now	22
50	Not spending enough time on study	21
321	Getting low grades	21
9	Having to ask parents for money	21
26	Losing my temper	20
159	Can't keep my mind on studies	20
117	Wanting to buy my own things	19
120	Needing a job during vacation	18
27	Taking some things too seriously	18
6	Needing to learn how to save money	17
81	Daydreaming	16
307	Getting into trouble	16
315	Wanting to leave home	16
46	Missing too many days of school	16
324	Afraid of failing in school	16

(Washington, 1973) p. 254

High School Journal, 1973, *56*, 248–257. Published by University of North Carolina Press.

Mooney Problem Check List, as itemized in Table 3.3, were "wanting to earn some of my own money" and "needed to find part-time job now." More than one-third of the top 16 problem statements concerned financial situations. Contrary to some studies (Morris, 1972) this indicates that truants, many of whom are from financially stressed families, recognize the financial demands placed upon their families and may choose to exclude themselves from school due to financial situations. Table 3.4 carefully ranks the problem areas which truants attempt to solve as defensively and effectively as possible.

The use of drugs among adolescents is argued as another characteristic of truants. Morris (1972) stated that the current drug culture is doing more than its share to increase truancy. Survey studies indicate that as many as one-third to one-half of the high school students have experimented with drugs. According to McDonald, a former New York State Supreme Court judge, the use of narcotics has decreased the motivation of adolescents toward educational pursuits (Morris, 1972).

The goal in dealing with truancy is not merely to return the child to school. Further establishment of personal meaning and fulfillment from school attendance must be attained. If the student continues to find frustration and failure in school, he will seek to alleviate these pressures. If avoidance behavior (truancy) is forbidden, the student may move toward more aggressive behaviors. The next section will deal with the foundations and characteristics of these aggressive behaviors.

Table 3.4. THE FREQUENCY OF RESPONSES CATEGORIZED INTO PROBLEM AREAS BY PUPILS CLASSIFIED AS TRUANTS (N = 56)

Rank	Problem Area	Frequency Totals
1.	ASW-Adjustment to School Work	310
2.	PPR-Personal-Psychological Relations	251
3.	FLE-Finances, Living Conditions, and Employment	250
4.	SPR-Social-Psychological Relations	217
5.	HF- Home and Family	213
6.	HPD- Health and Physical Development	189
7.	MR-Morals and Religions	179
8.	FVE-Future: Vocational and Educational	177
9.	SRA-Social and Recreational Activities	153
10.	CSM-Courtship, Sex and Marriage	146
11.	CTP-Curriculum and Teaching Procedures	141

(Washington, 1973) p. 254

High School Journal, 1973, *56*, 248–257. Published by University of North Carolina Press.

CLASSROOM, CORRIDOR, AND SCHOOL RELATED AGGRESSION

The dimensions of human personality present a mosaic not completely understood even by those who have made a lifework of its study. It is not uncommon to place personality traits on a continuum, with semantic differentials serving to identify the polar ends. Passivity and agressiveness are two adjectives used to differentiate human behavior, and rightly or wrongly, serve as references against which people are described.

In 1928, Wickham conducted a study which has since become a classic. He noted that teachers can identify aggressive youths as having problems which may be of an emotional origin. Furthermore, he found that passivity does not draw attention to youths, even when the emotional bases for such behavioral actions are more deviant. Wickham's data raised two issues which have generated a wealth of research throughout the years. First, what constitutes emotional disturbance (e.g., is a youth with a problem the same as a problem youth)? Second, what constitutes a reasonable system of observing and reporting behavior when it has a direct situational bearing? In short, it is possible to be rational 90% of the time, or for that matter 99% of the time. However, in serious conflict situations a person's behavior may be considered irrational 10% or 100% of the time.

A wealth of research attention from the areas of psychology and education has been directed to the subject of aggression. Historically aggression has been studied from biological and psychodynamic perspectives, and more recently by behavioral and learning theorists.

The term *aggression* has been variously defined, but three components of aggression are common to all the definitions: it is a behavioral act; it inflicts pain to another individual; and it violates a social norm. Some research has brought forth further dysfunction to the concept of aggression. Sears, Maccoby and Lewin (1957) distinguish between two forms: instrumental aggression and hostile aggression. Instrumental aggression is defined by acts manifested to satisfy wants or desires. On the other hand, hostile aggression is done to inflict pain or injury on another individual. In a more recent paper, Sears (1961) further delineated aspects of aggressive behavior, including antisocial aggression, self-aggression, prosocial aggression, projected aggression, and aggression anxiety.

One reason for the lack of progress in clarifying the concept of aggression is the lack of agreement on behaviors that can be distinctly labeled as aggressive (Feshbach and Feshbach, 1971). Also to be considered is the amount and intensity of aggressive behavior relative to the situation. The awareness of productive assertativeness has led to the development of training patterns to assist people in achieving certain levels of assertativeness therapeutically. What distinguishes appropriate assertativeness from aggression? From class to class, from teacher to teacher, the label, the restraints, the reinforcement must in fact be different because an accepted operational definition of aggression has not been forthcoming.

The changing concept and definition of aggression presents a significant problem when studying this type of behavior. Research on the topic decreases in value when the concept and definition differ from study to study. Furthermore, programs on the identification of causes and characteristics have also slowed. Keeping the definitional problems in mind, theories on etiological considerations and characteristics are reviewed.

Freud viewed aggressive behavior as an inherent drive of man. Each individual has what Freud labeled a Death Instinct, which if activated would lead to self-destructive behavior. Over the years the self-destructive drives create tension and anxiety within the individual. In order to neutralize the drives the individual directs these toward others in the form of aggressive acts. Dollard and associates (1939) articulated the Frustration Aggression hypothesis which changes the perspective of aggression from an innate response to more of a learned response. The Frustration Aggression approach suggests that aggressive acts are initially an instinctual response to a frustrating situation. Thus, frustration begets aggression. A revised theory of Miller (1941) acknowledged that frustration could lead to other learned behaviors including depression, withdrawal, anxiety, and aggression. According to Miller, the continued strength of aggressive acts is determined in part by reinforcement.

Behavioral theorists have viewed aggression as a learned response, primarily the product of reinforcement strategies. Sears (1958) noted that if aggressive behavior removes the frustrating stimulus, the probability of the aggressive act appearing again is increased. Lovaas (1961) investigated the verbal aggressive behavior of preschool children. One group of children was rewarded for being verbally aggressive to a doll figure, while a second group was rewarded for nonaggressive verbal remarks. Following reinforcement training, the children were given an opportunity to play with either a nonaggressive or aggressive toy. Consequently, the children who had been reinforced for verbal aggression used the aggressive toy significantly more often than the other children. The relationship between aggression and reinforcement indicates that aggression is controlled through the consequences which follow the act.

A social learning approach suggests that aggressive behavior is learned via the modeling or imitation of individuals in the environment (Bandura, 1970). A youth can learn a repetoire of aggressive responses through observing the behavior of aggressive individuals. As Feshbach and Feshbach stated (1971),

> An important point made by these modeling studies is that aggressive behaviors can be acquired without the prior performance and direct reinforcement of the behavior. (p. 368)

The antecedents which are purported to lead to aggression are more hypothesized than factual. Some theories underscore the nature of aggression as an inherent human characteristic. An alternative approach views aggression as a learned response through reinforcement or modeling of others. Additional information is needed on the etiology of aggression prior to the formation of any definitive conclusion. Research, however, has clarified some of the family and school characteristics of aggressive children and youth.

It has been commonly accepted that a youth's family experiences establish the favorable or unfavorable conditions for school participation. Family vacations, country trips, and exposure to different literary, musical, and artistic works provide the experiential constructs from which the child's early school success is related. If the parents have not equipped their children with an adequate social behavior and cognitive framework, poor performance in social and academic situations can be the consequence. Academic shortcomings and failures generate growing frustrations with the school, which may be expressed as classroom aggression and disruption. The problem is compounded when the academic difficulties are reported to the parents. Generally, parents regard the lack of success as an indication that further educational stimulation is a waste for the child whose increasingly bad achievement in school and unacceptable social behavior attest to his inability to cope with learning demands. The interrelationship of school and family necessitates a review of the influence of the family on the development of aggression.

The role of the family is central to all theories of aggression. Child development theorists view the family as the primary socialization institution, and no matter which theoretical perspective is considered, parents influence the development of aggression. For this reason, the study of family organization and parental characteristics has received extensive research. Research on family organization has concentrated on the effect of parental absence on the development of aggression. In a review, Hetherington and Martin (1972) noted a greater probability of antisocial and aggressive behaviors among males in homes where the father was absent. Additional support comes from the Cambridge Study on Delinquent Development, where Gibson (1969) reported a greater incidence of delinquency in father-absent homes. Reasons for the absence compound the problem. When the father is absent because of death or illness, the aggression is noted to a lesser degree. On the other hand, if divorce or desertion is evident, the aggression appears to a greater or more intense degree. Goldstein (1972) has hypothesized that in the father-absent home the mother is unable to fulfill both paternal and maternal roles. The father generally provides behavioral performance contingent love which leads to the development of prosocial behaviors. With his absence, this shaping process is lessened. In summary, paternal absence, particularly with respect to males, appears to be related to the development of aggression.

Personality and behavioral characteristics of the parents as related to aggression has been examined. Social learning theorists argue that children are socialized by observing the behavior of others. It follows, then, that similar aggressive traits would appear in parents and their children. Reseachers, in fact, have indicated that delinquents and aggressive children and parents who demonstrated these behaviors (Glueck and Glueck, 1950; Peterson, Quay, and Cameron, 1959). Youths who are reared in environments where the predominant mode of social interaction is characterized by aggressive behavior are likely to behave aggressively in school and social settings. Over the years repeated demonstration, observation, and modeling of aggressive actions makes efforts to attenuate the behavior, particularly at the secondary school level, exceedingly demanding.

Personality traits of parents were investigated by Feldhusen, Thurston, and Benning (1970) in a longitudinal study of third, sixth, and ninth grade youths who consistently displayed either aggressive-disruptive behavior or socially approved behavior. Aggressive-disruptive youths, when compared to peers whose behavior was identified as socially approved, were reported to have parents who displayed less overt affection. Consequently, these youths were inadequately supervised and disciplined. Families of aggressive-disruptive youths were not cohesive, were on lower educational and occupational levels, and were limited in community participation. On the Kvaraceus Scale (1950), a test used to predict delinquent behaviors, aggressive youth evidenced response patterns indicating proneness to delinquency. Academically these youths were significantly lower than the socially approved group on arithmetic and reading performance. Finally, the authors defined the aggressive-disruptive youth according to 18 primary behavioral characteristics:

> is quarrelsome, is sullen, is rude, is defiant, is resentful, steals, lies, is destructive, disrupts class, is a bully, has temper tantrums, is overly dominant, talks back, is cruel, is tardy or absent without excuse, uses profanity or obscenity, fights with other pupils, and deceptive.
>
> (Feldhausen, et al., 1970, p. 438)

In reviewing the differences between the aggressive and socially approved groups, Feldhusen, Thurston, and Benning (1970) noted that family and environmental differences were related to aggression. The importance of the preschool years, the family attitudes, and the youth's reinforcement history may possibly have established the circumstances precipitating behavior.

Some aggression in schools is issue-oriented to serve as a message to the school administrator or community. Havighurst, Smith, and Wilder

(1971) reported on a study of 350 high schools representing most of the 620 large cities in the United States. In response to a question regarding the frequency of physical confrontation between student and student, and student and faculty, student-student confrontations occurred 39% of the time. Student-faculty conflict occurred in 45% of the high schools. Conflict in the form of physical confrontation occurred for both student-student and student-faculty groups at a much higher rate in black/white mixed schools. Racial aggression or confrontation was not limited to isolated incidents between one or two youths. Groups of adolescents were involved in these racial incidents which would undermine the school activities for brief or long periods of time. School administrators noted that most of these conflict situations were short lived and produced disruptions for periods of up to one school day. Nevertheless, a majority of schools were victimized and these aggressive racial situations involved disruptions.

Besides aggression brought on by racial issues or confrontations, conflict situations between students and teachers are spurred on by youth wanting to convey a message. As Havighurst (1971) and associates noted,

> Conflict situations develop from substantive concerns. The substance at stake may be clearly articulated as an issue or demand, or it may be rather vaguely symbolized by the nature of the act of conflict itself. In some cases, the substance of the conflict and the form of expression are highly related. It is possible, for example, that when students strike particular classes they do so in order to express their displeasure with the instructional process in those classes. On the other hand, the act of striking classes may be simply a convenient act to give visibility to an ideological position which cannot readily be reduced to a specific demand. (p. 80)

The ideological concerns that led to the aggression varied from situation to situation. In middle-class all-white schools the primary issue was the dress code problem where students were challenging the school administration. Grave ideological issues arose in integrated schools where students protested racial decisions, community conditions, and administrative decisions.

The concept of alienation, while rooted in sociological theory and tradition, has in recent years been applied to educational concerns. The study of alienation among high school students has been a recent topic of research. Most notably, Warner and Hansen (1970) have argued that the primary cause of alienation among adolescents has been the increased tendency of society to treat individuals as commodities rather than people. It is hypothesized that alienation from the school milieu may be related to the increased incidence of aggression in secondary schools. Specifically, the greater the perceived alienation from school, the greater the likelihood that the youth will act aggressively in school.

Sociological authorities have offered theories to explain the development of alienation among individuals in society. Merton (1949) states that society not only creates the goals for which individuals should strive, but society also establishes and controls the acceptable modes of attaining those goals. As long as an individual receives satisfaction from the goals and enjoys the means required to reach them, an effective equilibrium will be maintained in the society. Alienation develops when one or both of these elements are blocked, or one becomes completely dominant over the other. Thus, when society completely controls the individual, a feeling of powerlessness develops, or when the individual cannot accept the norms of society he becomes normless. When both goals and norms mean little to the individual he feels isolated from the society. In today's society it would appear that these are situations in which many students find themselves. Specifically, some students are disconcordant with the goals set forth by the school administrators, or they do not possess the skills or inclination to utilize the acceptable means for goal attainment. Circumstances such as these breed alienation which may be manifested in aggressive behavior.

Warner and Hansen (1970) conducted a study to measure alienation among high school youths. Three attitudinal scales were administered to secondary school students: Dean's Scale of Alienation, the Tennessee Self-Concept Scale, and Taylor Manifest Anxiety Scale.

Dean's Scale of Alienation measures the students' perception of alienation and provides a total measure for alienation as well as scores on three aspects of alienation: powerlessness, normlessness, and social isolation. *Powerlessness* was described as feelings of not being able to understand or influence the outcomes of one's behavior. *Normlessness* was the feeling that society has no norms by which to live or that the norms that do exist do not apply to one's own life. *Social isolation* was described as the feeling of being all alone; of being separated from society. Alienation, according to Warner and Hansen (1970), refers to the individual's feeling of frustration caused by discrepancies between desires and expectations and the societal means and rewards. The Tennessee Self-Concept Scale consists of 100 self-descriptive items which the subject uses to identify his own beliefs or feelings about himself. The Taylor Manifest Anxiety Scale measures the students' level of anxiety in social situations.

Warner and Hansen (1970) reported that a significant relationship existed between alienation and a low self-concept. Alienated youth indicated they were skeptical of their ability, perceived themselves as undesirable, and had little self-confidence. Moreover, the alienated adolescent felt isolated from peers and school and felt powerless to change the situation or to control his own destiny. In describing this youth, Warner and Hansen (1970) stressed the fact that "in essence, he feels isolated from and different from the mainstream of his society" (p. 208). The alienated were further characterized by a high degree of anxiety. They were described as nervous, worrisome, inflexible individuals. The anxiety these individuals exhibit hinders their involvement in school related activities which reinforces their state of alienation. The cyclical pattern of a low self-concept, a high degree of anxiety, and alienation places these youths further and further apart from the acceptable school structures and functions. When you consider their personality characteristics, it is not surprising that these youths feel removed from society and powerless to change the situation. As the schools are not presently equipped to work with the alienated, they find themselves in a self-perpetuating situation. One of the writers of this chapter noted that he thought he knew what aggression and aggressive behaviors were until he had completed the review of the literature. It is a confusing topic to investigate, but it has concrete meaning when it occurs in the corridors, parking lot, or classroom of a school. The *it* is real. Aggression is simply an unwanted and undesired behavior display by one person.

It is probably the most undesirable behavior of which man is capable when it is extreme, because it is the cutting edge for violence and destruction, and produces general discomfort for others. There are self-aggressive behaviors, and there is certainly the need for aggressive acts to get things done. As was stated, the most profound aspect of aggression is the fear it imposes—that one has no control over one's self or one's property because of another. Probably the biggest worry of most secondary teachers is what to do when faced with inappropriate aggressive acts.

HIGH INCIDENCE SECONDARY YOUTH

The term *high incidence handicapped* refers to youths traditionally labeled as: learning disabled, mentally retarded, and behaviorally disordered. A discussion of secondary school age chronic disruptive youth would remain incomplete without reference to those who comprise the group of high incidence handicapped. The legal definition of handicapped youth varies from state to state. Therefore, the incidence and prevalence also varies. Inclusion of high incidence handicapped adolescents in a chapter on characteristics of chronic disruptive youth serves to acknowledge a relationship between youth with handicaps and youth in trouble. The physical, mental, emotional, and social disabilities of these youths make them likely candidates to perform disruptive acts in school. At the secondary school level students in conflict with the rules and regulations of the institution were historically viewed as juvenile offenders, chronic disruptive, and/or norm-violating youth, with minimal regard to the presence of other handicapping disabilities. As depicted in Figure 3.2, these groups were considered separable entities. In contrast to this view, one alternative suggests consider-

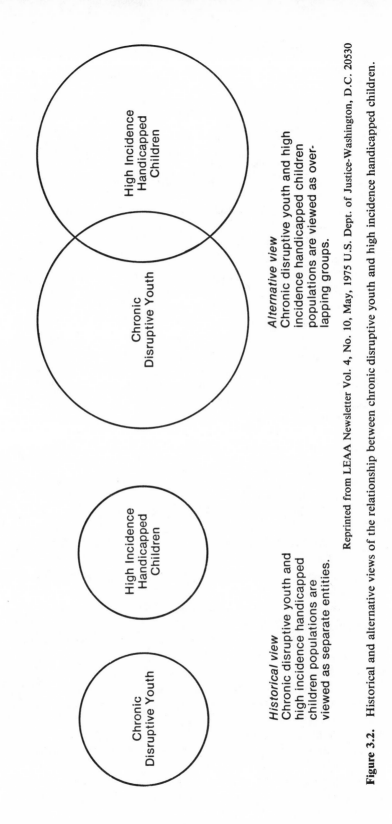

High Incidence
Handicapped
Children

Chronic
Disruptive Youth

Alternative view
Chronic disruptive youth and high
incidence handicapped children
populations are viewed as overlapping groups.

High Incidence
Handicapped
Children

Chronic
Disruptive Youth

Historical view
Chronic disruptive youth and
high incidence handicapped
children populations are
viewed as separate entities.

Reprinted from LEAA Newsletter Vol. 4, No. 10, May, 1975 U.S. Dept. of Justice-Washington, D.C. 20530

Figure 3.2. Historical and alternative views of the relationship between chronic disruptive youth and high incidence handicapped children.

able overlap between these two populations. Specifically, it is hypothesized that a significant number of youths labeled as chronic disruptive also possess academic, intellectual, and behavioral handicaps. Figure 3.2 illustrates the hypothesized relationship between chronic disruptive and high incidence handicapped youths.

Within special education a number of authorities have expended vast energies in attempting to concisely define specific populations of handicapped youths. The perseverance of these workers suggests that a viable definition is a prerequisite for successful programming. Although these differentiations may be quite academic, the reader's awareness of learning disabled, mentally retarded, and behaviorally disordered youths will be heightened by discussing each of the groups. A discussion of each type of high incidence population will provide the reader with a definition, the characteristics, and the prevalence of each group.

The teacher is forewarned that the historical emphasis in special education has been at the elementary school level, with only minimal interest developing quite recently at the secondary level. Parallel to this historical emphasis, researchers have made concentrated efforts in developing viable definitions, identifying behavioral characteristics, and estimating prevalence statistics of elementary age exceptional youths. Since it is logical to expect differences between elementary and secondary school populations, it is reasonable to assume that our source of knowledge is limited with respect to adolescent exceptional youth. Thus, much of the material cited in this section will reflect an elementary school bias, which underscores the need for special educators to place concentrated efforts at the secondary level.

A meaningful definition as to what constitutes a handicapped population serves many purposes. Communication within and among professional groups is facilitated with a common definition. Information can be more accurately exchanged in professional journals and books when agreement exists regarding the specific characteristics for a population. The value of research is further enhanced where investigators can discretely and consistently identify a select group of youths for study. Comparative research between groups of children on such issues as etiological factors, behavioral characteristics, and remedial strategies, provides more useful data when populations are clearly defined. Definitions are essential in placing youths in appropriate educational programs, and for funding purposes when individuals submit grants to federal and state agencies in search of financial support for programs, training, and research.

The definitions which follow were developed with elementary age children in mind, and the appropriateness of applying these definitions to secondary school youth should not go unchallenged. Questions basic to the validity and relevance of these definitions to adolescents are legion. Are definitions of learning disabilities, behavior disorders, and mental retardation more difficult to conceptualize and implement with older youth? When arriving at secondary schools should youths be classified as high incidence handicapped in the elementary school continue with that label? These and other questions must eventually be answered.

LEARNING DISABILITIES

Terminology in the field of learning disabilities has been flooded with controversy. A task force sponsored by the National Institute of Neurological Diseases and Blindness (N.I.H.) and the National Society for Crippled Children and Adults was formed in 1964 to study the issues of definition, terminology, and identification. The panel identified a total of 38 terms that had previously been used to identify children now labeled as learning disabled. A perusal of these terms reflects the lack of unamity in referring to these youths.

Definition

Association Deficit Pathology

Aggressive Behavior Disorder

Aphasoid Syndrome

Association Deficit Pathology

Attention Disorders

Cerebral Dysfunction

Character Impulse Disorder

Choreiform Syndrome

Clumsy Child Syndrome

Conceptually Handicapped

Diffuse Brain Damage

Dyslexia

Hyperkinetic Behavior Syndrome

Hyperkinetic Impulse Disorder

Hyperkinetic Syndrome

Hyperexcitability Syndrome

Hypolinetic Syndrome

Interjacent Child

Minimal Brain Damage

Minimal Brain Injury

Minimal Cerebral Damage

Minimal Cerebral Palsy

Minimal Chronic Brain Syndromes

Minor Brain Damage

Neurophrenia

Organic Behavior Disorder

Organic Brain Damage

Organic Brain Disease

Organic Brain Dysfunction

Organic Drivenness

Perceptual Cripple

Perceptually Handicapped

Primary Reading Retardation

Psychoneurological Learning Disorders

Specific Reading Disability

A historical review of terms used to define the learning disabled child reveals the problems inherent in the attempt to provide closure to an objective definition. Moreover, terms such as *minimal brain injury, perceptual cripple, shadow child, underachiever, learning disabled,* or *learning disordered,* underscore the ambiguity and lack of agreement within the field. Terms which fail to describe youth behaviorally in an instructional manner, especially when their respective definitions do not complement the purposes of a definition, tend to mitigate against the value of a definition.

The search for an adequate definition in the field of learning disabilities has moved through three distinct areas: brain-injured, minimal brain dysfunction, and specific learning disabilities (MacIntosh & Dunn, 1973). Strauss and Lehtinen, pioneers in the field of brain injury (many professionals associate brain injury and learning disabilities), in 1947 provided the term *brain-injured youth* and the following definition:

> A brain-injured child is a child who before, during, or after birth has received an injury to or suffered an infection of the brain. As a result of such organic impairment, defects of the neuromotor system may be present or absent. However, such a child may show disturbances in perception, thinking, emotional behavior, either separately or in combination. These disturbances prevent or impede a normal learning process.
>
> (Strauss & Lehtinen, 1947, p. 4)

Youths were classified as brain-injured according to behavioral and biological criteria. Behavioral considerations focused on the evidence of four factors: perceptual disorders, perseveration, thinking or conceptual disorders, and social-behavioral disorders. The biological criteria were limited to three characteristics: slight neurological signs, history of neurological impairment, and no history of mental retardation in the family. Criticism quickly followed, with the most vocal reaction from educators who were concerned with the inexact measures used to identify brain disorders, the stigmatizing effect of the term on the child, and the inability to relate specific brain injury to a learning disorder. Sarason (1949) questioned Strauss on the circularity of the term, in that the diagnosis of brain injury could be based primarily on behavior characteristics without any "hard" evidence of actual brain impairment.

The 1964 task force under the leadership of Clements advocated the term *minimal brain dysfunction.* The definition was as follows:

> The term "minimal brain dysfunction syndrome" refers in this paper to children of near average, average, or above average general intelligence with certain learning or behavioral disabilities ranging from mild to severe, which are associated with deviations of function of the central nervous system. These deviations may manifest themselves by various combinations of impairment in perception, conceptualization, language, memory, and control of attention, impulse, or motor function. Similar symptoms may or may not complicate the problems of children with cerebral palsy, epilepsy, mental retardation, blindness, or deafness. These aberrations may arise

from genetic variations, biochemical irregularities, perinatal brain insults or other illness or injuries sustained during the years which are critical for the development and maturation of the central nervous system, or from unknown causes.   (Clements, 1966, pp. 9–10)

Questions similar to those voiced over Strauss' term were raised with the label *minimal brain dysfunction*. Educators also predicted that by increasing Strauss' behavioral characteristics from 7 to 15 items, the term would become a catch-all phrase. Additionally, the definition was viewed as a pseudo-medical term and etiologically oriented. With these apparent problems, the definition was not widely accepted by educators.

The vocal reaction of educators and parents against the stigmatizing labels led to the development of the term *learning disability*. Although Kirk, in 1962, first coined the term learning disability, it was not until 1968 under the aegis of the National Advisory Committee on Handicapped Children that a suitable definition was brought forth. They defined this population of children as:

> Children with special learning disabilities exhibit a disorder in one or more of the basic psychological processes involved in understanding or in using spoken or written language. These may be manifested in disorders of listening, thinking, talking, reading, writing, spelling or arithmetic. They include conditions which have been referred to as perceptual handicaps, brain injury, minimal brain dysfunction, dyslexia, developmental aphasia, etc. They do not include learning problems which are due primarily to visual, hearing, or motor handicaps, to mental retardation, emotional disturbance or to environmental disadvantage.
> (National Advisory Committee on Handicapped Children, 1968, p. 38)

The definition has been criticized as being impractical for school use, ambiguous in wording, insufficiently educational in focus, and too long. At the heart of the issue is a basic concern: Can the definition of learning disabilities be operationalized? One approach to providing a viable definition is to identify the major characteristics and operationally define each. The current definition of learning disabilities, when succinctly read, isolates four major characteristics: intelligence, perceptual language deficit, academic achievement deficit, and exclusion. Operationally, this definition implies that when all of the following four characteristics are identified in a child, a learning disability is indicated.

1. *Normal intelligence.* The student is able to perform at or above the normal range (IQ = 85) on nonverbal measures which involve language conceptualization.

2. *Perceptual language deficit.* The student exhibits a deficit in perceptual language processing. Practically all learning-disability theories

hypothesize that if the perceptual reception of a stimulus is interfered with (and the symbolic quality of information distorted), lost prematurely due to faulty retention function, or improperly sequenced and arranged, a deficit in perceptual processing is indicated.

3. *Academic-achievement deficit.* The student exhibits an academic-achievement deficit in at least one subject area (e.g., reading, quantitative skills). Deficit is defined as an inability to score above a given percentile on standardized achievement tests measuring proficiency in that subject area.

4. *The absence of other primary handicapping conditions.* The student shows no evidence of visual or hearing impairment, mental retardation, severe cultural neglect, or severe emotional disturbance.   (Sabatino, 1973)

So far, the discussion has centered on problems in developing a viable definition of a learning disability. Controversy with the definition has confounded the work of many individuals in the field. Related to this issue is the adequacy of this definition for children with learning disabilities at the secondary school level. Specifically, will professionals using this definition be able to identify and diagnose secondary school aged youths as learning disabled? Are the four major components of the definition as critical with older children as has been the case with younger students? Examination of these questions suggests that for a number of reasons the efficacy of this definition with older youth is limited. Perceptual and language disabilities which impede the learning of nursery and elementary age children apparently do not play such a crucial role with increasing age (Belmont & Birch, 1963). Possibly the youth compensates for any perceptual and/or language handicap, thus, the deficits are not as evident. The reliability and validity of perceptual language tests are questionable as these tests were standardized on younger students and bear little relation to the tasks and situations demanded of secondary school adolescents. Also, many of the behavioral characteristics (e.g., hyperactivity, impulsivity) attributed to the learning disabled are assumed to decrease or disappear with puberty. Finally, as the student experiences more and more academic failure, the incidence of behavioral and affective disabilities increases.

In summary, we suggest that efforts be channeled into the following:

1. The development and operationalization of a definition that encompasses secondary school learning disabled children.

2. An examination of the perceptual, learning, and behavioral characteristics of this population and the delineation of the age differences accordingly.

3. An all out effort to identify viable diagnostic and remedial models for secondary school learning disabled youth.

Characteristics of learning disabilities

The major purpose of the 1966 task force headed by Clements (1966) was to develop a definition of learning disabilities. Related to this task was the establishment of a list of clinical symptoms or behaviors to identify such children. By reviewing over 100 publications the task force identified 15 major clinical categories which included over 50 characteristics. Of these, the 10 characteristics most frequently associated with learning disabilities are:

1. *Hyperactivity.* An excessive amount of motor behavior that is not demanded by the task and which is inappropriate to the setting. Generally disruptive to the adult or group in the environment.

2. *Perceptual-motor impairments.* Problems in coordinating stimulus input from the visual and auditory channels with appropriate motor behavior.

3. *Emotional liability.* Emotional responses which are inappropriate to the setting.

4. *General orientation deficits.* Clumsiness or awkwardness, fine and gross motor coordination problems.

5. *Disorders of attention.* Distractibility, inability to concentrate on a task for any length of time and perseveration. Inability to stop repeated motor or verbal behavior even though task requirements have been completed.

6. *Impulsivity.* Failure to think or reflect on the consequences of behavior.

7. *Disorders of memory or thinking.* Problems in recalling information either over a short- or long-term period. Difficulty in understanding conceptual and abstract problems.

8. *Specific learning disabilities.* Problems in arithmetic, reading, writing, and spelling.

9. *Disorders in speech and hearing.* Problems in remembering or understanding the spoken word, delayed speech articulation, or inappropriate use of grammar and vocabulary.

10. *Equivocal neurological signs.* The evidence of possible neurological problems (e.g., perceptual/motor problems) without clear "hard" signs of a definite central nervous system dysfunction.

The characteristics of secondary school learning disabled youth have not been fully investigated, which limits definitive statements concerning these characteristics. Some of the previously cited attributes may not be obvious at the secondary level, or may be compensated for, or may even be manifested as other problems. For example, maturation is assumed to ameliorate some of the problems associated with elementary aged children. Many teachers acknowledge that the rate of hyperactivity and perceptual impairments decrease with age. Conversely, other problems are more blatant with age, such as academic retardation and emotional disorders. Obviously what is needed is a longitudinal study investigating the behavioral characteristics of secondary school learning disabled youth.

Prevalence of learning disabilities

The task of obtaining accurate prevalence figures for any area of exceptionality is determined by the definition. Where agreement exists as to what constitutes a handicap, the prevalence figures from study to study tend to be accurate. In cases where disagreement is present, as in the area of learning disabilities, prevalence statistics vary from study to study. Estimates of the number of children with learning disabilities have ranged from 1% to upwards of 25% of the school population. Generally, the more stringent the definitional criteria, the more conservative the figure.

Based on a survey of 3,000 second grade children in eight Rocky Mountain states, Meier (1971) reported that 15% of the population were at least two years below grade expectancy. At Northwestern University, Myklebust and Boshes (1969) screened 2,800 children and found 15% to be learning disabled. However, with the inclusion of more stringent measures, the number of children identified decreased to 7%. A more conservative figure of 1–3% of the school aged population appeared in a report by the National Advisory Committee on Handicapped Children (1968). The United States Office of Education estimates that 314,000 youths, or 1.8% of the population at the secondary school level are learning disabled. As can be seen, the actual number of students who evidence a learning disability is not known. Nevertheless, even using a conservative figure the total number of students involved suggests the necessity for programming.

BEHAVIOR DISORDERS

The area of behavior disorders has been influenced by many professional disciplines, namely psychiatry, psychology, sociology, criminology, and education. Working independently, these disciplines added to our initial understanding and programming of youth with behavioral disorders. However, interdisciplinary disagreements regarding the etiology, diagnosis and treatment of behavior disorders have hampered efforts to share a common definition.

Definition

The area of behavioral disorders has been changing direction. Historically, at the turn of the century biological and genetic factors were viewed as the primary causal agents of deviant behavior, and the earliest definitions reflected these beliefs. By the 1920s, sociological factors conceived with the influences of culture, race, socioeconomic status, and community were considered the critical factors. Through the 1940s and 1950s, the psychodynamic approach which relies on interpsychic explanations of behavior became the predominant theory. Quasi-scientific terms such as *heightened anxiety, nervous disorder, psychosis,* and *defense mechanisms* were used to label, classify and define emotionally disturbed youth. In more recent years, behavioral and ecological approaches have gained wider acceptance in the educational community and have influenced recent definitions. In summary, the number of concerned disciplines involved with our changing knowledge and beliefs of what constitutes a behavior disorder has confounded efforts to provide a clear, concise definition of a behavior disorder.

A review of material published over the past decade (1966–1976) yielded 37 definitions of a behavior disorder. It is interesting to note that of all the definitions reviewed there was no mention of secondary school youth with behavior disorders. Moreover, no attempt was made to differentiate between younger children and older youth with behavior disorders. The citations ranged from psychiatrically oriented to behaviorally stated definitions. While these definitions do not share philosophical orientations there are points of agreement common to most of the definitions: (1) norm violation; (2) chronicity; (3) interpersonal relations; and (4) social and affective disabilities. A discussion of these points of congruence provides further understanding of authorities described as constituting a behavior disorder. In Table 3.5, the more frequently cited educational definitions are presented.

Norm Violation. Youth are judged and/or labeled as behaviorally disordered based on some assumed standard of normalcy. The crucial factor is the discrepancy between what is considered normal behavior and what is the child's current behavior. The greater the discrepancy between expectation and actual behavior, the greater the likelihood that the perceiver (i.e., adult) will rate the behavior as deviant. The relevance of the norm violation aspect to a definition of behavior disorders is articulated by Rhodes, whereby:

Table 3.5. DEFINITIONS OF BEHAVIOR DISORDERS

	Norm Violation	Chronicity	Interpersonal Relations	Social and Affective Development
Bower (1969)		The emotionally handicapped child demonstrates one or more of the following characteristics to a marked extent and over a period of time.	An inability to build or maintain satisfactory interpersonal relations with peers and teachers.	An inability to learn which cannot be explained by intellectual, sensory or health factors. A general pervasive mood of unhappiness or depression. A tendency to develop physical symptoms, pains, or fears associated with personal or school problems. Inappropriate types of behavior or feelings under normal conditions.
Kirk (1972)	Behavior disorder will be defined as a deviation from age-appropriate behavior which significantly interferes with		The lives of others	The child's own growth and development
Graubard (1973)	Which violate the perceivers expectations of appropriateness and which the perceiver wishes to see stopped	Behavioral disabilities are defined as a variety of excessive, chronic deviant behavior ranging from		Impulsive and aggressive to depressive and withdrawal acts

	Norm Violation	Chronicity	Interpersonal Relations	Social and Affective Development
Haring and Phillips (1962)			Emotionally disturbed children are children who have more or less serious problems with other people, peers, and authorities such as parents and teachers	Who are unhappy and unable to apply themselves in a manner commensurate with their abilities and interests
Reinert (1976)			The personal or educational development of his peers.	The child in conflict is defined as...the child whose manifest behavior has a deleterious effect on his personal or educational development and/or
Joint Commission on Mental Health of Children (1970)				An emotionally disturbed child is one whose progressive personality development is interfered with or arrested by a variety of factors so that he shows impairment in the capacity expected of him for his age and endowment: 1) for reasonably accurate perception of the world around him, 2) for impulse control,

	Norm Violation	Chronicity	Interpersonal Relations	Social and Affective Development
Morse (1975)		A disturbed pupil is one who is persistently unable to cope with reasonable school environment even though expectations are geared to his age and potential	His behavior may be 1) so disrupting as to violate the rights and educational growth of his peers, or he may 3) for satisfying and satisfactory relations with others,	4) for learning. 2) manifest social withdrawal, and/or 3) require an inordinate amount of depth of teacher involvement for control and emotional support.
Woody (1969)	The child who cannot or will not adjust to the socially acceptable norms for behavior and consequently		The learning efforts of his classmates, and interpersonal relations	Disrupts his own academic progress, and

> what is considered deviant, how it is designated, interpreted, and treated is viewed as much a function of the perceiver as of the behaver. (1967, p. 451)

Each individual as a parent, teacher, or clinician has a set of standards to evaluate the appropriateness of a youth's actions. These standards represent an end product of cultural experiences. Directly or indirectly, parents are influenced by the media, particularly popular magazines and child care books, which describe what behaviors emerge at specific age levels. Teacher training programs usually require an introductory course in child and adolescent development which provide the future educator with a global view of development. Obviously, each individual with different life experiences and training has developed a unique criterion of normalcy, which more than likely differs from other individuals. When one includes norm violation as a major construct of a behavior disorder several questions arise: What is normal behavior in children and youth? How can the clinician and novice distinguish between normal and aberrant behavior? In summary, although norm violation is crucial to most definitions of behavior disorders, the exact standards or meaning of normal behavior remains more subjective than objective.

Chronicity. Deviation from an acceptable behavioral code is a part of normal youth development. No youth completely escapes from affective or social difficulties. Some time during development each youth exhibits depression, anxiety, aggression, and other aberrant behaviors. What separates a normal amount of disturbed or disturbing behavior from an abnormal pattern is how chronic or persistent the deviant behavior pattern is for a period of time. Any youth who is behaviorally unable to adjust to the demands of the school or community, or continually fails to conform to rules is likely to be labeled a chronic disruptive youth.

Interpersonal relations. The inability to form and continue satisfactory meaningful relationships with others is a major component of a behavior disorder. Youths with healthy interpersonal skills can make friends, share their possessions with others, tolerate peer pressure, and work well with others. Behaviorally disordered children are unable to do these actions. Their behavior, rather than enhancing associations with peers and adults, places them at odds with other youths. Such youths are either ostracized or isolated by their peers, and in turn, they are either withdrawn or aggressive toward groups of youths and adults.

Social and affective disabilities. A social and affective disability refers to behaviors or internal conditions which, when manifested, interfere with the normal progression of development. Regardless of one's philosophical persuasion, it is in this area where agreement among theorists exists. A review of Table 3.5 clearly indicates that each definition acknowledges a social and/or affective disability. The behaviors included range from aggressive and impulsive acts to withdrawn and depressive behaviors.

No single definition has captivated the imagination of professionals in the field of behavior disorders. As discussed in the previous sections on learning disabilities, a definition is a prerequisite to effective diagnosis, classification, and treatment. Until a unified definition is forthcoming these issues will remain unresolved. In Table 3.5, we review the most quoted definitions, and identified the points of mutual agreement. Using these points of commonality, the following definition is posited as a viable alternative. A behavior disorder is defined as:

> the *chronic* display of behavior which is not adaptive to the *normal standards* of the environment, and generally draws attention to the individual which interferes with that individual's *social and affective development* and *interpersonal relations*.

Characteristics of behavior disorders

The problems associated with a definition of behavior disorders have made the task of identifying characteristics equally demanding. The range of labels encompassed under the rubic of the behaviorally disordered includes the autistic, schizophrenic, juvenile delinquent, socially maladjusted, mildly and severely emotionally disturbed. Lack of homogenity within the population of children labeled as behaviorally disordered has plagued the productive search for common characteristics. Keeping this in mind, the following discussion will be limited to the characteristics of youths with behavior problems found in public and private school settings.

Bower (1969) advanced a definition of behavior disorders (see Table 3.5) which has gained widespread acceptance among educators. Based on a longitudinal study of the behavioral disabilities of educationally handicapped youths, five major behavioral characteristics were identified. According to Bower, a behaviorally disordered youth will evidence one or more of the following characteristics:

1. An inability to learn which cannot be explained by intellectual, sensory, or health factors.

2. An inability to build or maintain satisfactory interpersonal relations with peers and teachers.

3. Inappropriate types of behavior or feelings under normal conditions.

4. A general, pervasive mood of unhappiness or depression.

5. A tendency to develop physical symptoms, pains, or fears associated with personal or school problems.

Quay (1966, 1972) developed a factor analytic approach to investigate the characteristics of these youths. The rationale for the factor analytic approach is that behavior disorders which share a significant number of common characteristics may be similar in etiology, diagnosis, and treatment. By using the statistical approach called factor analysis the researcher is able to identify the correlation or relationship between individual characteristics. Those items which correlate or cluster together may share a common etiology or be amenable to the same treatment. In a series of investigations, Quay & Werry (1972) consistently identified four behavioral dimensions: (1) conduct disorder; (2) personality disorder; (3) inadequacy-immaturity; and (4) socialized delinquent. The constituent characteristics of each dimension are:

1. *Conduct disorder.* The presence of physical and verbal aggression and inadequate interpersonal relations. Behaviors included are fighting, temper tantrums, attention seeking, impatience, disruptiveness, and disobedience.

2. *Personality disorder.* Characterized primarily by withdrawn or withdrawing behavior. Behaviors included are self-conciousness, hypersensitivity, depression, shyness, anxiety, fear, and feelings of inferiority.

3. *Inadequacy-immaturity.* Characterized by the consistent presence of behavior inappropriate to chronological age. Behaviors included are sluggishness, clumsiness, short-attention span, daydreaming, and passivity.

4. *Socialized delinquent.* Behaviors which reflect the child's membership or allegiance to a delinquent group. Behaviors included are truancy, stealing, and bad companions.

It is not known which characteristics are more prevalent at the secondary level. The majority of teacher attention is focused primarily on the disturbing quality of the behavior exhibited by the conducted disordered youth and socialized delinquent. On the other hand, adolescents with personality disorders or maturity problems may go unnoticed by the non-observant teacher.

Prevalence of behavior disorders

The prevalence of behavior disorders vary according to the definition, the agency reporting the figures, and the diagnostic measures used in the study (Clarizio and McCoy, 1976). Estimates have varied from a low of 1% to as high as 35% of the school aged population. The difficulties involved are clearly evident from the range of figures reported.

Based on teacher reports, self-ratings, and peer evaluations, Bower (1969) found that 10% of the school aged population evidenced enough social problems to be labeled behaviorally disordered. Shultz, Hirshoren, Manton, and Henderson (1971) surveyed directors of special education in the 50 states and the District of Columbia. The prevalence estimates ranged from 0.5% to 15% and seven states reported no prevalence figures. The most thorough review of prevalence figures was conducted for the Joint Commission on the Mental Health of Children by Glidewell and Swallow (1968) who reviewed 27 published studies that had appeared over the past 40 years. Their findings indicated that almost one-third of all elementary school age children evidence a mild behavior disorder, 10% need professional assistance, and 4% would be referred to special services. The United States Office of Education (Metz, 1973) estimates that approximately 2% of the elementary and 1% of the secondary school aged population are behaviorally disordered.

As with the other areas of exceptionality, minimal effort has been made to provide separate statistics for the secondary school population. Whatever the actual prevalence figure is, one point is clear. In each classroom across the nation there are probably one to three youths who are behaving in such a manner as to warrant some special assistance.

MENTAL RETARDATION

Mental retardation is a harsh, serious label which greatly influences the academic and social performance expectancies teachers place on youth. Most definitions, and certainly the ones adopted by state legislators in developing school reimbursement formulae, require tests to be administered. Therefore the operational definition used is simply the fact that on a standardized test, the mentally retarded person functions below the normal limits of intelligence. The danger inherent in accepting this definition derived from a test score is that one must accept the test and the test conditions as being unbiased culturally and linguistically. Secondly, the label suggests that even the mildly mentally retarded are not capable of learning at a normal rate the academic materials appropriate to children at the same chronological age. Thus, it provides an excuse to place them in special classes and lower expectancies to an inordinate degree.

Of the early definitions, the two most popular were presented by Tredgold (1939) and Doll (1941). Tredgold defined mental deficiency as:

> A state of incomplete development of such a kind and degree that the individual is incapable of adapting himself to the normal environment of his

> fellows in such a way as to maintain existence independently of supervision
> control, or external support. (Tredgold, 1939, p. 4)

Doll (1941) added greater specificity to the concept of mental retardation
with the following definition:

> We observe that six criteria by statement or implication have been generally
> considered essential to an adequate definition and concept. These are (1)
> social incompetence, (2) due to mental subnormality, (3) which has been
> developmentally arrested, (4) which obtains at maturity, (5) is of constitu-
> tional origin, and (6) is essentially incurable. (Doll, 1941, p. 215)

The inclusion of six criteria added more detail to the concept of mental
retardation, although questions emerged regarding the latter two points.
The etiology of mental retardation is no longer considered solely on the
basis of constitutional origin as proposed by Doll. Indeed, enough evidence
exists to postulate a multiple causality theory, with environmental factors
playing a crucial role in the development and maintenance of mental retardation, particularly with the educable mentally retarded group. Furthermore, the belief "once retarded always retarded" is not accurate. Workers
in the fields of education, psychology, and medicine now believe that given

Table 3.6. INTEGRAL COMPONENTS OF THE 1973 AAMD
DEFINITION ON MENTAL RETARDATION

Components	Definition
Mental retardation	Refers to a level of behavioral performance without reference to etiology. The term is descriptive of current behavior.
Intellectual functioning	Measured via one or more norm-referenced intelligence tests.
Significantly subaverage	Specifies performance *must* be more than two standard deviations from the mean.
Developmental period	Refers to the period between birth and 18 years.
Adaptive behavior	Degree to which the individual meets the standards of personal independence and social responsibility appropriate to his age and cultural group.
Deficits in adaptive behavior	Reflected in the following areas: sensory motor skills, communication skills, self-help skills, socialization, academic performance, reasoning and judgment, social skills, and vocational adjustment.

a properly timed treatment the condition of mental retardation is reversible at certain levels.

Recent efforts to define mental retardation have been championed by the American Association on Mental Deficiency (AAMD). In 1973, Grossman revised a manual on terminology and classification of mental retardation for the AAMD which was first edited by Heber (1961). The definition of mental retardation reads as:

> Mental retardation refers to significantly subaverage general intellectual functioning existing concurrently with deficits in adaptive behavior, and manifested during the developmental period. (p. 11)

Key components of the definition are elaborated upon in Table 3.6.

The 1973 AAMD manual also provided a classification system of mental retardation based on the severity of the handicap. Classification of an individual is determined by performance on a standardized test of intelligence and a measure of adaptive behavior. The four categories and their respective intelligence parameters are: mild (IQ 52–67); moderate (IQ 51–36); severe (IQ 35–20); and profound (IQ 17 and below).

The AAMD definition has gained widespread acceptance from individuals within the field of mental retardation. Robinson and Robinson (1976) have delineated the dimensions which account for this agreement. First, a designation of mental retardation describes only present behavior and makes no reference to later functioning. No attempt is made regarding prognosis of adult behavior. Retardation is considered in light of an individual's mastery of developmental tasks appropriate for that age. Also, the definition operationalizes the measurement of retardation by specifying intelligence scores at various levels. Finally, the definition affords a more conservative estimate of mental retardation by using a cut-off score of two standard deviations below the mean. This significantly reduces the number of individuals to be considered retarded and removes the *borderline* groups (IQ 85–70) from being labeled retarded.

The AAMD definition has not gone without its share of criticism. Clausen (1971) objected to the use of adaptive behavior because of the difficulties in the definition and measurement of adaptive behavior. Bijou (1966) questioned the concept and value of the term intelligence. According to Bijou, intelligence can only be inferred from behavior, and not measured directly.

Characteristics of mental retardation

In this section, the characteristics of the mildly mentally retarded are discussed. Data on the characteristics of this group has come from comparative studies of a group of mildly retarded youths and a group of average youths. Generally, the findings from comparative studies have consistently shown that the retarded group is deficient in many areas. It is important to note, however, that the discussion will focus on group characteristics. Any individual within the mental retardation population will not necessarily exhibit all the characteristics. Said another way, people with mental retardation are not a homogeneous group, for within the population not all individuals are equally deficient. The behavioral characteristics where retarded individuals show deficits include: (1) perceptual disorders; (2) interpersonal relations; (3) communication and speech disorders; (4) self-care skills; (5) academic retardation; (6) attention deficits; and (7) motor movement (Grossman, 1973).

Perceptual disorders. Perception refers to the reception and integration of stimuli into more meaningful units of information. Many theories of cognition account for the importance of accurate information processing for development. With respect to mildly retarded individuals, the relationship between learning and perceptual deficits is not clear. Some investigators have found brain-damaged retarded persons to be deficient in unimodal perception (e.g., visual perception), cross-modal integration (e.g., auditory-visual perception), selective perception, and perceptual integration and reproduction. Relatively little, however, is known regarding the perceptual integrities of the non-brain-damaged mildly retarded population.

Interpersonal relations. Social deficiencies in mildly retarded individuals appear to be related to the level of retardation. Mildly retarded persons at the lower level are reported to have difficulty accepting responsibility as group members; tend to feel uncomfortable in group settings; are conformists rather than leaders; and have not mastered the social customs of society, although complex social skills can be taught through proper treatment and guidance. Thus, the level of social functioning of each individual is related to the treatment programs received. Concern for the mildly retarded should focus then on the environment, particularly the school setting in which the child is placed.

Communication and speech disorders. The ability of the mildly retarded child and youth to communicate his needs is limited by speech and language deficits. Approximately two-thirds of all retarded individuals have some type of speech and/or communication deficit (Sirkin & Lyons, 1941). The specific deficits referred to are articulation disorders, syntax deficits, and a limited vocabulary, with articulation problems the most prevalent. The interaction between mental retardation and speech defects is not necessarily a causal relationship. Authorities view each as a separate phenomenon related to an overall retardation in development (Robinson & Robinson, 1976). However, the greater degree of retardation, the greater the severity of the speech defect. Speech and language stimulation can effectively attenuate these disorders, and a number of commercial programs are available (Dunn & Smith, 1965; Engelmann, Osborne, & Engelmann, 1969).

Self-care skills. Mildly mentally retarded youths master the necessary independent self-care skills, although they learn these behaviors more slowly than normal youths. The lower level functioning retarded individual learns self-care skills such as dressing, toileting, feeding, and other domestic accomplishments, but with greater difficulty. Appropriate self-care skills are learned, but the training involves a greater investment of time and effort than with average youths. Training involves the step-by-step introduction of skills, teaching through drill and repetition. Obviously, a significant expenditure of adult time is involved in the teaching of these skills.

Academic retardation. The pervasive intellectual retardation of these youths directly influences their academic achievement. Specifically, mildly retarded individuals are unable to achieve as well as average youths on academic tasks. However, mildly retarded youths can be expected to achieve up to their mental age expectancy. Based on the degree of retardation, predictions can be stated regarding the level of academic attainment. On tasks which demand abstract reasoning or inductive processing, the effects of retardation are more profound. Performance on such academic tasks as reading comprehension and arithmetic reasoning is hindered. For other subjects where practice and drill exercises are appropriate, the mildly retarded child can attain an acceptable level. For example, spelling and arithmetic computation are appropriate areas for repetition training, and the mildly retarded can become proficient and develop adequate skills.

Attention deficits. Mildly retarded individuals are frequently described as having disorders in two aspects of attention: the ability to sustain attention and to resist distracting stimuli. The ability to concentrate on the task at hand and also not be distracted by competing stimuli is a prerequisite to learning. Since attending to stimuli precedes the components of learning (i.e., perception, integration, and reproduction) a disability in this area confounds the whole learning process. Attention as a behavior, fortunately, can be learned and thus the mildly retarded can be taught to heighten their attending skills.

Motor skills. The inability to coordinate and/or orient motor acts within the environment is an additional characteristic of the retarded. It is important to note, however, that in motor skills, more than the other characteristics, the mildly retarded individual is most like the average youth. Generally, the more severe the retardation the greater the deficiency in motor skills. Deficiencies have been noted in gross motor activities (e.g., the inability to stop on command or control motor movements) and in fine motor skills (e.g., inability to write legibly). Fortunately, motor skills like other behaviors can be taught, and with appropriate instruction and training the retarded are able to master these behaviors.

Prevalence of mental retardation

The actual number of mentally retarded children and youth is not known, as prevalence statistics vary according to the technique used to collect the data. The most common methods used to estimate the number of mentally retarded persons are sampling social work agencies, reviewing census data, and analyzing case history files. Rarely are individual testing or interview sessions employed in these studies. Also, as the definitions of mental retardation have changed, the prevalence figures have varied accordingly. For example, the current AAMD definition (Grossman, 1973) with more stringent criteria reported a more conservative prevalence figure than the previous AAMD definition (Heber, 1961). Based on a review of 28 prevalence studies, Heber (1961) reported estimates ranged from 0.16% to 23% of the population.

In the two studies with official sanction, the President's Committee on Mental Retardation estimated an incidence figure of 3%; the United States Office of Education cited at the elementary school level 2.3% and 1.4% of the secondary level. The prevalence of mental retardation ranging from mild to moderate to profound and severe is approximately 75%, 20%, and 5%, respectively. Additional demographic data on the prevalence of mental retardation was outlined by Payne and Mercer (1975), who found:

1. A greater proportion of mental retardation at the school-aged years than at the preschool and adult years.
2. A greater proportion of mental retardation among males than females.
3. A greater proportion of mental retardation among minority groups.
4. A greater proportion of mental retardation among lower socio-economic groups.

CONCLUSION

The nation's secondary schools are faced with a difficult task. The task is to provide a breadth, continuum, or range of services and programs to enable adolescent youth to realize abilities to the fullest, and then achieve personal, social, and vocational productivity in a very competitive society. Almost everyone appears to agree with this basic concept, at least to the extent of giving it lip-service. Yet, schools are involved in curricula and methodology which appears to the adolescent to promote exactly the opposite. Students are assumed sufficiently alike to benefit from uniform teaching in fixed groups. The trouble is there are those students, truants, aggressors, vandals, dropouts, and high incidence youth, who will not, cannot, and perhaps should not, go along with such patterned learning.

For students who demonstrate an infrequent, negligible problem, the counselor can be responsible for restoration of normal school progress. Generally speaking, more severely troubled youth are often serviced through highly specialized programs and personnel. The intent of this chapter was to identify and discuss the characteristics and problems of chronic disruptive and norm-violating youth, a medial group who appear to fall through the cracks in existing secondary school programming.

What are the major descriptive characteristics of youth in trouble? The two dominant motives of vandals are financial or property gain, and personal emotional problems. Vandals tend to be academic underachievers with few interpersonal commitments (peer relations and acceptance is a significant exception), and little satisfactory emotional involvement with others. The prominent factors influencing dropouts are the attitudes of school administrators, lack of readiness for academic achievement, prejudice, cultural background, and irrelevant curriculum experiences. When repeated failure in school produces intolerable personal discomfort, the youth feels he has no other option but to leave school. Truancy and dropouts are parallel issues. Truants exhibit academic inabilities and personal-psychological problems of a less severe nature. It is often inferred that truants have a desire to learn, but with frustration from inadequate academic skills and personal problems, the truant feels the need to periodically exclude himself from the classroom and school. The aggressive-disruptive youth, due to a variety of causes, primarily displays the following behaviors: defiance, destruction, fighting, truancy, and profanity. High incidence secondary youth have perhaps the most extensively delineated mental and physical characteristics, which lead to subsequent emotional and social disabilities.

What does this mean for the classroom teacher? In dealing with youth in trouble, or potentially in trouble, the teacher can first work on prevention techniques at two levels. A trained awareness of characteristic backgrounds, behaviors, and motivating factors of the indicated secondary youth prepares the teacher to manage the classroom to effect minimal conflict. In addition, personalizing work and introducing pertinent focuses enables the teacher to avoid the boredom or frustration which often lead toward vandalism, dropping out, truancy, and disruptive behaviors. These two levels of prevention—awareness and individualization—require a distinct knowledge and understanding of the youth involved.

For the situations which prevention techniques do not circumvent, additional techniques need to be explored. Ultimately, the teacher helps the student perfect skills in becoming what he finds he can do successfully. That is, the teacher helps youth, in essence, to establish rapport with their dreams, which is no trivial task.

REFERENCES

Abbott, E., and Breckinridge, S. *Truancy and Non-Attendance in the Chicago Schools*. Chicago: University of Chicago Press, 1917.

Bandura, A. *Principles of Behavior Modification*. Englewood Cliffs, N.J.: Prentice Hall, 1970.

Belmont, L., and Birch, H. G. "Lateral Dominance and Right-Left Awareness in Normal Children." *Child Development* 34 (1963): 257–270.

Bijou, S. W. "A Functional Analysis of Retarded Development." *International Review of Research in Mental Retardation*, vol. 1. Edited by N. R. Ellis. New York: Academic Press, 1966.

Bledsoe, J. "Self-Concept of Children and Their Intelligence, Achievement, Interests, and Anxiety." *Children's Education* 43 (1967): 436–438.

Bower, E. M. *The Early Identification of Emotionally Handicapped Children in School*. 2nd ed. Springfield, Illinois: Thomas, 1969.

Brammer, L. M. "The Coming Revolt of High School Students." *NASSP Bulletin* 52 (1968): 13–21.

Brookover, W. B.; Erikson, E. L.; and Joiner, L. M. "Self-Concept of Ability and School Achievement." Office of Education, Cooperative Research Project No. 2831. East Lansing: Office of Research and Publications, Michigan State University, 1967.

Burke, N. S., and Simons, A. "Factors which Precipitate Dropouts and Delinquency." *Federal Probation* 29 (1965): 28–32.

Carmichael, S., and Hamilton, C. *Black Power: The Politics of Liberation in America*. New York: Vintage Books, 1967.

Charters, W. W., Jr. "Social Class and Intelligence Tests." *School Children in the Urban Slum*. Edited by J. I. Roberts. New York: The Free Press, 1967.

Clarizio, H. F., and McCoy G. F. *Behavior Disorders in Children*. 2nd ed. New York: Crowell, 1976.

Clausen, B. "Quo Vadis AAMD?" *Journal of Special Education* 6 (1971): 51–60.

Clements, S. D. "Minimal Brain Dysfunction in Children." NINDS Monograph No. 3, Public Health Service Bulletin No. 1415. Washington, D.C.: U.S. Department of Health, Education, and Welfare, 1966.

Cohen, D. K. "Immigration and the Schools." *Review of Educational Research* 40 (1970): 16.

Cohen, S. "Property Destruction: Motives and Meanings." *Vandalism*. Edited by C. Ward. London: Architectural Press, 1973.

Coleman, J. S. *Equality of Educational Opportunity*. Washington, D.C.: United States Government Printing Office, 1966.

Coleman, J. S. *The Adolescent Society*. New York: The Free Press of Glencoe, 1961.

Conant, D. *Slums and Suburbs*. New York: McGraw-Hill, 1961.

Cubberly, E. P. *Public Education in the United States*. Boston: Houghton-Mifflin Co., 1919.

Dauw, E. G. "Individual Instruction for Potential Dropouts." *NASSP Bulletin* 54 (1970): 9–21.

Doll, E. A. "The Essentials of an Inclusive Concept of Mental Deficiency." *American Journal of Mental Deficiency* 46 (1941): 214–219.

Dollard, J. C.; Dobb, L.; Miller, N.; Mowrev, D.; and Scars, R. *Frustration and Aggression*. New Haven: Yale University Press, 1939.

Douglass, H. R. "Effective Junior High School Program for Reducing the Number of Dropouts." *Contemporary Education* 41 (1969): 34–37.

Dunn, L. M., and Smith, J. O. *Peabody Language Development Kits*. Circle Pines, Minn: American Guidance Service, Level No. 1, 1965.

Engelmann, S.; Osborn, J.; and Engelmann, T. *Distar Language 1: An instructional system*. Chicago: Science Research Associates, 1969.

Feldhusen, J.; Thruston, J.; and Benning, J. "Aggressive Classroom Behavior and School Achievement." *Journal of Special Education* 4 (1970): 431–439.

Feshback, N., and Feshback, S. "Children's Aggression." *Young Children* 26 (1971): 364–377.

Fink, M. B. "Self-Concept as it Relates to Academic Achievement." *California Journal of Educational Research* 13 (1962): 57–62.

French, J. "Characteristics of High Ability Dropouts." *NASSP Bulletin* 53 (1969): 67–79.

Frost, J., and Hawkes, G. *The Disadvantaged Child*. Boston: Houghton-Mifflin Co., 1970.

Gibson, N. B. "Early Delinquency in Relation to Broken Homes." *Journal of Child Psychology and Psychiatry* 10 (1969): 195–204.

Glidewell, J., and Swallow, C. *The Prevalence of Maladjustment in Elementary Schools*. Chicago: University of Chicago Press, 1968.

Glueck, S., and Glueck, E. T. *Unraveling Juvenile Delinquency*. New York: Commonwealth Fund, 1950.

Goldman, N. "School Vandalism: A Socio-Psychological Study." *Education Digest* 26 (1960): 1–4.

Goldstein, H. S. "Internal Controls in Aggressive Children from Father-Present and Father-Absent Families." *Journal of Consulting and Clinical Psychology* 39 (1972): 512.

Graubard, P. S. "Children with Behavior Disabilities." *Exceptional Children in the Schools*. Edited by L. M. Dunn. New York: Holt, Rinehart, and Winston, 1973.

Grealy, J. I. "Criminal Activity in Schools—What's Being Done about it?" *NASSP Bulletin* 58 (1974): 73–78.

Grieder, C. "Vandalism Symptomatic of Our Societal Sickness." *Nation's Schools* 85 (1970): 10.

Grossman, H. J., ed. "Manual of Terminology and Classification in Mental Retardation." American Association on Mental Deficiency Special Publication Series No. 2, 1973.

Haring, N., and Phillips, L. *Educating Emotionally Disturbed Children*. New York: McGraw-Hill, 1962.

Havighurst, R.; Smith, F.; and Wilder, D. "Profile of a Large City High School—Student Activism and Conflict." *NASSP Bulletin* 55 (1971): 70–89.

Heber, R. F. "A Manual on Terminology and Classification in Mental Retardation." rev. ed. Monograph Supplement American Journal of Mental Deficiency (1961): 64.

Hetherington, E. M., and Martin, B. "Family Interaction and Psychopathology in Children." *Psychopathological disorders of childhood*. Edited by H. C. Quay and J. S. Werry. New York: Wiley, 1972.

Hiatt, J. "The Truant Problem and the Parental School." U. S. Bureau of Education Bulletin, 1915.

Hick, A. O. "School Attendance." *Education Research Bulletin* 3 (1933): 249.

Hoerlein, P. H. "How can Schools Control the Rising Incidence of Damage and Loss of School Property?" *Today's Education* 57 (1968): 31–32.

Jensen, A. R. "How Much Can We Boost IQ and Scholastic Achievement?" *Educational Review*, Harvard Educational Review, 1969.

Joint Commission on Mental Health of Children. *Crisis in Child Mental Health: Challenge for the 1970's*. New York: Harper and Row, 1970.

Kirk, S. A. *Educating Exception Children*. Boston: Houghton-Mifflin, 1962.

Kvaraceus, W. C. *The Kvaraceus Delinquency Proneness Rating Scale and Checklist*. New York: Harcourt, Brace and World, 1950.

Law Enforcement Assistance Administration *Newsletter*, "School Crime." Washington, D.C.: U.S. Dept. of Justice, 1975.

Lovaas, O. "Interaction Between Verbal and Nonverbal Behavior." *Child Development* 32 (1961): 329–336.

MacIntosh, D. K., and Dunn, L. M. " Children with Major Specific Learning Disabilities." *Exceptional Children in the Schools*. Edited by L. M. Dunn. New York: Holt, Rinehart, and Winston, 1973.

Martin, J. M. *Juvenile Vandalism: A Study of its Nature and Prevention*. Springfield, Illinois: Charles C. Thomas, 1961.

Meier, J. H. "Prevalence and Characteristics of Learning Disabilities Found in Second Grade Children." *Journal of Learning Disabilities* 4 (1971): 1–16.

Merton, R. *Social Theory and Social Structure*. Glencoe, Illinois: The Free Press, 1949.

Metz, A. S. "Number of Pupils with Handicaps in Local Public Schools, Spring 1970." U.S. Department of Health, Education, and Welfare, U.S. Government Printing Office, 1973.

Metz, A. S. "Statistics on Education of the Handicapped in Local Public Schools." U.S. Department of Health, Education, and Welfare, U.S. Government Printing Office, 1970.

Miller, N. E. "The Frustration-Aggression hypothesis." *Psychological Review* 48 (1941): 337–342.

Morris, G. T. "Youth in Trouble: The Truant." *Today's Education* 61 (1972): 41–42.

Morse, W. C. "The Education of Socially Maladjusted and Emotionally Disturbed Children." *Education of the Exception Children and Youth*. Edited by W. M. Cruickshank and G. O. Johnson. Englewood Cliffs, New Jersey: Prentice Hall, 1975.

Murdock, K. "A Study of Race Differences in New York City." *School and Society* 11 (1920): 149–150.

Myklebust, H. R., and Boshes, B. "Minimal Brain Damage in Children." Final Report, Contract 108–65–142, Neurological and Sensory Disease Control Program. Washington D.C.: Department of Health, Education, and Welfare, 1969.

National Advisory Committee on Handicapped Children. "Special Education for Handicapped Children." First Annual Report. Washington, D.C.: U.S. Department of Health, Education, and Welfare, January 31, 1968.

Payne, J. S., and Mercer, C. D. "Definition and Prevalence." *Mental Retardation*. Edited by J. M. Kaufman and J. S. Paine. Columbus, Ohio: Merrill, 1975.

Peterson, D. R.; Quay, H. C.; and Cameron, G. R. "Personality and Background Factors in Juvenile Delinquency as Inferred from Questionnaire Responses." *Journal of Consulting Psychology* 23 (1959): 395–399.

Quay, H. C. "Personality Patterns in Preadolescent Delinquent Boys." *Educational and Psychological Measurement* 26 (1966): 99–110.

Quay, H., and Werry, J. S. *Psychopathological Disorders of Childhood*. New York: John Wiley and Sons, 1972.

Reinert, H. R. *Children in Conflict: Educational Strategies for the Emotionally Disturbed and Behaviorally Disordered*. Saint Louis, Missouri: C. V. Makby, 1976.

Rhodes, W. C. "The Disturbed Child: A Problem of Ecological Management." *Exceptional Children* 33 (1967): 449–455.

Robinson, N. M., and Robinson, H. P. *The Mentally Retarded Child*. 2nd ed. New York: McGraw-Hill, 1976.

Ross, E. A. *Foundations of Sociology*. New York: The Macmillan Co., 1905.

Sabatino, D. A. "Learning Disabilities: A Problem in Definition Revisited." *Prise Reporter*, 1973.

Sarason, S. B. *Psychological Problems in Mental Deficiency*. New York: Harper, 1949.

Schreiber, D. "700,000 Dropouts." *American Education*, United States Department of Health, Education, and Welfare, Office of Education, 1968.

Schultz, E. W.; Hirshoren, A.; Manton, A. B.; and Henderson, R. A. "Special Education for the Emotionally Disturbed." *Exceptional Children* 38 (1971). 313.

Sears, R. R. "Personality Development in the Family." *The Child*. Edited by J. M. Seidman. New York: Holt, Rinehart, and Winston, 1958.

Sears, R. R. "Relation of Early Socialization Experiences to Aggression in Middle Childhood." *Journal of Abnormal Social Psychology* 63 (1961): 466–492.

Sears, R. R.; Maccoby, E. E.; and Levin, H. *Patterns of Child Rearing*. Evanston: Row-Peterson, 1957.

Shaw, M. C.; Edson, K; and Bell, H. "The Self-Concept of Bright Underachieving High School Students as Revealed by an Adjective Checklist." *Personnel and Guidance Journal* 39 (1960): 193–196.

Sirkin, J., and Lyons, W. "A Study of Speech Defects in Mental Deficiency." *American Journal of Mental Deficiency* 46 (1941): 74–80.

Strauss, A. A., and Lehtinen, L. E. *Psychopathological Education of the Brain Injured Child*. New York: Grune and Stratton, 1947.

Taylor, R. G. "Personality Traits and Discrepant Achievement: A Review." *Journal of Counseling Psychology* 11 (1964): 76–81.

Tredgold, A. F. *A Textbook of Mental Deficiency*. Baltimore: Wood, 1939.

U.S. Dept. of Health, Education, and Welfare—Education Division. *Digest of Education Statistics,* 1975. Washington, D.C.: U.S. Government Printing Office.

Warner, R., & Hansen, J. "The Relationship between Alienation and Other Demographic Variables among High School Students." *High School Journal* 56 (1970): 248–257.

Washington, R. "A Survey-Analysis of Problems Faced by Inner-city High School Students who have been Classified as Truants." *High School Journal* 56 (1973): 248–257.

Weiss, J. N. "Vandalism: An Environmental Concern." *NASSP Bulletin* 58 (1974): 6–9.

Wickham, E. *Children's Behavior and Teachers' Attitudes*. New York: The Commonwealth Fund, Division of Publications, 1928.

Woody, R. H. *Behavioral Problem Children in the Schools: Recognition, Diagnosis, and Behavioral Modification*. New York: Appleton-Century Crofts, 1969.

4

reading theory and research with problem adolescents and chronically disruptive youth

AUGUST J. MAUSER

Most researchers have cited evidence indicating school adjustment and academic problems more prevalent among chronically disruptive and delinquent youths than those youths who do not exhibit such behavioral characteristics. Jacobson (1974), Mauser (1974), Poremba (1976), Sabatino (1973), and Silberberg and Silberberg (1971) are recent contributors indicating that an inordinate prevalence of youth having reading disorders and/or learning disabilities will also have norm-violating behavior. These may be typed as either a socio-legal or a school-conduct nature, or both. To further argue the point that reading or learning disabilities contribute to chronic-disruptive behavior or that chronic-disruptive behavior leads to reading or learning disabilities is not the intent of this chapter. The intent is to direct the practitioner working with problem adolescents, to more efficient programming and implementation designs necessary to foster the growth of reading skills and abilities of such troubled youth. Most investigators have found that delinquency and other forms of disruptive behavior run correlary to poor school adjustment. Only the curriculum area associated with reading will be studied as a possible approach to prevention, and as a significant contributor to the positive adjustment of problem adolescents in an educational setting. No attempts will be made to examine the total school to establish it as a base in the development of delinquency.

Studies as early as Percival (1926), who examined the causes of school failure, suggest that 99% of those first grade children who are not promoted were failing one subject—reading. Thus, as the child progresses through the traditional educational lock step in reading, so does he progress in school in general terms. The trend to equate school promotion in grades three through six also has been heavily weighted toward the child's ability to read. A prophesy or prediction of eventual delinquent behavior was presented by Roman (1955), who cited that a progressive developmental triad occurs—reading retardation-truancy-delinquency.

Sullivan (1927), Lane and Witty (1934), Hill (1935), and Bond and Fendrick (1936) were all early researchers in the field of reading and delinquency. They report that this population, as a group, was significantly retarded in reading ability. Klasen (1972), in contrast, reported a relatively low percentage of her population of dyslexic children who were socially maladjusted in the sense of being chronically dishonest; guilty of theft, truancy, severe disciplinary problems; or evidencing other types of delinquent or criminal conducts. She pointed out that the 2.6% of her children who were dyslexic, and also had evidenced behavioral problems were considered to not be representative of the general population of retarded readers because of the group's young age.

Fabian (1955) found that 10% of the group he studied were problem readers in an unselected sample of school children. He observed that one-third of this group of problem readers were being referred for child guidance consultation. Almost two-thirds of the problem readers were foster children, and approximately 83% among his sample were cited as maladjusted youngsters. Tomkins (1963) found that 75% of the young delinquents who appear in court in New York were two or more years retarded in reading. Equally important was the fact that 50% of these cases had a reading retardation of five or more grade levels below chronological expectancy. Critchley (1968) stated similar ratios in analyzing the delinquency rates of 12- to 16-year-olds in Paris, France.

Klasner (1972) states that general estimates of the proportion of severe reading problems among asocial younsters range from 20% to no less than 83%. Wepman (1962), following a cause-effect point of view, warned that among potentially criminal, inter-city dwellers, those individuals experiencing reading failures are most likely to become antisocial.

The most sophisticated of all civilizations, past and present, has cited the reading-writing skill as the most important basis of communication. Whether one is reading and evaluating highly scientific literature or is perusing menus, traffic signs, and advertisements, the ability to read pervades much of our daily life. The individual who is unable to decode and understand the symbols within his environment soon acquires feelings of inadequacy. This type of individual may resort to isolation or more hostile and aggressive types of behavior. The behavior of problem adolescents, then, is often traceable to the earlier states paradigm of reading retardation-truancy-delinquency. Of utmost importance is the identification and remediation of reading problems in their gestational stages.

THEORIES AND MODELS OF READING

Before one can plan programmatic efforts to develop and maintain reading skills in problem adolescents, the worker in the field should be familiar with the various theories and models of reading acquisition. One of the most often quoted authorities is Dechant (1964) who lists the following multi-faceted characteristics of reading:

1. *Reading is a sensory process.* Reading requires the use of the senses, especially vision. The reader must react visually to the graphic symbols. The symbols themselves must be legible, the eyes must see clearly and singly, and the light must be adequate.

2. *Reading is a perceptual process.* Reading occurs when meaning is brought to graphic stimuli. It is a progressive apprehension of the meanings and ideas represented by a sequence of words. It includes seeing the word, recognizing the word, being aware of the word's meaning, and relating the word to its context. This is perception in its fullest sense.

3. *Reading is a response.* Reading is a system of responses made to some graphic stimuli. These include the vocal and/or subvocal muscular responses made at the sight of the word, the eye movements during reading, physical adaptations to the reading act such as postural changes, the critical and evaluative responses to what is being read, the emotional involvement of the reader, and meaningful reactions to the words.

4. *Reading is a learned response.* Reading is a response that must be learned by the child, and is under the control of the mechanisms of motivation and reinforcement.

5. *Reading is a developmental task.* Developmental tasks have one basic characteristic: the child's readiness for them depends on the child's general development. Reading is a difficult task, and there is a "most teachable moment" for beginning reading and for each of the specific skills in reading. The child's level of achievement in reading depends on his overall growth and development.

6. *Reading can be an interest.* Reading may become an interest or goal in its own right. It then may motivate other activity.

7. *Reading can be a learning process.* Reading may become one of the chief media for learning. The child can use reading to acquire knowledge and to change his own attitudes, ideals, and aspirations. Genuine reading involves integration and promotes the development of the reader. It opens up to him a world of ideas, takes him to distant lands, and lets him walk side by side with the great sagas of time.

8. *Reading is communication.* Reading is an active process. Communication from writer to reader occurs only if the reader can take meaning to the printed page. Without the reader, communication via the printed page is impossible.   (Dechant, 1964, pp. 1–2)

According to Williams (1973), the basic models of reading can be categorized as: (1) taxonomic; (2) psychometric; (3) psychological; (4) linguistic; and (5) transactional. All the theories and models presented will have merit in some cases, but total agreement among authorities covering all aspects of reading will probably not be found. Attention will be given to the problem adolescent's individual learning style and possession of the various types and degrees of cognitive regulators.

Taxonomic models

The taxonomic model system is exemplified in the work of William Gray (1960). This model categorizes the skills underlying reading into four major classes: (1) word perception, which includes pronunciation and meaning; (2) comprehension; (3) reaction and evaluation of ideas of the author; and (4) assimilation of what is read through a fusion of old ideas and information obtained through reading. Robinson (1966) expanded Gray's theory and added a fifth category, rate of reading, which can be adaptable to varying reading purposes. Also included in his writing was the differentiation of reading skills from process and from instructional procedures.

Psychometric models

Holmes (1953) has been a significant researcher in the development of the psychometric systems. The substrata-factor theory developed by Holmes has since been elaborated and refined by Singer (1970). The substrata analysis consists of administering to readily disturbed youth those test variables that, on the basis of theory and past research, seem to contribute to most of the variance in reading comprehension. He then analyzed into secondary factors those which identify a set of subtest variables. These secondary factors are considered as the significant contributors to the variance of each of the first-order factors. The major objective is to determine the nature of the combination of the hierarchically organized subsystems that form a working system for speed and power of reading. Clymer (1963) and Sparks and Mitzel (1966) have stated that the Holmes system does not constitute a theory per se in the true sense of the word, primarily on the grounds that it is nonpredictive.

Psychological models

The basic psychological models associated with reading can be grouped into (1) behavioral; (2) cognitive; and (3) information processing. *Behaviorally based models* have been strongly influenced by Skinner (1957). Skinner's writing did not deal significantly with reading, but has had an influence on the development of teaching techniques to enhance it. Skinner cites that reading behavior is described as vocal-verbal responses under the control of nonauditory verbal stimuli. He cites automatic reinforcement of reading activity based on the reader's interest. Appropriate units of instruction are described, as are discussions of the differences between the beginning reader and the skilled reader. Skinner's formulation of reading does not stress the nature of the written language as a code, as he compares reading behavior with behavior and mimicry. According to Skinner (1957):

> The automatic reinforcement of reading and interesting texts, however, has merely the effect of increasing the probability of the occurence of such behavior; it does not differentially reinforce correct forms at the phonetic level. (p. 53)

Staats (1968) is another leading proponent of the behaviorist point of view. His early work in reading was firmly entrenched within a strict operant-condition framework. The acquisition of reading, according to Staats, Staats, Schultz, and Wolf (1962), is discrimination training with certain verbal responses reinforced in the presence of certain verbal stimuli. The emphasis at that time was on the development of a system of reinforcers—generally tokens which could be exchanged for trinkets and edibles. Additionally, a discrimination learning apparatus along with cumulative records indicating the number of responses acquired were present in terms of materials necessary. The basic reading materials used were simply single letters or consonant-vowel combinations which were chosen to reduce response variation. The acknowledgment that reading was a language process was ignored in his early work. The more recent work of Staats, however, has been modified. He sees basic elementary reading as a process of instrumental discrimination, and he feels that reinforcement contingencies are appropriate for the acquisition of reading and further study of the processes involved. Staats, Brewer, and Gross (1970) describe reading as a complex cognitive skill, many of whose components must be developed on the basis of already learned more basic skills including language repertoires.

Gagne (1970) presents still another approach with a "learning" emphasis rather than a behavioral orientation. According to Gagne, there are eight distinct types of learning, ranging from signal learning to problem solving. Each is clearly distinguishable from the other, for it begins with a different state of the organism and ends with a different capability of performance. A hierarchical formation is associated with these eight learning types; the prerequisite for one type is that learning of the next lowest type is already established.

Planning sequences of instruction involves examining the learning structure of various content areas. According to Gagne (1970) these are broken down into smaller units of student competencies. His sequences are not "developmental," for people of all ages acquire simple kinds of learning. Rather, increasingly complex forms of learning build on simpler forms no matter what the age of the subject.

Gibson (1970) presents another *cognitive based model* rather than a behavioral approach to the psychological model. The cognitive theory is quite comprehensive and elaborative. It is basically divided into phases. The first phase skills include those that are fundamental to learning to read, namely speech and the *graphic act*. According to Gibson, for the normal child, written material is a second-order symbol system that decodes the speech; some competence in hearing and speaking must come first. Three aspects of language are stated as being significant: (1) the phonological; (2) the semantic; and (3) the syntactic. The youth must be able to extract the information from each of these aspects of language. The youth clearly must acquire a knowledge of the phonological rule system. He must also develop a basic conceptual system including relations, that is, same-different. The child must also have fundamental knowledge of syntax and morphology. According to the authors, the fundamental *graphic act* is scribbling, and the reinforcement for this activity comes from the opportunity to see the marks just made. The child develops awareness of graphic features, such as continuity, intersections, etc. The child will differentiate *writing* and *drawing* and then must differentiate the alphabet letters. This ability to differentiate two-dimensional forms increases with age.

A cognitive based approach heavily oriented toward Piagetian theory has been offered by Elkind, Horn and Schneider (1965). This provides a relatively sharp contrast to the behavioral model that was presented. Elkind concentrates primarily on the perceptual aspects of reading acquisition. His approach is based on the assumption that there are well differentiated stages of development and that the learning process or processes manifested by the child depends on his developmental level. According to Elkind et al. (1965), it is first necessary to diagnose the level, and then determine what processes are associated with that level. One of the first things the child must learn is that printed text is a representation, like speech, and that the markings on the printed page are arbitrary signs. It is postulated that this awareness develops according to the same principles as the awareness of the arbitrariness of signs in general. The perceptual processes that account for this development of fundamentals leads to an understanding of the development of reading in general. Elkind, unlike many others, denies the importance of discrimination and association of that aspect of perceptual growth. He feels that the processes involved in perceptual growth are concerned with the basic development of *decentration*. The young child's perception is centered in the sense that it is determined by the dominant aspects of the visual field-continuity, proximity, closure, etc. With age, according to Elkind et al., perception becomes increasingly decentered; that is, freed from the domination of the field effect.

Elkind et al. (1965) see all of the perceptual processes as embodying logic. These processes include (1) perceptual organization (the ability to rearrange mentally a stimulus array without acting physically on it); (2) perceptual schematization (the ability to organize parts and wholes so that they retain their unique identities without losing their independence); and (3) perceptual exploration (the ability to scan systematically an array or figure so that all its features are noted). Elkind (1965) has criticized look-say instruction on the grounds that it inhibits the development of a true whole-part schematization since it provides no training on analyzing parts of words.

Venezky and Kelsay (1970) present a model for reading skills that falls clearly within an *information-processing* framework. Visual scanning, the first of several postulated processes, is directed by (1) general knowledge of the reader; and (2) immediate knowledge from the material being read. According to the authors there are two types of immediate knowledge: what is deduced from the materials and thus creating expectancy, and what is obtained from where the eye is at that moment processing. There are two simultaneously operating forms of processing: syntactic semantic integration of what has just been scanned and forward scanning. Forward scanning is directed at the task of locating the largest manageable unit that can be chunked rapidly. The reader of the materials notes punctuation, for example, or phrase boundaries. When this unit is identified, forward scanning continues and the information of the unit already identified is then integrated or related to what has previously been stored. A word is identified via search of the associative word store, which contains frequently encountered words and word parts, and of the low frequency store (larger and less well organized). Using partial information on expectancies, matches are attempted. If there is a failure, more scanning is necessary. The good reader scans well; that is, he maintains a good balance between the two processes of integration and forward scanning, which must adapt to changes in the type of reading material and in the reader's purpose.

In terms of this information-processing model, the nonreading 6-year-old would have an empty letter store, no visual patterns in either word store, plus no knowledge of language in the real world. Input to the model would be first letter pairs, then words, etc. There is no distinction between integration and forward scanning in early stages of learning to read. The authors note, however, that important developmental changes in abilities may complicate the issue, and they pose some general questions about the actual nature of the relevant cognitive processes and their acquisition. Kelsay, Chapman, and Venezky (1971) have developed a basic skills test consisting of a large set of subtests related primarily to the three primary areas of the acquisition model. These subtests are designed to sample a skill in a variety of different contexts. An attempt is made to identify the underlying psychological processes involved in the ability. Five areas of cognitive functioning are tested: matching of visual forms, auditory-phonetic identification, letter-sound association, vocabulary knowledge, and general achievement. Preliminary results indicate that skill components, if narrowly defined, are quite independent. Performance on auditory matching, segmentation, and corresponding learning tests are poor. Visual perception skills are reasonably good, but cognitive abilities such as sequencing and memory for visual forms are not good.

Other researchers involved with the information-processing point of view include Roberts and Lundser (1968). Their writings point out that language has a dual character. It is representational and communicates meaning, and it is also behavioral. It includes a complex of skills that is comprised of a set of symbols which are interrelated in complex ways. Different sizes and arrangement of these units comprise the grammar. It has been stated that linguistic behavior involves concurrent activity at three levels: representational (semantic), grammatical, and perceptuo-motor (phonological). The establishment of reading skill depends on the acquisition of a high level of automatization at all three levels in relation to their interpretation of the written text. Reading is done in order to obtain information or reduce uncertainty. Information is also the effect of generating new uncertainty, so there is a cycle of uncertainty-information-new uncertainty.

Roberts and Lundser (1968) present a complex schematic representation of processes involved in reading, stressing their hierarchical and sequential relations. The importance of motivation is cited which is extraneous to the reading skill itself. The remaining elements represent decision processes of strategies, perceptuo-motor mechanisms, and active memory states or processes.

Another version of the information-processing point of view has been cited by Smith (1971). Like other theorists working within this framework, he concentrates on a description of the skilled reader. Smith's feature-analytic model proposes that (1) letter identification, (2) word identification, and (3) comprehension of meaning are three distinct tasks that can be performed independently on the same information. The identification of a single letter is achieved as a result of testing a sufficient number of features so that alternative responses are eliminated and uncertainty is reduced. Agreeing with Neisser (1967), Smith suggests a word identification is not necessarily based on prior letter identification. Rather, distinctive features directly provide the basis for word identification. In fact, according to this model, fewer visual features are required to discriminate a letter within a word than to discriminate a letter in isolation. By the same token, word identification can take place when there is insufficient information for identifying any of the individual letters. Word feature lists include information about location of feature.

Smith (1971) cites the concept of comprehension in the information-processing model. Comprehension of meaning is based on the same kind of feature analysis. The skilled reader uses information from the visual configuration plus information from context (for example, he has knowledge of semantic and syntactic constraints). Comprehension of meaning then will require less information than word identification. Consequently, it perceives word identification in normal skilled reading.

An interesting and valuable contribution by Smith is his analysis of how the information-processing capacities of the novice reader are taxed to a much greater extent than are those of the mature reader. According to Smith (1971) the beginner cannot often identify words and meanings directly. Instead, mediated identification is required. Mediated word identification involves mapping the word onto its sound pattern, which is then used as a basis for the identification of the word. Phonics rules are taught in order to maximize the translation from a visual configuration to acoustic configuration. In discerning the mediated meaning, word identification must occur so that there is a basis for comprehension. These mechanisms are disruptive because they overload the visual information-processing and memory systems. The beginner must learn to overcome these restrictions by utilizing the redundancies in written language (feature redundancy in individual letters; and orthographic redundancy). Until the beginning reader accomplishes this task, he must rely more heavily on the visual information that he picks up; therefore, he will read more slowly and with less comprehension than after he has learned to use the redundancies.

Linguistic models

The major limitation of the models presented to this point is that there appears to be an underemphasis on the structure of language. It is noted that there are statements in the literature within the previously presented models that reading is a language process. The major emphasis, though, is in terms of the psychological rather than the language structure variables.

The application of linguistics to reading was, until recently, fairly restricted. Bloomfield (1942) posited that irregularities in correspondence between orthography and speech should not be presented to beginning readers but that only regular correspondence should be presented. Fries (1963) was also concerned primarily with letter-sound relationships. Lefevre (1964) was among the first to point out the importance of syntactical cues, both intraword, such as inflections; and interword, such as sentence structure. One of Lefevre's major interests was in the cueing of intonation.

Great emphasis was placed on the difficulty in reading English because of its irregular grapheme-phoneme correspondence. Levin and Watson (1963) argued that a child should be trained on achievement variable correspondences from the beginning so that he could develop a prospect for diversity. Venezky and Weir (1966) demonstrated that there is considerable regularity between English orthography and oral language if one looks beyond the direct grapheme-phoneme relationship. The relationship between print and sound must be described in two steps. First, there are rules deriving lexical forms from the graphic input; and second, there are rules deriving the phonemic form from the lexical data. Chomsky and Halle (1968) also analyze the relationship in two levels, but for them these levels are the lexical and the phonetic. According to Chomsky and Halle, orthography is a nearly optimal representation of the lexical level of spoken English.

Recent notions about language development, especially as it has been described by those who work within the transformational grammar framework, have been of great interest to people working in reading. The rejection of a passive, receptive learner for one who is actively constructing his language (on the basis, it is sometimes argued, of innate knowledge of linguistic universals); the distinction between competence in performance; the analysis of grammatical structure, and other ideas have to lay the foundation for reading models that have a strong linguistic orientation.

Goodman (1970) has been influenced greatly by a *transformational-generative* theory. According to this author, reading is a constructive process involving active information processing. The reader who is knowledgeable about language brings his total experience to the reading task. Reading is a psycholinguistic process in which the reader decodes from the graphic stimulus not speech, but directly into the deep structure of the written material. In oral reading, he then encodes the meaning into speech. Since comprehension and communication are the goals of reading, the proficient reader may recode with modification and meaning the speech that contains transformational vocabulary and syntax. Three kinds of information are used simultaneously: graphic, syntactic, and semantic. As reading proficiency improves, the reader who has more control over language structure, better conceptual skills, more experience, and better sampling strategies, uses fewer and fewer graphic cues. Goodman argues that one cannot fractionate the reading process into component skills, either for research or for instruction, because the reader does not use all the information available in the text. He uses only enough to predict and decode the language structure.

Goodman's research is to look at *miscues* in reading. Miscues are occurrences of mismatches between the text and the reader's response. They are not errors, for some very good reading may involve miscues where meaning is not disturbed. Analysis of the miscues will lead to an understanding of the reader's strategies. In fact, instruction should be designed to maximize the sampling and hypothesis-testing strategies, rather than try to get the child to attend to more specific details of the text.

Clay (1968) and Weber (1970) have also investigated errors in oral reading. In general, studies indicate that most readers, even beginners, depend heavily on syntactical constraints. Fewer miscues are interpreted as being due to misperception of the graphic stimuli themselves. Goodman's (1968) 11-month study of six first-grade readers indicated uneven development in strong individual differences. In general, however, the more proficient children made "better" errors; that is, they demonstrated more complex processing and they showed more ability to correct their errors when they conflicted with their expectancies of meaning or language. Thus, language does control reading to a large extent. Goodman's model presumably operates both for the beginner and the proficient reader, but one must not assume that the processes are the same. The model is complex and it can be broken down into several alternative submodels so that it would represent the beginning reader versus the skilled. It could account for the differences in the individual reader that would occur as he read materials or varying levels of difficulty.

Ruddell (1970) has presented a model of communication that includes speech, writing, and listening. Using a transformational-grammar framework, language is seen to operate on several levels. First, there is a surface structure consisting of the relationship between morphophonemes and morphographemes. The second level consists of structural and semantic readings that lead to processing language for interpretation. The third level is a deep structure of language. The first level is important in considering the decoding process; all three levels are relevant in determining comprehension. According to Ruddell (1970), decoding is one of the central tasks in early reading instruction. He notes that children manage to pick up decoding skills from a variety of approaches, many of which stress quite different units. He speculates that there may be a relationship between the optimal unit for instruction and particular learned characteristics. The comprehension process involves relational meaning, both at the surface structure level and at the deep structure level. In addition, lexical meaning including the importance of context in determining semantic possibilities is important. The model also takes into account an individual's interests, attitudes, values, and cognitive strategies. As reading progresses, a child goes from learning the nature of the code of the writing system to learning to decode. As cognitive strategies develop, he should gain alternative ways of handling print besides decoding words. With a greater proficiency, the reader may move directly to meaning, relying less and less on the morphological system.

Ryan and Semmel (1969) stress the *transformational-grammar* framework and the fact that the child must have some degree of knowledge of grammar in order to take advantage of the irregularities that exist on an abstract level. They argue that the beginning reader has and uses to some extent, abstract rules about language structure. The child should be trained so he or she can use knowledge about language structure. The youth should be taught to use the rules known about language even more effectively in his or her reading. Instruction should stress the conceptual aspects, concentrating on the perceptual aspects, which would lead to absolute identification of letters and words that interfere with mature reading strategies.

The reading models based on psychological theories, which seem to represent all points of view about the nature of learning and development, comprehensive models based on linguistic analysis, seem to be found solely on transformational-generative grammar.

Transactional models

The transactional model of reading has been cited by Rosenblatt (1969). Adults' reactions to poems were studied in his research. The quality of experience that the reader is living through, under the stimulus of the text (the poems), is the goal of the reading. According to Rosenblatt, there is an active, two-way relationship between the reader and text. The *transaction* terminology underscores the importance of both elements in a dynamic relationship. The active seeking out of particular aspects of the text and the tentative interpretations and reinterpretations makes analysis closely related to the more typical cognitive point of view.

Williams succinctly summarizes the present state-of-the-art in terms of reading models:

1.   Models at present focus on cognitive aspects of reading; little attempt has been made to incorporate affective aspects into the model.

2.   Several different theoretical positions within psychology, representing a wide variety of points of view, have been used in the development of models of reading, whereas transformational-generative grammar is the only theory from linguistics that is represented in the recent attempts at comprehensive model building.

3.   There seems to be a rapprochement among theorists toward a view of reading as being a complex cognitive skill, the goal of which is obtaining information in the complex language system.

4.   Most models focus on the reading process per se. This is due in large part, of course, to the theorists' specific interest in skilled reading. However, the emphasis on proficient reading is also a result of the opinion that in order to understand the acquisition process, we must first study the skill as it appears in final form.

5.   Most models of the acquisition phase focus on decoding prerequisite abilities. The mechanisms involved in making correspondences between orthography and sound cannot, however, be characterized in terms of associative learning. Rather, basic knowledge is intimately involved as well as the utilization of complex active and perceptual strategies.

(Williams, 1973, p. 124)

CORRELATES OF SUCCESS AND FAILURE IN READING

Norm-violating youth, like other individuals involved in the process of reading, can be involved in an active rather than passive reading experience. Reading is not a single process, but it is the synthesizing of many processes culminating in a single act. The main purpose of this section is to point out some of the basic research conclusions and relate them to the total reading process of the chronically disruptive youth. Problem adolescents, as with nonhandicapped children, can be viewed along various dimensions. Before we review the more frequently encountered correlates of reading ability or lack of it, we must agree that problem adolescents will follow the total continuum and ranges of behaviors in all of the categories mentioned with the exception of the variables related to social adjustment behavioral characteristics which will obviously be low.

Variances within the stated correlates of reading ability may be related to the exhibited behaviors of problem adolescents and chronically disruptive youth. Among the more frequently encountered correlates of reading ability are: (1) intelligence, (2) mental age, (3) sex, (4) socioeconomic level, (5) language, (6) race, (7) personality, (8) attitude,

(9) physical growth, (10) perceptual skill, and (11) rate of learning. This listing represents only a few of the major reading correlates. Brief comments will be made about the more important ones which appear to have greater significance in studying the reading process of problem adolescents.

Intelligence quotient and mental age

The terms *intelligence quotient* (IQ) and *mental age* (MA) are usually used to express the results of tests of general intelligence. The IQ of a 12-year-old youth represents the ratio between his or her particular score on a given intelligence test and the score which an average individual of the same age would attain on the same test. In differentiating between MA and IQ, one might state IQ is a measure of mental growth, whereas MA might more appropriately be described as a level of mental maturity. Although there are exceptions, IQ's are generally thought to remain relatively stable as the individual grows older. MA, on the other hand, tends to increase at a rather constant pace until sometime in mid-adolescence. Consequently, MA seems to be a better short-range predictor of perforformance while IQ is more appropriate for accurate long-range prediction.

In viewing the IQ's and mental ages of problem adolescents, from a quantitative and qualitative point of view, the writing of Mauser (1974) has cited that the average IQ of delinquents was 95. This quotient falls within the national norm of average intelligence. Schlichter and Ratcliff (1971) compared 45 juvenile delinquents and 45 nondelinquents participating in a learning discrimination study. They found no significant difference in IQ levels. Ahlstrom and Havighurst (1971) conducted a longitudinal study that included black delinquents and white delinquents. They found the average IQ for black delinquents was 91 and the average for white delinquents was 94.

Although there is general agreement that intelligence is an important factor in developing reading proficiency, educators are divided about the extent of that importance. Over the years, of all the factors correlated with reading readiness and achievement, none has been more persistently or frequently studied than intelligence. This amount of knowledge and conflicting information about the importance of intelligence has tended to compound rather than clarify the issue. Some of the more pointed statements in the literature related to the importance of intelligence include Harris' statement (1970) that ". . . the most important single factor in reading readiness is general intelligence, which, being an average of many phases of mental growth, is significantly related to most of the other factors" (p. 12). Similarly, studies by Witty and Kopel (1936) concluded that an individual with a Binet IQ below 25 ordinarily will never reach a level of mental development sufficient to learn to read. Those individuals with an IQ score below 50 will experience difficulty in reading both abstract and other types of difficult material. Those invidvidual with IQ scores between 50 and 70 may ultimately be able to learn to read, but probably never above fourth-grade level. Whether the findings of Witty and Kopel (1936) are applicable today as they were in years past is doubtful. It is predicted that many interesting and surprising results will be reported related to the teaching of severe and profoundly retarded individuals' reading and mathematical skills.

Bond and Wagner (1966) cite the relationship between intelligence and reading abilities will vary from one academic level to another. Specifically, it was stated that the correlation between mental age is measured by individual Stanford-Binet tests and reading comprehension. The end of the first grade is approximately 0.35; at the end of the fifth grade it is approximately 0.60; during the high school years it approaches 0.80. Cohen and Glass (1968) found no significant relationship between IQ scores and reading ability in the first grade, but they found a significant relationship in the fourth grade.

In terms of problem adolescents, it is shown that the majority of the identified students will be in the upper primary and intermediate levels. The fruition of the frustration of such youngsters will probably culminate in the junior high or early high school years.

The importance of an adequate mental age in beginning reading is often noted. Morphett and Washburne (1931) conducted a classic study which pointed out that children whose mental ages were below 6 when they entered school usually failed the first grade. This study also reported that the proportion of failures dropped as mental age increased up to about 6½ years. In the same era, Gates (1937) disagreed with the Morphett-Washburne findings as he stated that other factors may be as important as mental age. His research indicated that the necessary mental age for reading is relative. He cited that class size, teaching procedures, and methods allow some children to read as early as age 4½, where others may begin to read as late as age 7. Gray (1956) also supported the mental age of 6 concept for beginning reading. He did state that materials, teaching procedures, and a variety of other factors may be more important than mental age. Gray (1956) noted that several European countries and Scotland had developed successful readers at the mental age of 5. One must caution interpreters of these results unless they analyze the language structure and symbolic structure of reading materials that are used in countries and environments reporting reading success at mental ages of 5 or below.

Although there is conflict of opinion about the exact nature of the relationship of IQ and MA to reading, certain points of agreement can be found that will have implications for working with problem adolescents.

1. IQ and MA are relatively good predictors of a child's minimal performance level. Barring other serious handicaps, most chil-

dren with mental ages of 6 can be taught to read at the first-grade level.

2. Most students who failed to succeed in reading in the first grade have mental ages below 6 years.

3. Although IQ and MA are important, other factors such as class size, motivation, and teaching procedures may be just as important to success in reading.

4. Even though IQ and MA are relatively sound predictors in most cases, they should never be used in isolation to determine expectations. The fact that a first grader has an IQ of 130 is no more of a guarantee that he will learn to read than the fact that a child with an IQ of 80 will not.

5. Correlations between IQ and reading scores tend to increase with age and grade level of the student. This is due largely to similarities in test items of the measuring instruments administered to ascertain supposedly different skills or traits. A high IQ score at the sixth-grade level is a much better predictor of reading performance than the same score at the first-grade level. This is due to the greater amount of nonverbal items included on the test for children at this lower level.

Socioeconomic factors

One of the significant factors most often correlated with reading achievement has been socioeconomic status. Problem adolescents may be members of any socioeconomic class, but it is estimated that the majority are from lower socioeconomic homes. Assuming that the greater number of problem adolescents will be members of the lower socioeconomic class, it is also understandable that there would be greater problems of reading, regardless of other factors. Early studies by Coleman (1940) and Gough (1946) cite a high relationship between socioeconomic status and reading ability. Riessman (1962) offers the rather conservative estimate that 15% to 20% of American school children have some degree of reading disability. His estimates of the number of reading disabled individuals, who are members of the lower socioeconomic classes and particularly the disadvantaged subpopulations, raised the incidence figures to 50%. Benson (1969) stated that the number of children with retardation in reading may include 10% to 20% of middle class children, but in most lower socioeconomic areas it may range as high as 80%.

The problem adolescent who comes to the educational environment from a home with malnutrition, poor health, crowded living conditions, unstable environment, and economic pressures undoubtedly will be at an extreme disadvantage. These are problems over which the teacher will have very little control. Additionally, there are a number of other reasons for poor achievement which may be associated with socioeconomic status. These factors may be discussed under the headings of (1) background experience, (2) level of motivation, (3) language.

Background experience

Chronically disruptive youth who do come from low socioeconomic levels are often said to lack academically relevant background experiences. The fact that their experiences are not the same as those of middle-class children or those represented in traditional teaching materials should not be misinterpreted as irrelevant to the academic experience. Many teachers have overlooked the fact that experiential backgrounds do exist in these children. These same teachers have failed to capitalize on the wealth of nontraditional experiences the child brings to the learning situation.

Hence, chronically disruptive youth are handicapped in many cases by their background experience. Since the educational system is geared toward middle-class standards with middle-class subject matter and vocabulary, the child who has never experienced these is at a disadvantage. Again, the problem adolescent from the lower socioeconomic class has fewer opportunities to travel, less books to handle, fewer magazines in his home, and fewer opportunities to meet people outside his immediate environment. Because of restricted social environment and economic limitations, many avenues of enrichment are closed to him. Frequently in the home of the chronically disruptive youth, both parents work and there is little opportunity for them to contribute to widening the child's experiences. In many other cases, because of social and economic pressures, parents simply contribute to additional neglect of the child. Consequently, this child may be attitudinally unprepared to accept the changes that accompany school. The author cautions that not all norm-violating youth come from negative environments, and advises that teachers be prepared to handle the unique problems of the more affluent youth included in the chronically disruptive category.

Level of motivation

To assume that all problem adolescents want to learn to read is unrealistic. Many problem adolescents come from homes in which the parents cannot read or feel reading is unimportant; therefore, the motivation for learning to read may be lacking. This is especially true of the chronically disruptive youth from low socioeconomic environments. They are less likely to see their parents, or other members of their family, and peer groups placing importance on reading and its related activities. Also, they are less likely to have opportunities to examine books, magazines, newspapers, etc., in their homes. They have neither the encouragement nor any reason to learn to read.

Past reading experiences for chronically disruptive youth have often-times been unrewarding experiences. This fact alone may be regarded as a significant point related to the reason why the children and adolescents are poorly motivated in the reading environment. The inadequate backgrounds that many of them come to school with deter levels of readiness. Because many of the problem adolescents come to the learning environment ill-prepared, they fail. Reading, too often, becomes equated with failure. Few, if any, individuals enjoy failing, so it not surprising that negative associations are built up and associated with the school and reading related activities. Rather than motivating children to read, constant failures motivate them to leave school and to assume the street behaviors of norm-violating youth. A later chapter will describe materials that contribute to the positive motivation of chronically disruptive youth in the learning situation.

Language

Another significant area related to the reading ability of problem adolescents is language. Students from low socioeconomic environments are oftentimes handicapped by their language and language patterns. This is not always the case but it does seem to surface more frequently in studying students from low socioeconomic environments. Chronically disruptive youth may often come to school with a language quite adequate for communication with his family and peers. This is not sufficient for the traditional school setting. The language of the home and community may not necessarily be the language of the school. Bernstein (1960) and Patin (1964) cite the *public* or *restricted* language that low socioeconomic students possess restricting the amount of formal or elaborative language consistently utilized. The student's public language is adequate for conveying simple items of information, making requests, or indicating agreement or disagreement. The public language is characterized by simple declaratory sentences in imperative spirit. Structural complexities, dependent clauses, and more elaborate speech patterns found in formal language are not in his public language. Since the language of the school is formal, the student from a low socioeconomic group is at a disadvantage from the beginning.

READING AS A SENSORY PROCESS

No matter how intelligent the chronically disruptive youth may be, or how psychologically ready the individual may be for reading, he cannot learn to read unless he has some way of experiencing the stimulus material. Reading begins as a sensory process. The cues and stimuli for reading come through the ears, eyes, and in the case of the severely visually impaired, through braille, and the fingers. The problem adolescent, if visually handicapped, will have additional burdens that may prevent him from progressing in reading. To say that a problem adolescent who is also visually handicapped will not learn to read would not be a true statement. The chronically disruptive, as other youth, have the remarkable ability to compensate. The proper interpretation should be that impairment in vision or hearing alone should not impede progress in all cases. Reading is a sensory process, but we do not intend to mean that it is only a sensory process. There are many factors involved in reading. Disability in reading is usually the result of a multiplicity of factors, some working singly or in combination. Visual weaknesses or hearing problems alone may not cause severe problems for the chronically disruptive youth, but he will rarely find either one standing in isolation. Most often they join with, or cause, other problems such as fatigue, restlessness, discomfort, poor self-image, etc., that may propel these youths into their maladaptive behavior performance.

Reading and vision

Dzik (1966) has been one of the foremost researchers primarily focusing on vision and the juvenile delinquent. He states that 85% to 90% of the students' learning is through eyesight and vision. Consequently, if his vision is poor, his chances of success in the classroom are poor. In his examination of 125 juvenile delinquents, he found that 94% were reading below their school grade level. Significantly, 54% failed the far-sighted vision test, 48% failed the near-vision test (14 inches), and 35% of the juvenile delinquent population failed both. Additionally, 53% failed perception (acquiring meaning from seeing) and 72% failed either one or more of the vision tests.

Reading begins with seeing—stimulus enters through the eye. At an early age, children begin to perform in a way that might loosely be called reading. The child begins to recognize that certain signs or symbols represent names of things. Later, they learn when certain signs and signals are put together, they represent talk. They begin to recognize and interpret billboards, road signs, labels, and so on. Reading books and printed materials is another matter. The question is often asked, "When are they ready to read such materials?" It might be better to state the question, "When is their vision ready?"

By the time the child reaches the age of 5 or 6 he is usually visually ready for reading books. At this age he has reached some competency in binocular coordination, depth perception, focus and re-focus, and changing fixations at will. Optometric research has indicated, though, that at this age he is generally far-sighted. Since children are individuals with individual patterns of growth and development, there are likely to be considered differences between pupils in any group of children.

Refractive errors are the most common type of visual disability. The child with a refractive error simply has eyes that are out of focus. Many first-grade children suffer from various degrees of one type of refractive error or another. Hyperopia (far-sightedness) is one type. Many schools still use the Snellen-type wall chart for testing vision. Consequently, many children are missed because this test does not measure near vision. The child with far-sightedness will be able to focus on objects, wall charts, blackboards, stop signs, and other large objects that he may experience, but will have difficulty when required to read from a book.

Myopia (near-sightedness) is the second type of refractive error. Myopia is less common in beginning readers and, except in extreme cases, appears to have little detrimental effect on reading. Some authorities feel that moderate myopia favors, rather than hinders, reading. Most reading first-graders read at a distance of 14 inches, which is well within arm's reach, so it is unlikely to be a problem.

Astigmatism, the third type of refractive error, is a condition of uneven focus of the eyes. Astigmatism may be present in addition to hypermetropic and myopic conditions. Astigmatism is not necessarily a major cause of reading disability but can be a contributing factor. As with other types of refractive errors it tends to create discomfort, tension, and disinterest in reading. The problem adolescent who possesses refractive errors will have additional sources of internal and external discomfort because of these vision problems.

Inadequate conversion and fusion deficiencies are also types of visual problems, but are much less frequent. It will generally take someone more highly trained to detect these problems. This fact alone gives credence to the recent plea by optometrists that thorough visual analysis should be made prior to entering any educational setting.

Diskan (1963) and Knox (1953) have presented a list of symptoms that are regarded as reliable for picking out visual defects that may eventually contribute to reading problems. The list of symptoms include: (1) facial contortions, (2) book held close to face, (3) tension during visual work, (4) tilting head, (5) head thrust forward, (6) body tense while looking at distant objects, (7) assuming poor sitting position, (8) moving head excessively while reading, (9) rubbing eyes frequently, (10) avoiding close visual work, and (11) losing place in reading. According to the authors, these overt symptoms combined with results from a screening test appear to be relatively good indicators of vision difficulty. Consequently, visual difficulty and difficulty in reading printed materials results.

As implied earlier, there are many studies suggesting no relationship between visual defects and reading disabilities. Among these are studies conducted by Witty and Kopel (1936), Betts and Austin (1941), Ball (1961), and Shearer (1966). On the contrary, Park and Burri (1943) stated that better readers had fewer than average visual deficiencies for their chronological and mental age groups. Poor readers had more than average visual deficiencies for their chronological and mental age groups. Betts (1934) and Spache and Tillman (1962) cited that fusion is directly related to reading problems. Additionally, studies relating reading disability and visual deficiencies include the research of Harris (1970), Kephart (1953), Eames (1965), and Dearborn and Anderson (1938).

Visual defects should be regarded as a possible cause or contributing factor of reading disability, depending on the individual. It may be totally unrelated to the reading performance of problem adolescents. However, all vision should be checked by a screening device, with a referral system for those who fail the screening.

Reading and hearing

The ability to hear sounds accurately is essential for learning to read efficiently. Durrell and Murphy (1953) state that almost every child with reading achievement below the first grade was handicapped with a marked inability to discriminate sounds and words. Bond (1935), in addition to Goetzinger, Dirks, and Baer (1960), conducted studies involving the matched pairs technique in an effort to determine differences in the performance of good and poor readers on selected auditory skills. Significant differences were found in each study between the two groups of readers in auditory discrimination. Thompson (1963), in a study of second graders, found that of the 24 best readers, 16 possessed adequate auditory discrimination upon entering the first grade. Of the 24 poorest readers, only 1 exhibited adequate discrimination skills at the beginning of grade one.

Low correlations between reading readiness skills and selected auditory skills in first-grade children were found by Gates and Bond (1936). Additional research questioning the relationship of auditory skills to reading ability was cited by Reynolds (1953) and Templin (1954).

Although the research related to auditory skills and reading is inconclusive, it is felt that it does have a significant role to play, especially when reading instruction in certain instances will rely on some sort of phonics or oral system of sounding out words. Whether the difficulty in hearing is due to physical reasons or due to cultural-dialectical differences, hearing ability will definitely influence the child's language and reading.

Cozad and Rousey (1966) studied the hearing and speech disorders among delinquent children. More than 5 times the normal incidence was reported. Additionally, there was a higher incidence of defective hearing among the boys than the girls. Among delinquent youth, speech disorders, which are at times related to hearing disorders, occurred nearly 12 times higher than the normal incidence. The incidence of speech disorders is high in all the categories rather than focusing specifically on articulation, stuttering, or other types of speech problems.

The beginning reader should be able to hear likenesses among letter sounds as they occur in words. The ability to detect words that begin and end with the same sound is important. Rhyming ability and the ability to determine words containing a given sound are also significant. Those children who cannot perform these tasks can be trained to do so. In those cases where auditory training is unsuccessful, a program emphasizing phonics approaches should not be implemented.

ASSESSING AND EVALUATING READING GROWTH OF PROBLEM ADOLESCENTS AND CHRONICALLY DISRUPTIVE YOUTH

It is of great importance that problem adolescents and chronically disruptive youth be thoroughly evaluated in an effort to provide the most direct and beneficial educational program. This section deals with some techniques that can be used to assess the cognitive reading achievement of problem adolescents, including: (1) group and individual tests, standardized and informal; (2) attitudinal measurement; and (3) criterion referenced tests for functional literacy. A variety of procedures will give an intelligent estimate of the level of materials which individual students can read successfully. Careful and continuous evaluations of reading abilities and disabilities cannot be overemphasized. Through continuous evaluation, program direction may ultimately evolve from a remedial to a compensatory type of program. Evaluation of problem adolescents in the reading area will not only be concerned with the individual skill development, but also the effect of reading instruction on the student's attitudes and reading habits.

Cognitive reading achievement can be measured by both standarized tests and informal (nonstandarized) instruments of techniques. Standarized tests are especially valuable in helping us compare our students' reading achievement with that of students in a national norm group. Informal reading tests are quite valuable in determining which of our available materials are best suited to the needs and achievement of individual students in our classes. By using informal tests, we can determine which of our available materials are on a student's frustrational reading level, which are on his instructional reading level, and which are on his independent reading level.

Materials that are on a student's *frustrational reading level* are normally too difficult to read even with the help of a teacher. Materials that are at his *instructional reading level* are suitable for him to read if he has guidance from a teacher. Materials on his *independent reading level* are easy enough for him to read on his own. It is imperative that the chronically disruptive and troubled youth, as other students, receive reading materials, textbooks, etc., at his instructional level. Other materials such as supplementary materials which the student reads with little or no guidance from the teacher, should be at his independent reading level. Rarely, and only when the student is intensely motivated, should the student read materials at his frustration reading level.

Standardized reading achievement tests

The number of different reading achievement tests on the market is large. Buros (1972) has provided a valuable service by periodically soliciting reviews of the various tests from reading specialists; including them in a collection of reviews of mental measurement instruments. Mauser (1976) has described over 300 assessment protocols suitable for use in the assessment and diagnosis of learning disabilities in children. Few of the reading achievement tests will be described in this section, as the number of tests is too large to do an adequate job. Regardless of which standardized reading achievement tests are used, Smith and Barrett (1974) have distinctly outlined some very practical criteria and questions related to standardized achievement tests:

1. Are the students who were used to gather normative data similar to our students and therefore likely to provide helpful comparisons?

2. Are the reading passages on the test good representations of the kind of reading material that the student must learn to read?

3. Are the tasks students are asked to perform good representations of what a good reader does when he is getting meaning from print?

4. Are the comprehension questions asked of students carefully constructed to measure different levels of thinking about significant aspects of the content of the material?

5. Are the strengths and weaknesses of one particular test in regard to the strengths and weaknesses of other available tests?

6. Is reading rate always measured as a rate of comprehension? A rate of reading score that does not take comprehension into consideration is meaningless.   (p. 171)

One of the most common types of information that the teacher of chronically disruptive youth has is the individual's IQ. If a teacher has IQ scores for his or her students, he or she has available the information to approximate how well each student should be reading:

$$\text{Reading Expectancy Grade} = \frac{IQ}{100} \times \text{years in school} + 1$$

or   (Bond and Tinker, 1967)

$$\text{Reading Expectancy Grade} = \frac{2\,MA + CA}{3} - 5.2$$

(Harris, 1970)

With this information, the teacher now has only the individual's reading expectancy grade. The teacher does not know the actual reading grade level of each student. Probably the best way of finding the reading grade level of a student is by administering a standardized reading test and using the grade scores supplied by the publisher. This appears to be a very simple task. However, the more one examines the many standardized reading tests available for teacher use, as well as the interpretations of grade scores supplied by publishers, the more complex a teacher's decisions become.

Different reading abilities are measured when we use different reading tests. There are two major categories for classifying reading tests: oral and silent. Some reputable oral tests measure only oral reading (no comprehension questions are asked). Obviously, different types of reading ability are being measured when students take such a test. The student takes a silent reading test in which he is asked to indicate synonyms or antonyms for words as well as to respond to study, skill, and comprehension questions.

To get the maximum amount of usable information from a reading test, a wise and selective choice of tests must be made. As a teacher of problem adolescents, one must determine what information is most important to know in relationship to a student's reading achievement. Standardized group tests are helpful to the teacher because they provide information on every child in his class. Achievement batteries such as the Iowa Test of Basic Skills (Spitzer, 1964) and the Stanford Achievement Test (Kelly, et al., 1964) can be used as initial screening devices. These tests usually give an estimate of general reading level and subscores in such areas as vocabularly, deriving paragraph meaning, and study skills. These tests do not identify specific strengths and weaknesses in reading. It is often a good idea to study the errors of individual youngsters to obtain some specific information on his performance. Many errors of the same type can alert the teacher to a possible problem. Unfortunately, a teacher seldom has time to do such detailed studies for every child in his class.

Group tests that focus specifically on reading include the Gates-MacGintie test (1964) or California Reading Test (1963). The administration of a reading test to those youngsters who have unusual results on their achievement battery can provide additional evidence to confirm or refute the additional scores. In most cases, reading survey tests are longer than the reading section of general achievement batteries, thus, they sample more reading behavior. Because of their greater length, they usually measure more consistently, and are advisable in assessing the general reading abilities of the chronically disruptive youth.

Group diagnostic tests such as the Stanford Diagnostic Reading Test (Karlsen, et al., 1966) and the Bond-Balow-Hoyt Silent Reading Diagnostic Test (1955) provide additional screening instruments. An example of a test to analyze specific skills in reading is the McCullough Word Analysis Test (1963). It must be noted that the previous tests mentioned involve a great amount of time and cost of administering, scoring, and interpreting such tests. It is cautioned that not all youngsters in the chronically disruptive catetory will need this degree of analysis.

Individual reading tests—oral and silent

Some individual instruments are primarily oral tests; others have an oral reading section but contain additional sections that enable the examiner to gather supplement specific diagnostic information. If a teacher would like to know how well her students compare with students nationally in oral reading, she might want to give a good oral reading test. If the teacher has been trained in giving an oral reading test, she may also be able to derive valuable diagnostic information from it. By observing a student's error patterns, a program can be set up for correcting his oral errors. Thus, the teacher might look at such behavioral characteristics as:

1. *Mispronunciation.* Are these patterns to the student's mispronunciations? Are there syllabication errors, certain types of errors, principally in word endings?

2. *Substitutions.* Does he misread words, usually putting in a synonym for the word given by the author?

3. *Omissions.* Does he skip words?

4. *Insertions.* Does he include words that are not the passage?

5. *Regressions.* Does he repeat words or phrases?

6. *Hesitations.* Does he pause for long periods of time?

7. *Punctuation errors.* Does he ignore punctuation?

Tests such as the Gray Oral Reading Test (1963) and the Gilmore Oral Reading Test (1952) are designed to provide a useful supplement to information gathered by silent reading tests. With these tests the teacher notes the child's ability to orally read paragraphs of increasing difficulty and answer questions concerning the content of what is read. The number of selections that can be read by a child during an administration of these tests limits the amount of reading behavior that can be sampled. Since oral reading tests must be administered individually, they are also rather demanding of teacher time. Additionally, oral reading requires several skills not necessary in silent reading, thereby increasing the difficulty of assessing only silent reading ability. It is noted that modifications of oral reading tests can be made. Such tests can also be used to assess silent reading comprehension and listening ability. For silent reading, the child is simply asked to read the paragraphs silently and answer the questions. Listening ability can be measured if the teacher reads the paragraph to the child and then asks him to answer comprehension questions.

Individual diagnostic tests can be used to assess the status and needs of those youngsters who require particularly detailed study. Individual diagnostic tests focus intensively on specific reading skills such as knowledge of initial consonants and synthesizing word parts. The disadvantage of the individual diagnostic test is that very few classroom teachers are trained to administer them. The Durrell Analysis of Reading Difficulty (1955) or the Spache Diagnostic Reading Scale (1963) are examples of individual diagnostic tests that can be used to assess the specific reading abilities and disabilities of problem adolescents. The time required to administer a complete individual diagnostic test makes tham somewhat impractical for the classroom teacher to use. (See Table 4.1 for some basic assessment protocols.)

Informal reading inventories

The Informal Reading Inventory (IRI) has become increasingly important in the evaluation of students' reading achievement. The individual reading inventory evolved from the lack of trust and faith in the available standardized reading achievement tests. The informal reading inventory has been used as a means of gathering information for grouping and individual diagnostic remedial work. Essentially, the IRI is a series of paragraphs rated in terms of reading difficulty. The selections to be read are often taken from a basal reader series. The IRI is administered by the classroom teacher to individual children. As the child reads a selection, allowed errors are recorded and word attack skills are noted by the teacher. Comprehension is usually checked immediately by several questions on the content of the selections. Frustration reading levels are easily detected as well as the recreational reading level. The instructional level may be somewhat more difficult to determine. Specific criteria have been associated with the informal reading inventory.

Table 4.1. INDIVIDUAL DIAGNOSTIC TESTS*

Title of Test	Age/Grade	Time	Description	Pub.
Bond-Balow-Hoyt Silent Reading Diagnostic Tests	grades 2–6	9:00–10:00	Group tests which measure silent reading abilities in 8 areas of word recognition: words in isolation, words in context, visual-structural analysis, syllabication, word synthesis, beginning sounds, ending sounds, vowel and consonant sounds. Tests should be administered in 3 sessions.	Lyons and Carnahan, Inc.
California Reading Test	grades 1–adult	0:23–1:08	This test battery yields two major scores for vocabulary and comprehension and a total score.	CTB/McGraw-Hill
Durrell Analysis of Reading Difficulty	grades 1–6	0:30–1:30	This test consists of 13 subtests: oral reading, silent reading, listening comprehension, word recognition and word analysis, naming letters, identifying letters, visual memory of words, hearing sounds in words, learning to hear sounds in words, learning rate, phonic spelling of words, spelling, and handwriting. It should be used with less severe cases.	Harcourt Brace Jovanovich, Inc.

*Adapted from Mauser, A. J. *Assessing the Learning Disabled.* San Rafael, California: Academic Therapy Publications, 1976. 95p.

continued

Title of Test	Age/Grade	Time	Description	Pub.
Gates-MacGinitie Reading Tests	grades 1–9	0:40–1:00	These tests consist of six different levels: primary A (grade 1); primary B (grade 2); and primary C (grade 3). These levels measure both vocabulary and comprehension. Primary CS (grades 2–3) measures speed and accuracy, vocabulary, and comprehension. Survey E covers the same categories for grades 7–9.	Teachers College Press
Gilmore Oral Reading Test	grades 1–8	0:15–0:20	This individually administered test consists of 10 paragraphs measuring comprehension, speed, and accuracy. It records pupil errors in: substitutions, mispronunciation, insertions, and omissions.	Harcourt Brace Jovanovich, Inc.
Gray Oral Reading Test	grades 1–adult	0:02–0:05	This test consists of 13 graded passages in each of four forms. It measures growth in oral reading, diagnoses reading difficulties, and assists with pupil placement in grades and reading groups.	Bobbs-Merrill Company, Inc.
McCullough Word Analysis Test	grades 4–6	8:10	These tests yield 10 scores: initial blends and diagraphs, phonetic discrimination, matching letters to vowel sounds, sounding whole	Personnel Research Institute

Title of Test	Age/Grade	Time	Description	Pub.
			words, interpreting phonetic symbols, phonetic analysis, dividing words into syllables, root words in affixed forms, structural analysis, and a total score. It should be administered in seven sessions.	
Spache Diagnostic Reading Scale	grades 1–adult	0:20–0:30	These individually administered tests identify reading deficiencies. They can be used with normal readers at the elementary level, and with retarded readers at the junior and senior high levels. The scales consist of three word-recognition lists, two reading passages, and eight supplementary phonics scores.	CTB/ McGraw-Hill
Stanford Diagnostic Reading Test	grades 2–8	1:50–2:00	This test identifies specific strengths and weaknesses in reading comprehension, vocabulary, syllabication, beginning and ending sounds, auditory skills, various aspects of phonetic analysis, and rate of reading. It should be administered in three sessions.	Harcourt Brace Jovanovich, Inc.

1.   The *independent level* is a level of supplementary dependent reading. The student should be able to read the book at home or at school without aid. The material should cause no difficulty. This is a level where oral reading and word calling is at 99% accuracy. The child will also comprehend 90% of the material.

2.   The *instructional level* is the actual teaching level. The reading material must be challenging and not too difficult. There is 95% accuracy in oral reading and word calling ability. Comprehension of content is 75% or higher.

3.   The *frustration level* is the level to be avoided. It is the lowest level of readability at which a child is able to understand. The material is too difficult and frustrates the pupil. There is less than 90% accuracy in oral reading and word calling. Comprehension is less than 50% and there are obvious distracting signs of tension and nervousness.

Increasing numbers of authorities in the field are challenging the percentages associated with required degree of accuracy in oral reading and comprehension that has been previously associated with informal reading inventories. This is especially true in the evaluation of reading performance of norm-violating youth.

Farr (1969) has been a proponent of the teacher construction of informal reading inventories. He supports the notion that when IRI's are used to plan an instruction, informal measurement procedures have more validity than do standardized tests. One of the major characteristics of the IRI which is attractive to most teachers is that the evaluation can be conducted with the same material as the student is using for instructional purposes. Teachers of chronically disruptive youth, as counselors and psychologists, must be aware of the IRI as a valuable evaluation technique.

The Cloze method of diagnosing comprehension

The Cloze technique has been used to evaluate the student's ability to comprehend certain materials. Bormuth (1962) suggests the deletion of every fifth word from a reading selection and asking students to fill in the blanks.

For middle-grade level students, the selection should be at least 500 words long if it is to provide a good notion of how well students are understanding the story line. Although certain purists will disagree, it is our belief that teachers who score Cloze exercises should accept reasonable replacements for the actual words that were deleted. Since Cloze procedure is only one kind of measure, it is actually only a rough estimation of comprehension ability.

In a 250-word passage, there would be 50 closures (every fifth word deleted). Each correct response counts for two percentage points. To be correct the student must supply the author's exact word, though it might be misspelled. That is the way the procedure has been standardized and that is the way the passage must be scored. Credit is not given for synonyms—what one person may consider a synonym another may not. The percentage score a student receives is used to determine his reading level for the passage.

58%–100% correct: independent level

44%– 57% correct: instructional level

0%– 43% correct: frustration level

The Bormuth-Cloze procedure is becoming increasingly popular with reading experts. Within the students' responses are evaluations of the author's style and technique as well as a revelation of the background of information and syntax of the students being tested. Workers with problem adolescents are encouraged to utilize Cloze techniques in their diagnostic reading programs.

Measuring attitudes

The attitudinal measurement of chronically disruptive youth toward reading materials is of utmost importance. Like comprehension, attitudes are difficult to measure. It is axiomatic that a student's affective response to reading selections is critical to becoming a reader. With this in mind, some kind of test measuring the problem adolescent's attitude to his reading experiences is an important aspect of the total evaluation process. If, in the process of learning to read, students learn to be bored with or even hate reading, the educational process is harmful rather than helpful to their growth in reading. Some individuals may actually feel that chronic problem behavior is based on these early negative experiences with reading.

Consistent measuring of attitudes toward reading is difficult if not impossible since the reading takes so many forms and means so many things to different students. For example, a student may enjoy reading the sports page or the comics of the local newspaper, but may be completely turned off by reading a library book to complete an English assignment. Whether or not the individual likes reading depends on what he is reading and for what purpose.

The most valid measures of a student's attitude toward reading would seem to be his response to individual selections. Since people tend to repeat pleasurable experiences and avoid unpleasant ones, we can assume that students who have more pleasurable than unpleasant reading experiences are probably learning to regard reading as a life-enrichment experience. The following scale has been useful in measuring students' attitudes toward reading selections. With possible modification, there is utility in its use for the norm-violating youth. One of the modifications might be to design rubber stamps with smiling faces equaling *strongly agree,* neutral faces equaling *uncertain,* and frowning faces equaling *strongly disagree.* A more descriptive scale for measuring attitudes is as follows:

1. I enjoyed reading this selection.

    ____Strongly Agree

    ____Agree

    ____Uncertain

    ____Disagree

    ____Strongly Disagree

2. This selection was boring.

    ____Strongly Agree

    ____Agree

    ____Uncertain

    ____Disagree

    ____Strongly Disagree

3. This selection held my attention.

    ____Strongly Agree

    ____Agree

    ____Uncertain

    ____Disagree

    ____Strongly Disagree

4. I disliked reading this selection.

    ____Strongly Agree

    ____Agree

    ____Uncertain

    ____Disagree

    ____Strongly Disagree

If the response choices are scored 5, 4, 3, 2, 1 for the positively stated items (numbers 1 and 3); and 1, 2, 3, 4, 5 for the negatively stated items (numbers 2 and 4); then a score of 20 would indicate the highest possible attitude; a score of 4, the lowest possible attitude. Numbers 1 and 3 can be checked against numbers 2 and 4 to determine the degree of consistency in the student's responses. The problem adolescent should not be expected to respond positively to all their reading experiences; but if the majority of their responses indicate negative attitudes against reading selections, something is wrong. One hopes that students would respond positively to most of the selections they read. If they are not in the reading program, it needs review and restructuring.

Criterion referenced testing for functional literacy

Criterion referenced testing is one of the most recent and fastest growing techniques for evaluating school achievement. Millman (1972) states that criterion referenced tests are used to measure performance against a specified criterion score without reference to the distribution of scores of others. This is in contrast to norm referenced tests which compare a student's score with others taking the test. The Individual Reading Inventory (IRI) was previously discussed when used with the child's existing reading materials as an example and modification of criterion referenced testing.

McDonald and Moorman described what may prove to have great promise for many norm-violating youths and their attempts to read. Although we take a most optimistic attitude toward the development of reading skills in problem adolescents, it is only reasonable to assume that some of these individuals will have extreme difficulty and possibly not reach a functional literacy, according to present-day standards. Standards of functional literacy are continuing to rise. Years ago literacy was regarded to fall at the fourth-grade level of ability. Many communities are beginning to designate the ninth-grade level of proficiency shall be regarded as the minimal level for functional literacy. McDonald and Moorman (1974) described twelve basic reading skills which an adult in higher society needs in order to function without handicaps. The twelve objectives comprise the basis of the Minimal Reading Proficiency Assessment (MRPA):

1. A functional reader will correctly identify stated main ideas.

2. A functional reader will correctly identify inferred main ideas.

3. A functional reader will correctly identify conclusions drawn from a stated and/or inferred main idea.

4. A functional reader will correctly identify stated supportive details.

5. A functional reader will correctly identify conclusions drawn from stated or inferred supportive details.

6. A functional reader will correctly identify stated and/or inferred sequences within selected contents.

7. A functional reader will correctly answer relationship questions such as cause and effect, fact and opinion, and/or time and space.

8. Given written directions, a functional reader will demonstrate the ability to follow those directions.

9. Given tasks using an index and/or table of contents, a functional reader will demonstrate the ability to complete the given task.

10. Given tasks using a dictionary, a functional reader will demonstrate the ability to complete the given task.

11. Given tasks for extracting information from graphs, tables, maps, charts, diagrams, pictures, and/or cartoons, a functional reader will demonstrate the ability to complete the given tasks.

12. Given tasks for using context clues, a functional reader will select an appropriate meaning for a given unfamiliar word.   (p. 364)

To measure student performance in the twelve skill areas, test items were developed. Derived from such sources as the daily newspaper, application blanks, contracts, drivers' manuals, city maps, and tax forms, over 150 test items were developed. Three criteria were established in selecting test items: (1) an item must relate to the student's interest; (2) an item must be answered correctly by approximately 75% of the students in the sample; and (3) an item should effectively discriminate between an adequate and inadequate reader. The preliminary research indicated this test is highly reliable and capable of isolating individual student reading deficiencies.

The chronically disruptive youth, when entering into or departing from an educational program in reading, may then be evaluated in terms of similar criterion-based functional literacy standards. Kelly (1974), in discussing survival literacy as it relates to understanding traffic signals, road maps, driver test manuals, lavatory signs, job want ads, and drug prescriptions, suggests the use of game types of devices to detect basic weaknesses and develop understanding of those concepts and basic areas necessary for present-day survival. His suggestions have much applicability and utility for problem adolescents with a severe reading disability.

INDIVIDUALIZING READING AND LEARNING
ENVIRONMENTS FOR CHRONICALLY DISRUPTIVE YOUTH

Placement decisions for chronically disruptive youth are based on a variety of factors. It is assumed that after thorough diagnosis and evaluation of the chronically disruptive youth's strengths and weaknesses, immediate action will take place to insure that specific recommendations related to his reading program will be fulfilled. As there will undoubtedly be a variety of patterns of reading behaviors, there must also be a variety of placement options that will include appropriate educational materials. Although much has been written about individual differences in children, we are still faced with a great amount of lip service and low levels of quality control related to educational placement of norm-violating youth.

The ancient axiom that success breeds success and failure breeds failure is still as true today as it was years ago. The environmental setting that one chooses to serve problem adolescents should be regarded as temporary in all cases. As problem adolescents change, other options must be available to them. Whatever environment is decided on, it must guarantee that the unique individual needs of chronically disruptive youth will be met in a more humanistic way than our conventional approaches which, in most cases, have been related to failure and boredom. Following are some descriptive terms often used in the field of reading that may additionally describe reading behavior of problem adolescents.

The retarded reader

Any student whose reading achievement is significantly below his grade placement may be called a retarded reader. This term indicates defective reading but does not limit the consequences that can develop from the use of it. Use of the term retardation has led to an erroneous connotation that implies the child is mentally retarded. The two concepts should not be confused.

The disabled reader

This term can be best applied to a student who is performing below his ability as measured by some test of general intelligence. Many educators stress the point that a certain arbitrary discrepancy must exist between achievement and potential. At one time, a two-year discrepancy was suggested as a lag sufficient to be considered a disability. Today, however, in dealing with young children we recognize that a child in first grade with a lag of even six months may experience enough difficulty to affect his personal/academic development.

The reluctant reader

A student who has the ability and *can* perform up to grade level but often does not, is called a reluctant reader. This student is usually erratic and inconsistent in his performance and does well in those subject areas he enjoys. When motivated, he achieves; when not motivated, he is usually called lazy by his teacher because of his erratic performance.

These terms are the most significant of all labels given to students with problems in reading. As indicated, a name alone does not amount to a means for approaching the problem. Instructionally, the labels used by the medical and educational professions are ambiguous. They often add to the problem of dealing with children who are experiencing difficulty.

Reading is a most important means for gaining skills, knowledge, attitudes, and values. Since norm-violating youth will differ greatly in their ability to deal with reading tasks, we will make short mention of some basic kinds of individual differences that will affect reading and contribute to the labeling process, which may determine the possible educational environment for chronically disruptive youth.

Experiences—past and present

Recognizing the fact that problem adolescents are different in many ways will lead us to regard that these differences are not discreet and isolated factors that can be studied under a microscope. Rather, the individual differences of chronically disruptive youth are enmeshed and interwoven into the life pattern of each of them. Each year in the life of the chronically disruptive youth adds to his uniqueness as a learner. This accumulation of life experiences which are oftentimes negative makes the teacher's job of identifying the child's special instructional needs more difficult.

Out-of-school experience, both past and present, are of extreme significance for problem adolescents in their relationship to the reading process. The uniqueness of these students is largely due to the type and richness of the everyday experiences they encounter. The experiences form the basis for all our concepts. Research has indicated that home environments that provide books, magazines, trips, good language patterns, parents who read, and other activities that require learning involvement tend to produce better readers. Chronically disruptive youth in most cases have been void of these past positive types of experiences. Negative experiences received from his home and community interactions can be related to self-concept deficiencies. Those experiences that build healthy egos and self-respect tend to make the complicated learning-reading progress for norm-violating youth a little easier.

Past and present school experiences of the chronically disruptive youth will have wide educational implications related to his success or failure. Varied and wide educational experiences conducted in the appropriate educational setting will have positive effects on the adjustment of problem adolescents. The more restricted and rigid the reading program or learning program for chronically disruptive youth, the more difficulty he will have in handling the total learning process. Placement decisions and teacher-ratio decisions, then, will definitely be affected by the experiential background of norm-violating youth who bring to the educational setting a set of behaviors fostered from and within this experiential background.

Differences within the student influencing placement

Although it is difficult to separate environmental or experiential factors from biological factors, many of the things done by chronically disruptive youth and other children relate back in some degree to biological heritage. Factors that may play a role in assignment to or formulation of a particular environment setting for problem adolescents and their reading problems will be discussed under the topics of (1) ability factors; (2) learning rates; and (3) fluctuation factors.

Educators and psychologists have many definitions for ability, but all recognize ability as an important factor in reading learning. Inherited ability is important because it helps us to (1) organize internally the incoming experiences we face daily; (2) adapt to our surroundings or external circumstances; and (3) assimilate and use our experiences to meet and cope with new situations and circumstances.

Much of the chronically disruptive youth's individual ability is determined by his biological endowments and his experiences within his environment. If inherent in the task of reading, there is a concern with bringing our knowledge and abilities to printed symbols, then our ability to both cope with and use symbols and to profit from experiences are necessary. The problem adolescent cannot take meaning from the symbols if he does not first have some understanding of the content he is to read. In the selection and design of an educational environment for norm-violating youth, the individual abilities of the student will not cause problems in reading unless the specific abilities are ignored or taken for granted.

As ability factors are important, we must also acknowledge that each chronically disruptive youth has his own learning rate. The learning rate of chronically disruptive youth, in many cases, will influence the time spent and duration factors associated with his educational placement. A learning rate of norm-violating youth varies in accordance with many factors. His health, interest, ability, prior knowledge of prerequisite skills, and the meaningfulness of the material he is expected to learn will effect the norm-violating youth's rate of learning. Problem adolescents cannot be typified as either slow, average, or rapid learners. Within a group of problem adolescents we will find individuals who exhibit learning rates associated with each of those categories. Certain chronically disruptive youth, regardless of the educational environment, will need more concrete and varied experiences than others. Many chronically disruptive youth possess superior reading skills and will need very little direct instruction or guidance by the teacher. Although there might be minimal direction on the part of the teacher in terms of instruction, the teacher must make frequent assessments in order to keep appraised of the pupil's present pace and level. Problem adolescents who possess significant emotional overlays will, in many cases, exhibit increased learning rates as these emotional contributors to learning failure are relieved. Many problem adolescents, like other students, may suffer from developmental lags. They oftentimes show rapid progression in reading or other areas in which they have been regarded as late bloomers. Most often these late bloomers are boys who appear to be slow learners in the first few grades. Often, difficulties tend to dissipate before the end of the fourth grade. One significant problem with the late bloomer concept is that too frequently parents of handicapped children, and in our particular case, chronically disruptive youth, develop false hopes for positive changes in behavior to happen. Probably the safest attitude to take is that we should make no wide generalizations about learning rate, but accept the fact that differences in problem adolescents do exist and must be considered when teaching reading in an appropriate personalized environment.

One of the most consistent descriptors of norm-violating youth is their behavioral fluctuation. Inconsistencies in interest, readiness, motivation, learning, drive, attention, and many other individual traits are qualities within the chronically disruptive youth that will affect reading progress, and possibly influence the individual's placement in a particular setting. Norm-violating youth are not always ready for new learning tasks. From time to time their behavioral characteristics work in direct opposition to any new learning activity. Chronically disruptive behavior from a cause-effect dilemma will contribute to peer relationship problems, home problems, personal problems, etc. Erratic and inconsistent behavior will influence placement decisions in terms of degree and kind of behavior.

REFERENCES

Ahlstrom, W. M., and Havighurst, R. J. *400 Losers*. San Francisco: Jossey-Bass, Inc. 1971.

Ball, E. A. "Visual Functioning in Reading Disability." *Education* 82 (1961): 175–178.

Benson, J. "Teaching Reading to the Culturally Different Child." *Readings on Reading*. Edited by Alfred R. Binter, John Diabal, and Leonard Kisi. Scranton, Pennsylvania: International Textbook Company, 1969.

Bernstein, B. "Language and Social Class." *British Journal of Sociology* 11 (1960): 271–276.

Betts, E. A. "A Physiological Approach to the Analysis of Reading Disability." *Educational Research Bulletin* (1934): 135–140, 163–173.

Betts, E. A., and Austin, A. S. *Visual Problems of School Children*. Chicago: Professional Press, 1941.

Bloomfield, L. "Linguistics and Reading." *Elementary English Review* 19 (1942): 125–130, 183–186.

Bond, G. L. *The Auditory and Speech Characteristics of Poor Readers*. New York: Bureau of Publications, Teachers College, Columbia University, 1935.

Bond, G., and Fendrick, P. "Delinquency and Reading." *Pedagogical Seminar and Journal of Genetic Psychology* 48 (1936): 236–243.

Bond, G. L., and Wagner, E. B. *Teaching the Child to Read*. New York: MacMillan, 1966.

Bormuth, J. R. Cloze Tests as Measures of Readability and Comprehension." Doctoral dissertation, Indiana University, 1962.

Buros, O. K. *The Seventh Mental Measurements Yearbook.* Highland Park, New Jersey: Gyphon Press, 1972.

Chomsky, N., and Halle, M. *Sound Pattern of English.* New York: Harper and Row, 1968.

Clay, M. M. "A Syntactic Analysis of Reading Errors." *Journal of Verbal Learning and Verbal Behaviors* 7 (1968): 434–438.

Clymer, T. "The Utility of Phonic Generalization in the Primary Grades." *The Reading Teacher* 16 (1963): 252–260.

Cohen, A., and Glass, G. G. "Lateral Dominance and Reading Ability." *The Reading Teacher* 21 (1968): 343–348.

Coleman, H. A. "The Relationship of Socioeconomic Status to the Performance of Junior High School Students." *The Journal of Experimental Education* 9 (1940).

Cozad, R., and Rousey, C. "Hearing and Speech Disorders among Delinquent Children." *Corrective Psychiatry and Journal of Social Therapy* 12 (1966): 250–255.

Critchley, M. "Reading Retardation, Dyslexia, and Delinquency." *British Journal of Psychiatry* 115 (1968): 1527–1547.

Dearborn, W. F., and Anderson, I. W. "Anisukonia as Related to Disability in Reading." *Journal of Experimental Psychology* 23 (1938): 559–577.

Dechant, E. U. *Improving the Teaching of Reading.* Englewood Cliffs, New Jersey: Prentice Hall, 1964.

Diskan, S. M. "Ego Problems in Children." *Postgraduate Medicine* 34 (1963): 168–178.

Durrell, D. D., and Murphy, H. A. "The Auditory Discrimination Factor in Reading Readiness and Reading Disability." *Education* 73 (1953): 556–560.

Dzik, D. "Vision and the Juvenile Delinquent." *Journal of the American Optometric Association* 37 (1966): 461–468.

Eames, T. H. "The Effect of Anisometropia on Reading Achievement." *American Journal of Optometry and Archives of American Academy of Optometry* 41 (1965): 700–702.

Elkind, D.; Horn, J.; and Schneider, G. "Modified Word Recognition, Reading Achievement, and Perception De-centralization." *Journal of Genetic Psychology* 107 (1965): 235–251.

Fabian, A. "Reading Disability: An Index of Pathology." *American Journal of Orthopsychiatry* 25 (1955): 319–329.

Farr, R. *Reading: What Can be Measured?* Newark, Delaware: International Reading Association, 1969.

Fries, C. C. *Linguistics and Reading.* New York: Holt, Rinehart, and Winston, 1963.

Gagne, R. M. *The Conditions of Learning.* 2nd ed. New York: Holt, Rinehart, and Winston, 1970.

Gates, A. I. "The Necessary Mental Age for Beginning Reading." *Elementary School Journal* 37 (1937): 497–508.

Gates, A. I., and Bond, G. L. "Relation of Handedness, Eye-Sighting, and Acuity Dominance to Reading." *Journal of Educational Psychology* 27 (1936): 455–456.

Gibson, E. J. "The Ontogeny of Reading." *American Psychologist* 25 (1970): 136–143.

Goetzinger, C. P.; Dirks, D. D.; and Baer, C. J. "Auditory Discrimination and Visual Perception in Good and Poor Readers." *Annals of Otology, Rhinology, and Laryngology* 69 (1960): 121–136.

Goodman, R. S. "Reading: A Psycholinguistic Guessing Game." *Theoretical Models and Processes of Reading.* Edited by H. Singer and R. B. Ruddell. Newark, Delaware: International Reading Association, 1970, 259–271.

Goodman, Y. M. "A Psycholinguistic Description of Observed Oral Reading Phenomenon in Selected Youth Beginning Readers." *Dissertation Abstracts* 29 (1968): 60.

Gough, H. G. "The Relationship of Socioeconomic Status to Personality Inventory and Achievement Test Scores." *Journal of Educational Psychology* 37 (1946): 535–536.

Gray, W. S. *The Teaching of Reading and Writing.* (A Unesco Report.) Chicago: Scott, Foresman, 1956.

Gray, W. S. "Reading and Physiology and Psychology of Reading." *Encyclopedia of Educational Research.* Edited by C. W. Harris. New York: MacMillan, 1960, 1086–1088.

Harris, A. J. *How to Increase Reading Ability.* New York: David McKay Company, Inc. 1970.

Hill, G. E. "Educational Attainment of Young Men Offenders." *Elementary School Journal* 36 (1935): 53–58.

Holmes, J. A. *The Substrata-Factors Theory of Reading.* Berkeley: California Book Company, 1953.

Jacobson, Frank. "Learning Disabilities and Juvenile Delinquency: A Demonstrated Relationship." *Handbook of Learning Disabilities.* Edited by Robert E. Weber. Englewood Cliffs, New Jersey: Prentice Hall, Inc., 1974.

Karlsen, B.; Madden, R.; and Gardner, E. *Stanford Diagnostic Reading Test.* New York: Harcourt, Brace, Jovanovich, 1966.

Kelly, L. P. "Survival Literacy: Teaching Reading to those with a Need to Know." *Journal of Reading* 17 (5) (February 1974): 352–355.

Kelly, T.; Madden, R.; Gardener, E.; and Rudman, H. *Stanford Achievement Test.* New York: Harcourt, Brace, Jovanovich, 1964.

Kelsay, R.; Chapman, R.; and Venezky, R. "How a Child Needs to Think to Learn to Read." *Cognition in Learning and Memory.* Edited by I. L. Gregg. New York: Wiley, 1971.

Kephart, N. C. "Visual Skills and their Relation to School Achievement." *American Journal of Ophthalmology* (Part 1) 36 (1953): 794–799.

Klasner, E. *The Syndrome of Specific Dyslexia.* Baltimore: University Park Press, 1972.

Knox, G. E. "Classroom Symptoms of Visual Difficulty." *Clinical Studies in Reading* (II Suppl. Educ. Monograph No. 77) (1953): 97–101.

Lane, H. A., and Witty, P. A. "Educational Attainment of Delinquent Boys." *Journal of Educational Psychology* 25 (1934): 695–702.

Lefevre, C. *Linguistics and the Teaching of Reading.* New York: McGraw-Hill, 1964.

Levin, H., and Watson, J. "The Learning Variable Grapheme to Phoneme Correspondences." (A Basic Research Program on Reading, Cooperative Research Project No. 639). Ithaca, New York: Cornell University, 1963.

Mauser, A. J. "Learning Disabilities and Delinquent Youth." *Academic Therapy Quarterly* 9 (6) (Summer 1974): 389–402.

Mauser, A. J. *Assessing the Learning Disabled.* San Rafael, California: Academic Therapy Publications, 1976.

McDonald, T. F., and Moorman, G. B. "Criterion Referenced Testing for Functional Literacy." *Journal of Reading* (February 1974): 363–366.

Millman, J. "Criterion Referenced Measurement: An Alternative." *The Reading Teacher* 26 (3) (December 1972): 278–281.

Morphett, M. V., and Washburne, C. "When Should Children Begin to Read?" *Elementary School Journal* 29 (1931): 496–503.

Neisser, U. *Cognitive Psychology.* New York: Appleton-Century-Crofts, 1967.

Park, G. E., and Burri, C. "The Relation of Various Eye Conditions and Reading Achievements." *Journal of Educational Psychology* 34 (1943): 290–299.

Patin, H. "Class and Casts in Urban Education." *Chicago School Journal* 45 (1964): 305–310.

Percival, W. P. "A Study of the Causes and Subjects of School Failure." Unpublished thesis, Teachers College, Columbia University, New York, 1926.

Poremba, C. "Learning Disabilities, Youth and Delinquency: Programs for Intervention." *Progress in Learning Disabilities,* edited by H. Myklebust. Vol. III, New York: Grune & Steatton, 1976, 123–149.

Reynolds, M. C. "A Study of Relationships between Auditory Characteristics and Specific Silent Reading Abilities." *Journal of Educational Research* 46 (1953): 439–449.

Riessman, F. *The Culturally Deprived Child.* New York: Harper and Row, 1962.

Roberts, G. R., and Lundser, E. A. "Reading and Learning to Read." *Development in Human Learning*. Edited by E. A. Lundser and J. F. Morris. New York: American Elsevier Publishing Company, 1968, 192–224.

Robinson, H. M. "The Major Aspects of Reading." *Reading: Seventy-five Years of Progress*. Edited by H. A. Robinson. Chicago: University of Chicago Press, 1966, 22–32.

Roman, M. "Tutorial Group Therapy, 1955." *Psychology in Teaching Reading*. Edited by H. P. Smith and E. V. Dechant. Englewood Cliffs, New Jersey: Prentice Hall, 1961.

Rosenblatt, L. M. "Towards a Transactional Theory of Reading." *Journal of Reading Behavior* 1 (1969): 31–49.

Ruddell, R. B. "Language Acquisition and the Reading Process." *Theoretical Models and Processes of Reading*. Edited by H. Singer and R. B. Ruddell. Newark, Delaware: International Reading Association, 1970, 1–19.

Ryan, E. B., and Semmel, M. I. "Reading as a Constructive Language Process." *Reading Research Quarterly* 4 (1969): 59–83.

Sabatino, D. A. "An Evaluation of Resource Rooms for Children with Learning Disabilities." *Journal of Learning Disabilities* 4 (1971): 84–93.

Sabatino, D. A. *Neglected and Delinquent Children*. Wilkes-Barre, Pennsylvania: Educational Development Center, Wilkes College, 1973.

Sabatino, D. A.; Mauser, A. J.; and Skok, J. "Educational Practices in Correctional Institutions." *Behavioral Disorders* 1 (1975): 21–26.

Schlichter, K. J., and Ratcliff, R. G. "Discrimination Learning in Juvenile Delinquents." *Journal of Abnormal Psychology* 77(1) (1971): 46–48.

Shearer, R. V. "Eye Findings in Children with Reading Difficulties." *Journal of Pediatric Ophthalmology* 3(4) (1966): 47–52.

Silberberg, M. C., and Silberberg, N. E. "School Achievement and Delinquency." *Review of Educational Research* 41(1) (February 1971).

Singer, H. "A Developmental Model of Speed of Receding in Grades Three through Six." *Theoretical Models and Processes of Reading,* edited by H. Singer and R. B. Ruddell. Newark, Delaware: International Reading Association, 1970, pp. 198–218.

Skinner, B. F. *Verbal Behavior*. New York: Appleton-Century-Crofts, 1957.

Smith, F. *Understanding Reading*. New York: Holt, Rinehart, and Winston, 1971.

Smith, R. J., and Barrett, T. C. *Teaching Reading in the Middle Grades*. Reading, Massachusetts: Addison-Wesley Publishing Co., 1974, 171–172.

Spache, G. D., and Tillman, C. E. "A Comparison of the Visual Profiles of Retarded and Nonretarded Readers." *Journal of Developmental Reading* 5 (1962): 101–109.

Sparks, J. A., and Mitzel, H. E. "A Reaction to Holmes' Basic Assumptions Underlying the Substrata-Factor Theory." *Reading Research Quarterly* 1 (1966): 137–145.

Spitzer, H. T., in collaboration with E. Horn, M. McBroom, H. A. Green, and E. F. Lindquist. *Iowa Every-Pupil Test of Basic Skills.* Boston: Houghton-Mifflin Co., 1964.

Staats, A. W. *Learning, Language, and Cognition.* New York: Holt, Rinehart, and Winston, 1968.

Staats, A. W.; Brewer, B. A.; and Gross, M. C. "Learning and Cognitive Development: Representative Samples, Cumulative-Hierarchical Learning, and Experimental-Longitudinal Models." *Monographs of the Society for Research in Child Development* 35 (1970): 1–85.

Staats, A. W.; Staats, C. K.; Schultz, R. E.; and Wolf, M. M. "The Conditioning of Reading Responses Using 'Extrinsic' Reinforcers." *Journal of Experimental Analysis of Behavior* 5 (1962): 33–40.

Sullivan, E. B. "Intelligence and Educational Achievement of Boys Entering Whittier State School." *Journal of Delinquency* 11 (1927): 23–38.

Templin, M. C. "Phonic Knowledge and its Relation to Spelling and Reading Achievement of Fourth-Grade Pupils." *Journal of Educational Research* 47 (1954): 441–454.

Thompson, B. B. A. "Longitudinal Study of Auditory Discrimination." *Journal of Educational Research* 56 (1963): 376–378.

Tomkins, C. "A Reporter at Large: The Last Skill Acquired." *The New Yorker* 1963. (Special printing of the Children's Neurological Development Program.)

Venezky, R. L., and Kelsay, R. C. "The Reading Competency Model." *Theoretical Models and Processes in Reading,* edited by H. Singer and R. B. Ruddell. Newark, Delaware: International Reading Association, 1970, pp. 273–291.

Venezky, R. L., and Weir, R. "A Study of Selected Spelling-to-Sound Correspondence Patterns." (Cooperative Research Project No. 3090) United States Office of Education, Stanford University, 1966.

Weber, R. M. "First Graders' Use of Grammatical Context in Reading." *Basic Studies on Reading.* Edited by H. Levin and J. P. Williams. New York: Basic Books, 1970, 147–163.

Wepman, J. "Dyslexia, Language and Concept Formation." *Reading Disability,* edited by J. Money. Baltimore: Johns Hopkins Press, 1962.

Williams, J. P. "Learning to Read: A Review of Theories and Models." *Reading Research Quarterly* 8(2) (Winter 1973): 121–146.

Witty, P., and Kopel, D. "Factors Associated with the Etiology of Reading Disability." *Journal of Educational Research* 29 (1936): 119–134.

5

institutionalization: history, influence, and the problem of recidivism

DAVID A. SABATINO

It is most difficult to review juvenile institutional programs and feel positive about how adults view youth. If the aims of society were noble in constructing institutions, far too frequently the good intentions were lost or confused at the program level. It is probably safe to summarize that the program components in most juvenile institutions for adjudicated youth reflect maintenance, not treatment. Countless institutional workers, both professional and paraprofessional, have worked timelessly to pave the way to successful societal adjustment for an equally countless number of youths. Their efforts have generally been unsuccessful, because the model used to obtain adjustment in the walls does not seem to transfer to public school and other community settings.

The history of institutionalization begins with the one-sided view that all crime is punishable, adult or juvenile. There was little differentiation among facilities for adults and juveniles until the mid-1800s. There was even less concern for programmatic differentiation, and that aspect may still be difficult to isolate. Consequently, the correctional educator has been kept fairly low in the pecking order of juvenile correctional workers. In fact, many juvenile institutions would place security and clinical treatment at the apex, and teachers and college workers at the base in any type of treatment hierarchically arranged. Yet, a review such as this one points out two facts. First, the history of institutions and the programs they offer generally yield low success rates if recidivism is the performance measure

181

used. Second, the only programs that demonstrated success are the academic and vocationally related school programs. They are only as successful as they are able to relate directly to sister facilities or other community agencies, particularly the public schools. If asked what kind of on-campus educational program is ideal, the answer would probably be one constructed with the public schools for those youths (approximately 25% that can go directly into vocational and college bound studies. The purpose is not to break their achievement output studies and reinforce their ability to compete with society at large. For the 75% who need remedial programs, the reader will sense that a traditional 1920 educational program still flourishes in the public schools. It is recommended this program be replaced with current special education delivery of service models, including special education teacher consultants, resource rooms, career information, work stations, job stations, and learning centers. After all, the reader must conclude that basic or regular education has already failed these youths; why should it persist? Indeed, a richer mix of remedial special, vocational, and career education seem to be the hope for the future.

THE DEVELOPMENT OF INSTITUTIONS

Institutions were first established in this country to protect society from the criminal class born to evil.

> The colonial period saw the eventual demise of corporal punishments (whipping, branding, the stocks) and of the punitive and deterrent rationale in the theory of "corrections." At this time, should the youthful offender be above the age of responsibility, as discussed earlier, he would be dealt with as an adult. The incidents of children being hanged occurred more frequently than one might imagine. Thus, as the confinement rather than punishment of adult offenders became the prevalent treatment mode, the youthful offender joined his adult counterpart within the institution.* (Atkinson, 1974, p. 174)

The approach adopted in this country of confining adolescent offenders to reformatories grew out of seventeenth-century houses of confinement in Europe and England. These were restricted habitats for the poor, unemployed, criminal prisoners and the insane. In 1684 the French government decreed that the houses of confinement should be divided into sectors for males and females if they were below the age of 25. That same decree specified that work was to occupy the greater portion of the day, accompanied by reading pious books. "They will be made to work

---

*Reprinted by permission of University of Michigan Press.

as long and as hard as their strength and situation will permit . . . will be punished by reduction of fuel, by increase of work, by imprisonment and other punishment customary in said hospitals, as the director shall see fit.''   (Foucault, 1973, p. 60)

> This first house of refuge was little more than a separate prison, walled, built upon the congregate (connected or single buildings) housing plan. Incarceration, not rehabilitation, was its primary purpose . . . The Phila-delphia House of Refuge was opened in 1828 along much the same lines as the other two, and for the same express purpose: to prevent youngsters from learning the vices of their criminal elders. . . The first nonpunitive reformatory, dedicated to the correction of destructive and vicious youths through proper guidance and tutelage, was opened in Westboro, Massachusetts, in 1848 under the direction of Dr. Samuel G. Howe. Utilizing a congregate housing plan, imbued with the nurture theory of behavior, influenced by the mood of urban disenchantment, this innova-tive approach to the treatment of youthful offenders was plagued with failure from its inception. Farmers in the area were unwilling to accept placement of children. Financial strains were aggravated by overcrowd-ing. Finally, a fire destroyed most of the institution in 1859. . . It was left to the Ohio State Reform School, established in 1854 under the direc-tion of another Howe, Dr. G. E. Howe, to successfully implement the new theories of behavior modification and socialization in a minimal security, unwalled cottage plan institution. This, the first true industrial school, stressed individualized treatment, practical technical or agricul-tural training, with strong doses of religion and physical education.*
>
> (Atkinson, 1974, pp. 174–175)

Prisons for youthful criminals became reform schools. Physicians dominated the correctional scene and therapeutic procedures to identify, diagnose, cure, and control the ''illness'' were initiated.

> The Whittier State School in Whittier, California, was originally opened in 1899. The school had eleven cottages on a 226-acre site. The superintendent of the facility was a physician; the assistant superintendent had only a high school education. The regular staff included eight school teachers, nine vocational instructors, three nurses, and thirty-eight group supervi-sors. The teachers were all certified by the state board of education, but there were no minimum qualifications for group supervisors. A psycholo-gist and psychiatric social worker were irregularly available to render clinical services to those children who had been singled out by the staff for psychiatric evaluation . . . The Boy's Vocational School in Lansing, Michigan, was originally opened under the auspices of the state correc-tions authority as an industrial school. The shift in title from industrial

---

*Reprinted by permission of University of Michigan Press.

> school to vocational school was an indication of the shift in emphasis
> from agricultural training to the teaching of skills more useful in the ur-
> ban environment.*   (Atkinson, 1974, p. 175)

As the medical cures failed, sociological research having identified the problems of the slums, broken homes, poverty, and a lack of employment skill
began to promote theories of supposed treatment. Reformatories were rede-
veloped to provide a family environment for parentless children.

For all practical purposes, the institutions for delinquent youth were
aimed at stabilizing society by removing deviant and dependent children.
Any concern for effectiveness of these traditional, outmoded, and bor-
rowed European practices was not a factor in their rapid establishment.
Rothman (1971, p. x, p. iii) states, "The almshouse and the orphan asylum,
the penitentiary, the reformatory, and the insane asylum, all represent an
effort to insure cohesion of the community in new and changing circumstances."

> Within a period of fifty years, beginning in the nineteenth century, not only
> was the penitentiary discovered and spread across the face of the colonies,
> but by 1860, twenty-eight of the thirty-three states had asylums for the
> insane. This development was coincidental with sudden rapid growth of the
> colonies and antedated only slightly the development of compulsory educa-
> tion and correctional programs for youth.   (Rhodes and Head, 1974, p. 27)

With the advent of the industrial revolution and urbanization, treatment at any cost was too slow and probably too ineffectual. Increased
governmental control growing out of depression-fighting mechanisms
mounted the juvenile court movement which went far beyond any thought
for special treatment. Institutions became symbols of the period, reflecting
the changes in society and, in particular, family life.

> One of the main forces behind the child-saving movement was a concern for
> the structure of family life and the proper socialization of young persons,
> since it was these concerns that had traditionally given purpose to a
> woman's life.   (Platt, 1969, pp. 26–27)

The child-saver movement became a permanent aspect of American
life when it was incorporated into the juvenile court system. The whole idea
of new categories of childhood social deviance, e.g., incorrigibility,
truancy, neglect, vicious and immoral behavior, were born.

---

*Reprinted with permission of University of Michigan Press.

> The juvenile-court movement went far beyond a concern for special treatment of adolescent offenders. It brought within the ambit of government control a set of youthful activities that had been previously ignored or dealt with on an informal basis. (Platt, 1969, p. 29)

Society rationalized the rapid growth of institutions as a measure to protect children against the hazards of life which they were not equipped developmentally to confront. "There is no lot as, we all know, so hopeless and helpless as that of a destitute orphan; its career of sin and ill, when neglected, is almost certain . . ." (Cincinnati Orphan Asylum, Annual Report for 1848, p. 3). The Boston Asylum and Reform School was constructed to provide for children suffering from "abodes of raggedness and want, where mingled with the cries of helpless need, the sounds of blasphemy assail your ears; and from example of father and of mother, the mouth of lisping childhood is taught to curse and revile" (Rothman, 1971, p. 170). By 1899 the child savers had already established the first juvenile court in Chicago. Again, the justification was still the same—that asylums and institutions were necessary for the moral treatment of helpless youth in preparing them for the great society promised in the American dream; when, in fact, the caretakers, as they preferred to call themselves, were attempting to revalue children who represented a value structure not condoned by general society.

By the early 1900s, child guidance clinics were beginning in Chicago and Boston. A new progressivism, weak minds and predispositions for evil had begun to give way to organized mental health movement. In 1921, a national conference on the prevention of juvenile delinquency was held. The outcome was the five-year demonstration request for child guidance clinics which yielded the famous Healy and Bronner Report (1926). For the first time, community treatment centers began to replace the idea of the asylum which essentially was operated on an out-of-sight, out-of-mind principle.

> The clinic or "center" had supplanted the asylum as the institutional defense against the menacing presence of irrationality without and within. We no longer needed to wall out this infectious menace. We now had the tools for threat-reduction through scientific labels, and isolate through programs of intervention. The populations at risk were still the destitute, the powerless, and the culturally different. The preferred image was still the character type, behavioral pattern and life style of "successful," "hard-working," "gratification-delaying," "stable" middle-class Anglo-Saxon culture-bearers living quietly behind the doors of their own homes, on their own property, in peaceful neighborhoods. Now, however, with the advent of social sciences, and the technologies of social services, there was an ob-

jectively validated rationale for one's character-trait and life-style preferences. There were indices of pathology determining who was not socially
and emotionally adapted. It was not a matter of arbitrary personal prejudice or social power. It was now a matter of science—the new national
Church; and thus the whole social institution of mental health came into
being. The partnership between bourgeois order and medicine, formed
around the threat of irrationality at the time of the Reformation and the dis-
appearance of the scourge of leprosy, moved away from the religious am-
biance of "moral treatment" into the aura of "public health." The powerful empirical antibodies of medical diagnosis and medical treatment would
now be applied to social ills, through the invasion of disorganized community members. Medical treatment provided further protection against the
contamination of the individual by individual through the psychological distance of the subject-object split maintained by modern science. Psychological mechanisms of displacement and projection were legitimized by this sep-
aration between the excitor and reactor. No longer did sane and insane
share sin in common. The disease was within the excitor, not a mutual bond
between excitor and reactor. The disease was communicable, but modern
asepsis was more powerful than stone walls for protection against this type
of transmission. No longer did the dominant culture-bearer have to look
into the mirror of irrationality and say, "We have seen the enemy and they
are us." Now, the threat to collective orderliness lay without.

(Rhodes and Head, 1974, p. 30)

Institutional growth continued to reflect society in general following
the great depression. The depression had brought what would eventually be
vocation education in the institution. Skills for gainful employment were
taught by having the youth take active roles in farming, shoe making, furni-
ture repair, etc. Vocational craftsmen, known as tradesmen, were employed
for the first time. No longer were incarcerated youths merely a source of
cheap labor within the institution. The work in the institution served to
teach skills that provided gainful employment upon release.

The First World War had alerted the American people to the number
of functional illiterates in this country. Research in the 1920s and 1930s
exposed the relationship between poor academic achievers and delinquency.
School programs teaching academic subject material in institutions began in
the 1920s. Remedial education was added in the 1930s, and special education in the 1940s. Special education was added to institutional programs emphasizing a concern for the mentally retarded delinquent and later those
with serious emotional disturbances.

World War II had brought new meaning to an old word. Rehabilitation of the returning veteran, wounded or suffering from the strain of com-
bat, through the veteran administration programs emphasized a number of
relatively previously unheard of therapies. Speech and language therapy,

physical and occupational therapy, and various forms of counseling and psychotherapy became household words. Institutional programs began to reflect these various therapeutic forms, especially those emphasizing counseling and psychotherapy. These approaches directed at modifying behaviors associated with delinquency were natural extensions of the sociological treatments of the early 1900s (teaching values and restricting family life by pioneering a home away from the poor-home model, which the sociologists agreed produced delinquency).

The psychological approach did not emphasize the generation of a healthy institutionalized "home" environment as had the sociological approach. The psychological approach attempted to produce a healthy person, capable of making good personal decisions not dependent upon a particular home environment. The prohibiting problem to the psychological approach was the extreme cost in providing individual and even group psychological-psychiatric treatment to incarcerated youth. A lack of professional manpower to work in institutions may have been based on the semi-militaristic disciplines and beliefs which existed in them. Finally, however, the evidence which seemed to result from psychological treatment was not always the most rewarding in favor of that treatment approach.

It would appear that in the development of institutions, they have completed a full cycle. They have tried almost all existing forms of treatment programs; beginning with instruction in moral principles through medical, sociological, educational, vocational, and psychological approaches leading to community participation. Probably, to a great extent, the public still sees a correctional institution as a place to punish crime and evil. Therefore, it is punishment of the person, not the behavioral act, that must, in the public eye, always be considered. In a civilized country one form of punishment is to remove a person from his daily routine and place him into a controlling environment for a period of time. Institutional correctional educators and administrators must be concerned with the question of whether time heals. They must also educate society to the realization that institutions have never served as a deterrent for crime, or habilitated or rehabilitated criminals. Institutions merely contain them, protecting society. The only hope for treatment is community treatment facilities, especially for youthful offenders. What is needed are more alternatives to those currently existing, and joint cooperative ventures between treatment agencies.

Institutional educational administrators and their staff must make decisions about the programs their institutions will offer. The problem with treatment programs in the past is that they were one-sided, one of a kind; *all* the youth had to fit the structured program. That never works. It appears that prescriptions of need based on a planned program for a given child are in order. They can be effective if an institution has the range of programs necessary to fit the program to the youth. Comprehensive programs for the 1970s to meet complex social-personal-cultural problems are necessary. The institution must become a part of the social order, not be separate from it.

Reynolds (1962) has described a hierarchy of special education programs that deserves our attention for two reasons. First, it plainly reveals that a youth should not be placed into an institutional program until every available aspect of community treatment is explored and eliminated as a possibility. It is simply not good enough to have residential institution and regular public school classes. A system of alternatives are needed between these two extremes. It is not appropriate to institutionalize a youth for his failure to conform to a regular class, regular school, or regular society—especially during a period of crisis in his life. Figure 5.1 provides a flow of the alternatives Reynolds deems important for handicapped children. Many of these same alternatives, interwoven between school and community, would make a set of salient features for adjudicated youth

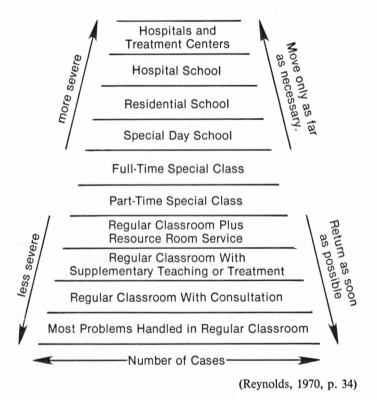

(Reynolds, 1970, p. 34)

Figure 5.1. Special Education Programs

The 1970s marked the period of prevention and community involvement with greater attention being paid to these aspects than ever before. Project Newgate, furlows, pre-release, and community treatment are common expressions in our current correctional conversations.

> The Highfields and Silverlake experiments have been well documented (McCorkle, Elias, and Bixby, 1958; Empey and Lubeck, 1971) as two of the more promising new approaches to institutional interventions. Both are aimed at normal, adjudicated delinquent boys of fifteen to eighteen years who have been diagnosed as having ecologically-based deviance problems. However, they differ in their approaches to the environmental intervention. Highfields has modified a modernized rural congregate plan for a small number of boys into a simulation of a real environment. Silverlake leaves the child within the troubling environment while utilizing peer group therapy to teach the boy to cope with that environment. Both emphasize "job training" and "career counseling and placement" as an integral part of their program. The primary treatment mode at Highfields has been the guided group interaction.* (Atkinson, 1974, p. 176)

The working institutional administrator has three major tasks in making community-based programs work. First, he must convince society that delinquency is a community problem, not a problem for a person or a family. Therefore, his efforts to educate the community at large on what he expects to do, is doing, and needs to do must be achieved.

> Perhaps the most touted new development in institutions has been the implementation of the "return to community" treatment mode through the halfway or group home concept.† (Atkinson, 1974, p. 176)

Second, he must continue to upgrade the institution's staff until they are capable of employing efforts directed at altering poorly-developed behavioral patterns or a lack of behavioral alternatives for chronically disruptive youth. Finally, he must work to facilitate articulation among all the agencies that teach a chronically disruptive youth the values of life. A liason of public, private, community, state, and federal relationships with single goal statements clearly communicated are the only way institutions can function in the societal mainstream. If the institution fails to achieve that position, it is merely a backdoor for society to close out its ugly members. If that is true, then we have not advanced in our belief of human nature since the Renaissance.

---

*Reprinted with permission of University of Michigan Press.

†Reprinted with permission of University of Michigan Press.

Current trends

Correctional educators and in particular, correctional administrators, must formulate a position as to their roles in the total correctional decision-making process. From state to state, the role of the institution varies depending on its decision-making autonomy and the very important interagency liaison among the agencies who focus on youth. Unlike the public schools, correction agencies serve the courts, the mental health system, the mental retardation program, the state's justice system, as well as relating to federal justice, local and state police, and public education. The juvenile judges, elected officials, are a political force that must be brought into the planning in any state. Correctional educators simply do not have the privilege to develop programs in isolation; nor do they have the right to administer existing programs in the absence of cooperative planning. In fact, working interagency councils appear to be an important consideration. The danger resulting from limited or poor interagency articulation is a disrupted flow of programs. That is a far cry from a continuum of services, beginning and ending in the communities. *The youth of any community are the responsibility of that community.* Norm-violating behaviors are not the sole responsibility of the youth, schools, courts, or other community agency. To rationalize, accuse another agency, or deny the complexity of this issue, is most certainly a by-product of the threat and jealousy imposed in the difficulty of offering the wide span of services which these youth need. Isolated program aspects force youth to fit programs, the danger being recidivism and restricted social learning which is learned for the purposes of passing through one setting with little transfer to another setting. The end goal is to achieve success in the program, not achieve adjustment directed toward successful living in the community.

To develop social programs, Graham (1962) stresses an active participation in legislation to help the lawmakers understand what is needed for tomorrow's citizens. His second consideration is that current programs must be accepted as community effort and responsibilities. As long as they are red brick buildings off someplace in another town, an "out-of-sight, out-of-mind" philosophy will prevail. Graham also notes that the most important aspect to achieve a balanced program is one with enough alternatives that offers something to every child without bending the child to fit the program.

DYNAMICS OF AN INSTITUTION

In 1965, Pulliam (Homans, 1975) described 16 major training departments responsible for specialized services to the residents:

1. Department of Clinical Services
2. Psychiatric Services Division
3. Psychological Services Division
4. Social Service Division
5. Religious Education Division
6. Cottage Life Division
7. Nursing Service Division
8. Academic Education Division
9. Vocational Education Division
10. Physical Education Division
11. Recreational Division
12. Department of Business Services
13. Fiscal and Personnel Division
14. Supply Division
15. Maintenance Division
16. Dietary Division

The dynamics of an institution certainly result from the goals for that institution, its purposes, and missions. Goffman (1961, p. 13) defined the *total institution* as a place of residence and work where a large number of like-situated individuals, cut off from the wider society for an appreciable period of time, together lead an enclosed, formally administered round of life. He lists five types of institutions.

1. Those established for the care of persons who are incapable of developing self-help skills which generate fully independent living.
2. Those established to care for persons incapable of self-care and who also provide a threat to society.
3. Those established to protect society from the inmate within.
4. Those established to accomplish a specific goal or mission—a military base is given as an example.
5. Those which are retreats from the world, for example, monasteries, etc.

One of the distinctions of a total institution is that all aspects of life are conducted in the same place, and under the same administrative provisions. That reality exists because institutions for delinquents have a small supervisory staff which manages a large number of residents. Therefore, unlike most social orders, the social mobility between the two strata is grossly restricted with the resulting social distance being prescribed in hard boundaries. The problem of the total institution is that the job of administrating it is a mechanical one. Thus, the people in it become objects whose lives are bent to fit a goal, a mission, a program, a place to work, a place to live. Most certainly the majority of institutions for delinquents fit that description, and not because they wish to do so.

The only common concern is how to institute and achieve behavioral change. What is frequently lost in the translation of human behavioral change is what aspects are natural or normal learning, and what change is relearning. Socialization is a normal developmental task that is learned naturally. Although it must be taught, it doesn't require relearning; just everyday exposure, well-taught by modeling. Many delinquent youths have not learned appropriate social values; therefore, models, values, and social, as well as adaptive skill behaviors must be taught. That is entirely different from focusing on resocialization which implies unlearning and relearning. Therefore, the massive lumping of youth into institutions on a geographic basis, through court assignment without thought of provisions for treatment, should be questioned. The differentiation of treatment by offering specialization in cottage living, school, vocational programs, or the type of treatment personnel available is highly desirable. At least three different types of institutions with a distinct type of staff can be identified:

1. The first type is one that provides for primary social learning. This facility would be primarily for young offenders who have no symptoms of psychopathology and have never had the opportunity to learn normative social values or adapt their social values to that of the larger society. (This is an educational facility.)

2. The second type is a people-changing institution which provides retraining. It assumes the youth has learned an unacceptable pattern of behavior and refuses to utilize an appropriate behavioral alternative. Frequently, job training and working through feelings about authority and hostility toward the larger social order are necessary. (This is an educational facility with a clinical treatment support staff.)

3. The third type is for those with mental, emotional, or physical handicaps that inhibit learning or relearning social, educational, or vocational skills. Brain injury, psychopathology, and mental retardation are examples of such problems. It is true that this would not be a high incidence of youth, but it is unquestionably a group who desires special consideration. In a study of poorly adjusting offenders in a large state institution, Truxal and Sabatino (1973) found that over one-half of the chronic referrals to that institution's behavior court had known histories of acute problems associated with neurological deficits, e.g., seizures, head injuries, recurring headaches, or severe illnesses resulting in comitose or semi-comitose conditions. (This is a clinical treatment facility

with a strong special education component for seriously emotionally disturbed youth.)

A major issue confronting the administrator of an institution for delinquent youth has been the inability to differentiate the youth diagnostically for treatment purposes. Generally, most youthful offenders receive similar treatment. The major variation is in the amount of treatment received, not the type. People-changing organizations which emphasize socialization seek to prepare persons to undertake normal social, educational, and other learning experiences within the institution. Resocialization requires the person to eradicate or undo previously learned behavior. Therefore, his or her corrective time must be longer, and the range of behaviors displayed will be more inappropriate, with a greater number of trial-and-error approximations to obtain a desired behavioral display. Most institutions are a mixture of the two treatment processes. School or educational programs are socializing processes. Clinical treatment, individual remediation, and one-on-one work experiences are used to obtain resocialization. Treatment of psychopathology requires a total therapeutic milieu which seldom exists in state facilities for adjudicated youth.

The question as to whether an institution can be both a custodial and treatment center must be answered in the negative. Why can't some children merely receive custodial maintenance, while others are offered the opportunity for treatment? If the institution is neatly divided in half, then it is possible. Generally speaking, the goals are so different that it is impossible to administer, budget, or recruit trained personnel for a custodial facility in a manner similar to a treatment facility.

Street, Vinter, and Perrow (1966) discuss the problem of institutions with multiple goals. They raise the issues that cause administrators difficulty in making judgments about what a program should be. The major problem that they cite is how various staff groups and segments in society interpret *rehabilitation* and *custody*. The inability of institutions with multiple goals is to define specific operational patterns, particularly when staff and residents are in discord over the purposes of the institution. They write:

> Research on the correctional institution typically has been addressed to contradictions between the requirements of the goals of confinement (custody) and of change (rehabilitation) . . . a problem that we have suggested constitutes a major characteristic of the people-changing organization.
>
> Several sources of difficulty arise in judging effectiveness in the case of the juvenile correctional institution. First, the relatively ambiguous dual

goals generate conflict and uncertainty both inside and outside. Various staff groups and special publics may give different interpretations to "rehabilitation" and "custody" and propose different priorities. Second, whatever the particular balance of official purposes, the generality and ambiguity of these goals fail to provide a clear-cut basis for deriving specific operational patterns—thereby stimulating contention over the most appropriate types of interaction between staff and inmates. Third, the relative absence of feedback information about the inmates' subsequent behavior prevents a choice of means based on demonstrable outcomes. Recidivism rates have been utilized, but the effects of the institutional experience are usually confounded with the influences of other social systems in which the releasees act. Moreover, crude rates of recommitment connot be used to assess the relative efficacy of differentiated practices within the institution.

These difficulties in judging effectiveness have a number of important consequences. We have suggested that the organization must develop an inferential way of making assessments. Perspectivism and an emphasis on ideologies are heightened and, because personnel subgroups adhere to somewhat different belief and value systems, there is likely to be conflict. This gives additional impetus to the focus on immediate inmate behavior. The process can be seen as a tendency toward goal displacement through an overemphasis on means. In more traditional institutions the shift of attention to internal processes results in an emphasis on procedures for control and stability and on protective architecture . . .*

(Street, Vinter, and Perrow, 1966, pp. 13–14)

It is interesting to note that Street, Vinter, and Perrow differentiate *people-processing* institutions from *people-changing* institutions. People-changing institutions establish the major goal of behavioral modification and develop all program efforts toward those ends. People-processing institutions focus on people, but mainly to serve them, providing sustenance and welfare; the major program effort is changing the environment for the achievement of that goal.

INSTITUTIONAL PROGRAM MODELS

Street, Vinter, and Perrow (1966) have described three different types of instructions on a custody-treatment continuum. These are:

Obedience/Conformity. Habits, respect for authority, and training in conformity are emphasized. The technique is conditioning. Obedience/conformity maintains undifferentiated views of its inmates, emphasizes immediate accommodation to external controls, and utilizes high levels of

---

*Reprinted with permission of MacMillan Publishing Company.

staff domination with many negative sanctions. It is the most custodial type of juvenile institution presently found in the United States, for humanitarian pressures have eliminated the incarceration-deprivation institution as a viable empirical type.

Re-education/Development. Inmates are to be changed through training. Changes in attitudes and values, acquisition of skills, the development of personal resources, and new social behaviors are sought. Compared to the obedience/conformity type, this type provides more gratifications and maintains closer staff-inmate relations.

Treatment. The treatment institution focuses on the psychological reconstitution of the individual. It seeks more thorough-going personality change than the other types. To this end it emphasizes gratifications and varied activities, with punishments relatively few and seldom severe. In the individual treatment-variant, considerable stress is placed on self-insight and two-person psychotherapeutic practices. In the milieu treatment-variant, attention is paid to both individual and social controls, the aim being not only to help the inmate resolve his personal problems but also to prepare him for community living.*

(Street, Vinter, and Perrow, 1966, p. 21)

FORMAL ORGANIZATION

The institution has two immediate environments to which it must relate. There is the world beyond the gate, especially those aspects which relate directly to the institution, such as juvenile courts, welfare agencies, public schools, legislative and executive branches of state government, department of corrections, etc. Second, internal to the institution are the cottages or residence halls, work stations, and treatment facilities and personnel. It is beyond the scope of this section to examine the *informal* organization of an institution, simply because every institution in the United States has a different informal organization. An informal organization is the communication system within any organization that does not parallel the formal table of organization. Theoretically, at least, the nearer the formal and informal organizations are in fact, the smoother the operation and the less conflict. Conflict within an institution is generally represented by snafus in the communication process. At least they are the symptoms. It is a belief held by many practicing administrators that communication breaks down for other reasons than just the fact that some one person isn't talking or writing to another in the same organization. That is the reason that communication difficulties are discussed as symptoms of the overall organization.

*Reprinted with permission of MacMillan Publishing Company.

THE EFFECTIVENESS OF INSTITUTIONAL PROGRAMS

The discussion thus far in this chapter has focused on the juvenile institution for adjudicated youth and its conceptual role in society. The question of how effective institutions have been has not been fully answered in the first part of this chapter. The issues associated with evaluating any program or faculty resides in measuring the output of that organization against its stated objectives or mission statements. The primary difficulty with institutions for adjudicated youth is isolating a usable output or performance measure. In the absence of agreement on what constitutes an acceptable performance measure, two such output perimeters are fairly obvious. These are: recidivism, or reduction in recidivism, which simply states that once a youth is released from an institution he does not reappear in that or another institution. The second is objective measurement of the effects of selected institutional programs. The remainder of this chapter will focus on these two considerations.

RECIDIVISM

Recidivism remains high in percentage from state to state. It is alarmingly high, exceeding 75% in many states. In the 1960 census, 45,000 youths were in institutions for delinquents. Another 33,000 under 20 years of age were in federal and state penitentiaries or reformation facilities. In addition, 12,000 were in detention homes, detention centers, or diagnostic and reception units. The serious question raised by the prevalence of recidivism reflects on the current practices of institutional management and resulting amelioration of norm-violating behaviors in troubled youth. One problem in the treatment of delinquency is the definitions of delinquency are vague and ambiguous. There has been a pronounced practice for treatment agencies to group delinquents together for rehabilitative purposes. In spite of the variation in youth classified as delinquent, the practice of homogeneous grouping in institutions continues, thus exposing the questionable nature of institutionalization as practiced, for norm-violating youth.

Most treatment agencies tend to function upon a primary rationale of economics. The greatest economic advantages of such programs occur merely as an artifact of the preexisting social organization of services. (Feldman, Wodarski, Goodman, & Flax, 1973). Feldman, Wodarski, Goodman, and Flax suggest "the ultimate economic efficacy of a program must depend primarily upon a single intention, namely, the extent to which the treatment program is successful in enabling clients to maintain long-term social adjustment in the open community.'' (p. 30.) However, as is so obviously apparent, available data does not validate the criterion, especially in the areas of antisocial children and juvenile delinquents.

In order to delimit the harmful effects of rehabilitation on the youth's self-concept as well as others' view of them, it would seem essential that such programs operate in an atmosphere where these effects are not transmitted. If treatment programs could function among peers not labeled as delinquent, their stigmatizing effects would be eliminated. The case against treatment via segregation is increasing. The awareness of concerned people needs to be shared, including the evolution data of accountable treatment programs.

In another study (Ganzer & Sarason, 1973) several variables were isolated and found to be directly associated with recidivism among juvenile delinquents. Recidivists got into trouble and were first institutionalized at younger ages, had lower estimated verbal intelligence, and were more frequently diagnosed as sociopathic personality than were non-recidivists. Females more frequently came from disrupted or disorganized families than did males. Background variables consisted of (1) marital status of neutral parents; (2) socioeconomic status; and (3) family contact with law enforcement agencies. Only a slightly greater proportion of recidivists than non-recidivists came from broken homes. Socioeconomic status was not related to recidivism for either sex, and there was no appreciable difference between recidivists and non-recidivists in family contacts with the police.

McClintock and Bottoms (1973) initiated a long term study on the reasons for the failure of the Borstal System to prevent recidivism in England. Their work commenced in 1962. It was primarily a research effort to understand the reasons institutional treatment was not achieving greater success. They found that age 18 was the median age for arrests and convictions of youthful offenders, representing 33% of the total number. A breakdown of nonviolent crimes committed by youth by category revealed that 35% were breaking offenses, and 29% were offenses against another person, which also included personal robbery. Table 5.1 provides the percent of offenders for each type of criminal activity.

McClintock and Bottoms (1973) also provide data on the length of criminal activity in relation to the offender's age (Table 5.2), age relationship between just correction and initial institutionalizations (Table 5.3), type of offense and evidence of criminal associations (Table 5.4), and distribution of offenders according to degree of previous recidivism and type of current offense (Table 5.5).

Younger offenders have shorter recorded periods of criminal activities. Older criminals, above 19, tend to demonstrate chronic criminal activities. The length of time between first conviction and sentencing decreases with age. It is generally true that most juvenile courts attempt to keep youthful first-time offenders from institutionalization. Minor thefts are higher for youth not associated with others, but robbery and thefts of major proportion generally occur with youths working in relationship to other youths, or even gang members. Except for violent crimes against another person, including robbery and nonpersonal robbery (property), all other crimes increase with the number of convictions.

Table 5.1. BREAKDOWN, BY CATEGORY, OF NONVIOLENT CRIMES COMMITTED BY YOUTH

	Main Categories of Crime	*Number of Offenders*	*Percent*
I.	Offenses against the person (including robbery)	88	(28.8)%
II.	Breaking offenses (not involving personal violence)	106	(34.6)%
III.	Thefts* (not connected with violence or breaking offenses)	57	(18.6)%
IV.	Theft or unlawful taking of motor vehicles (not involving other theft)	39	(12.8)%
V.	Damage to property	5	(1.6)%
VI.	Other crimes	11	(3.6)%
		306	(100.0)%

*Thefts here include frauds, false pretenses, and receiving stolen property. (McClintock & Bottoms, 1973, p. 13)

Treatment relevance

Martinson and his team delved (1974) into rehabilitation programs of the New York State Parole system. The author states: ". . . a rather bald summary of our findings: with few and isolated exceptions, the rehabilitative efforts that have been reported thus far have had no appreciable effect on recidivism." A previous study by New York State (1964) found that for young males as a whole, the degree of success achieved in the regular prison academic education program, as measured by changes in grade achievement levels, made no significant difference in recidivism rates. Jacobson (1965) studied a program of *skill reeducation* for institutionalized young males consisting of 10 weeks of daily discussions aimed at developing problem-solving skills. Overall, the program produced no improvement in recidivism rates.

Similarly, a study on vocational training was conducted by Zivan (1966) at the Children's Village in Dobbs Ferry, New York. There was a logical sequencing of steps in preparation for the youth's adequate adjustment in a vocation: assessment counseling, development counseling, and pre-placement counseling. In addition, they participated in an occupational orientation consisting of role-playing presentations via audio-visual aides, field trips, and talks by practitioners in various fields of work. Furthermore, the clients were prepared for work by participating in the Auxiliary Maintenance Corps, which performed various chores in the institution. After release from Children's Village, a boy in the special program received supportive aftercare and job placement aid. There was no difference in recidivism rates.

Table 5.2. LENGTH OF RECORDED CRIMINAL ACTIVITY IN RELATION TO OFFENDER'S AGE

Length of Criminal Record in Years	Younger Offenders (Aged Under 19)		Older Offenders (Aged 19 or 20)		Total	
	No.	%	No.	%	No.	%
less than 1	29		15		44	
		34.2		16.6		25.2
1 less than 2	22		11		33	
2 less than 3	15		18		33	
		14.8		21.6		18.3
3 less than 4	7		16		23	
4 less than 5	24		25		49	
		31.6		33.8		32.6
5 less than 6	23		28		51	
6 less than 7	14		10		24	
		13.4		10.8		12.1
7 less than 8	6		7		13	
8 less than 9	6		9		15	
		6.0		17.2		11.8
9 less than 10	3		10		13	
10+	—		8		8	
Totals	149	100.0	157	100.0	306	100.0
Mean Length	3.8		4.9		4.3	

(McClintock & Bottoms, 1973, p. 13)

Table 5.3. AGE OF THE OFFENDERS ON SENTENCE TO BORSTAL
SHOWN ACCORDING TO AGE AT FIRST CONVICTION

Age at First Conviction		Age at Sentence to Borstal				
		17 or less	18	19	20	Total
Less than 13	No.	22	25	25	13	85
	%	7.2	8.2	8.2	4.2	27.8
13 or 14	No.	10	28	30	12	80
	%	3.3	9.1	9.8	3.9	26.1
15 or 16	No.	12	22	17	18	69
	%	3.9	7.2	5.6	5.9	22.6
17 +	No.	5	25	20	22	72
	%	1.6	8.2	6.5	7.2	13.5
Totals	No.	49	100	92	65	306
	%	16.0	32.7	30.1	21.2	100.0

(McClintock & Bottoms, 1973, p. 15)

A question may be raised as to the viability of the content of vocational training programs to the offender's subsequent life outside the prison. Gearhart, Keith and Clemmons (1967) reported vocational education to be nonsignificant in affecting recidivism rates. However, they found when a trainee succeeded in finding a job related to his area of training, he had a slightly higher chance of becoming a successful parolee. Yet in a comprehensive special education program for institutionalized women in Milwaukee, in which practical and academic training, such as reading, writing, spelling, business filing, child care, and grooming was administered, there was no difference in the women's rates of recidivism (Kettering, 1965). There is substantial evidence that the relationship of the skill development programs and the offender's life outside the prison is at best a weak one. The only indication that such a relationship even exists is provided by those parolees who matriculate through the institutional training program and adapt successfully to vocational placement outside the prison. In these few cases, moreover, the success rates can be traced to the success of those offenders in the training programs, and very often self-motivation forces to pursue extra training. Consequently, recidivism cannot be attributed entirely to the nature of the training programs, that is, whether or not the training was indeed demonstrably relevant or irrelevant. Perhaps the type of educational and skill improvement doesn't have much to do with an individual's propensity to display disruptive behavior. In any case, to date, education, academic or vocational skill development have not reduced recidivism by rehabilitating criminals.

An interesting finding is that when programs which have been administered successfully in institutions are applied in a noninstitutional setting, the results are not encouraging (Martinson, 1974). This should explain something of the worth of such programs, assuming that the phenomena of deviant behavior is one which differs not in kind from normal behavior, but rather differs in degree. One study of a noninstitutional skill development program by Kovacs (1967), described the New Start Program in Denver, in which offenders participated in vocational training, role playing, programmed instruction, group counseling, college class attendance, and trips to art galleries and museums. Kovacs found no significant improvement in the recidivism rate among the noninstitutionalized persons over the incarcerated persons. Even in a case of milieu therapy programs (Empey, 1967) which developed strong controlling norms for the behavior of the group, the total results show no significant improvement in recidivism rates. However, Empey did find that both the youth in the program and those on regular probation did better than those in regular reformatories. Another study on nonresidential milieu therapy found not only that there was no significant improvement, but that the longer a youth participated in the treatment the worse he or she was likely to do afterwards. Feldman, et al. (1973) conducted a summer camp program consisting of antisocial and prosocial children. They found that sufficient training and a prosocial peer environment can maximize the positive effects of such an experience for antisocial youth. If one bad apple has an effect on the model for youth, then what effect does only one model have for youth already in trouble?

Individual counseling

Many workers in the field propose that the personal interaction with the offender focusing on those deeper problems that caused their maladjustment is the essence of a treatment program. However, upon examining programs incorporating personal counseling, it is difficult to find groups for enthusiasm. Two studies by Guttman (1963) at different institutions found counseling to be ineffective in reducing recidivism rates. In one of those studies the investigator found that such treatment was actually related to a slightly higher parole violation rate. Adams (1959b and 1961) also found a lack of improvement in parole revocation and suspension rates. A crucial factor in these two studies which place them at variance with previous studies is the meaning of successful treatment. Parsons (1967) believed the term successfully treated should be differentiated from simply being subjected to the treatment experience. Parson (1967) found boys better in com-

Table 5.4.   TYPE OF CURRENT OFFENSE SHOWN ACCORDING TO THE NUMBER OF CRIMINAL ASSOCIATES

Type of Current Offenses		"Major" Offenses (total)	Alone	In Pairs	In Groups	"Minor" Offenses (total)	Alone	In Pairs	In Groups
Robbery, etc.		58	9	19	30	2	1	1	—
Sex Crime		2	1	—	1	3	3	—	—
Violence (not with property)		11	5	—	6	12	3	3	6
Breaking Offenses		99+	28	33	37	7	—	5	2
Thefts, etc.		30	12	13	5	27	16	5	6
Taking Cars, etc.		23	12	8	3	16	6	9	1
Damage		4	1	2	1	1	—	—	1
Others		3	3	—	—	8	7	—	1
Totals	No.	230+	71	75	83	76	36	23	17
	%	100.0	30.9	32.6	36.1	100.0	47.4	30.3	22.3

Minor offenses were significantly more often committed alone - P <.01.

*"Major" offenses are as defined in the classification on p. 25. In violent offenses, attacks on strangers are treated as major, plus neighborhood and domestic offenses where weapons were used. See note 11, p. 437.

+ In one case of a major breaking offense, the number of associates was not recorded.

(McClintock & Bottoms, 1973, p. 17)

Table 5.5. DISTRIBUTION OF OFFENDERS ACCORDING TO DEGREE OF PREVIOUS RECIDIVISM AND TYPE OF CURRENT OFFENSE

Type of Current Offenses		Total Offenders	No. of Previous Occasions on Which Convicted			Proportion with 3 or more %
			Less than 3	3 or 4	5 or more	
Robbery, etc.	No.	60	27	18	15	
	%	100.0	45.0	30.0	25.0	55.0
Violence, etc.*	No.	28	5	8	5	
	%	100.0	53.6	28.6	17.8	46.4
Breaking	No.	106	14	33	59	
	%	100.0	13.2	31.1	55.7	86.8
Thefts, etc.	No.	57	8	21	28	
	%	100.0	14.0	36.9	49.1	86.0
Taking Cars, etc.	No.	39	4	14	21	
	%	100.0	10.3	35.9	53.8	89.7
Malicious Damage and others	No.	16	4	6	5	
	%	100.0	25.0	37.5	37.5	75.0
Totals	No.	306	72	100	134	
	%	100.0	23.5	32.7	43.8	76.5

*In this table the small number of sexual offenses has been included in the violence category. (McClintock & Bottoms, 1973, p. 19)

munity adjustment than nontreated boys. On the other hand, nonamenable boys who were treated, actually did *worse* than they would have done if they had received no treatment at all. This study suggests that a critical factor is properly selecting subjects. If subjects are not properly selected, counseling, or other programs for that matter, may do more harm than good.

The effects of psychotherapy (Adams, 1959a) administered by a psychiatrist or psychologist resulted in parole rates almost 2½ times higher than if such treatment were administered by a social worker without specialized training. Martinson (1974) felt the data provided a favorable outlook for alternative forms of individual therapy, and that counseling and casework programs may assume a primary role in rehabilitation. To suggest that this type of therapy is a favorable alternative is a grand assumption in view of the fact that there is a dearth of any steadfast workable programs and approaches established. The only American study which provides a direct measure of the effects of individual counseling—a study of California's Intensive Program which was psychodynamically oriented—found no improvement in recidivism rates. This study directly influenced the de-emphasis upon individual counseling in the California penal system.

Group counseling

Shelley and Johnson (1961) used a pragmatic casework program, directed toward the educational and vocational needs of institutionalized young adult males in a Michigan prison camp. After six months of treatment, those inmates possessing good attitudes were correlated with parole success. However, Shelley was not able to measure the direct impact of the counseling on recidivism rates.

Young female offenders were studied by Adams (1959a) and Taylor (1967). Adams found there was no improvement in treating girls by groups rather than individual methods. Taylor came to a very similar conclusion; aside from the finding that when girls treated by group therapy committed new offenses, they were less serious than the ones for which they had originally been incarcerated. Similarly, Truax, Wargo, and Silber (1966) found that girls subjected to group psychotherapy and then released were likely to spend less time reincarcerated in the future. However, this particular study points out a possibly essential ingredient for the success of any treatment program. The therapists in this program were chosen for their empathy and nonpossessive warmth; in other words, special personal attributes of the therapists. Thus, groups and individual counseling programs seem to work best when the subjects are amenable to treatment, and when the couselors are not only trained, but good people as well (Martinson, 1974).

Milieu therapy

The attempt to create a supportive, nonauthoritarian and nonregimented atmosphere, and enlist peer influence in the formation of constructive values is really too all-encompassing, and must, therefore, be used in conjunction with group and/or individual counseling. The aim of milieu therapy is to enable the inmate's whole environment to be directed toward true correction rather than toward custody or punishment. This kind of therapy with adult prisoners was reported as a failure in two studies: Robinson (1967) and Kassebaum, Ward, and Wilner (1971).

Out of five studies of milieu therapy administered to juveniles, Lavlicht (1962) and Jesness (1965) report that there was either no significant effect or that there was a short-term effect that wore off with passing time. Positive effects of milieu therapy are reported from the Highfields program. Freeman and Weeks (1956) and McCorkle, Elias, and Bixby (1958) reported that boys in the program had lower recidivism rates (as measured by parole revocation) than a similar group spending a longer time in the regular reformatory.

Pre-release programs

There is promising evidence that parole and probation may provide a key to the reduction of juvenile recidivism rates. A British study reported that when probation was granted more frequently, recidivism rates did not increase significantly (Wilkins, 1958). Another such study by the state of Michigan in 1963 reported that an expansion in the use of probation actually improved recidivism rates.

Babst, et al. (1965) compared a group of parolees, excluding convicted murderers and sex criminals, with a similar group that had been put on probation. He found that the probationers committed fewer violations if they were first offenders, and did no worse if they were recidivists. A major drawback to this study, however, is that the behavior of these groups was being measured by separate organizations—by probation officers for the probationers, and by parole officers for the parolees. It is not clear what the results would have been if subjects had been released directly to the parole organization without having experienced prison first. In the comparison of a suspended sentence plus probation for first offenders with a one-year prison sentence, only first offenders under 20 years of age did better on probation; those from 21 to 45 actually did worse (Shoham & Sandberg, 1964). Whereas Babst found parole rather than prison brought no improvement for recidivists, Shoham reported that for recidivists with four or more prior offenses, a suspended sentence was actually better, though the improvement was much less when the recidivists had committed a crime of violence.

While both the Babst and Shoham studies suggest the possible value of suspended sentences, probation, or parole for some offenders (though they contradict each other in telling us which offenders), there is a generally pessimistic conclusion concerning the limits of the effectiveness of treatment programs. They found that the personal characteristics of offenders—first offender status, age, or type of offense—were more important than the form of treatment in determining future recidivism. An offender with a favorable prognosis will do better than one without, it seems, no matter how the treatments (good, bad, enlightened or regressive) are distributed among them.

Martinson et al. undertook a six-month search of reports regarding attempts at rehabilitation made in correction systems of the United States and other countries from 1945 through 1967. The search resulted in 231 methodologically sound studies. He states, "With few and isolated exceptions, the rehabilitative efforts that have been reported so far have had no appreciable effect on recidivism.'' Some of the complications were:

1. The groups in the studies were exceedingly disparate, nullifying or certainly jeopardizing that what works for one kind of offender also works for others.

2. Little attempt was made to replicate studies, thus stability and reliability needed buttressing.

3. The term *recidivism rate* lacked consistency in what the term referred to; e.g., failure measures such as arrest rates or parole violation rates, or success measures such as favorable discharge from parole or probation.

> We have been able to draw very little on any systematic empirical knowledge about the success or failure that we have met when we *have* tried to rehabilitate offenders, with various treatments and in various institutional and noninstitutional settings. (Martinson, 74, p. 98)

Ferrell, Tokstad, Listella, and Jackson (1969) report on a program for defective delinquents in returning them to society through a sequenced set of activities. They describe the program as a re-educational process reflecting a model of the normal socialization process. The two basic assumptions were: (1) factors primarily inherent in the organism that were operative even within a normal environment; and (2) a non-normal childhood environment that provided either subnormal social stimulation or abnormal experiences during the socialization process. They write:

> In summary, the following have emerged as the chief characteristics of this treatment program for defective delinquents: (1) an assumption of normality of patients with respect to their dignity and capacity for rationality and responsibility; (2) confrontation of patients with and responsibility for effects of their own actions; (3) participation by patients and staff in decision-making; (4) an open system of communication; (5) flexibility and expansiveness of the role system. (p. 7)

The method of evaluating the effectiveness of the program was to analyze where residents went upon leaving the ward. All of the residents who no longer were on the ward were placed in a category described as: community environment (job placement with family); vocational training environment (halfway house); more open institutional environment (more freedom, less structure); similar institutional environment (similar freedom, structure); less open institutional environment (correctional institution); patient is AWOL and remains out.

A significantly greater number of patients were rehabilitated after the inception of the new program. Chi square was significant at better than the .01 level. One very important finding is that there were no significant differences in age or intelligence for those residents capable of successfully demonstrating good adjustment after leaving.

The state of Washington has developed a state Youth Development and Conservation Corps (YDCC). It was developed to conserve natural resources and human resources by giving young men the opportunity to develop vocational skills and personality traits. Twelve-man teams live and work for six-week periods in state parks. The youths are provided room, board, and $25 per week. They are selected because of delinquency problems. The age range is 14 to 21, with an average age of 16½. Girls are now included in the program. The courts, schools, and legislation consider the program to be a great success.

The court records of incarcerated girls in a Tennessee state institution for correction revealed that over 60% had been institutionalized because of truancy and incorrigibility. A treatment model designated *Educo-therapy,* utilizing the disciplines of both psychology and education as an intensive treatment program, was offered in solution. Educo-therapy has three phases or progressive levels. The three are: (1) behavior modification; (2) remedial education; and (3) ego-development.

> It was predicted that if a child could experience success in learning and find gratification and reinforcement in academic achievement, many of his maladaptive behaviors, which were in evidence within the classroom would be reduced or removed entirely. A subjective evaluation by the conservative institutional staff enthusiastically supported the belief that "educo-therapy" shaped academic learning and provided an effective means of coping with disruptive emotional behavior. A modified version of the pilot project has been incorporated into the regular program of this institution.
>
> (Rice, 1970, p. 25)

CONCLUSION

Institutions are necessary. However, they are not an end in themselves, a terminal point in a treatment program, or a solution to a community's inability to develop programs. An institution must be viewed as one type of facility in constructing a full array or continuum of program delivery options for youth in trouble. When an institution is devoid of programs, and is merely a catch-all for a cluster of humanity no one is quite sure what to do with, then that institution is a maintenance facility. It is clear that what it maintains is skill-building for new disruptive behaviors and antisocial activities. It is proposed that the public schools in the community in which the youth is dominated be the responsible treatment agent for a youth. Thus, if the youth is in the public school, alternative school, institution, or other community based program, the educational program remains the responsibility of his home school district.

REFERENCES

Adams, S. "Assessment of the Psychiatric Treatment Program: First Interim Report." Research Report No. 14, California Youth Authority, June 30, 1959a. Mimeographed.

Adams, S. "Assessment of the Psychiatric Treatment Program Phase I: Third Interim Report." Research No. 21, California Youth Authority, January 31, 1961. Mimeographed.

Adams, S. "Assessment of the Psychiatric Treatment Program: Second Interim Report." Research Report No. 15, California Youth Authority, December 13, 1959b. Mimeographed.

Alper, B., and Keller, O., Jr. *Halfway Houses: Community-Centered Correction of Treatment.* Lexington, Mass.: Heath, Lexington Books, 1970. Cited in W. C. Rhodes and S. Head *A Study of Child Variance,* Vol. 3. Ann Arbor, Michigan: 1974, p. 176.

Atkinson, L. "The Treatment of Deviance by the Legal-Correctional System: History." *A Study of Child Variance,* Vol. 3. Edited by W. C. Rhodes and S. Head. Ann Arbor, Michigan: The University of Michigan, 1974.

Babst, D. V., and Mannering, J. W. "Probation Versus Imprisonment for Similar Types of Offenders: A Comparison by Subsesquent Violations." *Journal of Research in Crime and Delinquency* 2(2) (1965) 60–71.

Cincinnati Orphan Asylum, Annual Report for 1848, p. 3.

Empey, L., and Lubeck, S. *Silverlake Experiment: Testing Delinquency Theory and Community Intervention.* Chicago: Aldine, 1971.

Empey, L. T. "Delinquency Theory and Recent Research." *Journal of Research in Crime and Delinquency* 4 (January 1967): 28–42.

Feldman, R. A., Wodarski, R.; Goodman, R.; and Flax, N. Prosocial and Antisocial Boys Together." *Social Work* 18(5) (1973): 26–36.

Feldman, R. A., et al. "Treating Delinquents in Traditional Agencies." *Social Work* 17 (1972): 71–78.

Ferrell, C. R.; Tokstad, L.; Listella, M.; and Jackson, S. "Influence of a Therapeutic Community on Behavior and Adjustment of Defective Delinquents." *Mental Retardation* 7(6): 6–9.

Foucault, M. *Madness and Civilization: A History of Insanity in the Age of Reason.* New York: Random House, 1973.

Freeman, H. E., and Weeks, H. A. "Analysis of a Program of Treatment of Delinquent Boys." *American Journal of Sociology* 62 (1956): 56–61.

Ganzer, V. J., and Sarason, I. G. "Variables Associated with Recidivism among Juvenile Delinquents." *Journal of Consulting and Clinical Psychology* 40 (1973): 1–5.

Gearhart, J. W.; Keith, H. L.; and Clemmons, G. "An Analysis of the Vocational Training Program in the Washington State Adult Correctional Institutions." Research Review No. 23. State of Washington, Department of Institutions, May 1967. Processed.

Goffman, E. *Asylums: Essays on the Social Situation of Mental Patients and Other Inmates.* New York: Anchor Books, 1961.

Graham, R. "Responsibility of Public Education for Exceptional Children." *Exceptional Children* 28 (1962): 255–259.

Guttman, E. S. "Effects of Short-term Psychiatric Treatment on Boys in Two California Youth Authority Institutions." Research Report No. 36, California Youth Authority, December 1963. Processed.

Healy, W., and Bronner, A. *Delinquents and Criminals, Their Making and Unmaking: Studies in Two American Cities.* Mountclair, N.Y.: Patterson Smith, 1926, reprint 1969.

Homans, J. *A Textbook of Surgery,* 6th ed. Springfield, Illinois: Charles C. Thomas Publisher, 1975.

Jacobson, F. and McGee, E. "Englewood Project: Re-education: A Radical Correction of Incarcerated Delinquents." Englewood, Colorado: 1965. Mimeographed.

Jesness, C. G. "The Fricot Ranch Study: Outcomes with Small Versus Large Living Groups in the Rehabilitation of Delinquents." Research Report No. 47, California Youth Authority, October 1, 1965. processed.

Kassebaum, G.; Ward, D.; and Wilner, D. *Prison Treatment and Parole Survival: An Empirical Assessment.* New York: Wiley, 1971.

Kettering, M. E. "Rehabilitation of Women in Milwaukee County Jail: An Exploratory Experiment." *Dissertation Abstracts* 9 (1965): 5426–5427 abstract.

Kovacs, F. W. "Evaluation and Final Report of the New Start Demonstration Project." Colorado Department of Employment, October 1967.

Lavlicht, J., et al. *Berkshire Frams Monographs* 1(1) (1962): 11–48.

Martinson, R. "What Works? Questions and Answers About Prison Reform." *The Public Interest* 35 (1974): 22–54.

McClintock, F. H., and Bottoms, A. E. "Aims and Methods of the Project." *Criminals Coming of Age.* London: Heinman Educational Books, Ltd., 1973.

McCorkle, L., Elias, A., and Bixby, F. *The Highfield's Story: A Unique Experiment in the Treatment of Juvenile Delinquency.* New York: Henry Holt and Co., 1958.

Parsons, R. W. "Relationship between Psychotherapy with Institutionalized Boys and Subsequent Community Adjustment." *Journal of Consulting Psychology* 31(2) (1967): 137–141.

Platt, A. "The Child Savers." *The Invention of Delinquency.* Chicago: University of Chicago Press, 1969.

Pulliam, J. C. "The Administrative Organization of the Training School." *Readings in the Administration of Institutions for Delinquent Youth.* Edited by W. E. Amos. Springfield, Illinois: Charles C. Thomas Co., 1965.

Reynolds, M. C. "A Framework for Considering Some Issues in Special Education." *Exceptional Children* 38 (1962): 367–370.

Reynolds, M. C. "A Framework for Considering Some Issues in Special Education." *The Process of Special Education Administration.* Edited by Charles H. Meisgeier and John D. King. Scranton, Pennsylvania: International Textbook Company, 1970.

Rhodes, W. C., and Tracy, W. "A Study in Child Variance." Service delivery systems conceptual project in emotional disturbances. Ann Arbor, Michigan: University of Michigan, 1972.

Rhodes, W. C., and Tracy, W. "A Study in Child Variance." vol. 3. Service delivery systems conceptual project in emotional disturbances. Ann Arbor, Michigan: University of Michigan, 1972.

Rice, R. D. "Educo-therapy: A New Approach to Delinquent Behavior." *Journal of Learning Disabilities* 3(1) (1970): 16–28.

Robinson, C., and Kevotkian, M. "Intensive Treatment Project: Phase II. Parole Outcome. Interim report." Research Report No. 27, California Department of Corrections, Youth and Adult Correctional Agency, January 1967. Mimeographed.

Rothman, P. *The Discovery of the Asylum.* Boston: Little, Brown, and Company, 1971.

Shelley, E. L. V., and Johnson, W. F., Jr. "Evaluating an Organized Counseling Service for Youthful Offenders. *Journal of Counseling Psychology* 8(4) (1961): 351–354.

Shoham, S., and Sandberg, M. "Suspended Sentences in Israel: An Evaluation of the Preventive Efficacy of Prospective Imprisonment." *Crime and Delinquency* 10(1) (1964): 74–83.

Silberburg, N. E., and Silberburg, M. C. "School Achievement and Delinquency." *Review of Educational Research* 41(1) (1971): 17–33.

Street, D.; Vinter, R. D.; and Perrow, C. *Organization for Treatment.* New York: The Free Press, Macmillan Publishing Co., 1966.

Study by New York State, Division of Parole, Department of Correction. "Parole Adjustment and Prior Educational Achievement of Male Adolescent Offenders, June 1957–June 1961." September 1964.

Taylor, A. J. W. "An Evaluation of Group Psychotherapy in a Girls' Borstal." *International Journal of Group Psychotherapy* 17(2) (1967): 168–177.

Truax, C. B.; Wargo, D. G.; and Silber, L. D. "Effects of Group Psychotherapy with High Adequate Empathy and Nonpossessive Warmth upon Female Institutionalized Delinquents." *Journal of Abnormal Psychology* 71(4) (1966): 267–274.

Truxal, J. R., and Sabatino, D. A. "A Comparison of Good and Poorly Adjusted Institutional Offenders." *Georgia Journal of Corrections* 2 (1973): 76–84.

Wilkins, L. T. "A Small Comparative Study of the Results of Probation." *British Journal of Delinquency* 8 (1958): 201–209.

Zivan, M. "Youth in Trouble: A Vocational Approach." Final Report of a research and demonstration project, May 31, 1961–August 31, 1966. Dobbs Ferry, New York: Children's Village, 1966. Processed.

6

administrative management of institutions and school programs for troubled youth

DAVID A. SABATINO

The primary function for most administrators is to perform budgetary and personnel decision making. *Administration is the act of facilitating for those involved in a program, to the degree various resources or constraints permit.* Therefore, a successful program has an established channel by which information central to that program is directed to the decision makers. The word *administration,* or the act of administering, is frequently preceded by an adjective. School administration, business administration, or clinical administration of treatment staff are three different types of administration thought to require an administrator to have a different training and experiential background. Yet, all three of these functions may be expected of one person in a private or public facility for delinquent youth. A more acute difficulty is that each of these functions may be performed by an administrator with or without budgetary control, or with or without ultimate responsibility for personnel management. The program area administrator is frequently subordinate to a general administrator. Institutional superintendents may be political appointees, business managers, or may have previous experience in only one aspect of corrections, e.g., a correctional officer. A public school administrator may be a generalist with no knowledge of norm-violating youth.

Therefore, one difficulty in administering an institution or school program for norm-violating youth is that most programs exist as a suborganization of structure within a budgetary and program environment which must reflect a total balance. Therefore, all program goals must mirror, to some degree, the will of the larger organization or be in conflict with those values. That means that programmatic administrators must understand the social organization pressures in which they find themselves. The fact that an institution may be administered by a Department of Welfare, Child Welfare, Corrections, Education, Mental Health, or other service bureaus for children will provide a definite set of constraints upon the type of suborganization of structures which comprise it. As a suborganization of a larger organizational framework (such as a local educational agency in a state system), an institution or school program for norm-violating youth may have serious constraints in exercising decision making at the level of responsibility imposed. The difficulties with serving more than one master are rather obvious. But the difficulty associated with interorganizational conflict becomes even more apparent when the reader realizes the potentiality of interorganizational conflict among treatment staff members, custody staff members, and educational personnel, or among special educators, regular educators, and vocational educators. If the term *conflict* seems a bit too strong to the reader, then a few hours should be spent in the shoes of an institutional administrator working within state structures, attempting to facilitate the most appropriate program for adjudicated youth. Bureaucracy is always difficult to understand. A much needed typewriter or set of school books can be held up for six months; as a new governor, after election or at the end of a legislative probe of fiscal crisis, freezes, then redirects resources, or reorganizes the operative structure into a new, untested one. Later, that same governor may authorize the immediate construction of a bowling alley. To develop programs that will alter and enrich the lives of troublesome or troubled youth is very frustrating work. It is to that frustration that we dedicate this chapter.

CURRENT STATE-OF-THE-ART

If a capable young man or woman were to ask how to prepare for a career as an administrator of a state or private program for adolescent youth, it would be difficult to answer. Any specific answer would and could generate arguments. For instance, there is a theory that all administrators should be prepared as generalists, since the act of administrating a program is merely one of decision making. The advocates of the generalist position would advance arguments that all administrative problems are similar in nature, and the structure or environment in which they occur is inconsequential. They feel that the content question is not an issue; that is, it makes no difference if the decision to be made concerns treatment, maintenance (food, clothing, and shelter), the public schools, an institution, the elementary levels, or secondary levels.

Obviously, opponents of the general administrative point of view base their arguments on the knowledge that an administrator must be well viewed in substantive content of his field. It is quite a different task to develop an administrative program in process than to describe the substantive content for that process. It is obvious that the two large divisions of a residential program are maintenance and treatment. Is group work a maintenance or treatment function? It is usually supervised by social workers skilled in group process, and has treatment intervention qualities, but frequently it occurs in cottages or residence halls after the evening meal. This issue, like so many others to be raised in this chapter, essentially is unanswerable unless put into the context of a given administrative framework.

Burrello (1973) has provided a current review in *Research and Theory in Special Education Administration*, stating, "In the area of special education administration, little research has been reported in the literature" (p. 229). Rucker (1971) has grouped the studies in special education administration into four areas:

1. Within-group studies—surveys of special education administrators' concern for a specific role or function they should or must perform.

2. Between-group studies—comparisons of special education administrators with other groups of administration, in areas of attitudes, perceptions, role, and function of specific job tasks, or job analyses.

3. Organizational climate studies—usually descriptive studies of a particular organization structure or pattern within a given type of administrative unit, e.g., school district, institution, etc.

4. Descriptive studies—a study of those factors which influence the development, role, or function of a specified aspect of a special education program or service.

Burrello (1973) concludes that special education administration is still in its early infancy and that the research to date has attempted to descriptively classify administrative phenomena into logical categories from which meaningful generalizations can be drawn.

Newman (1968) attempted to determine what tasks special education administrators performed based on: (1) actual performance, (2) ideal performance, and (3) relative importance of these tasks. He found no significant differences between what administrators actually did, and the tasks they felt should be performed. Newman found that very few data-based decisions were being made. He suggests that more direct observational research is needed. The relationship of the special education director to teaching activities determined how administrative tasks were ranked in order of importance, particularly planning, development, and evaluation of teachers. The attitude of other administrators toward the special education directors, and the role in the administrative hierarchy, also have a direct influence on ranking administrative tasks by the special education administrators.

If the complexities of administering special education programs can be reduced to a dichotomous relationship, the two horns of the dichotomy would be self-contained/custodial maintenance versus active regular-school/community integration. The custodial attitude is defined as a maintenance of the resident as a recipient throughout the treatment period. The view may be one of punishment for a crime, protection of the resident, or protection of society. A passive treatment plan may accompany custodial maintenance. Passive treatment may be regarded as time to think, good food, clean bed, work detail, and moral, spiritual, and social guidance. The term *passive treatment plan* is used to denote that the intervention is not differentiated from one resident to another in keeping with long-range treatment objectives. It focuses more on maintenance of a safe, clean, orderly environment; one that is easily understood and does not require active participation by the resident in behavioral change, or in solving any socioemotional, cultural, group, or gang problem the resident may bring to the situation.

Active regular-school/community intervention is defined as primarily viewing children's or adolescent's behavior in educational, vocational, psychological, and sociological terms within the school-community setting. The critical question is what constitutes the judgment that provides either a custodial or active treatment program. Most assuredly, different reasons would be elicited by different people. It is easy to rationalize the establishment of a custodial treatment program for certain valid reasons, such as a lack of treatment facilities, limited budget, or inability of the political or social system to accept an active treatment role. Whatever the reason, the main one which inhibits an active treatment process is the administrator's attitude and personal beliefs.

What other factors may be responsible for determining the administrator's response for an active treatment program? Two factors may be hypothesized. The most obvious is the knowledge for the content dimensions of what a treatment program should be. In other words, it may be that the more clinically, educationally, or vocationally trained the administrator, the more he will attempt to establish an active regular school treatment program. On the other hand, the less formal training or professional preparation that an administrator has in treatment aspects for chronic disruptive norm-violating youth, the more likely he will be to attempt to institute a custodial effort which requires far less administrative arrangement. Certainly, an active regular school treatment program is more costly in cash outlay (primarily in salaries for professional personnel) than a custodial maintenance program. However, the cost/benefit ratio of an active regular school treatment program may be much less.

Burrello (1969) studied five need categories of administrators, based upon Rotter's (1954) social learning theory. The five need categories were: (1) recognition status, (2) protection-dependence, (3) dominance, (4) independence, and (5) love and affection within professional situations. To test the validity of the theory, the staff of 50 directors of special education were asked to react to eight simulated situations, depicting administrators' need preferences in relationship to scores on a Behavior Preference Inventory (BPI). A significant relationship was found between an administrator's need preferences and his respective staff's ranking of administrative need preferences. It was concluded that the BPI apparently described the need values of special education administrators in approximately the same fashion as their instructional subordinates perceived them. Courtnage (1967) studied the relationship between opinions and attitudes of public school superintendents and special education directors in the same district. He found there was a strong agreement between the two groups of administrators regarding most responsibilities and issues of special education administrators. In another study, Parelius (1968) examined the perception of general administrators (superintendents) to directors of special education. There was no significant difference between the role-expectations of the two groups. There is little disagreement between directors of treatment programs and general administrators, on the outlook of the program's dimension. This would seem to indicate administrators feel a relatively high degree of job satisfaction.

Job satisfaction is generally defined as the extent to which a person perceives his needs to be satisfied by the entire job situation (Guion, 1958). Getzels, Lipham, and Campbell (1968) noted that "satisfaction results from the absence of role-personality conflicts—the individual is not required to do anything he does not want to do" (pp. 129–130). Support is provided for this definition in a discussion of a theoretical model of the organization as a social system by Guba and Bidwell (1957). These authors indicated satisfaction is a function of the two factors of expectations and needs. Expectations of the organization are goal oriented, and serve to limit and organize the behavior of individuals toward systematic goal accomplishment. Need dispositions of the individual stem from personological characteristics. Therefore, individual satisfaction is dependent on the congruency of needs and expectations as perceived by the individual. If these factors are congruent, satisfaction results; if they are not, dissatisfaction results.   (Guba and Bidwell, 1957, p. 433)

Bidwell (1955) empirically demonstrated a relationship between teacher satisfaction and the role expectations of administrators as perceived by the teachers. Additional investigators have shown that job satisfaction is related to individual need fulfillment. Rosen and Rosen (1955) suggested that "satisfaction results when the individual sees occurring what he desires to occur, and that dissatisfaction results when he does not" (p. 312). Schaeffer (1953) noted that there was a positive, direct relationship between job satisfaction and need satisfaction.

Ross and Zander (1957), in a study of employee turnover, noted that workers whose needs were being satisfied by the job were more likely to remain on the job, than those whose needs were not met. Gordon's (1955) research concluded that workers' self-estimated moral (job satisfaction) was strongly associated with need fulfillment. Blai (1962) also reported a positive and direct relationship between job satisfaction and the extent to which individual needs are satisfied by a position, i.e., the greater the needs satisfaction, the greater the job satisfaction.

Yuskiewicz (1971) examined the specific formulation presented by Guba and Bidwell, that is, the congruency of needs and expectations as related to job satisfaction, by utilizing pupil control ideology as the criterion. His postulates were that job satisfaction would be directly related to the congruency between teacher-pupil control ideology (individual need orientation and their perception of control ideology of teaching colleagues) and principals (perceived role expectations). Findings support the hypothesis (p. < 001) in all cases. Job satisfaction may be a two-way street. The institutional administrator may have to recognize the restrictions and find job satisfaction working with the confines of the organizational pressures placed on the institution, be they legislative, governmental, from the superintendent of correction, or from society in general.

Changing societal attitudes, or those of an institutional staff, to meet what the administrator considers important needs for the residents within the institution he administers may be a long, deliberate process that requires a great deal of preparation. If the dilemma is adapting to society's or some other administrator's view of one's role, as opposed to viewing oneself as a change agent, then the expectations for job satisfaction and treatment efforts could be on a collison course. The interaction between the nomothetic and idiographic dimensions of a social system have been clearly delineated in Getzels and Guba's (1957) model (see Figure 6.1). When the role-expectation of the institution and the personality-need disposition of the individual fail to be compatible, a clash between the two is almost inevitable.

The nomothetic dimension can be depicted in the following manner: social system→ institution→ role→ expectation→ institutional goal behavior. The role is considered to represent a specific position or function within the institution. These specific functions are defined in terms of role expectation. Role expectation delineates what an employee is expected to do under specified conditions.

The idiographic dimensions are the individual, his personality, and his need dispositions. The personality is a dynamic factor providing the individual with active characteristics. Need dispositions, according to Getzels and Guba, are "goal oriented and influence not only the goals which individuals will try to attain in a particular environment, but also the way in which he will perceive and cognitize the environment itself" (Getzels and Guba, 1957, p. 75). Need dispositions, in their conceptualization, are perceived as patterned or interrelated. Getzels and Guba (1957) summarized their description of the two dimensions of behavior in the social system by suggesting that "the one is conceived as a rising in institutional goals and fulfilling goal expectations; the other as rising individual goals and fulfilling personality dispositions." (p. 78)

Ray Graham (1962) outlined four necessities for the administrators of special education:

1. *Philosophy.* No organization is any better than its philosophy. And, if the philosophy of an organization is getting out of accepting responsibilty, it will find a way. (p. 255)

2. *Leadership.* Leadership inspires—it is creative and creativity is contagious. Leadership gives status and balance—it gets results. (p. 257)

3. *Organization.* In special education, organization starts with objectives. It includes lines of authority and methods of communication.

Normative (Nomothetical Dimensions)

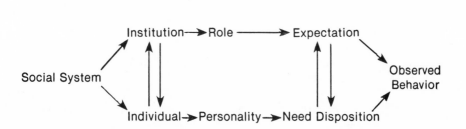

Personal (Idiographic Dimensions)

Figure 6.1.
Getzels' and Guba's Description of Educational Administration as a Social Process*

*Getzels, J. W., and Guba, E. G. *School Review* 65 (1957): 423–444. Reprinted with permission of University of Chicago Press.

It is more than facilities and personnel. In special education this means making special education as definite, as acceptable, as permanent, and as respected as is the third grade, reading, or geometry. (p. 257)

4. *The Look Ahead.* A planned future—programs of today must meet tomorrow's crisis and the future of the youth we serve. (p. 257)

The administrator of an institution is a middle man. He stands squarely between the youth his programs serve, the staff that serves them, and the governmental and child-oriented agencies which relate to the institution. In essence he must look both ways. If he fails to pay close attention to either one of these potential trouble sources, he will be in the proverbial washing machine wringer. Not that he cannot or would not be in the wringer some of the time anyway. State-level politics make most anything difficult, and yet, they are but one flank that must be covered if an administrator and his programs are to survive.

Pulliam (1965) writes:

The number of staff members reporting directly to the superintendent should be limited as much as possible. Some training schools operate with only two departments under the superintendent position—clinical services and business management. In addition, the superintendent's secretary and special committees report directly to the superintendent. Other training schools departmentalize down into education, recreation, special professional (including psychiatry, psychology, social work, and nursing), religion, cottage life, and business management.*   (Pulliam, 1965, p. 18)

The modern administrator must be able to prepare and interpret clear mission statements that personnel can understand as the guiding goals for an institution. If the governor's budget is so restrictive that it provides food, clothing, and shelter; and society (the residents of that state) have not yet heard of a pre-release program, the chances are that the institution in question is a custodial center. If the juvenile judges set the sentence and assign the youth, then there is little an administrator can do to effect behavioral change for a seriously emotionally disturbed youth. It is inappropriate for a custodial institution to expect, or even demand, treatment programs from a staff that does not have the preparation and is probably already overburdened. The role of an administrator in such a circumstance is to point out the problem to those who control the policy making or budget for that institution. But it seems hypocritical for an institutional facility to claim to be something that is impossible for it to be under realistic constraints of manpower, facility, or budget. Constraints will always exist in creating and maintaining needed programs. History frequently judges

---

*From Homans, John. *A Textbook of Surgery*, 6th ed., 1975. Courtesy of Charles C. Thomas Publisher, Springfield, Illinois.

administrators by their ability to order those constraints and promoting the efforts necessary to accomplish a task.

PLANNED CHANGE

There has been a great deal written about the administrator as a change agent. The reason is the rigidity which characterizes institutions once programs are initiated and staff employed. Once people learn about something—particularly if they have to manage it, or have some understanding as to why an expenditure is appropriated or an item on a purchase order necessary—they simply don't want to learn about a new program aspect which threatens to alter all they currently understand about that program effort.

Second and even more important, is a fact that most institutional administrators generally lack adequate evaluative data on how well their current programs are doing. Therefore, it is difficult to know what and how a program effort should receive additional support, or in fact be changed. To some extent, all programs of planned behavioral change, according to Suchman,

> . . . are required to provide "proof" of their legitimacy and effectiveness in order to justify public support. The demand for "proof of work" will vary depending upon such factors as degree of faith in authority and competition between opposing programs or objectives. The current proliferation of new types of social intervention which challenge traditional approaches . . . and which compete for both public and financial support are under constant pressure to show that they are better than established programs and deserve a larger proportion of available resources.   (Suchman, 1967, p. 54)

It is generally agreed that change must be planned and proceed in an orderly fashion. Personnel, their attitudes and comfort (freedom from threat), is the singularly most important ingredient to achieving planned change. Generally, the aspect most critical to achieving change is the time necessary to appraise all those who will pass judgment on, or relate to the program, to have the information they need. Achieving change in a democratic process is slow. That is not to say the democratic process is the only way. There are times when decisions must be made and even a well-informed staff cannot decide what should be accomplished. The administrator who makes the decision lives with the consequences. The administrator who fails to make decisions also lives with the consequences.

The key to planned change is the discussion time necessary to help the total staff understand the components necessary for the change and their reasons. Develop a prototype if possible, later test it, and support continued use of the program with evaluative data.

Stufflebeam, et al. (1971) have developed a planned change model which provides the details for executing the implementation of a new program. The major components are research, development, diffusion, and adoption.

Decision making

Administrators are decision makers. Passively or actively they make decisions simply because the absence of a decision is in fact a definitive policy statement in support of the status quo. Stufflebeam, et al. (1971) have outlined the making of a single decision as a complex process. They believe it to entail four distinct stages. These are: (1) becoming aware that a decision is needed, (2) designing the decision situation, (3) choosing among alternatives, and (4) acting upon the chosen alternatives. Stufflebeam (1972) provides an illustration of the decision-making process as he believes it should happen:

The Process of Decision Making

1. *Awareness*

   a. Identify programmed decision situations.

   b. Identify unmet needs and unsolved problems.

   c. Identify opportunities which could be used.

2. *Design*

   a. State the decision situation in question form.

   b. Specify authority and responsibility for making the decision.

   c. Formulate decision alternatives.

   d. Specify criteria which will be employed in assessing alternatives.

   e. Determine decision rules for use in selecting an alternative.

   f. Estimate the timing of the decision.

3. *Choice*

   a. Obtain and assess criterion information related to each decision alternative.

   b. Apply the decision rules.

   c. Reflect on the efficacy of the indicated choice.

   d. Confirm the indicated choice or reject it and recycle.

4. *Action*

   a. Fix responsibility for implementing the chosen alternative.

   b. Operationalize the selected alternative.

   c. Reflect on the face validity of the operationalized alternative.

   d. Execute the operationalized alternative, or recycle.

(Stufflebeam, *et al.,* 1971, p. 53)

TYPES OF FORMAL ORGANIZATION

The two basic administrative considerations in establishing an organizational structure within an institution are: (1) for facilitation of staffing pattern effectiveness; and (2) bringing into close physical and communication proximity, staff members who must relate if efficiency of operation is to be achieved. Generally, departmentalization with some degree of communication and coordinating autonomy provides for the second aspect of an organization.

The most essential types of departments are for custodial care and treatment. How these two essential components are further departmentalized depends on the size of the institution, its history, major goals and missions, existing staff, and especially key administrative or professional personnel. One administrative rule of thumb is that a chief administrator can have no more than five to seven subordinates reporting to him. If that rule is followed in constructing an organizational relationship, then size and function of the institution becomes the major consideration in establishing a table of organization. In a small facility a chief administrator may want to have an assistant director who, like he, is responsible for everything. They will operate more on a cabinet-level relationship than chief and assistant. This type of organization is not a very good one for many reasons. The reasons range from duplication of function to second guessing one another. Some small youth camps of about 20 employees with less than 100 residents do operate with such an organization. Larger and more complex institutions with multiple treatment programs will not operate effectively from such an organization platform. An example is provided in Figure 6.2.

Assistant directors can serve to direct the custody and treatment of an institution, permitting the administrator to be free to work with the

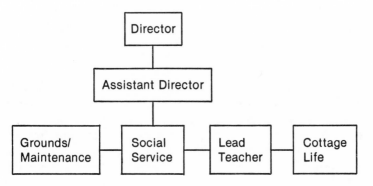

Figure 6.2.   Table of Organization - Type 1

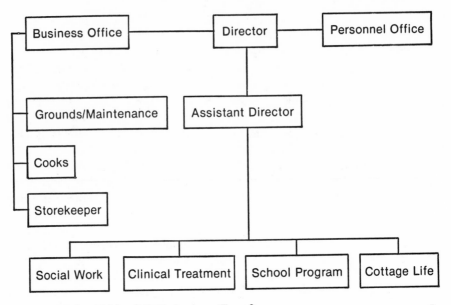

Figure 6.3. Table of Organization - Type 2

budget and recruit personnel. Figure 6.3 is an example of this type of organization.

The major difficulty with a Type 2 organization is the director is usually a business manager. The assistant director must, therefore, provide program leadership since the director is concerned with cost-efficient administration, and frequently not effective program development. The assistant director is also responsible for such a range of activities that he cannot possibly comprehend how they fit into an overall treatment milieu. Therefore, a custodial maintenance program is probably being facilitated, with the school program and custody emerging as the dominant factors. The role relationship of social service and clinical treatment becomes mechanical and low in priority in terms of an active treatment process. They will probably not be well integrated in either the school or custodial programs. Frequently, they are appendages to the institutional program.

There are many other types of organization structures. It is extremely difficult to find one that is better than another because tables of organizations must be built around the strengths and interests of existing staff, or for that matter, sometimes to compensate for the weaknesses of personnel or program. A very capable administrator upon being moved into a new position in a facility with a long history was asked how he would reorganize it. He answered automatically that his first year's work was to study the relationship of existing personnel to the table of organization in operation. It may be he felt that change for the mere sake of change was less than valuable, in fact, chaotic. Institutions, organizations, and administrative structures are people, or at least they reflect people. An effective table of organization reflects a balance between establishing departments. It maximizes communication between members of that department and achieves a relationship between department administrators that promotes the overall good of the resident over any department and program aspects. Therefore, one effective structure in administrative organization is to have fairly large multiple departments with program coordinators reporting to a director. The assistant director is a specialist with administrative skills. In a large organization, a director reports to an associate superintendent for treatment or custody. In a smaller-sized unit, the director reports directly to the chief administrator. Communication lines are kept clear by providing a cabinet-level meeting each week. Cabinet officers are staff officers above the coordinator level (superintendent, associate superintendents, and directors). Directors in turn have departmental meetings with total coordinators. Coordinators are line officers. More frequently, coordinators have program-level meetings. To augment new programs, prevent certain predictable problems, or quell problems in the making, core staff are identifed and brought together at the request of the associate superintendents. Core staff are directors and coordinators in either treatment or custody capacities. In other words each associate superintendent has an identifiable core staff which is made up of his line and staff officers (directors and coordinators). Bringing together core staff facilitates communication horizontally as well as vertically. Figure 6.4 presents a graphic representation of complex multiple departmental structures.

SYSTEMS ANALYSIS

What are the management alternatives for administering an institution, since the organization structures of institutions vary so greatly? Banghart (1969) writes:

> The field of educational administration is becoming concerned with the set of quantitative-scientific techniques that assist the educational administrator in the decision-making process. These techniques are customarily referred to under the term "systems analysis." (p. 3)

An administrator has two major options. First, he must be concerned with the care and well being of the residents. That means the building, meals, heating plant, and custodial staff must be provided and

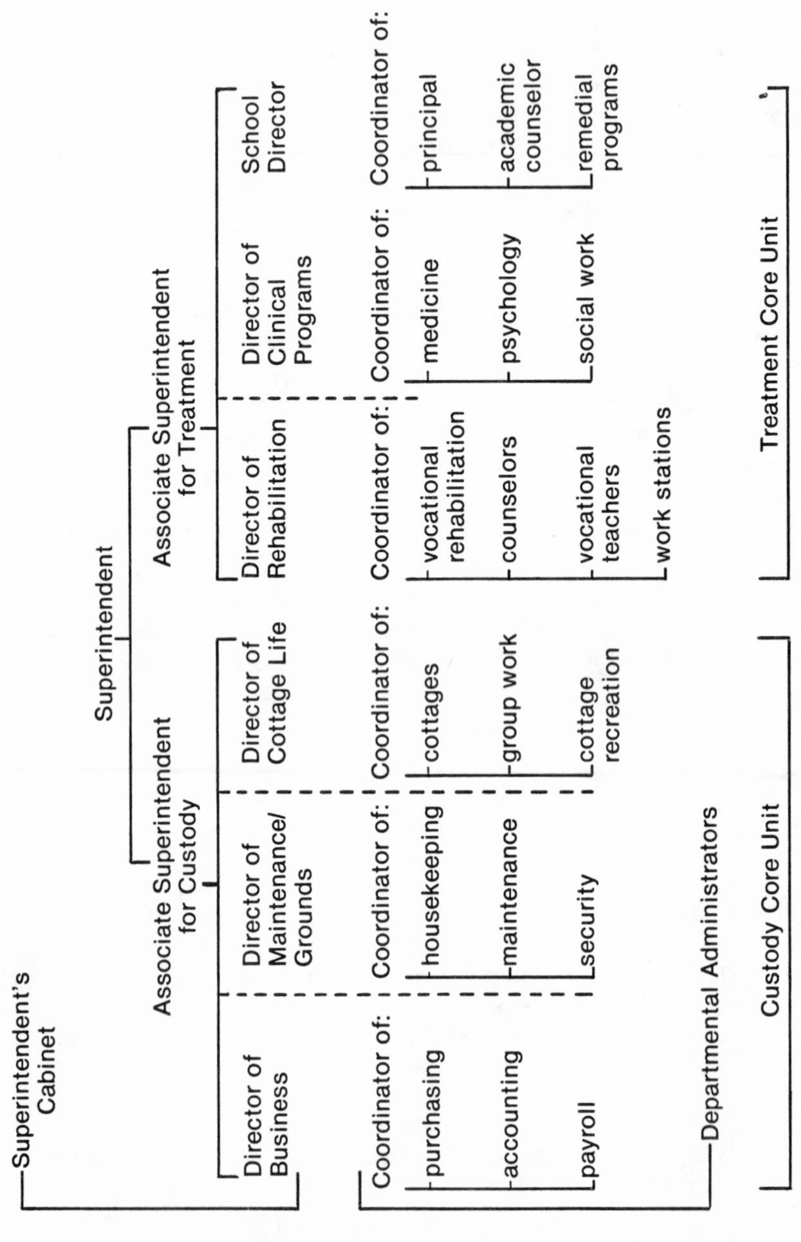

Superintendent's Cabinet

Superintendent

Associate Superintendent for Custody

Associate Superintendent for Treatment

Director of Business

Coordinator of:
- purchasing
- accounting
- payroll

Director of Maintenance/Grounds

Coordinator of:
- housekeeping
- maintenance
- security

Director of Cottage Life

Coordinator of:
- cottages
- group work
- cottage recreation

Director of Rehabilitation

Coordinator of:
- vocational rehabilitation
- counselors
- vocational teachers
- work stations

Director of Clinical Programs

Coordinator of:
- medicine
- psychology
- social work

School Director

Coordinator of:
- principal
- academic counselor
- remedial programs

Departmental Administrators

Custody Core Unit

Treatment Core Unit

Figure 6.4. Table of Organization - Type 3

maintained. The programs within the institution and the manner in which those programs are contiguously articulated with the real world are not always pressing issues. An administrator may elect to delegate or resolve himself of any concern for these programmatic aspects. The reason most commonly given is that in preparing and administering the budget, providing for the physical plant and essential custody personnel, a working administrator has all he can possibly do. That is why two associate or assistant superintendents under one chief administrator is a fairly common arrangement. One administers the custodial program, and one the treatment program. To prohibit warring between them, the chief decision maker must have the goals for the institution clearly in mind. If he does not have the overall goals, objectives, and means to achieve them tied into a well-thought through format, he will be administering from predictable crisis to predictable crisis. There must be some means of accounting for each of the goals and objectives as they relate to given aspects of the programs.

The concept of systems is useful in keeping the administrator informed on there his programs are, and what needs to be accomplished. Systems analysis is a quantitative-scientific tool for tracking program aspects and making decisions about them. It is hoped that most of the decisions made are based on evaluative date stemming from a pre-planned evaluation process. Two of the systems analysis techniques are: (1) Program Evaluation and Review Technique (PERT); and (2) Critical Path Method (CPM). Both techniques require institutional goals and program objectives to be laid out in a flow chart arrangement with the charting of events predicted until the end or terminal event is achieved. The network is an extension of the flow chart events. All activities have an onset, an activity path, and terminal or end objectives. It is a planning-evaluation guide to those goals the administrator wishes to accomplish. It gives him radar-detection-type instrumentation to verify his approach to selected goals.

Discussing systems, Banghart writes:

> The term *systems* carries the connotation on analysis and development . . . no comprehensive system development can take place without prior systems analysis. *Systems* . . . denotes all activities involved from the original analysis of the problem through the final implementation of recommendations . . . utilization of scientific mathematical techniques applied to organizational operations as part of management's decision-making activities. (Banghart, 1969, p. 20)

Lerner (1971) defines a system as:

> a set of objectives, together with relationships between the objects and between the characteristics of these objects. Systems analysis deals with

the selection of elements, relationships, and procedures to achieve specific objectives and purposes . . . A systems approach is extolled as a technique to prevent splintering and fragmentation of a field by bringing component parts, subsystems, or elements into a total relationship with each other . . . One goal of systems analysis is, in fact, to provide a means of crossing boundaries and of bringing diverse elements and operations and specialists toward a definite systems purpose. (p. 16)

Enormous administrative effort is expended each year identifying the sum of the parts of particular administrative problems. The character of an organization has many contributing aspects—the personalities and skills of its members, and the views maintained by those who use its services in an attempt to satisfy the reasons for its existence (credibility). To initiate any program effort without a game plan will soon lead to chaos. The inevitable problem of identifying the players in a game that is poorly understood and has no systematic rules of play is the same as taking a trip in a car to an unfamiliar spot without a road map. The roles of key staff members must be clearly delineated by all the organizational members of an institution, or confusion will result. The role differences between custody staff and treatment staff must be understood in achieving total program effort. When a classroom teacher recognizes a child with a serious reading problem, to whom does she direct the referral and what does she expect in return? Should a remedial program be in the school, clinic, or residence? These and other issues are the aspects that contribute to a total program, and they must be understood in light of coordinated program efforts.

As was said previously, there is a sharp distinction between program content and process. Program content is the substance that makes the wheels of an organization run. The process is the administrative or treatment structure which guides the operations; it is the frame, axle, and hubs upon which the wheels turn. A system design is not to be misconstrued as providing substantive considerations or instructional content to a program. Systems analysis provides a study of the process upon which the content is superimposed. Kipfer (1973) writes:

> One should keep in mind that the application of analysis is to *function* and not *content*. There is a great deal of disagreement in the field of special education relating to specific content areas. Kelly (1971) has described a special education paradigm listing basic postulates related to special educational functions, and uses the term *therapy* as synonymous with instruction. Kelly's basic postulates are:
>
> a. the major function of special education is therapy;
>
> b. therapy is effective only insofar as it accomplishes the basic purpose of special education, i.e., it induces desirable behavioral changes which are of eventual benefit to its subjects;

c. benefits of therapy can be observed in some way, but what is "desirable" is essentially dependent upon the social-cultural-teleological context of the therapeutic setting;

d. administrative-supervisory, research, and diagnostic functions of special education are ancillary to the major function of therapy;

e. ancillary functions must relate directly or indirectly to therapy; functional aspects which do not relate to therapy in some way may be regarded as spurious;

f. a comprehensive paradigm of the therapeutic process should relate to its ancillary functions to the extent that statements describing the processes of administration-supervision, research, and diagnosis can be derived from the original paradigm. (p.17)

Ryan describes the growth of correctional institutions in the United States as "haphazard and idiosyncratic" rather than "orderly and planned." It is her belief that a two-fold challenge exists in mandating and updating educational programs in institutions: (1) to maintain an effective, efficient educational system; and (2) to provide accountability of educational programs on decisions or policies being made in institutions. It is Ryan's view that

. . . corrections decision-makers must be prepared to answer to the citizenry, local governing bodies, state legislatures, and Congress when confronted with: "What were the intended outcomes of education in this correctional setting?" . . . To achieve this effectiveness, it is imperative for management to have an adequate knowledge of probable consequences before decisions are made.   (Ryan, 1972, p. 18)

Ryan has defined eight basic functions and the relationship between and among its functions in establishing a decision-making system for administrative management of educational programs in adult correctional institutions. These eight functions are: (1) conceptualizing the system; (2) monitoring the system philosophy and assessing needs; (3) defining goals and objectives; (4) processing information; (5) hypothesizing plans; (6) testing plans; (7) measuring outcomes; and (8) evaluating individuals and programs. Figure 6.3 provides a graphic display of the model Ryan recommends for the management of institutional educational programs. A working description of the eight elements in the systems flow is as follows:

1. *Conceptualize the System.* Basis for educational management is a description of the elements to identify relationships of the supersystem. This conceptualization of the system should set the stage for subsequent synthesis which will meet basic requirements of an effectively functioning

system by achieving wholeness of the elements, compatiblity between system and society in general, and congruence between system synthesis and purpose. (Ryan, 1969)

2. *Assess Needs.* A system cannot function effectively apart from the real-life environment of which it is a part. (Banathy, 1968). Social factors, cultural factors and values, provide the information along with an underlying philosophy which provides direction to educational management in correctional settings. Immediate and long-range goals are the factors influencing educational management. The end result of monitoring philosophy and assessing needs should be identification of problem areas and proposed means for alleviating them. The final step in analyzing of the situation should be a Go-No-Go decision in indicating whether the identified problem is amenable through the available programs.

3. *Define Mission, Goals, and Objectives.* The next task at hand is one of stating the mission and defining goals and objectives. The elements or functions must contribute effectively to achievement goals, and it is essential that educational management rest on a careful determination of the objectives. This includes an appropriate prioritization of goals and objectives.

4. *Process Information.* The feedback loop between process information and goals and objectives mandates an information-based control over proposed objectives. In each situation, feedback from processing information to defining goals and objectives will improve the system. The information acquired about learners, society-culture and existing institutional programs is analyzed and synthesized to form a basis for developing future goals and program directions.

5. *Formulate Hypotheses.* The crux of educational management lies in the design of educational plans. The educational plans formulated take the form of program specifications. Specification of limits to a program plan entails setting boundary conditions for performance. *Time* is a major factor in planning projects and the system design must be able to accommodate for time variation. *Information* constitutes an important constraint on design. The history of corrections is fraught with a lack of data to indicate long-term effectiveness of the system.

6. *Testing Hypothesized Plans.* The programs implemented and any alternative strategies to achieve the system goals must be tested for their effectiveness. Miller, et al. (1971) makes the point that strategies contain communication elements and that strategies which have been validated through feedback and control are the most reliable management techniques for achieving system goals. Strategies are developed to create learning environments and experiences. (Ryan, 1972, p. 25). It is to that end that prototype programs should be constructed and tested.

7. *Measuring Outcomes of System Operation.* Measurement of outcomes is a precondition to evaluation of program plans and validation of

the strategies implemented. Measurement must precede evaluation, as the data produced from measuring operations outcomes and products will provide the basis for judging system effectiveness.

8. *Evaluation of Individuals and Projects.* Evaluation is a process of determining the value of performance or assigning outputs. The results of evaluation are fed back into the system to modify it. It is from the evaluation data that management decisions in support or rejection of the educational program are made. (Ryan, 1972, pp. 24–25)

Program evaluation

The major dimension of any planning activity is the evaluation which determines the degree to which the objectives are being accomplished. Worthern and Sanders (1973) write: "Evaluation is one of the most widely discussed but little used processes in today's educational systems" (p. 1).

Stufflebeam, et al. (1971) define evaluation as

the process of delineating, obtaining, and providing useful information for judging decision alternatives. [(p. xxv). They add:] . . . The major reason evaluation is in difficulty is that knowledge of the decision-making process and of the methodologies for relating evaluation to decision making is woefully inadequate. (p. 16)

The few people with responsibility for funds ask why special children are "special" and, even more, whether special education is doing more for these children than the regular classroom can do. If we are to defend our programs, we must have facts. Increasing pressure is being placed on special educators to provide evidence that efforts with exceptional children are beneficial (Lessinger, 1971). If charged to communicate the effectiveness of their programs, they must (1) state precisely what outcomes the program is designed to facilitate; and (2) present evidence that the outcomes have, in fact, been produced. These demands on classroom teachers for accountability necessitate the use of an evaluation process; but the principles of evaluation may well be one area where preservice academic preparation is limited or nonexistent for most teachers.

Institutional administrators and the classroom teacher, faced with the day-to-day reality of changing the behavior of delinquent youth, do not need to learn another obtuse theoretical model or be overwhelmed by the academic prose in which most evaluation articles are written. Nor do they need what Ohrtman (1972) has aptly described as the "in and out researcher . . . gets two sets of kids, do A to one group and B to another, compare them, and one group does better at the .01 level—then off to the next project" (p. 377). Vergason (1973) and Jones (1973) have delineated many of the problems associated with the evaluation process. All too often there has been more effort required than value provided. Jones writes that before any school district should presume to devise a system of accountability for special education, the following questions should be answered:

1. What are the common and specific goals to which the administrator and the program are striving?

2. What student, community, or societal-need inventories are available, on paper, to indicate change strategies which should be undertaken?

3. What specific and measurable performance objectives have been written down that would enable outside agencies, the residents, and staff to understand the minimum expectations of the specific program efforts that relate to them?

4. What analysis of the existing delivery system is available to indicate that the current educational input approach is manageable as compared to the alternatives? (Jones, 1973, p. 632)

Vergason (1973) states that one area in which educators can be more definitive about their programs is that of standardized terminology. Stufflebeam (1972) has recently assumed a position similar to that of Scriven (1967) who defines the fundamental goal of evaluation as determining the value of a program or instructional activity. Originally, Stufflebeam (1968) saw evaluation as a systematic process of "delineating, obtaining, and providing useful information for judging decision alternatives" (p. 129). The CIPP (Context, Input, Process, and Product) model he developed represents a frame of reference for presenting alternatives to decision makers and can provide a classroom teacher with information about her program; but this evaluation model is too complex for daily use in the classroom.

Other evaluators have discussed plans for curriculum and course evaluation (Cronbach, 1963; Krathwohl, 1965; Lindvall, et al. 1964; Michael & Metfessel, 1967; and Popham, 1969), while still others have presented theoretical evaluation models (Atkin, 1969; Hammond, 1969; and Provus, 1969). These plans generally represent similar processes for conducting educational evaluations, but they do not offer a simplified procedure for the already over-burdened classroom teacher to use.

The term *evaluation* is not a good one because it increases anxiety without having a particular universal meaning. All sorts of atrocities have been accomplished in the name of evaluation. To reduce the ambiguity associated with the term, we are concerned with context evaluation, not personnel. In the next part of this chapter, evaluation procedures for describing program output, personnel effectiveness, and specific classroom delivery of objectives are discussed. The task of personnel evaluation is not a prerogative of an outside review (external to the institution). Personnel policies and the evaluation of people hired by an institution must be established in line with that individual's and institution's expectations for career development. Proger, Carfioli, and Kalapos, (1973) in a discussion of evaluating instructional materials, have made some very fitting remarks:

> The careless use of the term "evaluation" has led to misconceptualized models . . . An exhaustive description of characteristics of the learner, the material, the setting of instruction, and so on, does not constitute evaluation, although it is useful in delimiting the generalizabiltiy of evaluation results. Evaluation refers to the actual judgments that are made with regard to the quality of the material, its success in use with students, and other strengths or weaknesses. True materials evaluation implies that a definite position (favorable or unfavorable) is taken concerning the materials evaluated; neutrality is not a virtue. It is unfortunate that some evaluation models for materials have relied almost totally upon descriptive analyses of materials and have disregarded judgmental evaluations. Items on a materials-evaluation form that deal with description should be clearly labeled as such. The same should be done for items that concern judgmental evaluations. When this distinction is made, it is apparent how little (and that of poor quality) is being done in the genuine sense of materials evaluation.   (p. 272)

The above quote was not added to elicit support for making subjective or qualitative judgments. The point is that judgments will always be necessary, even when a criteria or standard is established. The crucial question is, "What is the standard or criteria and who is doing the evaluation?" In answer, begin by evaluating the content of the specific institutional program's objectives to determine the difference in what a program says it is doing, and what, in fact, it is doing in relationship to its objectives. The data can then be used to make a sound administrative decision reflecting an effort to plan for the future on the basis of the evidence revealed by the evaluation.

Goals and objectives

There are several goals (unmeasurable aims) and objectives (measurable) which are inherent in an institutional program. The main goal is to provide necessary program opportunities for youths to alter behavior at an optimum level and rate, with consideration for his ability, race, sex, socioeconomic level, and socioemotional development. The secondary goals are to provide continued support in the youth's efforts to achieve the skills necessary to leave the institution and perform normally in the community. Some other goal statements for institutionalized norm-violating youths are:

1. Isolate, segregate, or label as few children as possible from mainstreaming programs.

2. Keep the youth's school and community informed about his progress and needs in planning an orderly re-entry for him from institution to community.

3. Provide additional programmatic support for youths who experience difficulty adjusting to institutional programs.

4. Provide demonstration and inservice assistance to custodial and treatment staff to encourage and promote positive program climate.

5. Provide a value-learning system that will promote youths to make decisions concerning their lives that will ultimately reduce recidivism.

6. Provide continuous planning and monitoring of youths who have sufficiently serious problems that require institutionalization.

7. Provide continuous feedback to the youth and his family on his progress as he participates in various programs or service aspects.

8. Provide evaluation of all programs according to criteria established with a systematic procedure which denotes the quantitative and qualitative aspects for the program.

9. Provide a systematic diagnostic procedure that will permit identification of youth requiring unique programs.

10. Provide for the public image of the institution.

Objectives are measurable aspects that reflect the process and product of a given goal. An objective should state *what* is to occur, in what time frame (*when)* or order, and *how* it is to occur. Objectives must be specific to each factor or function listed in the task areas. This idea of specific objectives for each function, under a general program goal for a given task area, is rather self-explanatory in developing a program-planning guide. The first phase in evaluating a program is to carefully listen to what the administrators, teachers, and students say a program should accomplish. Two things should be carefully noted, as the information will later be compared to what the district's goals are. First, what is the attitude or commitment to the program? It should be understood that the people associated with the program also believe in it personally. The absence of such belief generates clichés and an air of triteness. Second, program constraints must be determined. The constraints of implementing a learning disabilities program are generally financial limitations; staff (level of training, type of training, ability); and the physical facilities that are currently available. The most important constraints are the attitudes within the system as well as those outside it, primarily the community.

All programs have to be developed within the budgetary framework and facilities available. It is possible, however, to make internal changes which could have a great effect on altering constraints. An example of a change of this nature might be the use of limited funds to employ a person to initiate a desired program in one cottage when it is desirable to have it in all cottages. But, it may be better for the sake of the program to provide an intensive effort at that one cottage for one year. As the program sells itself, budget will be added (or, if necessary, the person could be moved to another building the next year) until every cottage in the institution has an equal opportunity to benefit, as opposed to spreading one person too thin and obtaining a watered-down effort.

A simplified planning guide has the following dimensions:

1. Goal
2. Objective(s)
3. Strategies
4. Product/Outcome
5. Evaluation
6. Timeline with Date of Completion
7. Personnel
8. Cost/Benefit Ratio
9. Criteria or Standard

Evaluating program output

Accountability is a problem for all administrators. The demand and need for accountability in program evaluation is especially acute. The focus of this section is to provide administrators of institutions with guidelines for determining the effectiveness of their programs. A discussion of staff evaluation follows and finally, a simplified classroom evaluation process for teachers to self-critique their instructional activities concludes this section.

The need for program evaluation is the result of public demand for proof that programs and services to youth are effective and beneficial. Initial efforts in program evaluation focused on theory and the development of evaluation models with limited implementation. (Lilly, 1970). The following discussion hopefully will encourage administrators to lift program evaluation from paper and put into practice.

Evaluation has been defined by Stufflebeam et al. (1971) as "the process of delineating, obtaining, and providing useful information for judging decision alternatives" (p. 40). Program evaluation is more than cosmetic cardiac, judging the success or failure of a program on the enthusiasm of students, parents, and teachers. Program evaluation demands that actions (decisions) be based on systematically collected and analyzed information (data).

Stufflebeam (1969) conceptualizes such a plan:

Evaluation Design*

A. *Focusing the Evaluation*

1. Identify the major level(s) of decision making to be served, e.g., local, state, or national.

2. Project the decision situations to be served and describe each one in terms of its locus, focus, criticality, timing, and composition of alternatives for each level of decision making.

3. Define criteria for each decision situation by specifying variables for measurement and standards for use in the judgment of alternatives.

4. Define policies within which the evaluator must operate.

B. *Collection of Information*

1. Specify the source of the information to be collected.

2. Specify the instruments and methods for collecting the needed information.

3. Specify the sampling procedure to be employed.

4. Specify the conditions and schedule for information collection.

C. *Organization of Information*

1. Provide a format for the information which is to be collected.

2. Designate a means for performing the analysis.

D. *Analysis of Information*

1. Select the analytical procedures to be employed.

2. Designate a means for performing the analysis.

E. *Reporting of Information*

1. Define the audience for the evaluation reports.

2. Specify means for providing information to the audiences.

3. Specify the format for evaluation reports and/or reporting sessions.

4. Schedule the reporting of information.

F. *Administration of the Evaluation*

1. Summarize the evaluation schedule.

2. Define staff and requirements and plans for meeting these requirements.

---

*Reprinted from a paper delivered by Daniel Stufflebeam, "Evaluation as Enlightenment for Decision Making," at Sarasota, Florida: Association for Supervision and Curriculum Development, January 19, 1969, p. 48.

3. Specify means for meeting policy requirements for conduct of the evaluation.
4. Evaluate the potential of the evaluation design for providing information which is valid, reliable, credible, timely, and pervasive.
5. Specify and schedule means for periodic updating of the evaluation design.
6. Provide a budget for the total evaluation program.

Performance appraisal of personnel

One of the recurring difficulties in the performance appraisal of personnel involves the delineation of responsibility within the hierarchy of the chain of command. Traditionally, personnel are hired through a regional or state administrative structure. They are then assigned to an institution. To whom are they responsible? Technically, in terms of competencies, they are evaluated by departmental supervisors. However, their survival usually rests on public relation skills. The word *survival* is emphasized because most employees are evaluated in terms of their relationships with other staff, community, and finally the youth, rather than on the basis of the skills they possess. This is a sad commentary, but a true one.

The unresolved question remains *who* among the supervisory and departmental personnel will conduct the evaluation, and *how* the evaluation will be accomplished. It is even more important to determine expectations of each position and employee. Following are some guidelines which Redfern (1963) has suggested for principals to use with teachers. They are also applicable to supervisors involved in personnel appraisal.

1. Avoid the "boss complex." Help the teacher feel that the principal doesn't consider himself foremost as a member of the "administrative hierarchy."
2. Clarify the role of the principal and teacher in the evaluation setting.
3. Seek to establish that both the teacher and the principal should be primarily concerned with the educational welfare of the pupils rather than their own self-interest.
4. Be conscious that the evaluator's (principal) personality as well as that of the evaluatee (teacher)—good or bad—will have an influence upon achievable results in the conference.
5. Strive for unity in leadership effort and action among all administrators in the building.
6. Be willing to let the teacher express his feelings in the conference without risk of censure or reprisal even if they may be markedly different from those of the evaluator.
7. Provide for privacy.

8. Safeguard the confidential nature of any matter requiring it.

9. Avoid asking for opinions on the spot; allow time for consideration.

10. Strive for a climate of mutual respect.

11. Be prepared to take as well as to give.

12. Be honestly committed to the concept that teacher, principal, and supervisor are members of a team working for the best interests of a good educational program.

13. Take the initiative in encouraging the teacher to make constructive criticisms.

14. Provide the opportunity for the discussion of school problems.

15. Invite suggestions; when made, try to do something about them.

16. Don't give the teacher the brush-off when problems are presented.

17. Try to be aware of what the teacher is doing in his classes; be conversant with general developments in his field of specialization. Leave the technical aspects to the supervisor.

18. Don't talk too much; don't let the teacher talk too little.

(Redfern, 1963, pp. 45–46)

A simplistic program evaluation process

The evaluation process presented in Figure 6.5 can be viewed as a simplistic means of understanding what is happening in a given program. It contains three major stages: the pre-situational, the situational, and the post-situational. During the pre-situational stage, the goals and objectives of the program are defined.

During the situational stage, data are collected which allow judgments (evaluations) to be made (for example, statements about particular behavioral objectives which demonstrate attainment of the desired goals). This step is essential if the evaluation is to provide any information regarding objectives, goals, and their attainment. Such information may be collected by questionnaires, interviews, observation, etc. The information collected during this stage must be descriptively prepared so that its meaning and utility will be apparent. This involves representing graphically, or otherwise, the results of the valuations and defining the next step of the model. If the goals are not being met, the teacher can relate this information back to the first stage, and either new objectives can be formulated or new goals can be agreed upon. If, however, the goals are being met, the teacher then proceeds to the post-situational stage.

The post-situational stage involves determining which parts of the program are effective for obtaining the objectives and goals. The major function of this stage is to establish the relationship between the program goals and the successful achievement of objectives which lead to these goals.

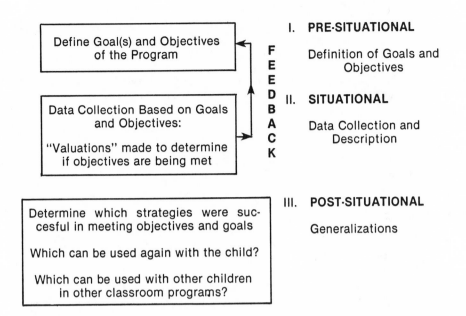

Figure 6.5. Evaluation Process   (Algozzine, Alper, and Sabatino, 1975, p. 35)

A practical evaluation design

The following example illustrates how the proposed evaluation design may be implemented by a teacher to evaluate a unit on word recognition skills for a norm-violating youth. While we are not recommending that a phonics approach be used to teach word recognition skills in all situations, we merely use it here as an illustrative example. The steps within each stage are not all-inclusive, but represent some possible choices in a sequenced flow of instructional activities.

Pre-situational stage

The purpose of this stage is to clearly state the goals and objectives.

1. Gather assessment information of the child from other personnel. (For example, check school records, test results, other teachers' reports, etc., to gather any information which might pertain to the overall goal.)

2. Administer teacher-made informal tests to determine child's level of functioning (response to previous instruction). (For example, the child can recognize letter combinations, but does not recognize words.)

3. Specify behaviors in need of remediation (recognizing initial consonant blends, for example).

4.   Specify instructional strategies (methods and materials) to be used in achieving the behavioral objectives (task analysis, behavior modification principles to be used, types of remedial materials to be used).

5.   Develop a hierarchy of sequential behavioral objectives based on the above information regarding the child's strengths and weaknesses. (For example, the child will recognize that *th, sh,* and *ch* represent different sounds and will then be able to identify these sounds orally from a series of words, i.e., shoe, choose, think, etc.) At this point the teacher will have defined her goal(s) within an instructional area and specified a sequence of behavioral objectives which should lead the child toward the mastery of the major aims of her instructional program.

Situational stage

The purpose of this stage is to collect and describe data based on the defined goals and objectives.

1.   Administer teacher-made, criterion-referenced tests to determine if the child has mastered the behavioral objectives being taught currently. (For example, the teacher presents a list of words. The child has to orally identify all the *sh* words with 80% accuracy.)

2.   Gather information from the child, his parents, other teachers, etc. This could be attitudinal information on study habits at home, etc.

3.   Consult with the resource teacher, supervisor, and/or school psychologist if necessary. Self-determination of the classroom climate (child-teacher-curriculum interaction) may be helpful at this point.

4.   Feedback this information to the original objectives in order to determine the student's performance in interacting with the curriculum according to the standards specified.

Post-situational stage

The purpose of this stage is to make comparisons, predictions, and generalizations based on the data obtained in the situational stage as it relates to achieving the desired goals.

1.   Administer criterion-referenced tests to determine where the child is functioning now in relation to the hierarchy of behavioral objectives. How do his strengths and weaknesses change as remediation is applied? What new goals and behavioral objectives seem appropriate? (For example, the child can now discriminate between *sh* and *ch* sounds within words, but cannot generalize this skill to reading orally words that contain the *sh* and *ch* blends.)

2. Determine which instructional strategies were successful with the child and which were not. Which ones, totally or in part, can be used again as the student initiates work on new goals and objectives? (For example, the child likes to work in small groups or with one other child, and has more success than when he is left to work by himself.)

Table 6.1. EVALUATION WORKSHEET

1. Pre-Situational Information

    What do you want the child to learn? (goal or objective)

    _____

    What does the child do now with regard to what he is to learn?

    _____

    What should you do to teach or enable his learning the stated goal or objective?

    _____

2. Situation Information

    What is the effect of teaching on the stated goal or objective (as determined by the child's performance)?

    _____

    Are modifications necessary at this point?

    ____ Yes. Is the strategy appropriate?____ Is your assessment of the child's skills appropriate?____ Are your goals and objectives appropriate?____

    ____ No. Go to the next stage.

3. Post-Situational Information

    What was the reason for the success?

    _____

    Which strategies were most successful with the child?

    _____

    Can this be generalized?_____

    Which strategies can be used again with the same child or with other children to teach other skills?

(Algozzine, Alper, and Sabatino, 1975, p. 39)

3. Determine which techniques might be successful for use with other children in the class (the teacher decides that task analysis, for example, can be used in many other instructional areas).

The answers to these questions provide the classroom teacher with evaluative information about her program. They tell her which aspects of her teaching plan were effective, and they allow her to keep records of the child's progress. Table 6.1 is an example of an evaluation worksheet which may be used by the teacher in order to carry out the instructional objectives proposed.

THE INSTITUTIONAL ADMINISTRATOR

Pulliam has described the institutional administrator's role and function in exacting terms.* He writes:

> The chief administrative officer or superintendent should be a person with a successful experience in work with children. Preferably, he should have a Master's degree in one of the social sciences and some experience in a supervisory-administrative capacity in a training school. This does not eliminate the person with more experience or unusual interest, who has less formal education. It does eliminate, however, the political appointee who is appointed superintendent for supporting the right man or party. The less-educated administrator will generally need a stronger department and division staff of well-educated and well-trained persons and will also need to be more willing to delegate responsibility in specialized areas.
>
> More superintendents are becoming "front men" for their institutions, devoting more time to dealing with matters from outside the institution, such as the parent agency, legislature, community leaders, newspapers, radio, television, and general public relations. When the superintendent takes the outside pressures off the clinical and business staff, these specialized employees are able to devote their full time and effort to matters more directly related to the children and the internal programs and problems of the institution. The superintendent actively participates in policy making decisions and chairs selected committees, leaving routine decisions and day-to-day operations to department heads and division chiefs.
>
> (Pulliam, 1965, p. 15)

This chapter has described the role and function of an administrator, working with institutional or public school programs for chronically disruptive youth. It was a state-of-the-art review. Historical facts and facets were discussed, as were the topics of decision making, planned

*From Homans, John, *A Textbook of Surgery, 6th Ed.,* 1975. Courtesy of Charles C. Thomas Publisher, Springfield, Illinois.

change, type of organizational models, systems analysis, evaluations processes, and the features of program accountability. It is obvious that a main ingredient is missing. Namely, information about the administrator—the person who assumes the responsibility for administering an institution.

Campbell, Corbally, and Ramseyer, (1966) in discussing the factors affecting administrative behavior, have said ". . . behavior is dependent upon the interaction of the conditions within the person and those which surround him" (p. 41). In essence, the man cannot be understood without understanding the job situation which in turn reflects the dimensions which characterize the man.

Sweitzer described five general responsibility patterns.

1. *Authority-Centered.* The authority-centered administrator sees his primary responsibility as achieving purposes through clarifying and carrying out the official policy adopted by the school board.

2. *Inner-Directed.* The inner-directed administrator conceives his primary responsibility to be modifying, improving, and interpreting policy and proceeding along lines he thinks will best meet the educational needs of the community.

3. *Work-Group-Oriented.* The work-group-oriented administrator considers his primary responsibility to be facilitating the cooperative development of group standards and procedures that tend to meet identified local needs.

4. *Individual-Centered.* The individual-centered administrator conceives his primary responsibility to be enabling individuals and groups to carry out their tasks, largely self-appointed and self-defined, with as little interference as possible.

5. *Other-Directed.* The other-directed administrator conceives his primary responsibility to be knowing as best he can the wishes of the people served, and seeing to it that the goals and procedures felt to be most worthwhile are officially adopted and then achieved.

(Sweitzer, 1958, p. 298)

Pallone, Rickard, and Hurley (1970) reviewed job satisfaction studies up until 1967. They found a great deal of support for the two-factor theory developed by Herzberg, Mausner, and Snyderman (1959). The difference in most traditional theories on job satisfaction and the two-factor theory is that job satisfaction has historically been considered as a linear continuum with the poles being satisfaction and dissatisfaction. Herzberg, et al. (1959) have posited that job satisfaction cannot be dealt with as degrees of satisfaction or dissatisfaction. There is, after all, a degree of satisfaction or dissatisfaction for any job. There are satisfiers, such as achievement, recognition, etc., and dissatisfiers. Satisfiers are intrinsic to the job content; dissatisfiers are extrinsic. Pallone, Rickard, and Hurley (1970) summarize their findings in three pointed statements.

1. There is insufficient evidence to support the two-factor theory that job satisfaction is generated by one set of variables, and dissatisfaction by another.

2. The relationship between job satisfaction and psychological and social needs is poorly understood. Some individuals satisfy many personal and social needs through work; others do not.

3. They do not support the widely held operational belief that job dissatisfaction leads to job or career change.   (p. 472)

These findings make considerable sense in light of Henrichs review. He believes that all job satisfaction research has been confronted by one serious problem. The problem is finding a suitable definition of job satisfaction which is such a broad, global term, that it must not be restricted to a specific task. He writes:

> . . . job satisfaction as a general construct roughly analogous to the often used by essentially undefined concept of "morale." Although the difficulties with the concept of morale were well outlined by Guion (1958), and as many as eight or nine different definitions were presented, the flavor of some complex of job attitudes reflecting overall favorable or unfavorable "morale" finds its way into much current-day research.
> (Henrichs, 1968, p. 479)

Vroom concludes:

a) There is a consistent negative relationship between overall satisfaction and turnover, though the correlation in the studies he cites are small.

b) There is an indication that absences and overall satisfaction are negatively correlated, though only to a moderate degree.

c) There is no simple relationship between overall job satisfaction and job performance.   (1964, p. 23)

Despite extensive use of the concept of overall job satisfaction, it would seem that the construct has provided only a minimum degree of precision in understanding the basis for various organization behaviors.

Vroom (1964) cites a list of factorial studies which have identified such variables as attitudes toward the company in general, promotional opportunities, specific job content, supervision, compensation, working conditions, and co-workers. Probably the most carefully conceived factorial research in job attitudes (Kendall, et al. 1963) utilizing the Job Description Index scale, generated five distinct factors. They were: promotional opportunities, job content, supervision, compensation, and co-workers. Sedlacek (1966) concludes from his extensive research that four factors—intrinsic, supervisor, social service, and financial advancement—empirically account for most of the common variance in job attitudes.

A general concept of morale is frequently demonstrated by factorial studies. It is not uncommon to obtain a general factor of overall job satisfaction characterized by significant factorial loadings for most variables in any data matrix. Dabas (1958) claims that a general factor exists in most morale surveys, reminding one of the classical discussions about the existence, or lack of existence, of a g-factor in mental ability.

Similarly, global measures of morale or job satisfaction have, up until now, not been useful research tools. These factors do play a role as broad indices. There is an evident need for research focusing on the components of job attitudes rather than attempting to utilize a global concept of general job satisfaction in trying to understand the dynamics of organizational behavior.

An analogy within the area of intellectual ability would seem to be appropriate for research dealing with industrial job satisfaction. While early efforts focused on the identification and measurement of general intelligence, more recent studies have concentrated on the identification of specific ability factors which must be understood in developing a comprehensive psychology of individual differences. Global measures of mental ability have not been as useful as differential measures in the understanding of human behavior.

Gruenfeld and Weissenberg (1970) have hypothesized that analytical and global perceivers would differ significantly among intrinsic and extrinsic sources of job satisfaction. The results showed that for global perceivers, intrinsic and extrinsic satisfactions correlated substantially with each other, and with overall job satisfaction; while for analytical perceivers, intrinsic and extrinsic satisfactions were independent and, as expected, only intrinsic satisfaction correlated with overall job satisfaction.

This study concludes that a consideration of individual differences may clarify some of the confusion surrounding the study of job satisfaction, particularly as defined by the two-factor theory of Herzberg, Mausner, and Snyderman (1959). By examining two groups which differed in cognitive style, Gruenfeld and Weissenberg demonstrated that these differences affected perceptions of potential rewards of the organization. This study also demonstrated why it was possible that some studies attempting to test the two-factor theory report that extrinsic rewards were related to overall satisfaction, and some intrinsic rewards were related to dissatisfaction, depending upon the subjects sample being assessed.

McCormick, Jeanneret, and Mecham (1972) have found that "job analysis resulted in the identification of reasonably meaningful job dimensions of human behaviors (and), . . . based on similar behaviors should have implications in terms of common aptitude requirements and corresponding rates of pay" (p. 346). The results indicate that aptitude requirements and rates of pay can be predicted reasonably well from such quantified job-analysis data, thus suggesting that conventional test-validation and job-evaluation procedures might sometimes be eliminated.

Herzberg's (1959) two-factor job satisfaction theory was the first significant step toward a multidimensional description of job attitudes at the professional level. Herzberg concluded from his study of engineers and accountants that only intrinsic work elements called *satisfiers* (recognition, achievement, accomplishment, responsibility, and advancement) could generate job satisfaction. Conversely, extrinsic elements, or *dissatisfiers* (supervision, wages, interpersonal relations, company policy, and working conditions) gave rise to job dissatisfaction. The roles of satisfier and dissatisfier were seen as independent—a satisfier could not evoke dissatisfaction nor could a dissatisfier give rise to job satisfaction.

However, further research testing the two-factor theory has convincingly shown that the intrinsic-extrinsic dichotomy does not adequately reflect the sources of positive and negative job attitudes. Both satisfiers and dissatisfiers appear to be aspects of job satisfaction and dissatisfaction. Wood and LeBold (1970) have found that using factor analysis (a 34-item questionnaire with 3,000 engineers) that job satisfaction is multidimensional. "A general job characteristic factor and a specific factor, Professional Challenge, tend to be related to job satisfaction. Five other factors were identified: Status, Autonomy, Professional Recognition, Interpersonal Relations, and Supervisory Relations." (p. 178)

The integration of the goals of an individual with the goals of his organization has been discussed in the literature. Numerous studies have described the conflict between individuals, especially professionals, and their organizations. (McKelvey, 1969). Most of these studies have viewed the conflict between professionals and organization as generally inevitable. The focus has been on the professional's responses to the conflict rather than on organizational conditions which might reduce the strains. In various fields, the socializing processes of educational institutions have been shown to increase the individual's identification with his profession.

Less is known about the development of organizational identification than is known about professional identification. Certain organizational conditions, such as reward structures and job design, appear to be linked to the member's organizational commitment. However, there has been little research on personal factors that might be related to identification, such as self-identity, personal values, and need satisfaction.

Iris and Barrett (1972) have studied the relations of job satisfaction, job importance, and life satisfaction measures in two samples of foremen differing in their level of job satisfaction. The results supported an interpretation of the relationship between job and life satisfaction. The relationship between satisfaction and pay was moderated by the favorability of the job situation. Those people who were in a work environment that provided little job satisfaction were more likely to be dissatisfied with other aspects of their life if they felt aspects of the job such as promotions, supervision, and work to be important for their job satisfaction. It would appear that when people are in a job situation that provides little job satisfaction, disavowing the importance of the job may be a healthy response.

Those who had given up any thoughts of advancing beyond the assembly line appeared to have better mental health than those who were still hoping for something better in life. In the same manner, the foremen in this investigation who were in an unsatisfactory job situation, but de-emphasized the importance of the various aspects of the job, tended to be satisfied with life and the job in general.

This finding supports some of Herzberg's (1959) work on the nature of pay and its dual role as a motivating factor. In an unfavorable job situation, satisfaction with pay comes to be a main determinant of overall job satisfaction. In a more favorable job environment, satisfaction with pay is not related to general job satisfaction, whereas the factors of promotion, co-worker, supervision, and work are related.

Research on the personnel selection of administrators has been of two main types. First, it analyzes senior executives in terms of their ability, personality, interpersonal relations, adjustment, values, etc. The result of this type of research has been to establish the fact that there are all kinds of executives; highly intellectual and not so intellectual, personalities varying from dominant to permissive, from outgoing to shy, from warm to aloof, from well-adjusted to those displaying obsessive and neurotic traits, from those who are materialistic to those having humanistic values. Second, research on personnel selection has attempted to analyze job demands against characteristics of the administrator, identifying some of the relevant dimensions of a job, and then finding ways to measure those dimensions. This approach has also failed to yield significant results, primarily because techniques for examining an executive's job have not been fruitful.

Cartwright and Zander (1968) suggest that the burdens and responsibilities of power may produce compassionate, rather than exploitive, behavior on the part of the administrator. There is the possibility that the administrative responsibility may produce other beneficial changes related to the administrator's view of the world. Administrative responsibility provides that individual with broadened and deepened understanding of himself and others. It is interesting to watch a person work through the ranks until he achieves an administrative position, at which time he changes his general perspective.

Rogow and Lasswell (1963) adopted a more neutral stand and maintained that the control of administrative responsibility neither leads to corruption nor to ennoblement. Rather, the connection between power and corruption depends on various combinations of individual ego needs and the type of social organization of which the individual is a member.

There are other social scientists who flatly believe that the very control of power induces individuals to act in an inequitable and exploitive manner toward the less powerful. (Sorokin & Lunden, 1959). The well-known observation of Lord Acton that "power tends to corrupt and absolute power corrupts absolutely" clearly reflects this point of view.

Kipnis (1972) studied the relationship between administrative control, self-esteem, and esteem for others in a simulated organization setting. Administrative responsibility caused subjects to (1) increase their attempts to influence the behavior of the less powerful; (2) devalue the worth of the performance of the less powerful; (3) attribute the cause of the less powerful's efforts to power controlled by themselves, rather than to the less powerful's motivations to do well; (4) view the less powerful as objects of manipulation; and (5) express a preference for the maintenance of psychological distance from the less powerful. No support was found for the prediction that the administrative responsibility elevated self-esteem.

It is suggested that administrative control triggers the following train of events: (1) With the control of power goes increased temptations to influence other's behavior; (2) As actual influence attempts increase, there arises the belief that the behavior of others is not self-controlled, but is caused by the power holder; (3) Hence, a devaluation of their performance occurs. In addition, with increased influence attempts, forces are generated within the more powerful to (4) Increase psychological distance from the less powerful and view them as objects of manipulation.

The findings on the relationship between control of resources and frequency of influence also suggest a link between two alternate views of administrative responsibility. The first view describes power in terms of the control of resources, which provides the power holder with the potential to influence others. The second view places greater emphasis on the exercise of power as a process of forcing or persuading others to carry out some behavior they would otherwise not do. Those who view the exercise of power as a manifestation of personality also stress the manipulative aspects of interpersonal relations. For example, McClelland (1969) defines need for power as "concern about having influence over others" (p. 143). Yet clearly there is a difference between power defined as a dimension of social interaction, where the emphasis is on dominance and the manipulation of others, and power defined as the control of resources.

Corruption can also refer to the way in which the control of power changes the power holder's self-perceptions and his perceptions of others. Interestingly enough, power holders frequently believe themselves exempt from common morality. This view has come down through history in several forms. Machiavelli, for instance, argued that it is necessary for a prince to learn how not to be good. A recent study of business executives (Sorokin & Lunden, 1959) similarly found power holders leading a double life with reference to morality—having one set of moral values for the office and a second for the home. Sorokin believes that the very possession of vast power tends to demoralize the power holder.

These changes in self-regard appear to occur for several reasons that are of concern to psychologists. First, the power holder finds that he is able to influence others because of the power he controls. Such compliance may lead the power holder to believe that his ideas and views are superior to other persons. Second, the power holder tends to be the recipient of flattery and well wishes from the less powerful. This flattery may also contribute to the idea that he is something special. Finally, it may be that the control of resources demands that the individual adopt a morality consistent with the kinds of power he controls. For instance, Galbraith (1967) has said that managers in large corporations are practically forced to make decisions which minimize risks to corporate investments, despite the fact that these decisions violate laws and the general welfare of the public. Thus, the morality that develops is designed to protect and extend corporate power and resources. Frequently, administrative power forces the administrator to ignore conventional morality.

Schwyhart and Smith (1972) investigated the nature of job involvement and its relationship to other variables with 149 male middle managers in one company. A replication group contained 58 subjects. Both company satisfaction and job involvement were measured using 20-item Likert scales. A significant linear relationship between the two was found in both groups. Because only the first factor—job ambition—was consistent with previous research, it was concluded that the factor structure of job involvement is occupationally specific. The results were interpreted as supporting the idea that importance of the job to a worker's self-image is associated with his satisfaction with the company.

Knowing how important a job is to a worker's self-image does not tell us why the job is important to him or what job behaviors or involvement may be related. Theories of work motivation are relevant to these questions. According to Vroom (1964), the self-image is reinforced, and the correlation between job performance and job satisfaction is increased when job performance is matched to the ability the worker values and possesses. Performance of workers has repeatedly been higher for those who were ego-involved in their jobs than for those who were not. The correlation between job satisfaction and perceived opportunity for self-expression was highest among workers who were highly involved in their jobs.

The job involvement concept has been shown to be positively related to the perceived importance of, desired amount of, and existence of opportunities for the attainment of esteem, autonomy, and self-actualization goals of middle managers. (Maurer, 1967). If the attainment of such goals is prerequisite to becoming involved, then turnover should be higher among less involved workers. It has been found that job satisfaction increases with the opportunities for recognition and autonomy, and persons achieving in the eyes of their companies are less likely to resign. (Ross and Zander, 1957).

Gemmill and Heisler (1972) found a relationship between an individual's control over his environment, job satisfaction, and performance. More specifically, the study indicates that the greater the belief in one's ability to influence the environment, the lower is the reported job strain and the higher is the reported job satisfaction and positional mobility. Managers who believe in their ability to control their environment, when confronted by job strain-evoking situations, are more likely to initiate attempts at improving the situation. To the extent that such attempts are successful, job strain is reduced and their belief reinforced. A history of success in overcoming job strain-evoking situations could also lead them to feel less bothered when confronted by such a situation. The relationship between the environmental control orientations of managers and positional mobility may be explained by the fact that managers who view control as external may be more likely to perceive promotion as a chance occurrence, thus being less inclined to focus upon the acquisition of necessary skills and techniques. It might be expected that managers who occupy higher organizational positions and who are more upwardly mobile (experience greater total positional mobility) would be more internally-oriented.

The concepts of organizational climate serve as a useful framework for tying together some of the diverse individual and organizational approaches to behavior. One purpose of research on reward policies is to demonstrate how differently reward policies may effect effort. Not only can the interorganizational differences be examined as a function of reward system, but also the differences in the way individuals relate to the organization.

Extrinsic rewards may be viewed as causes of effort which are moderated by the effort-reward policies and procedures of organizations. Effort is an interaction of both individual variables (the degree to which rewards are valued) and organizational climate or reward variables (the degree to which effort is rewarded with valued rewards).

It follows that measures of individuals may be valid predictors of behavior in some organizational settings but not in others. In terms of the path-goal (effort-reward) model, it is hypothesized that personal intrinsic values will be positively related to effort, and effort will be greater where the individual is rewarded with extrinsic rewards he values. Not only would effort be highest in organizations where it was rewarded with pay, but those people most highly valuing pay in that organization would be the ones working the hardest. There is, however, no relationship between the value of pay and effort. For those who most highly value intrinsic rewards or feelings, satisfaction with pay for high effort allows for self-reinforcement. Thus, it was found that those working the hardest not only most highly value various intrinsic rewards, they are also most satisfied with their pay.

Hodgkinson reported on work which attempted to correlate values assumed to be essential to the administrative process and social perceptions in the organization. He used Halpin's Organization Climate Description Questionnaire and value scales developed by Scott. He sampled 40 public schools with a total sample size of 8,707 teachers and administrators. He advanced five major hypotheses:

1. The hierarchical levels of an organization are reflected in differences of values and value orientations for the role incumbents. That is, values vary with status.

2. Staff value orientations are significantly correlated with social interaction perceptions.

3. Staff and leader values and value orientations are related to the concept of authenticity as expounded by A. W. Halpin (1966, pp. 203–204). Halpin was of the opinion that the two dimensions of Thrust and Esprit, as measured on his OCDQ instrument, represented the best indices of authenticity. He was, however, vague as to the precise nature of the term.

4. Inner-direction and other-direction (in the sense explicated) are directly or inversely related to the "openness" of organizational climate.

5. A biographical hypothesis: Age, sex, and length of service in the organization are predictive of value orientation.

(Hodgkinson, 1970, p. 00)

His findings suggest that values and social perceptions are related. There is evidence to support the hypothesis that values change with progression in the organizational hierarchy. Promoted teachers have value orientations which are different from their colleagues at the time of promotion; promoted teachers have value orientations which become different from their colleagues as a result of promotion; and as suggested above, promoted teachers have a flexibility of value orientation, which is an explanatory factor in observed changes at different hierarchical levels in the organizational structure.

The value of kindness discriminates between the role of teachers and administrators and between younger and older teachers, young female teachers being the most concerned about this value. The older and more experienced the teacher, the more important the value of loyalty tends to be. Some evidence indicated that newly appointed administrators stressed this value, but that it declined in importance with length of service. The value of academic achievement did not appear to be especially high to one group. Religiousness and physical development appeared to be of greater significance to the organization. The values of creativity and independence discriminate between organizational roles with administrators and older teachers.

To summarize, it would appear that personal factors such as intelligence and so-called organizational abilities are not important to the administrative function if a reasonable amount of skill is present. The influences from the administrator as a person, and the influences on the administrator from the job, as they become integrative forces, are the essential ingredients. Social values do change as one climbs the organizational hierarchy and especially as they are confronted with organizational pressures. It is not true that administrators use their power ruthlessly, or in fact, that power corrupts! The opposite is more likely to occur. As they feel a responsibility for people, administrators become more humanistic. The age-old struggle between humanistic and organizational values is not even an operable concept today, especially for an administrator faced with procuring behavioral change as the major product of his organization. Modern institutions do not need mechanisms to fix personnel and budgetary problems. They need active programmatic leadership, another pair of dirty hands, understanding and working for those who work in a program.

Educational administrators are decision makers above all else. Former President Truman's "the buck stops here" adage is most appropriate. Leadership has many different qualities. The three major ones are simply to be a good listener, weigh the matter, and decide a course of action. The modern institutional or special education administrators are working members of an organization; they must be a part of that organizational structure, representing all of its subparts, seeing them as organized wholes.

The practicing institutional or special education administrator must not only solve the problem, but must also assist in phrasing the question relating the problem to be solved. The reactor-to-crisis role must be laid to rest; the dimension of active planning must be surfaced. Ramos has a paragraph in "Models of Man and Administrative Theory" which is worthy of more than one reading. He writes:

> Administrative theory can no longer legitimize the functional rationality of the organization as it largely has done. . . What brings about the crisis in today's organizations is the fact that by design and operation, they still assume that old scarcities continue to be basic, while in fact contemporary man is aware of critical scarcities belonging to another order, i.e., related to needs beyond the level of simple survival. (19) Thus, the Social Darwinism that has traditionally validated management theory and practice has become outdated by the force of circumstances. (Ramos, 1972, p. 245)

CONCLUSION

This chapter presents a balance between the two major dimensions facing special-school or correctional administrators: social pressures and personnel needs. The attitudes and beliefs society maintains concerning institutional programs were explored since the current state-of-the-art for specialized services and programs reflects may historic antecedents. Special-education or correctional administrators constantly confront these two dimensions in developing and maintaining programs. That is, they must prepare, educate, and stimulate to action the professional staff and the community at large on the nature of their programs. And, they must develop skills necessary to undertake the daily job of administering an institutional program which entails planned change, the dynamics of administration, decision making, institutional program models, types of organization, modern systems analysis, formats for program, and personnel evaluation.

REFERENCES

Algozzine, R. F.; Alper, K. J.; and Sabatino, D. A. *A Simplified Evaluation Process for Classroom Teachers,* 1975.

Atkin, M. C. "Evaluation Theory Development." *Evaluation Comment* (1969): 2–7.

Banathy, B. *Instructional System.* Palo Alto, California: Fearon, 1968.

Banghart, F. W. *Educational Systems Analysis.* London: The MacMillan Company, 1969.

Bidwell, D. E. "The Administrative Role and Satisfaction of Teachers." *Journal of Educational Sociology* 29 (1955): 41–47.

Blai, B., Jr. "An Occupational Study of Job Satisfaction and Need Satisfaction." Unpublished doctoral dissertation, Temple University, 1962.

Burrello, L. C. "The Development and Validation of the Behavior Preference Inventory, based upon Rotter's Social Learning Theory for use with Special Education Administrators." Doctoral dissertation, Syracuse University. Ann Arbor, Mich.: University Microfilms, 1969. No. 70–14, 718.

Burrello, L. C. "Research and Theory in Special Education Administration." *The First Review of Special Education,* vol. 2. Philadelphia: JSE Press, 1973.

Campbell, R.; Corbally, J.; and Ramseyer, J. *Introduction to Educational Administration.* 3rd ed. Boston: Allyn and Bacon, 1966.

Cartwright, D., and Zander, A. *Group Dynamics.* 3rd ed. New York: Harper, 1968.

Courtnage, L. E. "School Administrator's Attitudes and Opinions Concerning the Public School's Responsibility in Providing Education for Exceptional Children." Doctoral dissertation, Colorado State College. Ann Arbor, Mich.: University Microfilms, 1967, No. 67–13, 672.

Cronbach, L. J. "Course Improvement through Evaluation." *Teachers College Record* 64 (1963): 674-683.

Dabas, Z. S. "The Dimensions of Morale: An Item Factorization of the SRA Employee Inventory." *Personnel Psychology* 31 (1958): 217-234.

Galbraith, J. K. *The New Industrial State*. Boston: Houghton-Mifflin, 1967.

Gemmill, G. R., and Heisler, W. J. "Fatalism as a Factor in Managerial Job Satisfaction, Job Strain, and Mobility. *Personnel Psychology* 25 (1972): 2, 241-250

Getzels, J. W., and Guba, E. G. "Social Behavior and the Administrative Process." *School Review* 65 (1957): 423-444.

Getzels, J. W.; Lipham, J. M.; and Campbell, R. F. *Educational Administration as a Social Process*. New York: Harper and Row, 1968.

Gordon, C. J. "A Factor Analysis of Human Needs and Industrial Morale." *Personnel Psychology* 3 (1955): 1-18.

Graham, R. "Responsibility of Public Education for Exceptional Children." *Exceptional Children* 28 (1962): 255-259.

Gruenfeld, L. W., and Weissenberg, P. "Field Independence and Articulation of Sources of Job Satisfaction. *Journal of Applied Psychology* 54 (1970): 424-426.

Guba, E., and Bidwell, D. E. *Administrative Relationships: Teacher Effectiveness, Teacher Satisfaction, and Administrative Behavior*. Chicago: University of Chicago, 1957.

Guion, R. M. "Industrial Morale (a symposium), the Problem of Terminology." *Personnel Psychology* 11 (1958): 59-64.

Halpin, A. *Theory and Research in Administration*. New York: MacMillan, 1966.

Hammond, R. "Context Evaluation of Instruction in Local School Districts." *Educational Technology* 9 (1969): 13-18.

Henrichs, J. R. "A Replicated Study of Job Satisfaction Dimensions." *Personnel Psychology* 21 (1968): 479-503.

Herzberg, E.; Mausner, B.; and Snyderman, B. B. *The Motivation to Work*. 2nd ed. New York: Wiley, 1959.

Hodgkinson, C. "Organizational Influence on Value Systems." *Educational Administration Quarterly* 6 (1970): 46-55.

Homans, J. *A Textbook of Surgery*. 6th ed. Springfield, Illinois: Charles C. Thomas, Publisher, 1975.

Iris, B., and Barrett, G. V. "Some Relations between Job and Life Satisfaction and Job Importance." *Journal of Applied Psychology* 56 (1972): 301-304.

Jones, R. L. "Accountability in Special Education: Some Problems." *Exceptional Children* (1973): 631-642.

Kendall, L. M.; Smith, P. C.; Hulin, H. F.; and Locke, E. A. "Cornell Study of Job Satisfaction: I.V. The Relative Validity of the Job Descriptive Index and other Methods of Measurement of Job Satisfaction." Ithaca, New York: Cornell University, 1963.

Kipfer, B. "Conceptualizing an Administrative Management System for Special Education." *Educational Technology* 13 (1973): 16-21.

Kipnis, D. "Does Power Corrupt?" *Journal of Personality and Social Psychology* 24 (1) (1972): 33-41.

Krathwohl, D. R. "Stating Objectives Appropriately for Program, for Curriculum, and for Instructional Materials Development." *Journal of Teacher Education* 12 (1965): 83-92.

Lerner, J. W. *Children with Learning Disabilities.* Boston: Houghton Mifflin, 1971.

Lessinger, L. "Accountability: Its Implications for the Teacher." *The Teacher's Handbook.* Edited by D. W. Allen. Glenview, Illinois: Scott Foresman, 1971.

Lilly, M. S. "Special Education: A Teapot in a Tempest." *Exceptional Children* 1 (1970): 43-49.

Lindvall, C. M.; Nardozza, S.; and Felton, M. "The Importance of Specific Objectives in Curriculum Development." *Defining Educational Objectives.* Edited by C. M. Lindvall. Pittsburgh Press, 1964.

Maurer, J. G. "The Relationship of Work Role Involvement to Job Characteristics with Higher-Order Need Satisfaction Potential. Doctoral dissertation, Michigan State University. Ann Arbor, Mich.: University Microfilms, 1967, No. 68-4182.

McClelland, D. C. "The Two Faces of Power." *Journal of International Affairs* 24 (1969): 141-154.

McCormick, E. J.; Jeanneret, P. R.; and Mecham, R. C. "A Study of Job Characteristics and Job Dimensions as Based on the Position Analysis Questionnaire (PAQ)." *Journal of Applied Psychology* 56 (1972): 347-368.

McKelvey, W. "Exceptional Noncomplementarity and Style of Interaction between Professional and Organization." *Administrative Science Quarterly* 14 (1969): 21-32.

Michael, W. B., and Metfessel, N. S. "A Paradigm for Developing Valid, Measurable Objectives in the Evaluation of Educational Programs in Colleges and Universities." *Educational and Psychological Measurement* 27 (1967): 373-383.

Miller, D. "Policy Formulation and Policy Implementation Relationships in an Educational System." *Strategies of Educational Planning.* Edited by R. Kraft. Florida State University, 1969.

Newman, K. S. "Tasks of the Administration of Programs of Special Education in Selected Public School Systems with Public Populations between 13,000 and 30,000." Doctoral dissertation, Arizona State University. Ann Arbor, Mich.: University Microfilms, 1968, No. 68-15, 012.

Ohrtman, W. F. "One More Instant Solution Coming Up." *Journal of Special Education* 6 (1972): 377-478.

Pallone, N. J.; Rickard, F. S.; and Hurley, R. B. "Job Satisfaction Research of 1966-1967." *The Personnel and Guidance Journal* 48 (1970): 469-478.

Parelius, A. M. "A Study of the Role Expectations of Special Education Directors in Oregon." Doctoral dissertation, University of Oregon. Ann Arbor, Mich.: University Microfilms, 1968, No. 70–9463.

Popham, W. J. "Objectives and Instruction." *Instructional Objectives.* American educational research association, monograph series on curriculum evaluation, no. 3. Chicago: Rand McNally and Co., 1969.

Proger, B. B.; Carfioli, J.; and Kalapos, R. L. "A Neglected Area of Accountability: The Failure of Instructional Materials Evaluation and a Solution." *The Journal of Special Education* (1973): 269–279.

Provus, N. M. *Teaching for Relevance: An Inservice Training Program.* Chicago: Whitehall, 1969.

Pulliam, J. S. "The Administrative Organization of the Training School." *Readings in the administration of institutions for delinquent youth.* Edited by W. E. Amos. Springfield, Ill.: Charles C. Thomas Co., 1965, pp. 15–16. Reference: Courtesy Charles C. Thomas Publisher, Springfield, Illinois.

Ramos, A. G. "Models of Man and Administrative Theory." *Public Administration and Review* 32 (1972): 3, 241–246.

Redfern, G. B. *How to Appraise Teacher Performance.* Columbus, Ohio: School Management Institute, 1963.

Rogow, A. A., and Lasswell, H. D. *Power Corruption and Rectitude.* Englewood Cliffs, N.J.: Prentice-Hall, 1963.

Rosen, R. A., and Rosen, H. "A Suggested Modification in Job Satisfaction Surveys." *Personnel Psychology* 1 (1955): 303–304.

Ross, L. C. and Zander, A. "Need Satisfaction and Employee Turnover." *Personnel Psychology* 10 (1957): 327–338.

Rotter, J. B. *Social Learning and Clinical Psychology.* Englewood Cliffs, N.J.: Prentice-Hall, 1954.

Rucker, C. Administration of special education dissertations, completed and in progress. Columbus, Ohio: General Special Education Administration Consortium, University Council for Education Administration, 1971.

Ryan, T. "Systems Techniques for Programs of Counseling and Counselor Education." *Educational Technology* 9 (1969): 7–17.

Ryan, T. A. "Educational Management by Systems Techniques in Correctional Institutions." *Educational Technology* 12 (1972): 18–26.

Schaeffer, R. H. "Job Satisfaction as Related to Need Satisfaction." *Psychological Monographs* 67 (1953): 1–29.

Schwyhart, W. R., and Smith, P. C. "Factors in the Job Involvement of Middle Managers." *Journal of Applied Psychology* 56 (1972): 3, 227–233.

Scriven, M. "The Method of Evaluation." *Curriculum Evaluation.* Edited by R. E. Stake. American Educational Research Association Monograph Series on Evaluation, No. 1. Chicago: Rand McNally and Co., 1967.

Sedlacek, W. E. *An Empirical Description of Available Theory and Research on Job Satisfaction.* Chicago: Midwestern Psychological Association, 1966.

Sorokin, P. A., and Lunden, W. A. *Power and Morality: Who Shall Guard the Guardians?* Boston: Sargent, 1959.

Stufflebeam, D. L. "Evaluation as Enlightenment for Decision Making." Address at working conference on assessment theory. The Commission on Assessment of Educational Outcomes. The Association for Supervision and Curriculum Development, Sarasota, Fla., 1968.

Stufflebeam, D. L. The Relevance of the CIPP Evaluation Model for Educational Accountability. Unpublished manuscript. The Ohio State Evaluation Center, 1972.

Stufflebeam, D. L.; Foley, W. J.; Gephart, W. J.; Guba, E. G.; Hammond, R. L.; Merriman, H. O.; and Provus, M. M. *Educational Evaluation and Decision Making.* Itasca, Ill.: F. E. Peacock Publishers, Inc., 1971.

Suchman, E. A. *Evaluative Research.* New York: Russell Sage Foundation, 1967.

Sweitzer, R. E. "The Superintendent's Role in Improving Instruction." *Administrators Notebook* (1958).

Vergason, G. A. "Accountability in Special Education." *Exceptional Children* (1973): 367–373.

Vroom, V. H. *Work and Motivation.* New York: John Wiley and Sons, 1964.

Wood, D. A., and LeBold, W. K. "The Multivariate Nature of Professional Job Satisfaction." *Personnel Psychology* 23 (1970): 2, 173–189.

Worthern, B. R., and Sanders, J. R. eds. *Educational Evaluation: Theory and Practice.* Worthington, Ohio: Charles A. Jones, 1973.

Yuskiewicz, F. P. Pupil Control Ideology and Job Satisfaction of Public School Teachers. Unpublished doctoral dissertation. The Pennsylvania State University, 1971.

7

psychosocial/educational assessment of juvenile delinquents

R. WAYNE JONES AND ROBERT L. BLANEY

Correctional facilities for juveniles have typically been more effective in labeling chronically disruptive youth as unworthy than they have been in providing these individuals with alternative paths to acceptable life styles. Yet the public assumes that correctional facilities for juveniles will be effective in altering an individual so that upon his return to society he will be less likely to conflict with established laws. A review of the effectiveness of these institutions in meeting this expectation strongly suggests that juvenile delinquent facilities, like adult penal facilities, are excessively expensive and, moreover, are exceptionally ineffective. The current Governor of California, Edmund G. Brown, Jr., has stated that these institutions "don't rehabilitate, they don't deter, they don't punish, they don't protect" (1975, p. 53). Almost everyone now connected with criminal justice systems, including lawyers, judges, criminologists, correctional officials, and even the inmates themselves are acknowledging openly that rehabilitation in prison is not effective work for most. It is estimated that the United States spends approximately one billion dollars a year to confine and correct 220,000 convicted offenders in state and federal prisons. At least half of these offenders return to these or similar facilities in neighboring states after their release.

If the purpose of juvenile correctional facilities is, in part, the rehabilitation of delinquents, then the specification of an appropriate treatment program becomes a critical factor. Such treatment programs should emphasize the development of effective coping skills which are consistent with the demands of society. An adequate self-concept has been hypothesized as one important factor in the development of effective coping skills and is necessary for the assumption of appropriate adult roles in society. (Brookover, 1967). Treatment goals in correctional facilities should take the form of realistic feedback to improve an individual's self-concept rather than to enhance feelings of inadequacy.

Unfortunately, most institutions for juvenile delinquents do not have highly individualized treatment regimes specifically directed toward remediation of the individual deficits or problems of a specified youth. Generally speaking, facilities provide a general educational program apart from or as part of a more specified clinical treatment program. The educational program is usually based on a standard state-approved curriculum, and herein lies a dilemma: a number of studies (Farls, 1967; and Jones & Strowig, 1968) have suggested education to be the single most important factor affecting the development of self-concept. But while most correctional facilities do provide some sort of educational program, that program is based on a standard curriculum that is typically the very source of academic difficulty for the male delinquent. (Sabatino, Mauser & Skok, 1975).

The educational programs available in correctional facilities for juvenile offenders are potentially the basis for effective individualized treatment regimes. However, if such programs are to be effective in reaching state treatment goals, important modifications must be made. For example, it is essential that for each individual the appropriate entry instructional/academic level in all subject matters (especially reading, math computation, and spelling) be specified. No student can be expected to succeed at instructional levels that are incongruous with his current levels of ability. In addition, careful attention should be given to the student's learning rate, as well as to other individual strengths and weaknesses in his learning style. The most effective means for obtaining the information necessary for the development of an appropriate individualized educational program would be by psychosocial/educational evaluation. Adequate psychosocial/educational assessment can, at the very least, delineate an individual's present level of ability in school content areas and predict learning rate and potential intellectual capacity.

Effective clinical treatment programs should be based on the information collected by a comprehensive psychosocial/educational assessment of norm-violating youths. The constraints of time and lack of fully qualified personnel may make the implementation of all the following suggestions difficult, but comprehensive psychosocial/educational evaluation during the initial period of adjudication could make programs for delinquents significantly more instrumental in producing positive behavior change.

The purpose of psychosocial/educational diagnosis is to describe the learning and behavioral characteristics of each youth so as to tailor-match remedial and treatment programs for specific problems. The type of diagnostic information obtained on incoming adjudicated delinquents will vary from one institutional facility to another, but almost all institutional facilities have some type of intake procedures. This is particularly true for the majority of correctional centers across the United States containing some aspects of an educational program. However, the specific procedures which characterize intake assessments have been shown to be exceptionally variable (Sabatino, Mauser & Skok, 1975). If intake diagnostic and assessment procedures of either a psychological or psychoeducational nature are to be meaningful, they must lead to alternative routes for treatment and/or education. In addition, all the collected data should provide predictive information on the age-old problem of recidivism.

Neither the courts nor the majority of treatment centers for adjudicated delinquents have fully qualified professional staff. The number of qualified penal psychiatrists is small. Ph.D.-level psychologists working on more than a consultative basis to the majority of facilities are exceptionally rare. (Meninger, 1968). The staffs of most facilities lack social workers or similarly trained personnel who can collect family and environmental histories. The majority of facilities rely on Masters-level counselors or psychologists to conduct intake interviews, record histories, assess court transcripts, and conduct the intitial psychosocial/psychoeducational assessment.

If delinquent incarceration is viewed as purely punishment, then there is no valid or logical reason for psychosocial/educational assessment. On the other hand, if treatment philosophy prevails as the main purpose of incarceration, headlining the major mission of preparing the individual to take an appropriate societal role upon return to his original environment, such assessment becomes vital. Evaluation of a variety of variables and/or deficit states which may have led the individual into the original conflict with societal norms and the resultant conviction and loss of civil liberties becomes totally essential. Psychosocial evaluation should provide the correctional facility staff with information that will effectively match assignments of an individual to (1) more appropriate and effective treatment regimes, including choice of psycho-therapeutic technique, milieu variables, and peer associates; and (2) the selection of an appropriate educational entry level for school placement, including a precise and detailed evaluation of possible areas for academic remediation, encompassing the degree to which curriculum and instruction must be individualized.

In addition to an urgent need for more effective evaluation and assessment of youth at the time of court adjudication, there continues to exist a need for improved precision in society's prediction of delinquency, thereby increasing the likelihood of prevention. More precise information on adjudicated youth may give new or expanded direction to delinquency prediction assessment techniques. The following section will review research on the three major existing instruments or procedures which have been used in the United States for predicting delinquency. The subsequent section will propose a model for psychosocial/educational assessment.

PROBLEMS IN THE PREDICTION OF DELINQUENCY

The difficulty in specifying the exact nature of juvenile delinquency has caused a number of problems in the development of instruments for the assessment, diagnosis, and prediction of delinquency. Any definition of delinquency is necessarily contextual in nature. A commonly held definition states the phenomenon to be the commission of repeated acts of a kind which, when committed by persons beyond the statutory juvenile court age of 16, are punishable as crimes (either felonies or misdemeanors). Such a definition is premised upon legal factors, and such factors usually vary from community to community depending upon the social norms and attitudes of that community. Thus, an offense which might designate a particular youth to be delinquent in one community may in fact not be considered a criminal offense in another. It is frequently a youth's failure to comply with a unique set of social norms that determines juvenile delinquency. Factors involved may change from situation to situation. Thus, because of sociocultural variability in defining juvenile delinquency, the specification of unique personality traits associated with juvenile delinquency is a difficult if not impossible problem.

McDavid (1968, 1974) suggests that crime and delinquency may be viewed as two sorts of behaviors: asocial and antisocial. Asocial behavior refers to an individual's inability to control certain behavioral impulses that arise from relatively normal motivation. Although such behavior is unacceptable socially, it is most likely the result of an individual's failure to learn acceptable socially defined behaviors. The behavior itself cannot be viewed as a direct and purposeful attack upon society; rather, the individual simply fails to learn to monitor his behavior through the inhibition of socially unacceptable acts.

Antisocial behavior, on the other hand, represents a purposeful and direct attack upon society. There is a premeditated, intentional factor in antisocial behavior that is absent in asocial behavior. Both asocial and antisocial behaviors may be serious unacceptable behaviors. Violent aggressive behavior can provide an example of the distinction between these two types of behaviors. Feelings of aggression may generally be considered as a normal consequence of frustration. The socialization process encourages the inhibition of relatively normal aggressive impulses through socially acceptable releases such as football, boxing, etc. When this socialization process fails to control the aggressive behavior of a particular individual, the individual may respond to aggressive impulses in a socially unacceptable manner. Although socially unacceptable behavior may take a number of expressive forms, it cannot be inferred that this behavior represents an intentional attack upon society. Excessive aggressive behavior may simply represent the failure of the socialization process to provide appropriate outlets for difficult-to-explain feelings. This failure of the individual to control or inhibit such impulses would still be appropriately referred to as asocial behavior.

On the other hand, the individual who experiences frustration and consequently sees himself as a victim of society's interference with his own personal objectives may be impelled to attack society directly. Such behavior would take the form of carefully planned crimes such as forgery, extortion, or premeditated assault. Asocial behavior is typically seen in the senselessness of many adolescent crimes such as the theft of a small amount of money, the theft of an auto for a brief joy ride rather than its resale, or pointless vandalism.

Although the various crimes committed by juvenile delinquents are both antisocial and asocial according to the distinction specified by McDavid, the greatest number of these crimes would seem to belong to the category of asocial behavior. It is interesting to note, however, that although most juvenile delinquents are initially adjudicated for what might be termed a foolish asocial crime, many of these youths become repeated offenders and subsequent crimes are of a decidedly antisocial nature. That is to say, a youth arrested for a relatively petty offense may well be later arrested for far more serious and premeditated crimes.

Considerable research has been undertaken in recent years to develop instruments useful in predicting juvenile delinquency. The reasoning behind such research has been the need for a method of identifying and treating the potential delinquent. Such reasoning is indeed sound; there could be no better deterrent to juvenile delinquency than the ability to detect those youths who evidence a high probability of delinquent behavior before such behavior occurs. Unfortunately, those instruments available have to date proven to be far from successful in identifying the potential delinquent. For a number of reasons the development of an assessment instrument capable of predicting juvenile delinquency has proven difficult. Some of these reasons characterize the development of any standardized predictive instrument.

The development of an instrument to predict delinquency is based on the notion that a configuration of personality traits is common to most juvenile delinquents. Thus, the basic problems in the development of a predictive instrument are first, the specification of the nature of those unique traits; and second, the development of effective techniques for measuring those particular traits. In addition, there are problems associated with the development of an instrument which can be administered effectively and economically to the appropriate populations. Furthermore, the validation of such an instrument is difficult but critical. These problems have all contributed to hindering or retarding the development of a valid and reliable instrument effective in the prediction of juvenile delinquency.

The accuracy of any predictive instrument is dependent on a number of factors. Because delinquency is typically an adolescent phenomenon, the problem arises as to when it is possible to detect or assess those traits which indicate a propensity toward delinquency. If an instrument is to be an effective predictor, then there should be no appearance of critical etiological factors after the assessment has been undertaken. Further prediction must be based on the nature of some trait which is relatively stable at the time it is measured and which remains stable as the subject matures. The identification of these traits and the assessment procedures have proven uniquely difficult problems for the production of an instrument predicting delinquency.

Some theorists (Glueck, 1950) claim that their instrument may be administered as early as age 6, but it is difficult to believe that significant factors within the family cannot change appreciably in the six or so years before adolescence. Other writers, such as Reckless, Denitz, and Kay (1957), argue that age 12 is the earliest age at which a reasonable prediction may be made about future adolescent behavior. Their selection of age 12 is based on a number of factors: (1) it is the age commonly considered to be the beginning of adolescence; (2) before this age, few cases are ever resolved in court; (3) around age 12, children generally enter junior high or high schools in most American cities; and (4) early adolescence is also generally considered to be the time of life when young people begin to verbalize about themselves and effectively utilize self-expression and self-reporting instruments making assessment more feasible.

Ethnic and racial composition of the normative population must also be considered and given special attention in an instrument produced to predict delinquency. A review of the literature on assessment instruments in this field indicates that most standardization procedures have failed to utilize a reasonable population sample for norming their predictive instruments.

Perhaps the most severe criticism of those instruments which have been developed and used in predicting delinquency is the lack of acceptable empirical validation of their predictive ability. Unfortunately, the validation techniques employed have retrospectively utilized populations of delinquent and nondelinquent youths. It is essential, however, that prospective application be given to different, independent samples in order to properly evaluate the instrument's ability to predict delinquency. Before reviewing these specific validation studies, a more detailed discussion of the predictive instruments available should be undertaken.

Despite the difficulties associated with their construction, a number of assessment instruments for predicting juvenile delinquency are available. Some of the instruments have been designed with this specific purpose in mind. Other techniques have proven amenable for assessing prosocial and antisocial behavior in varying degrees, and thus of predicting potential delinquency.

ASSESSMENT INSTRUMENTATION FOR PREDICTING DELINQUENCY

The following section discusses those instruments which have been used in extensive longitudinal predictive research studies. Three instruments are reviewed: the Gluecks' Social Prediction Scale, the Kvaraceus Delinquency Proneness Scale, and the Minnesota Multiphasic Personality Inventory.

Glueck's social prediction scale

It would be worthwhile to first examine the Glueck's Juvenile Delinquency Scale because of the important contribution made by these researchers to the literature on juvenile delinquency. The Gluecks initially designed three scales for predictive purposes. The first was a scale of interpersonal family factors, later known as the Social Prediction Scale. The second was a scale of character structure traits which was based upon a projective technique, the Rorschach InkBlot Test. The third scale dealt with temperament traits which were determined as the result of a psychiatric interview. The development of these three predictive scales was based upon those factors which were found to discriminate sharply between 500 delinquents and 500 nondelinquents. The three scales were later abridged to one, the Social Prediction Scale, and it has been this scale which has undergone intensive and long-term evaluation.

The nature of this Gluecks' Social Prediction Scale requires factual and observed data on five subtest variables to be obtained by trained home interviewers. The interviews recorded the following:

1. Discipline of the boy by his father
2. Supervision of the boy by his mother

3. Affection of the father for the boy
4. Affection of the mother for the boy
5. Cohesiveness of the family unit

The initial validation study on the prediction of delinquency utilizing the Social Prediction Scale was obtained on a sample of 224 Caucasian boys who were entering the first grade in the school year 1952–1953. This sample was later increased by the addition of another 76 boys. A comprehensive follow-up study of all the boys in this evaluation provided the predictive criterion data on this particular instrument.

The initial five-factor scale has been reduced to a two-factor and a three-factor scale. The three-factor scale includes: (1) discipline of the boy by his father; (2) supervision of the boy by his mother; and a measure of (3) family cohesiveness. The two-factor scale retains only supervision of the boy by his mother and a measure of family cohesiveness. It is suggested by the investigators that these two instruments are more refined than the earlier five-factor scale. After nine years of study and evaluation, the Gluecks' Social Prediction Scale has evidenced moderately good predictability between potential delinquents and nondelinquents. Validity data accumulated over the nine years indicate that the three-factor scale obtains 70% accuracy in predicting delinquency and 85% accuracy in predicting nondelinquency.

Despite the fairly high degree accuracy with which the Glueck's Social Prediction Scale has predicted delinquency and nondelinquency, a number of criticisms have been raised concerning the construction of these scales. One major criticism concerns the fact that a family rating approach is in itself a cumbersome, time-consuming, and expensive process. It is frequently not practical to require individual assessment of the family situation by a trained social worker. Other criticisms concern the nature of the construction of the test itself. For example, the studies used in the development of this particular prediction table were all completed in a restricted, high-delinquency area in New York City. In addition, the rating techniques used by the social workers in the assessment of these five major variables are subjective. The inherent subjectivity in these ratings can be seen in variables such as family cohesiveness and supervision. These particular factors are highly culturally dependent and often have little significance in lower-class families. Finally, the statistical treatment given the data accumulated by the Gluecks has been assailed on a number of accounts with frequent claims that invalid statistical treatments were involved.

Although many concurrent (matching control and known delinquent populations) validation studies of the Gluecks' Social Prediction Scale have been undertaken, very little data have been provided on the actual predictive validation of this instrument. Only two prospective studies other than those conducted by the Gluecks themselves appear to have been undertaken. These are the Maximum Benefits Project, which was initiated in Washington, D.C., in 1954, and the New York City Youth Board Project, which is reviewed in the writings of Whelan (1954). The obtained data indicate that in neither project was the Gluecks' Scale able to efficiently predict delinquents as opposed to nondelinquents. In fairness to the Glueck's Scale, it should be pointed out that circumstances surrounding the use of this scale were not ideal. The Maximum Benefits Project was not designed specifically to validate the Gluecks' Social Prediction Scale of delinquency. The Scale was administered to a random sample of boys entering first grade. Serious questions arise, of course, as to whether or not the Gluecks' Social Prediction Scale can accurately be used to detect delinquency proneness in children five to six years of age. Despite the authors' claim of validity for boys as young as age six, it should be noted that the instrument was, in fact, originally standardized on boys whose ages ranged from 11 to 17 years. In any event, predictive validation support for the Gluecks' work was not provided by the Maximum Benefits Project.

It would seem that the New York City Youth Board Study would provide the necessary criteria for adequate validation of the Gluecks' delinquency prediction scale. This project was longitudinal in nature and used first grade boys from high delinquency areas in which Negro and Puerto Rican children composed a large population. Under such circumstances this investigation held forth the possibility of a very rigorous test of the Social Prediction Scale. It also would allow a measure of potential generalization to racial and ethnic groups since the scale was originally derived from a Caucasian sample.

The study's results are unfortunately discouraging. Whelan (1954) reports that abbreviated tables of the Social Prediction Scale do not do an adequate job in identifying potential delinquents. In using the abbreviated three-factor scale (introduced midway in the study), correct prediction was obtained in 84.8% of the cases, but the forecast was that some 98.77% of the boys would be nondelinquent. These results suggest that there is a serious difficulty here. The Gluecks' Prediction Scale identified 70 of the 221 boys in the sample (31.7%) as potential delinquents requiring treatment. Such treatment efforts would, in fact, be unnecessary for 46 of the boys of two-thirds of the treatment group. In addition, one-fifth of the potential delinquents are missed by the Gluecks' screening device and would not receive appropriate treatment. (Voss, 1963). The question in this case may be whether any agency interested in the prediction of delinquency can afford to use such an unreliable measuring device. The three-factor scale, which was not the original instrument, was introduced in the middle of the experiment. As previously mentioned, the three-factor scale was comprised of mother supervision, father's discipline, and cohesiveness of the family.

The substitution was made because it was felt this particular scale was more accurate than the initial five-factor scale.

A number of other limitations of the Gluecks' instrument are cited by Voss (1963). Most of these criticisms concern the construction and standardization of the scale using an equal number of delinquents and nondelinquents (extreme population). Voss points out that samples of broader populations are needed to approximate the actual delinquency rates. This condition is necessary to construct a prediction scale containing prognostic power. Concerning the applicability to other racial and ethnic groups, aside from the original Caucasian sample, Voss reports that the predictive accuracy for the Gluecks' Scale was 100% for Caucasian and Puerto Rican boys and 92.6% for Negro boys predicted to be nondelinquents. On the other hand, the accuracy of the table was very low in its ability to predict potential delinquents. The predictability for Caucasians was 22.2%; for Negroes, 36%; and for Puerto Ricans, 36.4%. These predictions were correct in 76.5% of the cases (169 of the 221 cases studied). If these results can be assumed to reflect the actual predictive capacity of this instrument, then one must necessarily conclude the validity of the Gluecks' prognostic instrument is at best confined to use with lower-class Caucasian males. Voss (1963) concludes that the Gluecks have, in fact, not found a valid predictive instrument for juvenile delinquency. What they have developed is a prognostic tool which is only in the first stage of development, namely the establishment of criteria. The instrument awaits the next stage which involves the application of the criteria prospectively to independent new samples.

The Kvaraceus delinquency proneness checklist and rating scale

Two major diagnostic instruments for prediction of juvenile delinquency have been devised by Kvaraceus (1961). One, the Kvaraceus Delinquency Proneness Checklist is comprised of 70 background variables which delinquents are hypothesized to have. The form is generally filled out by the adolescent's teacher and requires a yes-no response to test items.

The second, the Kvaraceus Delinquency Rating Scale, utilizes a nonverbal test format consisting of 62 circles divided into four quadrants with a stimulus picture in each quadrant. The subject is asked to select which of the four pictures he prefers and which he likes least. This technique is similar to a four-choice multiple-choice question.

Validity data have been gathered in a detailed, three-year study on 1,594 students in a predominantly lower socioeconomic black junior high school, grades 7 through 9, and also on a small sample of retarded youths in special classes. Criterion data were determined by the behavioral adjustments made by individuals in this sample to school, neighborhood, and community over a predetermined time. Predictive efficiency of these instruments was studied by sex and grade using a 4-point scale. Sample subjects were classified according to categories: (1) never offending, (2) minor violations in school, (3) minor violations in school and community, and (4) serious offenses, including police and court records. Despite the care taken with the validation procedures of this particular instrument, an unfortunate lack of consistency in the data indicates that caution must be exercised in the employment of this particular instrument for decision making. One component in the validation procedure included a comparison between teacher nominations for potential delinquency as compared with the efficacy of this particular instrument in predicting potential delinquent behavior. Teacher nominations proved to be, in some situations, as efficient, and in others, more effective, as predictors of future delinquency.

A number of research studies have been undertaken using the instruments designed by Kvaraceus. Through these studies (including Balogh, 1958; Bechtold, 1964; Clements, 1967; and Kvaraceus, 1961), the general research conclusion indicates that the most immediate need is for a long-term validation study. These studies have indicated that the Kvaraceus Delinquency (KD) Scale and Checklist are relatively valid predictive instruments for use in the prevention of delinquency. One must keep in mind the predominantly Negro and lower-class composition of the standardization populations.

Kvaraceus' own validation of the nonverbal form of the KD Scale indicated that the nonverbal scale is not yet ready to be used in a school-community program of delinquency prevention. Kvaraceus (1961) makes note of several factors which he suggests are worth further attention in predicting delinquency tendency. First, he suggests that reading ability must be taken into account as one symptom closely associated with the delinquency syndrome. Thus, close attention to poor readers during the middle school years may enable school personnel to focus on a group of youngsters who are perhaps already, or potentially soon to be displaying behavioral disturbances. In addition, Kvaraceus emphasizes that behavior rating by experienced teachers in some cases showed more promise of predictive ability than the KD Proneness Non-verbal Rating Scale. In summary, the findings concerning the Kvaraceus juvenile delinquency prediction tools all seem to indicate that, like those of other instruments discussed, there remains a strong need for long-term, randomly sampled prospective validation studies.

Minnesota multiphasic personality inventory

The Minnesota Multiphasic Personality Inventory (MMPI) has become a standard reference measure in determining personality profiles. Although not designed specifically for purposes of predicting juvenile delinquency, the MMPI has been used for these purposes. Briefly, this instrument developed by Hathaway and McKinley (1943) consists of individual and group administration forms and yields 14 specific subscores delineating a number of traits reflecting states of abnormal mental health. The instrument is comprised of 550 statements and cover a wide range of subject matter from physical conditions of the individual being tested to his moral and social attitude. Statements are responded to as *true, false* or *cannot say.* The test rarely takes longer than 90 minutes to administer and can be completed in a period as brief as 30 minutes. No supervision is generally required other than assurance of optimal cooperation from the subject; however, reading comprehension of approximately eighth-grade level is necessary.

For a number of reasons, the MMPI is not well-suited as an instrument to predict juvenile law violation. The MMPI is a measure of an individual's response, rather than a strict test of psychopathology. Test interpretation is difficult and requires sophistication on the part of the test administrator. Other criticism concerns the fact that the test was designed and standardized for the age range of 16 years and older. When used with a younger subject population, the MMPI loses a good deal of its sensitivity because of the inability of younger individuals to read and fully understand the items. Many of the test items would be inappropriate, or would appear so to a young subject. In addition, many teachers and parents object to specific questions regarding sexual activities and fantasy.

Despite these limitations, a number of studies have been undertaken using the MMPI as a predictor of potential delinquent tendencies. Hathaway and Monachesi (1951) have reviewed the various studies in which the MMPI was used as a predictive instrument. Hathaway and Monachesi themselves undertook a two-year followup study of high school boys and girls who had been administered the MMPI. Their sample population included 4,000 students. The initial 4,000 students examined, 591 had been arrested by the police or had court contact or both. An examination of the MMPI profiles of these delinquents indicated several patterns which showed promise in their ability to predict delinquent behavior. The best predictors of antisocial behaviors were elevated scores on Scale 4—Psychopathic Deviate, and Scale 9—Hypomania. These two scales have been shown to be predictive of delinquency on certain cases.

Another interesting finding reported was that those adolescents whose MMPI profiles indicated no high deviation and were thereby indicated to be normal are very unlikely to be found delinquent. The nondelinquency prediction seems to be more substantiated in the data than does any specific pattern of scales for positive prediction of delinquency.

The greatest difficulty in predicting delinquency concerns the ambiguous middle group, indicated by any evaluative instrument in which demarcation between delinquency and nondelinquency is difficult and yet must be made. With respect to this problem, Hathaway and Monachesi note that it is probably not possible to identify such an individual within the confines of a single testing procedure, but rather determination of such inclinations would most likely depend on a careful evaluation of circumstances precipitating a social behavior. This is to say, the tendency toward delinquency in the cases of such individuals would be variable. In this middle group of juveniles, Hathaway and Monachesi propose that the individual is acted upon by environmental circumstances. It is these particular circumstances which must be further evaluated in order to make any accurate predictions.

VARIABLES IN PSYCHOSOCIAL/EDUCATIONAL ASSESSMENT

If appropriate comprehensive treatment programs are to be planned for adjudicated disruptive youth, psychosocial/educational assessment should include measures of a number of variables. These variables would minimally include assessment of the following categories:

1. Intellectual Capacity
2. Medical and Neurological Evaluation
3. Language Development
   a. Diagnosis of reading skills
   b. Diagnosis of mathematical computation
   c. Diagnosis of spelling ability
4. Academic Achievement Levels
   a. Standardized achievement tests
   b. Study and organizational skills evaluation
5. Personality and Self-Concept Evaluation
6. Vocational Interest Pattern Assessment

Intellectual capacity

An estimate of intellectual capacity is needed for a number of reasons in the assessment of individual cognitive and social development. Educators can most accurately use such scores to predict rate of learning. Individual measures of intelligence, such as the Wechsler Intelligence Scales and the Stanford-Binet provide psychologists and educators with detailed estimates of capacity in a number of content areas. In the normal adolescent there occur relatively even patterns of development as reflected by intelligence test subscores. In disturbed adolescents, however, these patterns show clusters of strengths and weaknesses. Awareness of individual variability can make a skilled teacher more competent in the selection of teaching techniques and materials which utilize the strengths of the given individual in overcoming apparent deficits.

Current data, collected from both adult penal institutions and records available on juvenile facilities, note the disproportionate number of incarcerated individuals who are found to be in the borderline or mentally retarded range. An individual limited in intellectual capacity is frequently unable to understand or to reason adequately in dealing with the environment. Such an individual frequently makes errors in judgment, is more easily swayed and influenced by others, and seems to lack the capacity for long-term planning.

Special education has demonstrated, however, that individuals with less than average intelligence can be educated to become self-sufficient. In vocationally-oriented or uniquely structured academic classes, many such individuals make considerable gains developing marketable skills that improve employment enlargement. Their general social functioning and capacity to meet societal demands can also be improved. For these reasons one must caution against any restriction to educational programs for adolescents with less than average intelligence. Even more care should be taken to avoid labeling individuals, particularly if no specific remediation program follows such classification.

The measurement of intelligence has always raised considerable questions. The most reliable and theoretically valid tests of intelligence (including the Wechsler Adult Intelligence Scale, the Wechsler Intelligence Scale for Children—R (revised), or the Stanford-Binet, Forms L–M) must be administered by a trained psychometrist. These instruments usually require approximately one hour or longer for administration. There are other available tests which purport to provide derived IQ scores, but these tests sample far fewer behaviors and thus, are basically screening tests. The Slossen Intelligence Test is a widely used instrument requiring approximately 30 minutes to administer. A number of the items on the SIT are drawn from the Stanford-Binet and some from the Wechsler Scales. The Peabody Picture Vocabulary Test is a screening intelligence test which taps only receptive vocabulary. Paper-and-pencil IQ tests, such as the Otis-Lennon or the Henmon-Nelson Tests of Mental Ability and numerous others, require a reading level at approximately fifth to seventh grade before validity can be ascertained. Further, a paper-and-pencil intelligence testing is only as accurate as the test conditions under which it is administered. During an individually administered test the examiner can monitor the motivational level of an individual and pull from him information that he might not otherwise offer. On a paper-and-pencil test, particularly where there are multiple-choice items, many individuals who have had poor experiences in school merely mark answers to be finished with an unpleasant task. They fail to realize the consequences of an invalid score.

Culture-free intelligence tests, more recently labeled culture fair tests, are both difficult to find and at best only fair to the culture on which they are standardized. The early attempts at avoiding language have not proved successful. For example, the Raven's Progressive Matrices, the Kohs Block Design Tests, and even the Leighter International Performance Scale are still heavily influenced by social class and school experience. Because many delinquents have a very erratic school record and frequently come from low socioeconomic status families, screening intelligence test instruments are of limited value. Furthermore, such measurements may lack meaningful data for important decision making by staff. Individual estimates of intelligence are clearly the preferred mode of assessment.

Medical and neurological evaluation

A thorough medical evaluation should be a standard component of admission procedures. Because many norm-violating youth grow up in families with limited financial resources, they may need extensive medical attention. Attention should be paid to sensory problems in vision and hearing. Body weight and height should receive careful evaluation with dietary recommendations becoming a part of a total program for adjudicated youth. Allergy reactions may be possible behavior-triggering components. Sex and health education may be critically important and require guided discussion and instruction. Acne reactions and medical guidance for reducing skin eruptions may likewise be of extreme importance in a defined adolescent population.

Careful attention should be paid during initial medical examination and psychoeducational assessment for possible neurological handicaps. The epileptic and seizure-prone individual makes up a far greater proportion of adjudicated adults than is found in the general populations. The typical explanation for this observation is that incarcerated individuals lack the capacity to delay gratification and have low frustration tolerance or excitation limits. Such an organic-based syndrome is characterized by quick or sudden anger outbursts, difficulty in maintaining delay components for gratification, and general impulsivity. Unfortunately, no totally valid psychological test is available to specify neurological malfunction. Possible diagnostic techniques continue to receive considerable attention, particularly in the work of Ralph Reitan at the University of Indiana, as well as numerous other investigators such as Larry Hartlege at the University of Georgia Medical School. These investigators are developing a series of examination procedures which attempt to specify localization of brain damage or variation in brain function (Halstead, 1947; Reitan, 1964). Numerous tests and tasks are involved in the examination procedure but the approach includes considerable emphasis on laterality or brain hemispheric dominance; repetition capacity such as in finger tapping; balance; and sensory recognition including touch, trace, feel, and grasping components of object recognition (Hartlage and Lucas, 1973). At this time, both the administration and interpretation of instruments designed to detect neurological dysfunction (Halstead, 1947; Reitan, 1964). Numerous tests and tasks are working in penal institutions. The procedures usually require a coordinated staff of physicians, psychologists, and laboratory technicians found only at medical schools or elaborate hospital settings in large urban centers.

Psychologists have frequently relied on the use of tests such as the Bender-Gestalt or other geometric copying tasks (Development Test of Visual Motor Integration, Rutgers Drawing Test, The Winterhaven Test) for one estimate of possible interference in motor coordination. The reliability of such diagnosis remains somewhat less than desirable. In general, however, these tests can detect the individual who demonstrates deficits in fine muscle motor control coordination which suggest neurological dysfunction. The occurrence of severe motor deficits on one of the above instruments should lead to a more extensive examination by a neurologist who could recommend medication or other forms of appropriate treatment.

Careful history may provide further significant clues in detecting neurological disorders. Fainting or blackout spells, the occurrence of a serious head injury, chronic and/or consistent headache patterns, marked difference in appetite or sleep patterns, and sudden change in behavior may give indications warranting more extensive medical examination.

Language development

The public school system in the United States is essentially a lock-step grade system which children enter around age six and are usually graduated from between the ages of 17 and 19. Success in the system is predicted on mastery of basic language skills in reading, written expression, and math. It is expected that most children with an average IQ would make such grade progress in a linear fashion. A large number of children with developmental language lags whose individual needs are not met by the grade system nonetheless remain locked into that system. The capacity to individualize academic programs depending on the specific language levels of children is a concept widely discussed, but unfortunately less frequently implemented.

Throughout the research literature the academic achievement levels of institutionalized male delinquents have pointed to serious under-achievement. It is now estimated that perhaps as many as 70% of ad-judicated male delinquents have mild to severe learning disabilities. In a recent sample by Sabatino, Mauser, and Skok (1975) 60% of delinquents were reported to have less than a 2.5 grade level reading comprehension score while their chronological ages ranged from 12 to 17. Ability to read, write, and perform simple math computations are essential skills required by contemporary society. Individuals handicapped in these areas are always frustrated as well as existing at a decided disadvantage. The severe reading problems which characterize so many males in the popu-lation deserve paramount attention during the average six- to nine-month period of incarceration.

The average delinquent is decidedly not interested in school. He frequently has a high truancy record. School failure is another frequent component. These parameters are often the result of early problems in mastering reading and other basic language foundations. One study by Shore, Massimo, and Ricks (1965) strongly suggests that lowered recidi-vism follows a marked enhancement of self-concept; but the essential precursor of an improved self-concept is bringing the literacy skills, par-ticularly reading, up to meaningful societal levels, somewhere between fifth and seventh grade. Individuals in our society who cannot read at a minimum fifth-grade level are seriously handicapped. They are unable to read sufficiently to get driver's licenses, complete employment forms, understand newspaper headlines, even to follow directions printed in buildings and other areas for travel. They are illiterate in the broadest sense of that term and severely handicapped in their interaction with others. The frustrations and anger, as well as the constant sense of inade-quacy, engendered by this deficit appear to be the prime motivators for the antisocial behavior described by McCandless and McDavid (1962).

Diagnosis of reading skills

The diagnosis of reading skills can be accomplished quite easily. The process of reading is more than mere calling of words; it requires com-prehension, that is, an understanding of content. Speed of reading, memory capacity when reading silently, as well as oral fluency skills, are all important aspects of reading assessment when making educational prognosis for adjudicated norm violators. There are a number of effective test instruments including standardized achievement tests which essentially monitor an individual's ability to read words of increasing difficulty. The most accurate indices are individual informal reading tests. The informal reading inventory asks an individual to read aloud to an examiner. Examples of these instruments are the Gray Oral Reading

Test (Grades 1 through 12), the Durrell-Analysis of Reading Difficulty (Grades 1 through 7), and the Gates McKillop Reading Diagnostic Tests (Grades 1 through 8). The basic requirement is that the individual be able to read and comprehend a paragraph of a certain grade level difficulty. If he can read with 80% accuracy on both decoding (word calling) and comprehension skills, it is assumed that he can essentially read at that given grade level. (Woodcock, 1973). If a student can read adequately at seventh-grade level or better, no further exploration of reading in needed. If he cannot read adequately, it may be necessary to utilize more intensive diagnostic approaches measuring whole word recognition, usually utilizing Dolch lists of words at varying grade levels and phonetic word decoding skills. One should measure various comprehension levels following both oral and silent reading, as well as listening comprehension, as in the test framework of the Durrell-Analysis of Reading Difficulty.

The Woodcock Reading Mastery Tests is a comprehension reading diagnostic battery determining vocabulary level, word recognition, and comprehension skills. This test requires 30 to 40 minutes for administration and provides the teacher responsible for reading with a detailed analysis of strengths and weaknesses in the reading process as well as appropriate entry level for instructional material. The broad dimensions of the reading process should be more commonly included in initial assessment procedures than is the grade-level score reported by the Wide Range Achievement Test, which is only an estimate of phonetic decoding ability.

The classroom level of reading instruction should be carefully tailored to the individual's needs. In recent decades there has been an explosion of materials designed for poor readers. These materials typically are comprised of low vocabulary level but high interest content which should increase their effectiveness with older students who are poor readers.

Diagnosis of mathematical computation

Determining an appropriate instructional level for mathematics is for the most part dependent on standardized achievement test scores. Only recently has there been the introduction of more elaborate measures for diagnosis of math ability, particularly for the primary school grades. The Key Math Diagnostic Arithmetic Test is an example of a commercially available screening instrument covering a wide variety of practical and applied mathematics. The test takes approximately 35 minutes for administration. Subtests measure addition, subtraction, multiplication, and division, as well as the other general components of math. It also evaluates metric units, time, money, change, and word problem solution. A total of 17 variables or math activities are delineated by specific grade-level proficiencies. The number of delinquents who do not have an adequate understanding of time units and money is large; many also lack a conceptual understanding of mileage units, distance, rate, and other applied math components which underlie the ability to study advanced science courses offered in high school. These are technical language handicaps which prevent such students from being able to compete in certain school courses, but more importantly, block avenues for particular jobs and careers.

Key Math should be administered by the school personnel responsible for math instruction. The math portion of the Wide Range Achievement Test is also a viable screening estimate of general math capacity. Grade-level math ability may be liably assessed in standardized achievement tests. The shortcoming of the achievement test estimate is the lack of specificity of developmental gaps in math ability which may be present or their inclusion of practical application of math such as making change.

The practical understanding of math is a pressing problem for delinquents. The need for algebra, geometry, and trigonometry courses is less important in facilities for disruptive youth. The most urgent need is to raise practical knowledge of math applications so that these students can carry on effective commerce, thus cope with day-to-day economics required in our society.

Diagnosis of spelling ability

Spelling skills remain one of the most neglected diagnostic areas in all psychometric evaluations. Few diagnostic instruments provide adequate measures of spelling ability, yet the majority of graded material in school requires written answers. The inability to express in writing what one may know is a decided disadvantage.

Careful attention should be made by teachers that an individual can spell sufficiently to express his ideas in writing. One can rarely spell better than he can read. Many adjudicated adolescents will show as much as a two-year lag in spelling below their reading comprehension level. Schools have frequently made this problem worse by some teacher's careful attention to correct spelling and by repetitive drill for practice of errors.

The spelling test on the Wide Range Achievement Test and the spelling test on the Durrell-Analysis of Reading Difficulty are both useful guides to approximate grade placement. The standardized achievement tests, such as the Stanford and the Metropolitan, evaluate spelling at the middle school years and high school years by a student's ability to correctly spot a misspelled word, but do not include in their batteries the actual written component. Many students may be able to tell you that a word is incorrectly spelled but will be unable themselves to spell it correctly. Criterion reference instruments developed by individual schools may be the most appropriate manner for evaluating a student's capacity to express knowledge by writing. It is not that the attainment of a particular grade level should be stressed in spelling, but rather teachers should ensure that students have sufficient capacity to express their written ideas at their level of reading comprehension.

Academic achievement levels

Standardized achievement tests

Standardized achievements tests are the most commonly utilized measures of academic performance levels in public schools as well as in the majority of institutions for delinquents. Standardized group achievement tests consist of samples of content-oriented questions presented in a multiple-choice format which require grade-level reading ability. They are usually administered with time limitations. A review of the specifications of tests would indicate that these instruments are basically power tests. The time dimensions are primarily used because additional time does not increase the accuracy score for the majority of students. Examples of standardized group achievement tests would include the Stanford Achievement Test Battery, the Metropolitan Achievement Test Battery, and the Iowa Test of Basic Skills, but there exist numerous others. These tests are usually designed at specific grade levels for the elementary school children and two or more forms for the high school student. The number of subscales on such achievement tests range from 7 to 10 or more. The amount of time provided for the completion of the total battery is between 6 and 11 hours.

The high school battery would be the most appropriate achievement test for the grade level of most adjudicated delinquents. However, the reading levels of many delinquents indicate that they would be unable to adequately understand either the directions or the questions. Minimum reading comprehension level requirement for understanding high school level standardized achievement tests is at least seventh grade and preferably higher.

These tests are highly inappropriate for children who have either poor school attendance records and/or serious language problems. The survey by Sabatino, et al. (1975) found that more than half of male delinquents were reported to be reading at less that 2.5 grade level. Depressed reading ability would preclude the use of the high school level achievement tests. In cases of suspected reading difficulty, a comprehensive reading test would be a far more meaningful diagnostic instrument for selecting beginning instructional level than would an achievement test. Frequently confused with detailed achievement tests such as the Stanford and the

Metropolitan achievement batteries is the Wide Range Achievement Test (WRAT). The WRAT is a screening instrument measuring word pronunciation (which the authors label *reading*), math computation, and spelling ability. Thus, this test, while normed on a large number of individuals, tends to overestimate by one year or more the elementary grade equivalent scores obtained on the more inclusive standardized achievement tests. The WRAT is frequently used because it can be administered quickly. Being only a screening instrument, it requires somewhere between 10 and 15 minutes for the average student to complete. The nature of the WRAT, then, suggests it to be inappropriate in determining estimates for entry level instruction or measurement of academic gain.

A final note of caution should be made. The average student does not show progressive grade-level gains throughout the high school years. Whereas grade-level scores for the elementary school level are generally associated with average proficiency, as one approaches the middle school years there is a decided ceiling effect. Only a smaller percentage of college-bound students continue to show yearly gains throughout high school. Percentile scores become more accurate indicators of average gain. During early adolescence there is also an increasing correlation between general intellectual capacity and achievement levels. The shift in source of variance is more than that directly attributable to classroom instructional activities. As stated previously, minimal reading competencies of approximately eighth-grade level are required for successful completion of any of the high school achievement batteries. Students who do not possess this level of reading comprehension will always score considerably lower on these instruments, despite the fact that they may know the correct answer when questioned orally.

The usefulness of standardized achievement tests lies in their ability to provide grade-level equivalencies for a variety of subject areas. One must be careful, however, in selecting appropriate entry level textbooks on the basis of these scores, because these tests assume a series of instructional progressions which are not always followed by different textbook authors.

Study and organizational skills evaluation

When planning educational programs for adjudicated delinquents, teachers and psychologists should evaluate a student's abili.y to organize material, his ability to scan material for useful facts, his reading speed, and his general approach to study matters. The poor school records of most delinquents allows one to predict that, as a group, they are weaker than the average high school student in terms of their ability to draw main ideas and to sequence important facts. They also usually lack the ability to take notes, outline, and condense material. These are effective skills in making academic tasks less difficult, but luckily may be acquired through instruction and practice. Study skills assessment is overlooked by the majority of diagnostic procedures. While this area may not require assessment at time of intake, it should be carefully monitored by teachers as they work with students, and individual attention to study skill deficits should be made early during incarceration. Improved study skills combined with an appropriate individualized curriculum could hopefully increase a student's motivation toward school accomplishment.

Several formal psychometric measures of study skills are available. The high school battery of the Metropolitan Achievement Tests provides measures of study skills in language and social studies. These measures are more accurately an estimate of an individual's capacity to follow printed directions or understand information presented in different forms such as tables or graphs. The test is valid only if the client possesses at least eighth-grade reading proficiency.

Study skills are included in the Comprehension Tests of Basic Skills with four separate grade levels between second grade and high school. These tests measure the ability of students to use library references, encyclopedias, maps, graphs, and charts. Unfortunately, the tests do not deal with the process of effective study or attitude toward school. Research suggests that minimal reading skills of at least mid-third grade level are required for even the lowest level of the test.

Several study skills evaluation tests exist for high school students who anticipate college entrance. These instruments would include the Cornell Critical Thinking Test and the Study Skills Test: McGraw-Hill Basic Skills System. These tests are appropriate only for students achieving at eleventh-grade level equivalents or higher.

The Diagnostic Evaluation of Study Skills, a self-report instrument developed by McDavid (1976) holds excellent potential for guiding teachers toward correction of deficits in an adolescent's approach to try schoolwork or something similar. The instrument attempts to pinpoint the level of skills development in the following areas: (1) Goal setting; (2) Motivation and values; (3) Budgeting time and scheduling; (4) Resistance to distraction; (5) Concentration and attention; (6) Learning and memorizing; (7) Reading; (8) Listening; (9) Taking notes; (10) Writing; and (11) Taking tests and examinations. These skills have been found to be well developed in students who achieve in high school and anticipate college attendance; and markedly deficient in underachieving high school students.

Personality assessment

Definitive assessment of personality dimensions remains an enigma to most practicing clinicians. Most agree that the personality makeup of individuals strongly contributes to their behavior patterns and their predictability, and should be an essential dimension in a full diagnostic profile for a given individual. Unfortunately, there are few concise and comprehensive measures of personality which can be used reliably with any population.

Projective techniques have frequently been used to differentiate between normalcy and the clinical diagnosis of severe neurosis and psychosis. Instruments such as the Rorschach InkBlot Test, the Thematic Apperception Test, and numerous others require one or more hours for administration. The administration and interpretation of these techniques usually require doctoral-level training in clinical psychology and considerable experience. Even the predictive or mechanical scoring systems as used by Kvaraceus in utilization of responses on the Rorschach InkBlot Test remain cumbersome, time-consuming, and difficult administrative tasks for the majority of psychologists or counselors responsible for such services in institutions. These techniques have low reliability and questionable construct validity, and do not appear to be promising practical approaches to the problems of delinquents.

Target behavior assessment has been suggested by Paul (1966) and Ullman and Krasner (1965) as an appropriate behavioral method for the categorization of individuals who may then require more extensive and in-depth interview and/or clinical assessment. One can predict with certainty that a significant number of inmates in juvenile facilities have serious emotional problems. At least a portion of these would be more appropriately placed in facilities for the emotionally disturbed rather than facilities for behavior correction which essentially characterizes youth development centers. Target assessment techniques include observation of interpersonal relationships, behavioral consistency, classroom awareness, and other behavioral indices which could be gathered by individuals working with the client. The authors emphasize that there are difficulties associated with such approaches. Careful base rate recording and communication between different professional staff are required as they interact with a given client across time. The practical information collected, however, is directly usable by a staff for planning and/or reacting to the problems of a given delinquent.

A number of paper-and-pencil personality assessment instruments have been discussed previously in the section of this chapter reviewing efforts to predict delinquency. Such inventories designed to measure personality development are frequently used with adults. The most commonly used instrument is the Minnesota Multiphasic Personality Inventory. As described earlier in this chapter, the test is read and answered by the subject. The inventory takes an hour or more and requires at least an eighth-grade reading comprehension level. These requirements make the instrument inappropriate for the majority of clients in facilities for juveniles. Further, interpretation is a multifactor comparison and cannot be done on the basis of scores alone. The MMPI and other paper-and-pencil indices of personality pathology may provide more inappropriate classification labels rather than useful insights for the staff personnel working with disruptive youth. Considerable caution must be exercised in the use of such tests, both in terms of the time and cost expenditure and the possibility of inappropriate application.

Locus of control can be attributed to oneself or the environment, and the extent to which one feels in control of his life appears to be an important variable. The measurement of this dimension has developed in terms of the internal/external (I/E) scale by Rotter (1966). A children's I/E Scale has been developed by Norwicki and Strickland (1973) which could have useful application, considering the academic levels of most delinquents in many institutions. The scale can be read by the individual or administered orally. Such internal/external measurement is utilized frequently in current research. In general, findings indicate the more internalized one is, the less likely he is to be swayed by his environment or by the influence of his peers. One's reliance on internal mechanisms has been shown to be an important dimension for the effectiveness of psychotherapy. Unfortunately, the average delinquent generally scores high on the externalization component of this measurement. But those individuals who show change toward an internalized state are usually considered to be showing positive progress and improvement. More research is certainly needed, particularly with delinquents for the construct validity of this scale with regard to prediction of future recidivism. It is a promising approach however, and one that should receive careful attention, particularly for problem children referred after their initial psychosocial evaluation and for individuals who are returning to youth development facilities.

The following tests for measurement of personality diagnosis and classification represent a selection of instruments with characteristics which should prove to be valuable for better understanding of problem youth.

The California Psychological Inventory (CPI) developed by Gough (1959) is designed to measure those character traits which arise directly and necessarily from interpersonal interaction. The assessment of these traits is then hypothesized to allow for the understanding and prediction of social behavior in any situation in any culture. The CPI is comprised of 18 subtests which in turn consist of a total of 480 test items. Almost half of these items are taken from the MMPI. Items are responded to in a true-false manner. The CPI is designed to assess the psychological adjustment of youths 13 years of age and older.

The original open-ended design of the CPI would allow for the addition of new scales as needed, but none were added. Rather, Gough elected to utilize linear combinations of the existing 18 scales for applied prediction purposes. The regression equations formulated on the basis of the original scales include ones to predict parole outcome, and social maturity versus delinquency. A major criticism of the CPI concerns the high inter-correlation of the subtests. Factor analysis does not support the hypothesis that the subtests are independent measures of personality variables. In addition to its redundancy and lack of parsimony, the CPI is criticized for a failure to include a sufficient number of duplicated items to allow for scoring of response consistency and response validity. Although the CPI is well normed, test-retest reliabilities are only moderate, ranging from 0.58 to 0.75 over a one-year period.

In the CPI's favor is the fact that it is one of the few personality inventories with enough empirical research collected to allow a user to evaluate its probable utility in an educational setting. However, the large number of scales makes the CPI difficult to interpret conceptually and cumbersome to use in counseling. The advanced reading level required to complete CPI also reduces its effectiveness in use with potentially delinquent populations.

The California Life Goals Evaluation Schedules, developed by Hahn (1966), are scales which attempt to determine an individual's desired future conditions. Based on an assessment of an individual's economic, social, and political attitudes, the California Life Goals Evaluation Schedules claim to determine directions of motivation. There are 10 schedules (or life goals) which investigate constructs. These include esteem, profit, fame, power, leadership, security, social service, interesting experiences, self-expression, and independence. The test contains a total of 150 highly debatable statements; the subject responds on a 5-point scale ranging from strongly agree to strongly disagree. After responses are scored, a profile is drawn up on the basis of the 10 life goals.

For a number of reasons, the California Life Goals Evaluation Schedules appear to be still in the experimental phase. The author indicates that norms, reliabilities, and validities are still tentative. In addition, it is not yet clear whether or not the 15 items on each scale comprise an adequate sampling of the concept. Because this instrument has been designed for use with individuals 15 years of age and over, the reading level of this test would most likely require revision downward to be of major use with delinquent populations.

The California Test of Personality (Thorpe, Clark, and Tiegs, 1953) consists of a series of five questionnaires designed to measure personal and social adjustment components in children. Each of the five components is designed for a specific age range, including 3 years of age through kindergarten, 4 through 8 years of age, 7 through 10 years of age, 9 through 16 years of age, and adults. The five components are basically uniform throughout this series. A major advantage of this particular test is the fact that it may be administered to groups, although individual oral administration is recommended for the primary scale.

The nature of the scales is generally directed toward items assessing self-adjustment and social adjustment. The self-adjustment scale is divided into six subtests which examine self-reliance, personal worth, personal freedom, feeling of belonging, withdrawing tendencies, and nervous symptoms. The social adjustment scale is also based on six subtests which investigate social standards, social skills, antisocial tendencies, family relations, school relations, and community relations.

Norms are provided for the evaluation of scores yielded by these particular tests. Anastasi (1968) suggests that internal consistency reliabilities are reasonably satisfactory for the total score yielded and also for the two subtotals. Self-adjustment and social adjustment are clearly important in predicting and diagnosing delinquency. Again, however, no careful studies utilizing the California Test of Personality have been reported with incidence data for delinquents.

A practical method of identifying emotionally disturbed children from within a general school population is offered by Lambert and Bower (1961) in their Two-Step Process for Identifying Emotionally Handicapped Pupils. Initially, a screening procedure is undertaken to identify children having difficulty in school because of suspected emotional disabilities. This procedure is followed by further identification of those children within this selected group whose emotional difficulties appear to be causing them extreme adjustment problems in school. The initial screening involves three types of measures designed to gather information regarding the child's interaction in the classroom. Specifically, these three measures involve the teacher's perception of the pupil's behavior on a day-to-day basis, perception by the classmates of their fellow pupils' school behavior, and the child's self-perception. Those students who score above a certain rank on any two or three screening measures are indicated as likely to be handicapped emotionally and are thus referred for further diagnostic treatment. This selected group generally includes approximately 10–15% of the school population. Forms were designed to allow for use at primary, elementary, and secondary grade levels.

A distinct drawback to the use of the Two-Step Process for Identifying Emotionally Handicapped Pupils is that it requires massive amounts of paper work. The validity of these particular screening processes has been subject to many different tests. According to Bower (1960), some 9 out of 10 children who were identified through the screening procedures in this two-step process were found, on the basis of individual followup study, to have emotional problems ranging from moderate to severe. The authors of the Two-Step Process for Identifying Emotionally Handicapped Pupils also claim it to be sensitive in detecting moderate to serious emotional problems in children who are not readily identifiable and who, thus, have not been reported as requiring assistance from school psychology personnel. One can readily anticipate that a significant number of such students will be delinquents, but to date no defined population incidence data are available.

The Ego Ideal and Conscience Development Test (EICDT) developed by Cassel (1969) has two forms and is a paper-and-pencil instrument consisting of nine subtests: (1) home and family; (2) inner development; (3) community relations; (4) rules and law; (5) school and education; (6) romance and psychosexual; (7) economic sufficiency; (8) self-actualization; and (9) a total score across other subtests. The instrument attempts to discriminate between delinquents and nondelinquents in their ego ideal development. Unfortunately, this instrument is low in test validity. The premise of the test is that the ego ideal and consequent conscience development in delinquents is markedly different from the development of such constructs in nondelinquents. Although there is some evidence that this device can distinguish delinquent and nondelinquent youth (Reise, 1969), further reliability and validity studies must be conducted before concluding that this instrument is assessing a phenomenon that does, in fact, exist.

Behavior Cards, developed by Stodgill (1949), are designed to provide a structured interview technique to assist in distinguishing potentially delinquent children. This instrument requires the subject to sort 150 cards which describe specific behaviors. Sorting is done on the basis of whether or not the described behavior is characteristic of the individual. In addition to the advantages gained by allowing for an interview, the Behavior Cards also are well suited to use with a potentially delinquent population in that they require only a fourth-grade reading level.

Average reliability coefficient between items was reported to be 0.68 and 0.72 for two groups of male delinquents, and 0.52 for a group of female delinquents. Validation and normative data are on small samples and no data are available to date on nondelinquent populations. Despite the relatively inadequate norming, validation, and reliability procedures undertaken for this instrument, the Behavior Cards seem worthy of further research, particularly concerning their potential clinical value where individual assessment techniques are required.

The Hostility and Direction of Hostility Questionnaire (HDHQ) is an instrument developed in Britain by Caine, Foulds, and Hope (1967). The major assumption on which the HDHQ is based is the hypothesis that aggression and severity of emotional disorder are highly related. Unfortunately, this speculation remains unfounded. No research data exist at this time to substantiate the relationship between emotional disturbance and aggression.

The nature of this particular instrument encompasses items taken from the Minnesota Multiphasic Personality Inventory, used on the basis of their face validity to assess five selected traits. The five subtests assessed variables of hostile acting out, criticism of others, projected delusional hostility (paranoia), self-criticism, and guilt. The reliability of this 51-item test is predictably low. Correlations between these five subscores and factor analysis of the intercorrelations suggest the existence of two main factors. The amount of hostility is determined by the sum of the five scores. The direction of hostility (intra- versus extra-punitive) is indicated by comparing the first three subtests with the last two.

The instruments reviewed thus far have been predominantly paper-and-pencil self-reporting instruments or instruments completed as the result of personal interviews. The Hand Test, in contrast to the above instruments, is an individual projective test. Individual projective tests are not frequently used in the assessment of potential juvenile delinquency for a number of reasons. Often such instruments do not report reliabilities or validities, and they generally fail to serve as instruments that are capable of producing valuable empirical data in response to research questions. A notable exception, however, appears to be this instrument.

The Hand Test, developed by Wagner in 1959, is aimed chiefly at adults but may also be successfully used with children as young as six years of age. The test consists of ten cards, nine of which show hands drawn in various positions and a tenth card which is blank. In addition to the standard cards for use with individuals, there now exists a group administered form which has been designed for experimental use.

Wagner's initial interest was the development of a projective technique to reveal aggression. He contends that the hand represents a natural medium by which important tendencies toward hostility and aggressiveness can be reflected. A subject's responses to the Hand Test as explained in the manual are classified into one or another of 15 formal scoring categories such as affection, dependence, exhibitionism, aggressive tension, etc.

Attempts to indicate any validity criterion of the Hand Test have been based to date on the ability to discriminate between individual subjects. Data collected indicate the following results in the use of this particular instrument. Wagner (1962) found that interpersonal, active, maladjustive, and withdrawal responses scored from the Hand Test successfully differentiated a population of 50 male schizophrenics from 50 college students. Use of the Hand Test was also the basis for the differentiation between 60 schizophrenics and 40 neurotics using a matched-pair design with this test.

Further study using this instrument (Bricklin, Protrowski & Wagner, 1962) described and compared differences in number and percentages of responses as well as other scoring categories for groups of normals, neurotics, schizophrenics, prison inmates, organics, and epileptics. Findings indicated that normals had the highest number of absolute responses, inmates the lowest; and epileptic patients gave the greatest number and percentage of problematic responses. Although these findings with adults need replication with juvenile offenders, the findings are provocative.

Self-concept

Researchers have recently indicated that several variables not normally assessed psychosocial assessment are important for understanding both the past history of delinquents and assisting them in developing strengths and skills which would reduce recidivism. Self-concept has been shown to be an important variable for distinguishing between antisocial individuals and those who take pride in both their own accomplishments and their position within society. People who feel inadequate, lack confidence in their own capacity, and are angry and frustrated by their deficits rather than confident in their capacities are high-risk individuals not only for crime but for mental disturbance. Several formal tests for measurement of self-concept exist and the following are among the more practical instruments for the norm-violating population.

The Tennessee Self-Concept Test (TSCS) purports to measure personal, family, social-ethic, and other aspects of self. The TSCS consists of 100 self-description items. Ninety of these items assess self-concept; the remaining 10 items assess self-criticism. Fourteen scores are derived in the Counseling Form which is felt to be suitable for feedback to the client. The same items are utilized in a more specific fashion to general scores on 30 dimensions on the Clinical and Research Form. The TSCS correlates high, with measures of anxiety such as the Taylor Manifest Anxiety Scale. The lack of appropriate factor analytic studies leaves open the question of whether the TSCS can validly generate 14 to 30 separate measures from a pool of only 100 items. The scale requires a seventh-grade reading level and has surprisingly good reliability. Time for administration is 30 to 45 minutes. The results are difficult to hand score but computer scoring is available. Interpretation is complex but does provide normed estimates of areas of normalcy or felt inferiority, and important scores of self-concept, which could be valuable in remediation efforts.

The Test of Social Intelligence is a measure of an individual's social cognition which involves the process of knowing or understanding other persons, their thinking, and their feeling. The test derives from Guilford's Structure of the Intellect. Reliability is variable on subtests but generally adequate. Responses require choosing multiple-choice formats of pictures or cartoons. A drawback is that normative data are based on a sample of eleventh-grade middle-class students; no populations of adjudicated youth have been studied. The instrument does hold promise, however, for improving a client's perception of others and a possible influence toward better self-understanding.

Several tests which are widely used with adult populations hold some promise for older delinquent populations. Unfortunately, like the MMPI, these paper-and-pencil instruments require reading levels of eighth grade or better. Such instruments would include the Edwards Personal Preference Schedule or the Thorndike Dimensions of Temperament. These instruments measure an individual's personality traits attempting to describe his basic behavior response. As such, they contribute to a fuller understanding of personality and self-concept development. The majority of delinquents lack sufficient experience in given situations to respond to a number of items. Each test requires an hour or longer to complete. Although these could provide useful resources in select cases, they are unlikely to be of value for most norm-violating youths.

Vocational interest pattern assessment

Complete assessment of psychosocial variables in populations of adjudicated youth should at least include some component of eventual interest in vocations or occupations. There are evident minimal academic competencies required for many occupations, and a realistic understanding of one's skills is indispensable in realistic planning. Interview or discussion approaches to monitoring an individual's anticipated work goals are frequent roles of counselors. Paper-and-pencil surveys are also used with success in college populations and certain groups of high school students. These approaches must be used cautiously, however, with delinquents.

The Strong Vocational Interest Blank for Men and for Women and the newly revised Strong-Campbell Vocational Interest Blank are the most widely used surveys of vocational interests. Unfortunately, these instruments are designed to monitor the emerging interests of older adolescents and young adults. Norms are provided only for individuals sixteen and older. Required reading comprehension is minimally eighth grade. Specific vocabulary and diversity of experience more typically acquired in middle-class families are necessary. The response profile can be hand scored, but it is moderately expensive. The Strong Vocational Interest Blank would be primarily useful for only the unusual delinquent; that is, one with above average high-school level literacy skills and vocational aspirations regarding activities of professional or managerial responsibility.

The Kuder General Interest Survey (KGIS) is a relatively new instrument which is more useful for the average incarcerated juvenile male population than the Revised Kuder Preference Record or the Strong Vocational Interest Battery. The KGIS is designated for grades 6 to 12. Required reading level has been kept simple and can be easily understood by adolescents with sixth-grade reading comprehension skills. Preferences for 10 work activities are scored. These include outdoor, mechanical, computational, scientific, persuasive, artistic, literary, musical, social service, and clerical. Profiles can be hand scored or machine scored. Considering the age and technical work experience of the majority of adjudicated delinquents, the more elaborate and refined dimensions of the Kuder Occupational Interest Survey require more experience and vocational knowledge than this population would possess.

A number of tests such as the Minnesota Vocational Interest Inventory require experience and/or minimal knowledge about the world of work. These tests require precise vocabulary and considerable information about vocations. They are standardized on populations of young adults; thus, they are not generally appropriate for the age group represented by adjudicated delinquents.

No vocational interest pattern instruments have been used extensively with adjudicated disruptive youth with longitudinal followup to measure their effectiveness. Clearly, such research activities are sorely needed. It may well be the diversity of literacy skills in incarcerated juvenile populations is such that it precludes heavy reliance on paper-and-pencil inventory profiles which have proved useful with graduating high school seniors and college populations.

Work evaluation or the work sample method utilized by vocational rehabilitation agencies is more likely to be of primary value for assessment of vocational potential. Work evaluation may also allow the incarcerated individual an opportunity to understand in a practical sense the variety of work experiences available to him. Technical and vocational education will increasingly become more viable as an avenue to adult financial independence for increasing percentages of our population in the United States. This pattern has been evident over the past 15 years. For the majority of adjudicated delinquents with their generally hostile attitude toward school achievement, vocational training may be a far more positive experience with realistic support.

The work sample approach to vocational evaluation is a mock-up or an abbreviated work activity that closely resembles the actual industrial operation. Work samples are often referred to as *work tasks, job samples,* or *prevocational tasks.* The work sample technique is an attempt to bring the individual into a simulated work situation. By simulating the actual job, the individual being evaluated is projected into a realistic industrial situation. Evaluation can thus be more effective than an aptitude test, and can be particularly useful with individuals who have educational or language handicaps. (Rosenberg, 1973).

There is considerable interest in the field of vocational rehabilitation to improve the quality of work samples as an evaluation technique for predicting work skill and potential. During the past twenty years a variety of work samples have been developed.

Jewish Employment and Vocational Service (J.E.V.S.)

Since 1958, the Philadelphia Jewish Employment Service has been working on a series of graded industrial tasks to assess individual abilities. In 1963–1965, a series of work samples were developed specifically for use with disadvantaged youth. This series consists of 28 sample tasks designed to measure potential skill in 14 general industrial categories: assembly-disassembly, bindery, clerical, display and printing, electrical, industrial housekeeping, layout design and drafting, mailroom, mechanical, packing, sorting, structural development, textile and tailoring, and metal work.

The evaluation procedure requires two weeks. The client begins with the simplest of the 28 work tasks—the assembling of three different sizes of nuts, bolts, and washers. Successive tasks become increasingly more complex, requiring the individual to perform such jobs as letter signs; couple sections of pipe; solder a square of tin; take apart and reassemble a step ladder, a door lock, and a telephone; perform varying electrical tasks; and weigh letters and boxes to compute postal rates. Each individual work sample is rated for time and quality on a 5 point scale for nine apptitudinal factors: G (general intelligence); V (verbal ability); N (numerical ability); S (spatial relations); P (form perception); Q (clerical ability); K (motor coordination); F (finger dexterity); and M (manual dexterity).

The Singer-Graflex vocational evaluation system

Developed by the Singer Corporation, this evaluation approach uses an audiovisual machine to present programmed instructions for the performance of certain work tasks. Work tasks have been developed in 10 occupational areas: basic tools, bench assembly; drafting; electrical wiring; plumbing and pipe fitting; carpentry and woodworking; refrigeration, heating and air conditioning; soldering and welding; office and sales clerk; and needle trades. For each occupational area, there is a work station which contains a teaching machine with film strip, synchronized tape cassette, and specific tools and supplies to complete the work task. The Singer-Graflex System is presently undergoing field testing and normative data are being collected to establish scoring criteria.

The TOWER work sample approach

The TOWER System (Testing, Orientation, and Work Evaluation in Rehabilitation) was developed as a means of predicting vocational skills in the handicapped. TOWER is a system of reality testing, employing work tasks in a simulated work environment. The system includes 13 broad areas of vocational evaluation: clerical, drafting, electronics assembly, jewelry manufacturing, leather goods, lettering, machine shop, mail clerk, optical mechanics, pantograph, sewing machine operating, workshop assembling, and welding. Each area covers a number of related occupations, thereby providing a total of more than 100 different tasks or tests.

During evaluation a client attempts several different jobs representing all phases of an occupational area. To determine manual dexterity for jewelry work, for example, he is exposed to jewelry filing, tracing, piercing, plier work, cutting, soldering, and polishing. If a client fails to perform effectively on one of the simpler sequences, he may be given no further tests in this area. In most occupational areas the last test in a given occupation involves the use of every tool from the preceding tasks. When confronted with a task involving a basic hand tool, a client is shown how to use the tool in the execution of a purposeful task through written and oral instruction. Once acquainted with the use of the tool, the client is given a task to perform and is rated for that specific task. This approach guides the client through various activities and helps him avoid mistakes.

The TOWER vocational evaluation program also provides for the observation of other factors which are important in determining work potential. Work habits and work tolerance are determined through exposure to meaningful tasks. Relevant aspects of a client's personality are seen in the permissive atmosphere of the evaluation process. By requiring a client to perform many jobs over an extended period, qualities such as flexibility and pliability can be assessed. However, the use of written instructions and the high skill level of the evaluated areas restrict the use of TOWER with low literate and mentally retarded clients. (Botterbusch, 1976).

General Aptitude Test Battery (GATB)

The General Aptitude Test Battery, developed for use in the occupational counseling program of the United States Training and Employment Services, is designed to measure aptitudes important to success in a number of occupations. The battery consists of 15 measures, 11 of which are paper-and-pencil tests and 4 which require the manipulation of small pegs and washers. The GATB is generally considered suitable for individuals 16 years of age and older who can read and understand English. A form of the GATB known as the Nonreading Aptitude Test Battery has been designed for individuals unable to read sufficiently well to take the GATB (as indicated by a special screening instrument designed for the purpose of detecting poor and nonreaders).

The GATB is not like a work sample, but the tests were designed to indicate aptitudes required for successful job performance. The complete battery takes approximately 2¼ hours to complete. Nine scores are obtained, including intelligence, verbal ability, numerical ability, spatial ability, form perception, clerical perception, motor coordination, finger dexterity, and manual dexterity. The interpretation of these scores is made using an accompanying GATB manual. Access to the tests and test components, as well as normative scales for interpretation, is limited to official governmental agencies or approved centers.

Several additional work-evaluation systems have been produced in recent years. These new approaches have generally been standardized on special populations. The McCarron-Dial Work Evaluation System is designed primarily for mentally retarded adolescents and young adults. It incorporates standard intelligence tests into a work sample battery and other psychometric approaches. The Talent Assessment Programs (TAP) consist of a battery of perceptual and dexterity tests designed to measure gross, fine finger, and manual dexterity. The Valpar Component Work Sample consists of 12 individual work samples and a list of 17 worker characteristics which can be tailor-selected for a specific employment opportunity or population. These materials are expensive and little research is available regarding their effectiveness. The Wide Range Employment Sample Test (WREST) is primarily designed to assess the manipulation and dexterity abilities of the client. Its application may be most useful with a sheltered workshop population.

A comparison of seven vocational evaluation systems has been made available by the Stout Vocational Rehabilitative Institute. (Botterbusch, 1976). For psychologists desiring more detailed information, this publication provides a table contrast component comparing time factors, cost, form of tabulated results, etc. Many facilities for delinquents will need to include in their staffs a trained counselor in working evaluation. This approach, however, is exceptionally practical and holds potential for important components of life adjustment needed by delinquents.

CONCLUSION

Psychosocial assessment of youth convicted of minor and/or major societal norm violation remains an individual problem. Only in the broadest terms in major areas of assessment can a model be described. The changeable nature of adolescents during the maturation process is itself a major hurdle. The lack of assessment instruments designed for the somewhat unique problems of adjudicated youth is also a major drawback. Only by more thorough and appropriate entry assessment can facilities prepare and offer programs effective in changing the behavior patterns of such youth. Each youth brings his own personal history and attributes; each in his own way needs particular constellations of education and treatment programs. It is anticipated that the psychosocial assessment procedures described in this chapter can move programs closer to that goal.

REFERENCES

Anastasi, A. *Psychological Testing.* 3rd ed. New York: The MacMillan Co., 196

Balogh, J. "Juvenile Delinquency Proneness: A Study of Prediction a s Involved in Delinquent Phenomena." *Journal of Criminal Law, Crimino o y, and Police Science* 48 (1958): 615-618.

Bechtold, M. L. "Validation and the KD Scale and Checklist as a Prediction of Delinquent Proneness." *Journal of Experimental Education* 32 (1964): 413-416.

Botterbusch, K. F., "A Comparison of Seven Vocational Evaluational Systems." Materials Development Center, Stout Vocational Rehabilitations Institute, University of Wisconsin, Stout, Nenomomie, Wisconsin, 1976: p. 48.

Bower, E. M. *Early Identification of Emotionally Handicapped Children in the School.* Springfield, Illinois: Charles C. Thomas, 1960.

Bricklin, B.; Protrowski, Z.; and Wagner, E. *The Hand Test: A New Projective Test with Special Reference to the Prediction of Overt Aggressive Behavior.* Springfield, Illinois: Charles C. Thomas, 1962.

Brookover, W. B. *Self-Concept of Ability and School Achievement. III. Relationship of Self-Concept to Achievement in School.* U.S. Office of Education, Cooperative Research Project No. 2831. East Lansing, Michigan: Office of Research and Publications, Michigan State University, 1967.

Brown, E. G., *Time Magazine* July 22, 1975: p. 53.

Caine, T. M.; Foulds, G. A.; and Hope, K. *Hostility and Direction of Hostility Questionnaire.* London, England: University of London Press, Ltd., 1967.

Cassel, R. *Ego Ideal and Conscience Development Test.* Hollywood, California: Monitor, 1969.

Clements, S. D. "The Predictive Utility of Three Delinquency Proneness Measures." *Dissertation Abstracts* 20 (March 1967): 3827.

Farls, R. J. "High and Low Achievement of Intellectually Average Intermediate Grade Students Related to the Self-Concept and Social Approval." *Dissertation Abstracts* 28 (1967) 1205 (Abstract).

Gluekc, E. "Spotting Potential Delinquents—Can it be Done?" *Federal Probation* 20 (1956): 7-13.

Glueck, E., and Glueck, S. *Unraveling Juvenile Delinquency.* Cambridge, Massachusetts: Harvard University Press, 1950.

Gough, E. H. *California Psychological Inventory.* Palo Alto, California: Consulting Psychologists Press, Inc., 1959.

Hahn, M. E. *The California Life Goals' Evaluation Schedules.* Los Angeles: Western Psychological Services, 1966.

Halstead, W. C. *Brain and Intelligence.* Chicago: University of Chicago Press, 1947.

Hartlage, L. C., and Lucas, D. G. *Mental Development Evaluation of the Pediatric Patient.* Springfield, Illinois: Charles C. Thomas, 1973.

Hathaway, S. R., and McKinley, C. *The Minnesota Multiphasic Personality Inventory.* New York: Psychological Corporation, 1943.

Hathaway, S. R., and Monachesi, E. D. *Analyzing and Predicting Juvenile Delinquency with the MMPI.* Minneapolis: University of Minnesota Press, 1951.

Jones J. G., and Strowig, R. W. "Adolescent Identity and Self-Perception as Predictors of Scholastic Achievements. *Journal of Educational Research* 62 (1968): 78–82.

Kvaraceus, W. C. *Kvaraceus Delinquency Proneness Rating Scale and Checklist.* New York: World Book Company, 1953.

Kvaraceus, W. C. "Forecasting Delinquency: A Three-Year Experiment." *Exceptional Children* 27 (1961): 429–435.

Lambert, N. M., and Bower, E. M. *Bower's Two-Step Process for Identifying Emotionally Handicapped Pupils.* Princeton, New Jersey: Educational Testing Service, 1961.

McCandless, B. R., and McDavid, J. "Psychological Theory, Research, and Juvenile Delinquency." *Journal of Criminal Law, Criminology, and Police Science* 53 (1962): 1–14.

McDavid, J. *Social Psychology.* New York: Harper and Row, 1968.

McDavid, John. *Diagnostic Evaluation of Study Skills.* Atlanta, Georgia: Atlanta Achievement Center, 100 Northcreek, Atlanta, Georgia, 1976.

Meninger, K. *The Crime of Punishment.* New York: Viking Press, 1968.

Norwicki, J. S., and Strickland, B. R. "A Locus of Control Scale for Children." *Journal of Consulting and Clinical Psychology* 40 (1973): 1–8.

Paul, G. L. *Insight vs. Desensitization in Psychotherapy.* Stanford, California: Stanford University Press, 1966.

Reckless, W. C.; Denitz, S.; and Kay, B. "The Self-Component in Potential Delinquency and Potential Nondelinquency." *American Sociological Review* 22 (1957): 566–570.

Reise, M. W. A Comparison between Delinquent Youth and Typical Individuals on the Ego Ideal and Conscience Development Test. Unpublished master's thesis, University of Wisconsin, 1969.

Reitan, R. M. "Psychological Deficits Resulting from Cerebral Lesions in Man." *The Frontal Granular Cortex and Behavior.* Edited by J. M Warren and K. Akert. New York: McGraw-Hill, 1964: 295–312.

Rosenberg, B. "The Work Sample Approach to Vocational Evaluation." *Vocational Evaluation for Rehabilitation Services.* Edited by R. E. Hardy and J. G. Cull. Springfield, Illinois: Charles C. Thomas, 1973.

Rotter, J. B. "Generalized Expectancies for Internal Versus External Control of Reinforcement." *Psychological Monographs* 80 (1966) (1, Whole No. 609).

Sabatino, D.; Mauser, A.; and Skok, J. A Survey of Institutional Educational Programs for Delinquents in the United States. Paper read at Annual Neglected/Delinquent Conference of Pennsylvania: Pocono Manor, Pennsylvania. June, 1975.

Shore, M. F.; Massimo, J. L.; and Ricks, D. F. "A Factor Analytic Study of Psychotherapeutic Change in Delinquent Boys." *Journal of Clinical Psychology* 21 (1965): 208–212.

Stodgill, R. M. *Behavior Cards: A Test Interview for Delinquent Children.* New York: Psychological Corporation, 1949.

Thorpe, L. P.; Clark, W. W.; and Tiegs, E. W. *California Test of Personality.* Monterey, California: California Test Bureau, 1953.

Ullman, P., and Krasner, L. eds. Case Studies in Behavior Modification. New York: Holt, Rinehart, and Winston, 1965.

Voss, H. "The Predictive Efficiency of the Gluecks' Social Prediction Table." *Journal of Criminal Law, Criminology, and Police Science* 54 (1963): 421–430.

Wagner, E. *The Hand Test.* Akron, Ohio: Mark James Co., 1959.

Wagner, E. Application of the Hand Test Indicators of Antisocial Action Tendencies in Adults to Teenage Juvenile Delinquency. Paper read at the Educational Psychology Association, April 1962.

Whelan, R. W. An experiment in predictive delinquency. *Journal of Criminal Law, Criminology, and Police Science* 45 (1954): 432–441.

Woodcock, R. W. *Woodcock Reading Mastery Test Manual.* Circle Pines, Minnesota: American Guidance Publishers, 1973.

TESTS AND PUBLISHERS

Behavior Cards: A Test Interview for Delinquent Children. Psychological Corporation, New York.

Bender-Gestalt Test. Western Psychological Services, Los Angeles, California.

Bower's Two-Step Process for Identifying Emotionally Handicapped Pupils. Educational Testing Service, Princeton, New Jersey.

The California Life Goals' Evaluation Schedules. Western Psychological Services, Los Angeles, California.

California Psychological Inventory. Consulting Psychologists Press, Inc., Palo Alto, California.

California Test of Personality. Test Bureau, Monterey, California.

Comprehension Tests of Basic Skills. McGraw-Hill Book Company, New York.

The Cornell Critical Thinking Test. Critical Thinking Project, Urbana, Illinois.

Developmental Test of Visual-Motor Integration. Follett Educational Corporation, Chicago, Illinois.

Durrell Listening-Reading Series. Harcourt, Brace, Jovanovich, Inc., New York.

Edwards Personal Preference Schedule. Psychological Corporation, New York.

Ego Ideal and Conscience Development Test. Monitor, Hollywood, California.

Gates-McKillop Reading Diagnostic Test. Teachers College Press, Teachers College, Columbia University, New York.

Gluecks' Social Prediction Scale. Harvard University Press, Cambridge, Massachusetts.

The Hand Test. Mark James Company, Akron, Ohio.

The Hand Test: A New Projective Test with Special Reference to the Prediction of Overt Aggressive Behavior. Charles C Thomas, Springfield, Illinois.

Henmon-Nelson Tests of Mental Ability. Houghton-Mifflin Co., Boston, Massachusetts.

Hostility and Direction of Hostility Questionnaire. University of London Press, Ltd., London, England.

Iowa Test of Basic Skills. Iowa Education Bureau, Ames, Iowa.

Journal of Clinical Psychology. 1958.

Key Math Diagnostic Arithmetic Test. American Guidance Services, Minneapolis, Minnesota.

Kohs Block Design Tests. C. H. Sterling Co., Chicago, Illinois.

Kuder General Interest Survey. Science Research Associates, Inc., Chicago, Illinois.

Kuder Occupational Interest Survey. Science Research Associates, Inc., Chicago, Illinois.

Kvaraceus Delinquency Proneness Rating Scale and Checklist. World Book Company, New York.

Leighter International Performance Scale. C. W. Stoelting, Chicago, Illinois.

Metropolitan Achievement Tests. 1931.

Minnesota Multiphasic Personality Inventory. Psychological Corporation, New York.

Minnesota Vocational Interest Inventory. Psychological Corporation, New York.

Otis-Lennon Mental Ability Test. Harcourt, Brace, Jovanovich, Inc., New York.

Peabody Picture Vocabulary Test. American Guidance Service, Inc., Circle Pines, Minnesota.

The Porters Maze Test. Psychological Corporation, New York.

Progressive Matrices. Psychological Corporation, New York.

Rorschach InkBlot Test. Greene and Stratton, Inc., New York.

The Rutgers Drawing Test. Anna Spiesman Starr, Highland Park, New Jersey.

Scale for Evaluating the School Behavior of Children, Ten to Fifteen. Psychological Corporation, New York.

Slossen Intelligence Test. Slossen Educational Publications, East Aurora, New York.

SRA Achievement Series: Work-Study Skills. Scientific Research Associates, Chicago, Illinois.

Stanford Achievement Test. Harcourt, Brace, Jovanovich, Inc., New York.

Stanford-Binet Intelligence Scale. Third Review. Houghton-Mifflin Company, Boston, Massachusetts.

Strong Vocational Interest Blank for Men. Stanford University Press, Stanford, California.

Strong Vocational Interest Blank for Women. Stanford University Press, Stanford, California.

Study Skills Test. McGraw-Hill Book Company, Inc., New York.

Taylor Manifest Anxiety Scales. Journal of Clinical Psychology, 1949, Vol. 16.

Tennessee Self-Concept Scale. Counselor Recordings and Tests, Nashville, Tennessee.

Test of Social Intelligence. Sheridan Psychological Services, Inc., Beverly Hills, California.

Thematic Apperception Test. Harvard University Press, Cambridge, Massachusetts.

Thorndike Dimensions of Temperament. Psychological Corporation, New York.

Unraveling Juvenile Delinquency. Harvard University Press, Cambridge, Massachusetts.

Wechsler Adult Intelligence Scale. Psychological Corporation, New York.

Wechsler Intelligence Scale for Children. Psychological Corporation, New York.

Wide Range Achievement Test. Guidance Associates, Austin, Texas.

Woodcock Reading Mastery Diagnostic Test. American Guidance Services, Minneapolis, Minnesota.

8

informal assessment of secondary youth in trouble

TED L. MILLER, DAVID A. SABATINO, AND LES STERNBERG

This chapter assumes the position that formal assessment procedures (those consisting largely of standardized tests described in the preceding chapter) are insufficient to adequately describe behavior or to form the basis for instructional and/or behavioral change in an educational setting. In most instances, the practitioner, that person most directly involved with youth in trouble, requires both frequent data and data that are program specific. Formal testing provides an initial understanding of the individual's current psychological and educational attributes in relationship to a comparison group. These data are, however, frequently unwieldy for formulating and evaluating specific educational intervention strategies. Also, formal test results may generally be regarded as age (developmentally) specific, and are not tolerant of any but the most abrupt behavior or learning skill changes.

In the case of troubled youth, abundant evidence suggests that conventional instructional methods have generally failed to be effective in promoting acceptable behavior in the classroom or corridor; alternate instructional strategies must be implemented. In viewing alternate educational methods for special education, Smith (1969) expressed several opinions. First, he asserted that the goal of education should be to facilitate the growth of the student in multiple domains. Among these domains are the social, emotional, and intellectual capabilities demanded by the community in which the student will eventually reside. Second, he indicated that vast differences are to be found in the demonstrated behaviors of students in any classroom, even classrooms ostensibly made homogenous on the basis of ability grouping. In order to cope with these givens, Smith further asserted that a teacher must have frequent and specific assessment data on a multitude of competency measures.

Smith and his colleagues expressed doubt for the ability of standardized psychoeducational measures to meet this task for at least two reasons. First, many schools are not favored financially and the performance of extensive psychoeducational diagnosis is an impossibility. Unfortunately, this factor holds at least equally true for the juvenile correctional system (see Chapter 7). Second, and perhaps even more crucial, is the value of even the best formal test results for educational purposes. Unlike the first issue there is considerable disagreement on this matter. Some educators hold psychometric analysis to be without parallel for value in the education of students, while others ignore' or persistently downplay the use of formal testing. Perhaps the largest group of educators take a moderate stance, choosing to pragmatically utilize information of value and ignore that which has less utility in establishing an instructional objective. Each extensive group testing programs are quite likely to be circumvented by omission, should the data provided not be acceptable for use by the teacher. Simply raising the intensity of the ongoing testing programs, thereby changing the quantitative but not qualitative aspects of the data, is not likely to provide success.

A number of factors contribute to the teacher's perception of the educational value of a specific test. Initially, a test must be involved in a dimension (e.g., intelligence, scholastic aptitude, language ability) that is acceptable by the teacher as relevant to learning in the classroom. It is unlikely that a test labeled "Attitudinal Awareness of Crabgrass" would gain much credance with fourth grade teachers, though it might prove of value to agronomists. Despite this obvious statement it remains advisable for practitioners who use tests to recognize what is purportedly being measured. Even in instances where construct validity is high it may be that the test constructor's notion of the nature of a given trait (e.g., intelligence, language capacity) is somewhat different than what is required in the classroom at that moment. Any given learner aptitude might be defined and measured three different ways on three separate tests. Simply accepting the construct label on a formal test will not always provide the practitioner with usable information.

> Here we are dealing with validity issues. Recall that at least four forms of validity can be identified. Face validity refers to the relationship of the instrument's appearance and purpose; the "Attitudinal Awareness of Crabgrass" test cited earlier has little face relationship to educational measurement. Content validity is a measure of a test's ability to sample a

universe of related tasks. Criterion validity is essentially the ability of a test to extrapolate to some future situation, i.e., prediction. Construct validity is a measure of the test's purported ability to identify and measure some hypothetical construct-intelligence, aptitude, language reception, etc.

Face validity is perhaps of the least importance, indeed it is violated frequently in psychological practice as, for example, in projective testing. Content validity is important in assessment if the purpose of assessment is to adequately sample and generalize to a larger domain. If the instructor requires information or a student's ability to spell typical fourth-grade words, a sampling procedure is important. But if, in assessment, the purpose is to determine if the word *truck* can be spelled, content validity is not essential. Either the word can or cannot be spelled, however, in this process, spelling *truck* does not suggest the student can spell any other word. Criterion validity is necessary if we wish to predict future skills, abilities or attributes; it is not necessary for measuring current functioning, i.e., answering the question, "Can the student spell *truck*?" Construct ability is essential for measurement of hypothesized inner constructs, e.g., intelligence. But, as Smith (1969) has pointed out, such representations do not necessarily yield the ability to program, only the ability to relate in individual's presumed quantity of something in relation to others. These concepts of validity are of extreme importance in traditional test construction given the purposes for which such tests are intended. How the concepts are particularly important for many aspects of informal assessment is a moot question.

Assuming that a formal test measures what it purports to measure (one form of validity), and that it does so consistently (reliability), is a rather large assumption.

Reliability can be thought of as the consistency of measurement possessed by an assessment instrument. Much has been written about reliability and a detailed review is beyond the scope of this chapter. However, reliability is pivotal in its ability: (1) to affect the validity of a test; and (2) to modify the precision attributed to a particular score. Reliability is expressed by a correlation coefficient, a number ranging from -1.0 to +1.0. The square of the correlation coefficient provides a direct measure of the amount of variation between two scores that can be accounted for. Thus, a test with a reliability of 0.80 can only account for 64% (0.80^2) of the variance seen between the tests.

It would be desirable, of course, to have a reliability of +1.0 as *any change* in score between two test administrations would have meaning, i.e., each score would be a true score, not an estimation. Anything less than +1.0 forces interpretation by use of the Standard Error of Measurement (SEM), a static between the observed score and a hypothetical true score. This procedure can be seen as necessary, but it has the unfortunate side effect of requiring large observed differences in scores before the scores can be taken as truly different. The size of the SEM is directly proportional to the reliability of a test, is one reason why Nummaly (1967) suggested that a desirable test reliability is in the area of +0.90 to +0.95. However, a review of several tests and their component subscales (Ysseldyke 1973) indicated that many tests do not approach 0.90, indeed that is the exception. Since the utility of a correlation is based on its square (0.80 = 64%; 0.90 = 81%), it may be seen that the reliability of many formal tests is quite inadequate for continual measurement of program effectiveness.

Some practitioners will argue that the reliability of formal measures is as high as can currently be achieved and, therefore, is superior to teacher-made (criterion-referenced) tools. This is only true dependent upon the *domain* to be inferred to. If a test purports to measure intelligence, language recep-tivists, or other traits that presumably encompass many potential skills, this is probably true. If, however, a finite set of skills are to be measured, this is not true. To illustrate, if the teacher wishes to know if student X can perform two specific, two-digit additions, test reliability can become very high as only minimal error will occur. If the domain (potential test items) is increased to all possible two-digit combinations, the probability of a lowered reliability increases since the potential for error increases in relation to the size of the domain. We are, of course, asking two separate questions here, but this distinction is important in the concept of norm-referenced and criterion-referenced testing and the sequential teaching process that employs task analysis.

Objectively viewed, it is sometimes difficult to understand the value of specific scores or profiles yielded by even the most commonly ad-ministered tests. For example, the Wecshler Intelligence Scale for Children (WISC), one of the most frequently used formal intelligence tests, has been shown to be a good indicator of g or general intelligence (Cohen, 1959). But the results of Cohen's work and other similar studies have yielded some disquieting data. In its development, the WISC was based on the premise that intelligence is composed of more than a single property, hence multiple tasks are required to adequately sample and accurately measure the con-struct. Accordingly, the test was developed to include the use of twelve sub-scales which produce verbal, performance, and composite intelligence quotients. Theoretically, such subscales should provide indices to the indi-vidual's capacity and learning style, that is, the structure of intelligence.

The disquieting aspect of Cohen's (1959) study is that the twelve scales did not emerge as distinct units. The technique of factor analysis that was used in the study (a correlational procedure that identifies groupings or clusters of similar items) yielded data that suggested only four identifiable dimensions in the test. Further, these dimensions seemed to be tapping char-acteristics that were not suggested by the 12 subscale names. In view of this we might suspect "pattern analysis" (clinical interpretation based on patterns of high and low scores within the WISC subscales) to be a most onerous task and one that is difficult to support. Sattler (1974), therefore, advocates this procedure by only the most highly trained specialist under the most rigorous conditions as the test data may be dubious except as a global measure of general intelligence.

The problem faced by WISC users is a general problem fully explored in a recent book (Gearheart & Willenberg, 1974). These authors reviewed the psychometric bases of many tests and provided a description of well over 50 instruments that measure intelligence, social maturity, auditory discrimination, visual perception, personality, and many aspects of potential interest to educators. Yet following this review of test instruments which is noted as being devoted to teacher application of tests, there is little discussion on the methodology for the use of test data in the daily classroom instruction. A major conclusion is that many tests currently in use in educational circumstances simply do not have extensive bearing on the ongoing activities of most classrooms. At best they seem to function as selectors, serving as gauges to an individual's performance in relation to others. Once interpersonalogical comparisons are accomplished, however well, many formal tests seem to have little further value (see Glaser, 1970, p. 77).

This distinction in test purpose is apparent in a recent review (Carver, 1974) that defines tests to be of two types, those that are primarily *psychometric* and those primarily *edumetric* in purpose. A psychometric test is one whose major purpose is to measure individual differences, a traditional tenet of the psychological and educational test. By contract, an edumetric test is one whose major function is to measure individual educational performance in terms of the academic skill of behavior management necessary to achieve a new growth pattern for that youth. In essence, psychometric tests measure inter-individual differences while edumetric tests measure intra-individual differences. The distinction between these approaches has sometimes been referred to as one of *norm-referenced* (Popham, 1971) and *criterion-referenced** tests (Glaser & Nitko, 1971, p. 653), although Carver (1974) suggests that distinction to be a confusing one as criterion tests also evaluate performance in relation to some standard.

Regardless of the terminology used, it is important to note that major differences occur in interpretation and use of the test data. In Carver's words, raw scores from psychometric tests are never interpreted

---

*A norm-referenced instrument is one designed to identify an individual on some trait or capacity in relationship to distribution of that trait or skill in a population of many persons. It can be shown that the distribution of most personological traits, for example intelligence, are spread throughout the population following a normal distribution. Recognizing this fact, it is possible to place, with considerable accuracy, an individual's score in relation to place, with considerable accuracy, an individual's score in relation to all other persons scores. This is, in fact, the major purpose of normed based tests. By contrast, a criterion-referenced instrument is designed to measure an individual's capacity to accomplish some specific activity. No effort is made to relate that performance to the performance of others; only the measurement of success to the criterion is considered important.

because the score itself means nothing unless it is compared to an average score [while] the edumetric score has meaning in relationship to a criterion, objective, or scale that is independent of individual differences. . . . It appears that psychologists have been giving away sound psychometric tests to education for many years when education really needed sound edumetric tests.   (Carver, 1974, pp. 515–518)

Similar thoughts have been echoed by Gagne (1970, p. 123) and Wittrock (1970, p. 10).

Other factors further contribute to the teacher's hesitancy to strongly embrace formal test data. There are major questions to be answered about the purposes to which data are put and the fairness of that process. Both psychology and education are endowed with a heavy influence of Aristotilean logic and more than a semblance of scientific thought. Accordingly, much emphasis is placed on the identification, classification, and grouping of *subunits* (e.g., organic elements, electrons, height, weight, intelligence, etc.). Such similar subunits are thought to be more recognizable and understandable, whereupon, *reassembly* permits an organization that is acceptable to the manipulator. There are difficulties with this concept when applied to educational settings. First, human beings do not respond as predictably as inorganic molecules, for example. They are much more responsive to the effects of the context of their peculiar situation (i.e., environment). Further, they are more susceptable to *multiple determinism,* the interactive and cumulative effects of many inputs. Formal assessment techniques seem to have ignored or glossed over these factors both by defining the structures that are to be measured as internal to the youth, and for conducting assessment in laboratory-like situations away from the natural setting of behavior where the multiple determined events could occur. The ramifications of ignoring these factors, and their consequences, will be apparent when we consider the ecology of assessment.

Second, and probably of more immediate influence in educational practice, is the criteria chosen for classroom grouping. Historically, this was accomplished through the use of such denominators as age or years of schooling. As the concept of individual differences in ability became prominent and universal education became the norm in this country, psychometric tests, measuring intelligence or aptitudes, became the basis for diagnostic labels. (See Chapter 1 for a discussion on labeling.) Although this practice may be useful in some instances, there are potential hazards; foremost of these are the dual possibilities of misclassification by legitimate standards or the misclassification of students for socio-political control.

As an example, tremendous controversy has recently arisen over the use of intelligence tests as determiners of placement for minority students in special classes. This is not a new event in the relationship of psychometrics and education. Cronbach (1975) indicates that the debate over the use of intelligence tests is at least five decades old, considerably predating the current controversy. Despite the longevity of this debate, Sattler's (1974) review of the literature concerning the testing of minority children suggests a general conclusion: many intelligence tests and aspects of the general administration procedure can be unfair as a result of the insensitivity of the test or the examiners, or the way in which a test result is used. Unfortunately we do not yet know what is fair or unfair nor do we have proper procedures for ameliorative action.* Attempts to improve standardized tests have been responsible and prolific, yet much uncertainty remains to be resolved before psychometric tests can be seen as unswervingly fair when used to classify and predict. The simple fact remains that formal, psychometric tests have been criticized by both professional and lay citizenry. Thus, the major historical functions of psychometric assessment, that of sorting and classifying, are no longer as acceptable as they once were. In assessment, the more pressing current question is what can be done instructionally with an adolescent?

While recent strides have lessened some potential for misuse (e.g., the Family Rights and Privacy Act of 1975, the enforcement of informed consent prior to evaluation, a tightened ethical posture within professional societies) a threat remains in many persons eyes. This potential for unfairness, coupled with a seeming inability to provide many useful educational functions, has led some instructors to reduce the attention given to such tests. Still, the teachers' need for daily information in the instructional process is apparent and real. Assessment processes that can be classed as informal may provide an immediate means toward removing the threat of formal tests and fulfilling the multiple requirements of classroom programming.

To summarize, the term *informal assessment* will be used operationally in this chapter to mean any instrument or procedure that is used by the practitioner for edumetric purpose. Examples of procedures that fulfill the intent of informal assessment as defined here would include, but not be limited to, checklists, interviews, tests that parallel current (daily) instruction, anecdotal records, and systematic observational procedures—so long as each remains directed at an edumetric purpose. Of these alternatives, the emphasis in this chapter will be given to the theoretical rationale and

---

*If, for example, intelligence tests are put to an edumetric purpose we have seen that their potential for educational programming is small. Thus, a major role for intelligence tests (and many other common instruments) is that of predicting future performance. Psychometric tests can be shown to be good predictors in a large proportion of the group instances in which they are used, but on an individual basis this accuracy breaks down. Some individuals will not be fairly treated even with 1% error. Seldomly is this accuracy achieved, thus "bias" has been claimed. But bias is not a single notion. No less than *five* models of test bias have been reviewed (Linn, 1972) each with separate assumptions that are not without socio-philosophical consequences. Thus, eliminating bias in prediction is a much greater task than the simple sampling problem that is sometimes suggested.

methodology for observational systems. Given this orientation to informal assessment, let us now consider some concepts in ecology and the relevance of the concept of ecology to informal assessment.

ECOLOGICAL THEORY AND INFORMAL ASSESSMENT

There are many possible models of classroom teaching (Joyce & Weil, 1972). Each distinct model tends to emphasize some specific aspect or combination of aspects from learning or organizational theory. In turn, each model contains underlying assumptions about the nature of curricula, how and what material and information is to be learned, the role of the teacher, the school as an organization, and the purpose and structure of the classroom. While each model has produced adherents and detractors, and each seems divergent from the other, many commonalities can be seen to exist if the classroom and the activities that are ongoing within it are viewed as an *ecological system.*

Ecology and system are two words which are used very frequently in both diverse professional literatures and more daily fare. Without careful scrutiny, one is apt to equate ecology to a clean environment and systems to a conceptual unit containing many small parts. Unfortunately, the use of these terms in even detailed professional literature is sometimes confusing, for in actuality the terms are often used in an assuming manner that promotes ambiguity. Strictly speaking, Wittaker (1970) states ecology is a branch of biology that emphasizes "the study of living systems in relation to environment" (p. v). Buckley (1968) suggested the definition of a system to be:

> a complex of elements or components directly or indirectly related in a causal network, such that each component is related to at least some others in a more or less stable way within a particular period of time. (p. 41)

Kaufman, speaking for the planning of educational systems, has suggested that a system can be thought of as:

> The sum total of parts working independently and working together to achieve required results or outcomes based on needs. (p. 1)

Thus, at their core, systems essentially speak of the interrelatedness of components, the belief that each unit in some way influences and is influenced by the next. The concept of ecology simply extends thought to the view of living things.

It is not difficult to extend this thinking to the classroom. The classroom obviously constitutes an ecological system since it contains living things each acted on and acted upon by multiple aspects of the environment. Although this interactional process is extremely complex and poorly understood, it may be seen that events simply do not occur in isolation, without cause or devoid of extended effect. Instead, events occur as a result of the complex interrelatedness of the components of subsystems. For example, Kounin (1970) became interested in classroom discipline by an event that illustrates this concept:

> While lecturing, I glanced around the room and noticed a student in the back row intently reading a newspaper that he was holding completely unfolded in front of himself. Contrary to what I advocated in the course, I angrily reprimanded him without diagnosis or understanding.
>
> The reprimand succeeded. He stopped reading the newspaper, or at least did not hold it completely unfolded in midair. But, the major observable impact seemed to be upon other members of the class. Side glances to others ceased, whispers stopped, eyes went from windows or the instructor to notebooks on the desks.   (p. 1)

What had happened in this instance was a classroom example of the interrelatedness and interdependence of units in an ecosystem. The behaviors of many tangentially related components were altered by the direct action of a single unit upon another unit. Simply put, the effects of a single action are not felt only at the intended point of impact. Ripple effects spread behavioral reactions throughout the system. Such a process has spawned an increasing interest in the study of behavior in relationship to the environmental context in which it occurs.

Barker and Wright (1955) and Barker (1963, 1968) undertook a preliminary investigation of the ecological basis for behavior. These investigations were initiated as the result of growing disillusionment with the type of behavioral data produced by experimental methodology, and recognition that the data of naturally occurring situations and experimental situations are not similar (Barker, Dembo, & Lewin, 1943; Labov, 1970). As a rule, the behavioral sciences have developed elaborate constructs that purport to describe the causal factors of specific behaviors, yet little is known about the natural occurrence of observable behaviors. Paraphrasing Sells (1963), a dearth of information exists outside artificially constructed situations (the laboratory) with specific classes of subjects (chicks, rats, pigeons, and college students). Little is known of such potentially valuable behavioral indices as frequency of laughter, conversation time with peers, number of encounters with specific environmental objects or situations, etc.

Barker and his colleagues were interested in such naturally occurring events and the development of processes to capture them. Accordingly, their efforts led to several concepts, among them the *behavioral setting,* the *specimen record,* and the process of *episoding.* The behavioral setting can be thought of as a collection of time, place, and object properties that seemingly direct or coerce the behaviors that are seen to occur. Specimen records are detailed, carefully written reports that describe the behavioral events objectively and without interpretation. Episoding is one methodology for the analysis of specimen records.

In *Midwest and Its Children* (1955), Barker and Wright began a series of intense longitudinal studies which employed these methods. From this investigation the environment was seen to be more than merely a passive influence or context for the behavior that occurred. An understanding of the ecology of a situation became very important to understanding behavior. Barker (1968) relates:

> When, early in our work at the Field Station, we made long records of children's behavior in real life settings in accordance with a traditional person-centered approach, we found that some attributes of behavior varied less across children within settings than across settings within the days of children. We found, in short, that we could predict some aspects of children's behavior more adequately from knowledge of the behavior characteristics of the drug store, arithmetic classes, and basketball games they inhabited than from knowledge of the behavior tendencies of particular children. **(p. 4)**

Studies with handicapped children (For example, Rausch, Farbman, & Llewellyn, 1960) have confirmed similar results, and on the basis of this it could justifiably be stated that an understanding of behavior is incomplete and inappropriate unless some attempt is made to consider the ecology within which that behavior takes place. Valid assessment procedures must make allowances for the ecology of the behavior to be recorded, and such data can only be collected from the natural environment.

Bersoff (1973) recognized this requirement and suggested that the psychosituational assessment should replace the psychoeducational assessment. He indicated that a return to a test definition that emphasizes systematic observation and description is in order, one that is "rooted to environmental events, relevant to the current functioning of an individual, and appropriate for assessing behavior change" (p. 895). These characteristics can be viewed as inherent in informal assessment.

An increasing number of authors (Mischel, 1968; Altman, 1975; Mehrabian & Russell, 1974; Proshansky, Ittelson, & Rivlin, 1970) have paid considerable attention to the effects of the environment on behavior. Williams (1967), examined the relationship of student's sense of obligation for high school activities to the size of the school and the student's marginality. Obligation was defined as a feeling of "I ought" or "I must," with reference to attending school based activities, while a series of measures (e.g., grades) operationally yielded regular and marginal student groups. He then identified the number of behavioral settings in large and small schools and the number of students available to fill those settings. In situations where a small proportion of students to settings were found, students performing marginally in the academic setting were much more likely to be accepted and readily incorporated into the mainstream of the ecology. Powerful school setting influences were similarly emphasized by Wicker (1969a), who reported that the amount of information recalled from a school based setting was directly proportional to the size of the school. A conclusion that could be read from both the Williams (1967) and Wicker (1969) studies is that in situations where a low student population to behavioral setting ratio is evident, individuals not only learn more of the situation but are more likely to be readily included into its ongoing behavior patterns. These general studies emphasize the importance of informal ecologically sensitive assessment within the classroom.

Swap (1974) took the position (after Rhodes, 1970) that classroom disturbances are the result of the interaction of person and environment. Drawing upon models of development proposed by Erikson (1963, 1964) and Hewitt (1968) she proposed specific environmental adaptations that could be implemented in the classroom. Both Erikson's and Hewitt's models are hierarchical schemes that relate the early stages of development as a series of sequential tasks, each stage dependent on the mastery of earlier stages. Failure to negotiate a stage will result in characteristic symptomology which Swap (1974) labeled triggering behaviors (see Table 8.1). Many of these behaviors might well be thought of as a characteristic of youth in trouble and would, from a psychodynamic perspective, represent failure to adequately resolve a developmental stage.

An interesting aspect of Swap's conceptualization is the use of two schemas that describe behavior; an *internal* representation (Erikson's and Hewitt's stages) based on developmental constructs, and the *behavioral-environmental mismatch* (after Rhodes, 1970). While internal representation might prove useful in formulating some ameliorative strategies, it might be equally possible and effective to attack behavior change with environmental adaptations devoid of internally based constraints. Look-

Table 8.1. A DEVELOPMENTAL VIEW OF DISTURBING BEHAVIORS IN THE CLASSROOM AND APPROPRIATE TEACHER RESPONSES

Developmental Stages		Triggering Behaviors	Adaptive Environmental Response
Erikson	*Hewett*		
Basic trust versus mistrust	Attention	Withdrawal Self stimulation Inability to focus attention Preoccupation with fantasy Inability to form close relationships	Establish climate of safety and predictability Accept and reward child's limited responses Provide one to one relationship
	Response	Inability or unwillingness to respond to familiar stimuli Fear of failure, phobias	Limit competition Provide simple tasks at which child can be successful
Autonomy versus shame and doubt	Order	Inability to complete tasks Compulsive trials Disruptive outbursts Intolerance of frustration Defiance of authority Distractibility Destruction of products	Provide structured learning environment Set clear expectations for student behavior and follow through consistently Require finished products Establish a firm one to one relationship Design a curriculum activity with a specific starting point in a series of steps leading to a conclusion Set up peer activities of a simple design

Developmental Stages		Triggering Behaviors	Adaptive Environmental Response
Erikson	*Hewett*		
Initiative versus	Exploratory	Extreme dependence Fear of looking, exploring Overzealous exploration	Provide multisensory experiences Build a framework for "orderly exploration" Teach child to plan and evaluate Encourage "discovery" activities
Industry versus inferiority	Social	Low self esteem Isolation Difficulty with sharing, completion Inappropriate social behaviors Aggression, teasing	Set up group projects Experiment with crossage teaching Educate children about their own values and attitudes Provide communication exercises
	Mastery, achievement	Low achievement Overly dependent on others' approval or initiative	Provide wide range of learning activities and methods Cultivate students' interests Encourage self evaluation

Swap, 1974, reproduced with permission.

ing again at Table 8.1, notice that at Erikson's stage of *autonomy versus shame and doubt* Hewitt proposed a stage labeled *order*. Both stages have coincidental triggering behaviors such as inability to complete tasks, compulsive rituals, disruptive outbursts, etc. Swap's proposed environmental adaptations were to provide structured learning environments, set clear expectations, etc. These resulting actions seem quite appropriate, but only slightly more logical in light of the stage constructs. In fact, the suggested procedures might have evolved as easily based on a clear record of the behaviors that occurred, the responses to them and the observable outcomes. In other words, the hierarchical model is not essential to the implementation of ecological strategies.

If the ecological emphasis is of such importance to the classroom and informal assessment, and obviously we take the position that it is, what have been major stumbling blocks to its successful implementation? Hunt (1975) has explored the seeming professional reticence to accept the person-environment paradigm which can be defined as the "coordination of individual difference and environmental effects (p. 209). Several factors were noted, the most common being the attempts of most researchers to view ATI (aptitude treatment interactions) designs strictly in the statistical sense of a significant disordinal interaction.* Unfortunately, the ATI does not occur with the frequency that might be expected because normative scores are required to meet the assumption of the experimental model by which ATI's have been evaluated. That is, true individual differences (n = 1) in relationship to the aspects of a specific environment or treatment strategy have not been explored. In Hunt's (1975) opinion, such a narrow concept of ATI has greatly reduced its usefulness and proven effectiveness.

The reasons for restricted definitions of ATI's have been termed by Hunt (1975) as the myth of general effects [and the] myth of personal consistency (p. 212). Both myths are long held bastions of formal testing; the first holding that general principles of behavior can be applied to all persons, the second suggesting that characteristics of an individual are stable across time and situation (i.e., a reluctance to accept environmental influence). Hunt challenged both doctrines and proposed a

---

*According to Ysseldyke (1973), the concept of an aptitude treatment interaction is based upon the premise that specific personological variables, aptitudes (IQ, figure ground perception) should respond differentially to specific treatment (instructional) strategies. Thus, the goal of an ATI research strategy is not to raise all youth's scores but to raise them selectively by matching specific treatments to psycho-educational profiles. The resulting graphic plot of this event would be a significant disordinal interaction psycho-educational profile A doing well with method A but not B, psycho-educational profile B doing well with B but not A. The matching, then, of profile and instructional formal would form the basis of individualized "prescriptive" instruction.

remedy to the situation based essentially on the individuality of the learner. In his view one does not ask which approach is better but rather, given an individual student with idiosyncratic learning characteristics, which approach is most likely to produce the greatest success? Thus, a careful, specific analysis of the individual's learning preferences, not necessarily capability, is essential for constructing the most appropriate learning environment.

Thus far we have attempted to contrast aspects of formal and informal assessment, and make a sound case for the inclusion of ecological considerations in any theoretical or practical attempt at informal assessment. The two discussions that immediately follow will expand upon and provide additional emphasis on the development of informal assessment procedures. The first discussion will provide a model for the development of a criterion-referenced program of instruction. The term *criterion* has been used in place of *edumetric* because it is more familiar and because it connotes mastery to criterion not merely change in the learner's demonstrated acquisition. If the reader feels uncomfortable with the terminology, *edumetric* can be substituted, bearing in mind the above distinction. Whichever terminology is used it will be apparent that a powerful paradigm for learning is presented, but that its utility rests in great measure on the extent of consistent feedback to teacher and student. The collection of that data is highly dependent on informal procedures.

The second of the three remaining sections will focus on the pivotal interactions between teacher and youth; possibly the single most significant aspect of the classroom ecology. These interactional processes will be shown to be not only influential but subject to modification, hence ameliorative action. Again, successful modification can only occur in the presence of consistent data flow, the dimensions of which have not yet been trapped by conventional assessment techniques. By default, informal techniques are required.

The final section of this chapter will be devoted to the integration of the concepts presented and the development of informal assessment techniques. The reader anticipating a cookbook or panacea will no doubt be disappointed; there is no single cure for any situation requiring informal assessment. What *is* available are guides for the creation of informal assessment tools and a suggested process for the practitioners use of the data. We have termed this process the Individual Achievement Monitoring System (IAMS) and will attempt to indicate the necessity of such a system in the development of an Individual Program Plan (IPP). In addition, we hope to make explicit the significance of informal assessment to the monitoring system.

CRITERION-REFERENCED ASSESSMENT

Assumptions

Criterion-referenced assessment operates from three basic assumptions: (1) It is not important to know the relative standing of a youngster in relation to other youngsters of the same age group, it is only important to understand the placement of a youngster in regard to the instructional program he is going to pursue; (2) It is not important to classify a youth by label (i.e., chronic disruptive, learning disabled, mentally handicapped), only to classify the youngster in terms of instructional objectives or tasks that he should be directed toward; and (3) It is not enough to diagnose a youth in terms of strengths and weaknesses, one should always consider an accurate prescription from the diagnosis.

This last assumption probably represents the most controversial issue in all forms of assessment. Recently, formal norm-referenced tests have come under considerable attack regarding the issue of whether or not test results lead directly to any useful amelioration procedures. Ysseldyke (1973) indicates that current norm-referenced test results do indeed produce a diagnostic statement. However, it appears as if what succeeds in an instructional program with a youngster does not depend on what the youngster's formal diagnostic profile happens to be. In other words, effective instructional programming does not stem from effective formal diagnostic procedures. However, as Ysseldyke concludes, the issue is not whether educators forget diagnosis, but rather that they discover, develop, and implement alternative assessment procedures which produce the "accurate" prescription. This would, in essence, prevent instructional programming from operating on a purely trial-and-error basis.

Planning criterion-referenced assessment

There are a number of ways in which a teacher can produce a criterion-referenced assessment device. However, with every criterion-referenced assessment or test device, there must be a conjunctive instructional program or guide. This then produced what will be referred to as a criterion-referenced program.

As mentioned above, there are two parts to a criterion-referenced program: its instructional section and the test section. By design, the criterion-referenced test should link directly to the criterion-referenced instructional section. The key to the link is the use of instructional objectives. These are usually statements of what the youngster is going to do (behavior), what he is going to produce (product), and how well he is going to perform (criterion or measurement statement). Therefore, the criterion-referenced test is made up of a number of test items which measure the youngster's attainment of different instructional objectives. If the youth does not display attainment of a specific objective during the test situation, he is merely directed toward that instructional objective in the instructional section of the criterion-referenced program.

This, obviously, is a very simplistic analysis of what is involved in criterion-referenced programs. A number of questions arise immediately: What and how many instructional objectives should a teacher develop for each student? What is the correct sequencing of instructional objectives? Can instructional objectives be the same for all youngsters? If many instructional objectives are developed, and a test item is made for each objective, would not the test be burdensome for both the teacher and youngster?

Perhaps the answers to all these questions can be best handled by explaining the development of a model criterion-referenced program. Again, it must be emphasized that this is not the only way to develop such a program. Also, every model program has its own assumptions. The key assumption of the following model is that there are no content differences in curriculum between different subgroups of students. That is, a reading or mathematics curriculum for a mentally handicapped child is the same as for a normal child. The differences are in how far each will progress through the curriculum and how each will be taught individual instructional objectives.

Steps in criterion-referenced program development: A model

Step I: The teacher must determine what general programs he or she wishes to place in a criterion-referenced format. Obviously, many teachers deal with more than one area of curriculum. However, for the sake of brevity, we will assume that a teacher wishes to develop a criterion-referenced mathematics program. He or she next determines the general goal of that program for all his or her students. Such a goal might be "to establish developmental skills across mathematics areas." The goal statement is only important insofar as to keep the teacher on target in developing instructional objectives leading to the goal.

Step II. The teacher should now compile a *developmental sequence* of instructional objectives which, when completed in whole or part, will dictate whether the youngster has or has not attained the general goal. The sequence is determined by a task analysis process. That is, the educator should determine what instructional objective should come first, second, third, etc., and assume that in order for the youth to display attainment of the third objective, he must have instruction in, or have showed prior attainment of, the preceding objectives. The initial and final objective developed should reflect direct instructional experiences with the youth in the educational arena. That is, the span of instructional objectives should be from "too easy" to "too difficult." This will somewhat guarantee the usability of the system with many different youngsters.

Obviously, the number of instructional objectives developed could be infinite. This would occur if the teacher begins to task analyze the objectives in terms of behavior, product, and criteria (e.g., "the student will point to the same picture of a car" and "the student will say the word *same*" are completely different objectives). It is therefore suggested in this model that the teacher focuses upon content or concepts that can be sequenced, and determine sequenced instructional objectives for these. For example, the mathematical concept of number property of sets might be considered. Following is a proposed sequential list of concepts leading toward the one considered, and instructional objectives for each.

Concept	Instructional Objective
one-to-one correspondence	The student will demonstrate 1-to-1 correspondence of set member.
equality of sets	The student will recognize equal sets (same number and same kind of objects).
equivalent sets	The student will recognize equivalent sets (same in number only).
more than	The student will discriminate sets in terms of "more than."
less than	The student will discriminate sets in terms of "less than."
number property of sets	The student will recognize number property of sets without counting.

Notice that instructional objectives, in this case, are somewhat different from those mentioned previously. The behavior and product sections are present but are nonspecific. Also, no criterion section is evident. The reason for these differences are two-fold. First, this procedure should decrease the number of objectives needed in the program. Second, the criterion level for each objective should be determined to obtain mastery of the objectives the youth can experience as success. For example, the teacher might decide for the entire program that an adolescent will not move from one objective to another until he has shown a correct response ten times in succession for each objective .

Step III. Once the sequence of instructional objectives is completed, the teacher may wish to delineate how he or she will pursue instructions in each objective. Again, the way in which objectives are written in the model does not indicate how the teacher will instruct, only what the student will do. Therefore, the teacher should describe briefly for each objective, the suggested ways or enabling steps that will be used. The more enabling steps developed, the more flexible the program is for different youngsters (in that all youngsters do not learn or display acquisition of objectives in the same way). For example, the following shows the link between an instructional objective and enabling steps.

Instructional Objective	*Suggested Enabling Steps*
The student will demonstrate 1 to 1 correspondence of set member.	(a) Teacher constructs set of objects placing them in a group one at a time as learner watches. Gives learner some objects and says, "Make a group just like mine."
	(b) Teacher shows learner picture of group of objects. Gives him cutouts of all objects, plus additional cutout objects. Says, "Make a group just like mine."

Step IV. Once the sequence of instructional objectives and delineation of enabling steps is completed, the basic criterion-referenced instructional section is completed. Now a criterion-referenced test or assessment device can be used to determine where in an instructional program an individual youngster should be placed (i.e., what specific objectives have or have not been attained). Obviously, even with this model, a large number of instructional objectives would have been developed. To create one test item for each instructional objective would indeed produce a burdensome criterion-referenced test. Therefore, a better practice is to collapse specific sequences of instructional objectives into individual global objectives and use the latter as test items. For example, taking the sequence of concepts and corresponding instructional objectives mentioned previously, one might look at that sequence as indicative of the global objective "the student will demonstrate the ability to manipulate sets." What the teacher must determine is a test item or observable behavior which will coincide with this global objective and which, if evidenced by the learner, will indicate that he has attained all the individual instructional objectives contained within that global objective. Perhaps the easiest way to do this is to rely on the task analysis of concepts. That is, take the last instructional objective in sequence per global objective (in this case, "The student will recognize number property of sets without counting.") for that objective. If the youngster fails the test item, or gives observable evidence of inaccuracy, he or she would subsequently be directed back into the program at the first objective in sequence for the global objective.

All queries should be derived so that there is no question as to the correctness or incorrectness of a response. This can be done by delineating specifically what the teacher does or presents in the querying situation, and also what the learner must do in response. For example, the following shows a measure of the global objective "The student will demonstrate the ability to describe sets" with the last instructional objective in sequence being "The student will differentiate between empty and non-empty sets.

Teacher Input	*Teacher Output*
Present learner with 3 sets of objectives as follows: 　one empty set 　two sets of 3 to 5 objects Verbally request learner to tell you about each group. Present one group at a time.	Verbally describes groups as requested (e.g., learner tells teacher that set is empty or says group consists of sum larger, blue sequence, etc. Teacher does *not* need to mention number of objects.).

Strengths and limitations of criterion-referenced assessment

The most obvious strength of criterion-referenced assessment is the direct linkage between evaluation and prescription. However, what is perhaps just as noteworthy is the adaptability of this system to individual student monitoring. Given a predetermined sequence of instructional objectives as well as a delineation of enabling steps, a teacher can pinpoint the position of a student within the framework of the instructional objectives (i.e., what the student has accomplished). The teacher can also determine and record the procedure(s) that helped the student attain the objectives (i.e., what the teacher did in the instructional setting). Yet another strength of the system is the possibility of checking and validating the progress of a student through the instructional section of the criterion-referenced program by continuous assessment. Therefore, assessment is not devoted to placement, but can be used as a continuous monitoring tool replacing the outworn pre-post testing format.

The major limitation of criterion-referenced assessment is that it is a totally task oriented device. It is used solely to evaluate a student's mastery of specific tasks, and in doing so, helps formulate a process for instruction. It remains possible that a student cannot show the mastery of a specific task because of the mode of the question (teacher writes rather than states questions) or another situational variable that interacts with individual characteristics. Therefore, informal assessment emphasizing task analysis should be used in conjunction with some measure of the youth's preference and strengths for learning.

There are at least two dimensions to be accomplished in this. The first is a traditional psychometrically ascertainment of normative status on personal characteristics and academic achievement skills. Second, to augment the formal assessment techniques, it is wise to consider task analysis with the direct observation of pupil-classroom ecology relationships. Direct informal measurement of responses to various situations of the classroom may prove more valuable in determining learner preferences than formal measurement of underlying constructs presumed to affect learning. At the very least, such informal measures can form a basis for testing instructional hypotheses formulated from norm-referenced data.

OBSERVATION IN THE CLASSROOM

Teacher observation and the evaluation process

The task at hand is to examine the changing view of the teacher's role in student assessment and the decision-making process. Traditionally, the teacher's role or function has been to provide the student with a reasonable human relationship and the opportunity to grow through academic accomplishment and social learning. It is also the role and responsibility of the teacher to identify those children whose academic achievement is minimal. This responsibility seems deceptively simple. The traditional scan-the-gradebook approach—looking for those repeated failures is a worn-out means of identifying minimal achievers, for in such an approach the fact is that the student must first fail before being identified.

In view of the shortcomings of the traditional approach to evaluation, it has become necessary to develop other measures for teachers to identify minimal achieving students. Before these other measures of teacher evaluation can be instituted we believe it is necessary that:

1. Schools reexamine how the curriculum, methodology, and experiences can be bent to enhance growth and minimize failure.

2. Teachers learn observational skills.

3. Teachers become more open about their feelings toward disruptive adolescents as externalization of attitudes is pivotal in changing negative feelings.   (William, 1969)

While this section cannot address itself to all three issues it will direct much effort to the second point, that of the development and use of observation skills. This emphasis in teacher evaluation is required *before* the student becomes lost to debilitating anxiety stemming from a lack of achievement and arbitrary judgmental standards. A new role for student evaluation is thus seen as crucial to the schools, particularly those dealing with troubled youth. In this view, Perticone (1972) makes several points:

> —That evaluation is not an end product. It is a means by which a child may be aided to learn. If evaluation serves only to distinguish high achievers from low achievers, the process can hardly be regarded as one which contributes much to a child's education.

> —That evaluation is a continuous process. It is not a discrete act that occurs only at the moment when the teacher assigns a grade to a child's work. On the contrary, opportunities for evaluation are present whenever the child can be observed by the alert teacher.

> —That teachers who engage in systematic observation for the purpose of evaluating a student *before* his grade is assigned are often able to identify the minimal achievers before they are overwhelmed by failure. (p. 23)

Perticone's evaluational approach focuses on the *what* and the *why* of the minimal achiever, as well as the *who*. By developing insights into the what and why through systematic observation, the teacher's ability to recognize individual educational needs and the ability to satisfy those needs are greatly enhanced (Coon & Burpee, 1967).

Approaches to observational systems

Direct classroom observation can be both elusive and deceptively simple. Cartwright and Cartwright (1974) used observation in a manner closely resembling the dictionary meaning of simply watching. Without doubt, such action is useful in many situations. However, when we speak of observation in this chapter, we are referring to a systematically structured procedure that makes explicit the rules of what and how events will be recorded. This specifically structured, categorical approach, is referred to as an *observation system,* and usually proceeds in one of two ways. The first of these, *participant observation,* is that form in which the observer and the person or persons observed are in interaction with one another. An ideal example is the teacher in the classroom attempting to identify and record the behavior of children while conducting a lesson. It is difficult to be systematic in this process and usually a rigorous observation system is not used. If a categorical system is used, it should be kept simple; recording may have to be accomplished with hand-held counters, clipboards, or the like. On the other hand, in conducting *nonparticipant observation*, the observer takes great care to avoid the attention of, or interaction with, the person or persons being observed. Observation may be conducted through a one-way mirror, or the observer may attempt to gradually become a "part of the scenery" as related by Wright (1967). At any rate, in addition to employing a systematic record, the observer is to be as unobtrusive as possible in the making of records.

Classroom circumstances have made use of both these techniques. Participant observation might include the teacher's record of the number of times an individual responds to teacher prompting, or the number of interactions between teacher and student. The use of this approach is open to the teacher continuously; there are few circumstances in which it cannot be used. However, it is subject to the pitfalls described earlier. Unobtrusive observation is currently limited in use because it requires either the teacher's recording of a behavior while independent of the classroom ecology or the assistance of at least one other person. The data tend, however, to have much greater authority for decision making and accountability. In the habilitation of troubled youth, the utility of unobtrusive observation could make the process cost effective.

The questions that are to be answered by observation cannot be independent of the specific methodology used. For example, participant observation can address many potential questions, but it also encounters a major problem. That is, one must assume that the observer's presence alters the observed ecology, particularly so when the observer is a key to the ongoing events. If the teacher is the participant observer, questions can only be addressed that are prefaced with the statement, "With the teacher present and engaged in producing and recording behavior, what is going on here?"

Unobtrusive measures can better attempt a measure of the "natural ecology," those events that unfold without influence of measurement methodology. If the teacher is present, teaching is the primary activity; he or she can be devoted to conducting the class in a natural manner and less potentially disruptive activities are evident (e.g., recording data on paper). Second, unobtrusive measures can observe the ecology as it undergoes shifts in material or in personnel; events can continue to be recorded even if the teacher or varying numbers of students leave. Such records may later prove of considerable value in analysis. To reemphasize, the question asked must dictate the choice of methodology.

Recently, a number of guidelines have emerged for the development of research-based (Altman, 1974; Johnson & Bolstad, 1973) and classroom-based observation systems (Cartwright & Cartwright, 1974). A number of such systems have been cataloged and are available to both practitioner and researcher (Simon & Boyer, 1970). Most of these efforts are devoted to systematic, unobtrusive systems, and represent a growing interest in this methodology. We have previously detailed the necessity of looking at the ecology or milieu of a situation and the recording of observable behavior to delimit academic change. The resurgence of the use of observation systems can be seen as an outgrowth of this emphasis and the movement away from a trait-based theory in psychology (as described by Bersoff, 1973).

Guides for constructing and using observation systems

In its simplest sense, an observation system usually consists of 3 to 10 categories of behavior. Though there are exceptions, categories are usually made mutually exclusive, that is two categories of behavior cannot occur simultaneously. In a single stage system, behaviors are usually arranged as such:

SINGLE STAGE SYSTEM

Behavior 1

Behavior 2

Behavior 3 ————————Recording Arrangement————————

Behavior 4

Behavior N

In such a system, the observer simply records the pre-arranged behaviors. More elaborate systems have been developed, for example, in a two stage system additional information is taken:

TWO STAGE SYSTEM

Behavior 1 Level 1

Level 2

Level 3

Level 4

Behavior N	Level 1	
	Level 2	
	Level 3	
	Level 4	

Thus, not only is the occurrence of a behavior recorded but also some additional information about it is collected. For example, Behavior 1 (raises hand) with Level 1 (lethargically) or Level 2 (quickly), etc. Usually, systems of this complexity are augmented by electronic measurement, and are more often found in research than application.

Other practical considerations of observational systems include specifying the *target* and the *behavioral sampling technique*. For example, given a particular question, is the target of observation to be only a single student, that student and the teacher, some collection of students or other grouping? This distinction must be made prior to beginning the construction of an observational system and again, it is greatly associated with the question of interest to the teacher. The second issue, behavioral sampling, refers to how the record is to be taken once the system is devised. Two methods are most commonly used, *time sample* and *event recording*. Time sample simply refers to the case when a datum bit is taken in a specified chronological sequence, as when a category of behavior is marked every five seconds. Event recording simply refers to the situation in which a specific behavior is recorded only when it appears. Theoretically, a recording session could yield no data should the behavior specified in the system not occur. In that instance, even though the observer might continually monitor a classroom, no data would be taken because the pre-specified behaviors did not occur and all other behaviors were ignored.

A final note concerns the selection of items, rater agreement and rater reliability. Despite the method used, it is vital for the behaviors to be observable and well defined, not requiring inference or speculation. Consider the difference in observer identification difficulty with the following roughly equivalent category:

Aggressive	*Strikes or Verbally Attacks Another Child*
(not behaviorally distinct, requires inference)	(behaviorally observable, defines actions)

While even the second example requires some interpretation, the judgment required of the observer is made considerably smaller. In an observational sequence, this is extremely important. Greater specificity would contribute to the ease of the observer's task (strikes Susy on the arm) but could also narrow the data to a ridiculously specific and useless level. A descriptive but recordable level of behavior must be used.

Observer reliability and agreement are two concepts that must be addressed. Consider a teacher-developed observation system with five categories, A–E, for which two persons have agreed to function as observers. High agreement would occur if both observers recorded the same categories in viewing specific behaviors. This could be used as one measure of adequately defined categories. High reliability would occur if the observers could consistently label "identical" behaviors to appropriate categories. It would be possible to have high agreement between observers but low reliability. Efforts need be made to assure the teacher that the defined categories are measured the same throughout the session (reliability) and that observers are in agreement upon labeling the behavior they see (inter-rater agreement). Without this, the data that is obtained must be viewed with suspicion. Simple procedures to calculate agreement and reliability can be found in Johnson and Bolstad (1973). Normally, acceptable agreement and reliability can be obtained quite quickly through inservice preparation of staff. Usually, this is accomplished by defining the behaviors to be observed, and calculating staff's agreement/reliability while observing preconstructed stimulus video-tapes.

Observational systems for use with troubled youth

A number of observational systems have been developed and extensively tested in the habilitation of troubled youth. Previously we have spoken of the need to develop specific systems in response to specific problem situations, and this is often the best procedure. However, the systems reported here are useful in a multitude of circumstances and can provide an excellent point of departure in informal evaluation.

Flanders' System of Interaction Analysis (Flanders, 1970) exemplifies a system which records the behavior of both teachers and students. Its categories are described in Table 8.2. Notice that records are kept of both teacher and pupil responses. A potentially valuable aspect of this system is the analysis of student response to teacher category, i.e., the study of the interaction of the two categories. Understanding this relationship can provide clues to guide the teacher's behavior during lessons.

The Indiana Behavioral Management System (Fink & Semmel, 1971) is primarily involved with affective pupil behavior and teacher behavior management techniques. It is concerned with the behaviors of both teacher and students, but records the behavior of only one child at any given time. The categories of this system are described in Table 8.3.

Table 8.2. CATEGORIES FROM THE FLANDERS' SYSTEM OF INTERACTION ANALYSIS

Teacher Talk Categories	Student Talk Categories
Accepts feelings	Student response
Praises or encourages	Student initiated talk
Accepts ideas	Silence or confusion
Asks questions	
Lectures	
Gives directions	
Criticizes or justifies authority	

Flanders. 1970 exerpt from *Focus on Exceptional Children* 5 (December 1973): 2. Reproduced with permission.

Table 8.3. CATEGORIES FROM THE INDIANA BEHAVIOR MANAGEMENT SYSTEM 11 (IBMS-11)

Pupil Categories	Teacher Categories
On-task	On-task
Self-involvement	Demand
Noise	Value-law
Verbal interaction	Conditioned stimulus
Physical interaction	Criticism
Verbal aggression	Punishment
Physical aggression	Empathy
Verbal resistance	Interpretive
Physical resistance	Humor
	Consequences
	Redirection
	Probing

Fink and Semmel. 1971 excerpt from *Focus on Exceptional Children* 5 (December 1973): 2.

The Teacher Practices Observation Record (Brown, 1970) concentrates exclusively on teacher behavior. Its categories are concerned with the nature of the situation (locating the center of attention), the nature of the problem, the development of ideas, and the use of subject matter. Figure 8.1 outlines the various steps in the teacher self-development process using observation systems.

Dayton (1967) developed an observational system which he termed the Pupil Classroom Behavior Scale: Elementary and High School Grades. The described purpose was to create a scale or criterion measure of the "effectiveness of various procedures for providing pupil personnel services to elementary school children" (p. 1). Thus, the scale was developed in the interest of the adjustment of students and within the context of the what and the why in recognizing educational needs. This scale, however, has not been recommended for individual assessment but for research.

The Behavior Problem Checklist (Quay & Peterson, 1967) is unlike other scales in that the judgment requires the teacher to assess the extent to which he or she judges the behavior to be a problem rather than the frequency or typicality. The manual presents reliability and validity data along with norms for both sexes. Research in the development and subsequent use of this Checklist suggests that a reasonably reliable assessment tool has been created, one that differentiates between children with emotional disturbances, specific learning defects, and normals. However, no data is available that directly relates factor scores and achievement measures within a normal group.

The Pupil Behavior Inventory (Vinter, et al., 1968) is said to measure the "behavioral and attitudinal factors which affect the degree of success a pupil will have in accomplishing his educational objectives" (p. 1). The authors see the scale as identifying problems of interest to those concerned with special educational programs. No norms are present, yet the Pupil Behavior Inventory seems to be a very useable scale as a result of the ease of scoring and administration. The reliability and validity data are adequate but it is one of few scales designed for high school-aged youngsters.

Werry and Quay (1969) have provided specific directions and definitions which can be associated with a shorthand method of reporting behaviors. The following identifies not only specific disrupting events but also detailed instructions for obtaining a frequency count on deviant classroom behavior.

It may be seen from this review that relatively few systems are directly applicable and, indeed, it is the current authors' bias that specific systems be created by the teacher to quantify particular situations. Previous sections have provided an overview of the mechanics of observation systems and some applicable examples. One further component, a scheme for the creation of categories, would be useful. Unfortunately no single guide will fit all situations, although Fink (1970) provided a tentative and seemingly useful format. It is outlined herein as a final note on observation before turning to the issue of monitory student behavior.

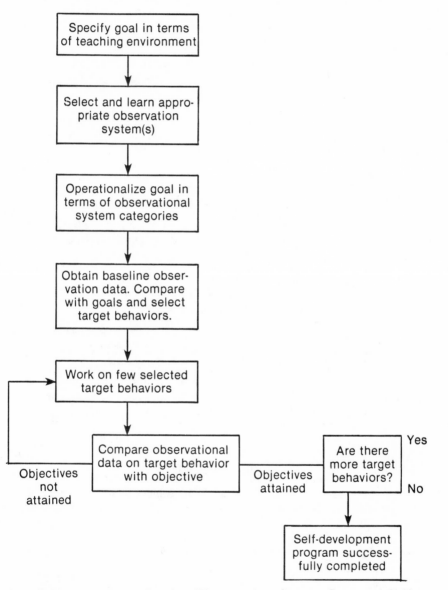

Semmel, M. I., and Thiagarajan, S., 1973 excerpt from *Focus on Exceptional Children* 5 (December 1973): 11.

Figure 8.1. Steps in Teacher Self-Development Using Observation Systems

Definitions of Observations	There are three classes of observations: deviant behavior, on task behavior, and teacher contact.

Symbol and Description	1. *Deviant behavior.* This is defined as any behavior which contravenes any explicit rule under which the class or individual child operates. Therefore, it is imperative to determine what the rules are in a given classroom before undertaking any observations.
	Behavioral Definition

Symbol and Description	Behavioral Definition
X Out of Seat	This is defined as any situation in which the normal seating behavior *does not* occur.
Physical Contact or Disturbing Others Directly	Any physical contact initiated or reciprocated between the child under observation and another person independent of the intent of the child (aggression or affection).
N Audible Noise	Any nonvocal, nonrespiratory noise which is clearly audible, and which is not an integral part of a nondeviant activity.
↗ 90 Degree Turn, Seated	A youth must be seated and the turn of the head and/or body must be more than 89 degrees from the desk which is the reference point.
V Vocalization	A vocalization or other respiratory noise such as a whistle which is not task related and which is not physiological (this includes normal cough or sneeze).
I Isolation (i.e., for deviant behavior)	The youth has been sent out of the room as a punishment or has been placed in the time-out room.
0 Other Deviant Behaviors	Include here behaviors which do not fit easily into a category above and also behaviors which are situational rather than absolutely deviant.

Symbol and Description	2. *On task-off task activity.* This is defined as an attempt to assess the youth's attention to the designated task.
	Behavioral Definition

// Activity while engaged in some other activity which is either clearly deviant or not the assigned one for more than 5 seconds.	This generally occurs after time has elapsed, for example when the teacher comes up and admonishes the youth.

Symbol and Description	Behavioral Definition
D Daydreaming— here the child is off task for more than 5 seconds but does so by daydream- ing or staring into space rather than some active endeavor.	This type of behavior is very uncommon in conduct problem children.

	3. *Teacher contact.* Teacher is defined as any adult person who is interacting with the children rather than just observ- ing them.
Symbol and Description	Behavioral Description
T	Teacher initiated contact (no instigation on part of child)
t	Child initiated (include both questions, etc. Add teacher re- sponding to deviant behavior)
T & t	Positive contact (judged by what teacher does)
T & t	Negative contact (Note: T ought not to occur!)

Note: Recording something above the dotted line for Deviant Behavior and something below it for on task behavior are obligatory for every cell. Teacher contact is of course added only when it occurs.   (Werry & Quay, 1969, p. 461-470)

Teacher Categories:

Three task categories are defined, each of which reflects a different process of involving students in task activities: unilateral direction giving, induced student participation, and feedback. Teacher nontask, or control categories, are viewed as having one covert and four overt response sets. One additional category is reserved for "no interaction."

The convert response set comprises two categories: *planned ignoring,* which is viewed as a positive control technique; and *incapacity.* The first of the four overt response groups of categories is seen as a series of verbal control actions on an authoritative-interpretive continuum. Thus, at one extreme, the category *authoritative* represents verbal interpretation that limits pupil participation. It represents teacher behavior that is commanding, rationalizing, and critical. At the other extreme, the causal category reflects verbal interaction which actively engages the student in the consideration and solution of a problem. Commonly, this means the use of life-space interview techniques. Between the extremes, three cate- gories are used: change tone, which primarily reflects the use of humor to effect behavior change; appeal to value/law, designed for the control technique which resorts to established rules and values; and surface behavior response, which deals with behavior at a minimally interpretive level.

The second group of overt response categories is designed for behavior which involves physical or spatial manipulation of students or their surroundings. This includes: exclusion of students from class; the use of "quiet rooms;" internal physical or personal rearrangement of students in relation to each other or the teacher; or the teacher's own manipulations, such as words, smiles, and gestures. The third group requires lower order incentives used for control of deviant behavior, such as tallied reward and punishment categories. The fourth overt response group accounts for the use of task expectations or activities which refocus attention on the current task as a means of deviant behavior control.

Pupil Categories:

Pupil categories were developed on the basis of the assumptions operative within the teacher categories. Nontask activities are considered along a number of dimensions. These include the nonaggressive acts contained within self involvement as well as generalized verbal and physical interaction. Aggressive acts are characterized in four ways: verbal aggression, generalized disturbing, refusal/resistive, and verbal and physical interaction. Verbal and physical interaction and aggression are further subdivided according to whether the behavior is directed towards self, peers, or teachers.

The reader is encouraged to consult the original source for greater · detail.

Individual achievement monitoring systems (IAMS)

The monitoring of a student's academic achievement progress is really an effort that should be conducted at several levels. Initially, we suggest that a multiple level IAMS can be thought of as having a most inclusive or general level that represents the development of an Individual Program Plan (IPP). We further suggest that this most general level of watching a student's progress is not sufficient for the teacher's daily classroom program. A monitoring system that will produce both a useful daily instructional statement and provide data for a yearly review is necessary.

The IPP is essentially a yearly statement that specifies the goals of educational treatment and resources necessary to provide instructional intervention. This process has been described for handicapped populations as an Individual Educational Plan (Tracy, Gibbins, Kladder, & Daggy, 1974).

The IPP formulation was derived from a systems model that made allowance for legal guidelines in remedial activity, such as the necessity for inclusion of all concerned parties in placement decisions and the continual sharing of information. The heart of the material is based on the belief that the IPP must be developed, systematically evaluated, and modified to fit the changing conditions of the situation, requirements of the learner, and goals of the educational process.

Tracy, et al. (1974) were concerned primarily with the accountability of a student's progress at the total program level. Figure 8.2 provides an overview of this most inclusive monitoring process. Briefly, it is presumed that a referral will proceed when some disturbing event is beyond the current academic situations ability to provide effective service. At this point, a case conference of all concerned parties is drawn, questions concerning the problem are raised, and informed consent is secured in order that specific efforts (particularly formal testing) may be conducted.

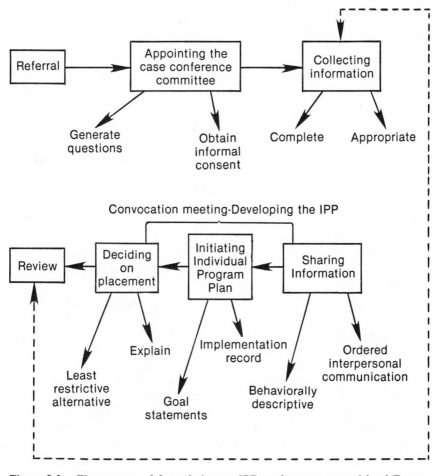

Figure 8.2. The process of formulating an IPP at the most general level Tracy, Gibbins, Kladder, and Daggy, 1974; reproduced with permission.

Following the case conference, a complete and appropriate assessment is conducted and specialists may be involved as agreed upon in line with the questions generated. A general shotgun analysis is avoided as data are collected only to respond to the specific questions agreed on earlier at the case conference.

Upon completion of these stages a second convocation of teacher, parents and specialists is drawn with three tasks to be completed; the sharing of the acquired information, the initiation of the IPP, and a decision upon the placement of the youth. Note that the sharing of information is ordered—all person's comments are sought—and every effort is made for adhering to behaviorally descriptive communication. The IPP that evolves represents a written contract of goals, procedures to be utilized, and resources to be expended; while step three of this convocation is a decision on the physical location for IPP implementation. In general, it is thought that implementation should take place in a situation that is as close to the normal as possible (the least restrictive environment) but that can achieve the specialized requirements of the IPP. Finally, the schema makes provisions for a review of student progress and the collection of additional information.

The formulation presented must be considered as a monitoring system at the most general level, an attempt to provide an abbreviated record of a student's progress. It is a basic statement of what is to be accomplished and under what specific conditions. Further, it provides an opportunity for all issues to be addressed in an ethical manner. Adhering to this format will provide a most equitable and logical procedure for looking at a youth's target behavior, although it does not directly provide a monitoring system useful for the teacher's day to day decision making. In short, the IPP provides the orientation, background information, professional-parental support, and general evaluation that allows the teacher the freedom to develop a specific learning situation.

Reconsider Figure 8.2. Notice that the teacher has, upon completion of the paradigm goal statements, a placement decision and/or technical assistance, and a large battery of data from formally administered tests. Following the second conference, but before the review, lies the time period in which the instructor will attempt to implement procedures in line with the plan. This is the teaching context for which we earlier proposed a criterion-referenced program of instruction. Recall that in the criterion-referenced model the teacher required continuous data for daily effective instruction. However, in the original process shown in Figure 8.1, a review of all data is to take place probably no more frequently than once yearly. This time cycle, while exhaustive of the specialized personnel time found in most situations, is simply not effective for daily instructional decisions. A complete IAMS must be multiple level, making proviso for both daily and long term monitoring; the first to guide the teacher in the daily instructional sequence, the second to assure appropriate student growth in the conditions established and mutually agreed to in the formulation of the IPP. Neither by itself is sufficient.

Figure 8.3 presents a framework for the teacher that will allow an integration of all available data, provide several avenues of instruction, and the daily monitoring of progress. This level of the IAMS is the most specific and is directed solely at the instructional sequence conducted in the daily implementation of the IPP. A close relationship of the two levels of the IAMS is evident however, as the instructional goals of the IPP at the most global level form the basis for the daily IAMS activities. In different circumstances or with different youth, both the number and specificity of the goals mentioned in the IPP may vary. As a guide, these goals must be evaluatable and realistically stated at the case conference. If this does not occur, the daily level of the IAMS will be excessively complex and difficult, resulting in a taxing situation for the instructor.

In the instructional sequence shown in Figure 8.3, separate goals are attacked simultaneously but not necessarily by similar means. Since goals may be quite different, and therefore emphasize different content, teacher or learner characteristics, group dynamics, etc., identical teaching and monitoring activities cannot take place across all goals. However, the process for developing the activities, per goal, is identical. In this example, we have charted the process for a single goal. Beginning at the top left hand corner of Figure 8.3, notice that strong familiarization with the results of formal analysis is required, particularly so with the initial instructional attempt. As we have seen, interpretation of this data is difficult. However, we suggest that at the least, such data will help pinpoint the level of entrance into the curricula and perhaps reveal some data on the learner's strengths or preferences that can be used in teaching.

Critical requirement at this stage is the adequate task analysis of the goal. Task analysis (Bateman, 1971; Mager, 1962) may be thought of as the identification of subtasks or prerequisite skills that the student must be able to accomplish before some larger skill can be achieved. Teaching thus concentrates upon developing student mastery to criterion on each subtask and, when attained, recombing the mastered subtasks to develop the total skill. For example, in a shop class, the goal of instruction might be for the student to drive a nail properly. Possible subtasks might be recognition of a hammer, nail, and wood; proper gripping of the equipment; correct swinging motion of the hand; and awareness of when the nail is firmly seated into the wood. This example is, of course, quite simple. However, it serves to emphasize the importance of the teachers presenting *learnable* units to the student. In more complex learning situations, such as reading, the task analysis process becomes even more crucial. However, in each learning exercise (driving a nail, reading) a goal must be set and the specific components of that goal must be identified, taught, and reassembled. The concept of task analysis, then, is useful across many learning situations, for it specifies for the instructor what to teach and in what order to do it.

When attempting to task analyze a goal, the instructor should be aware that no matter what subtask is chosen, it could always be made smaller or larger to fit a specific situation. There is no set of values by which to determine the original specificity of the tasks. Instead, the instructor's initial decision as to the level of the tasks must be on a best guess basis, possibly augmented by past experience and formal assessment data. Later, during the course of the process outlined in Figure 8.3, the teacher will attain more information about the accuracy of the level chosen and the advisability of resetting the level. However, all subtasks developed, regardless of level, must be behaviorally specific. That is, they must state the conditions under which a behavior will be observed and what observed behaviors will be taken as evidence of subgoal learning. The criterion to be met by the student must be prespecified for it will represent the percentage of accuracy under specified conditions that is acceptable for building toward the overall learning goal. While some margin for error must be allowed, it is wise to set subgoal mastery levels quite high if the final goal is to be achieved. A 60% mastery in letter recognition (subtask) is not likely to allow a correspondingly high mastery of word recognition (goal).

Following the consideration of formal test data, completion of task analysis, and presetting of acceptance (criterion) levels, the instructor is ready to conduct the lesson. The instructor has not only some indices of the students learning characteristics, but also possesses a firm grip on what and how the material is to be taught. Two informal evaluation measures are now necessary to complete the instructional strategy presented in Figure 8.3.

The first of these measures is the teacher-made criterion test. Such a test will provide an index to the percentage of subgoal mastery and, if skillfully written, can provide clues to the sources of student error in the subtasks. Records of these tests can be constructed in bar graph or histograph form and will provide both a record of progress and feedback to the learner. Such feedback has often been found to support or increase the learning rate.

Despite the usefulness of teacher-made criterion tests, such informal evaluation methods tend to ignore student learning characteristics and situational aspects of the classroom. Because of this, it is advisable to have a second informal measure, an observational record of the instructional events that occurred during teaching. Usually teachers will only be able to give approximations of what occurred in a lesson. Subjectively they may believe that a particular instructional method was carried through as planned, when in actuality it was not. This discrepancy frequently occurs

Cartwright, C. A., and Cartwright, G. P. *Developing Observational Skills.* New York: McGraw Hill, 1974.

Carver, R. P. "Two Dimension of Tests: Psychometric and Edumetric." *American Psychologist* 29 (1974): 512-518.

Cohen, J. "The Factoral Structure of the WISC at ages 7-6, l0-6, and 13-6." *Journal of Consulting Psychology* 23 (1959): 285-299.

Coon, F., and Burpee, L. "The Role of Observations in Special Education." *Teaching Educationally Handicapped Children.* Edited by John Arena. San Rafael, California: Academic Therapy Publications, 1967.

Craig, W. N., and Collins, J. L. "Communication Patterns in Classes for Deaf Students." *Exceptional Children* 37 (1970): 283-289.

Cronbach, L. J. "Five Decades of Public Controversy over Mental Testing." *American Psychologist* 30 (1975): 1-14.

Dayton, C. M. "Technical Manual: Pupil Classroom Behavior Scale." College Park, Maryland: University of Maryland Research Center of the Interprofessional Research Commission on Pupil Personnel Services, 1967.

Erikson, E. *Childhood and Society.* 2nd ed. New York: Norton, 1963.

Erikson, E. *Insight and Responsibility.* New York: Norton, 1964.

Fink, A. H. "An Analysis of Teacher-Pupil Interaction in Classes for the Emotionally Handicapped." Unpublished doctoral dissertation, University of Michigan, 1970.

Fink, A. H. and Semmel, M. I. 1971 excerpt from *Focus on Exceptional Children* 5 (7) (Dec. 1973): 2.

Flanders. 1970 excerpt from *Focus on Exceptional Children* 5 (7) (Dec. 1973): 2.

Gagne, R. M. "Instructional Variables and Learning Outcomes." *The Evaluation of Instruction.* Edited by M. C. Wittrock and D. E. Wiley. New York: Holt, Rinehart and Winston, 1970.

Gearheart, B. R., and Willenberg, E. D. *Application of Pupil Assessment Information: For the Special Education Teacher.* Denver: Love Publishing Co., 1974.

Glaser, R. "Evaluation of Instruction and Changing Educational Models." *The Evaluation of Instruction.* Edited by M. C. Wittrock and D. E. Wiley. New York: Holt, Rinehart, and Winston, 1970.

Glaser, R., and Nitko, A. J. "Measurement in Learning and Instruction." *Educational Measurement.* Edited by R. L. Thorndike. Washington, D.C.: American Council on Education, 1971.

Hewitt, F. *The Emotionally Disturbed Child in the Classroom.* Boston: Allyn and Bacon, 1968.

Hunt, D. E. "Person Environment Interaction: A Challenge Found Wanting Before it was Tried." *Review of Educational Research* 45 (1975): 209-230.

Johnson, S. M., and Bolstad, O. P. "Methodological Issues in Naturalistic Observation: Some Problems and Solutions for Field Research." *Behavior Change.* Edited by H. Hamerlynek and H. Marsh. Champaign, Illinois: Research Press, 1973.

Joyce, B., and Weil, M. *Models of Teaching*. Englewood Cliffs: Prentice Hall, 1972.

Kaufman, R. A. *Educational Systems Planning*. Englewood Cliffs: Prentice Hall, 1972.

Kounin, J. S. *Discipline and Group Management in Classrooms*. New York: Holt, Rinehart, and Winston, 1970.

Labov, W. "The Language of Nonstandard English. *Language and Poverty*. Edited by F. Williams. Chicago: Markham, 1970.

Linn, R. L. "Fair Test Use in Selection." *Review of Educational Research* 43 (1973): 139-161.

Mager, R. F. *Preparing Instructional Objectives*. Belmont, California: Fearon Publishers, 1962.

Mehrabian, A., and Russell, J. A. *An Approach to Environmental Psychology*. Cambridge, Massachusetts: MIT Press, 1974.

Mischel, W. *Personality and Assessment*. New York: John Wiley and Sons, 1968.

Perticone, E. X. "The Observant Teacher." *Academic Therapy* (7)1 (Fall, 1972): 21-26.

Popham, W. J. *Criteria Referenced Measurement: An Introduction*. Englewood Cliffs, New Jersey: Educational Technology Publications, 1971.

Proshansky, H. M.; Ittelson, W. H.; and Rivlin, L. G., eds. *Environmental Psychology: Man and his Physical Setting*. New York: Holt, Rinehart, and Winston, 1970.

Quay, H. C., and Peterson, D. R. "Manual for the Behavior Problem Checklist." Champaign, Illinois: Children's Research Center, University of Illinois, 1967.

Rausch, H.; Farbman, I.; and Llewellyn, L. "Person, Setting, and Change in Social Interaction. *Human Relations* 13 (1960): 305-332.

Rhodes, W. C. "A Community Participation Analysis of Emotional Disturbance." *Exceptional Children* 40 (1970): 309-314.

Sattler, J. M. *Assessment of Children's Intelligence*. Philadelphia: W. B. Saunders Co., 1974.

Sells, S. B. "An Interactionish Looks at the Environment." *American Psychologist* 18 (1963): 696-702.

Semmel, M. I., and Thiagarajan, S. 1973 excerpt from *Focus on Exceptional Children* 5(7) (Dec. 1973): 11.

Simon, A., and Boyer, E. G., eds. *Mirrors for Behavior II: An Anthology of Observation Instruments*. Vols. A and B. Philadelphia: Classroom Interaction Newsletter, c/o Research for Better Schools, 1970.

Smith, R. M. *Teacher Diagnosis of Educational Difficulties*. Columbus, Ohio: Charles E. Merrill, 1969.

Swap, S. M. "Disturbing Classroom Behaviors: A Developmental and Ecological View. *Exceptional Children* 41 (1974): 163-172.

Tracy, M. L.; Gibbins, S.; Kladder, F. W.; and Daggy, W. *Case Conference: A Simulation and Source Book*. Ann Arbor: University of Michigan Press, 1974.

Vinter, R. D.; Sarri, R. C.; Vorwaller, D. J.; and Schafer, W. E. "Pupil Behavior Inventory: A Manual for Administration and Scoring." Ann Arbor, Michigan: Campus Publishers, 1968.

Werry, J. S., and Quay, H. C. "Observing Classroom Behavior of Elementary School Children." *Exceptional Children* 35 (1969): 461–470.

Wicker, A. W. "Cognitive Complexity, School Size, and Participation in School Behavior Settings: A Test of the Frequency of Interaction Hypothesis." *Journal of Educational Psychology* 60 (1969): 200–203.

William, M. "Disturbed Children in the Classroom." *Today's Education* 58 (April 1969): 4, 20.

Williams, E. P. "Sense of Obligation to High School Activities as related to School Size and Marginality of Student." *Child Development* 38 (1967): 1246–1260.

Wittaker, R. H. *Communities and Ecosystems*. New York: Macmillan, 1970.

Wittrock, M. C. "The Evaluation of Instruction: Cause and Effect Relations in Naturalistic Data." *The Evaluation of instruction*. Edited by N. C. Wittrock and D. E. Wiley. New York: Holt, Rinehart, and Winston, 1970.

Wright, H. F. *Recording and Analyzing Child Behavior*. New York: Harper and Row, 1967.

Yesseldyke, J. E. "Diagnostic-Prescriptive Research: The Search for Aptitude Treatment Interactions." Edited by L. Mann and D. A. Sabatino. *The First Review of Special Education*. Philadelphia: JSE press, 1973.

subject index

author index